The Sufi Saint of Jam

The Sunni saint cult and shrine of Ahmad-i Jam has endured for 900 years. The shrine and its Sufi shaykhs secured patronage from Mongols, Kartids, Tamerlane, and Timurids. The cult and shrine complex started sliding into decline when Iran's shahs took the Shi'i path in 1501, but are today enjoying a renaissance under the (Shi'i) Islamic Republic of Iran. The shrine's eclectic architectural ensemble has been renovated with private and public funds, and expertise from Iran's Cultural Heritage Organization. Two seminaries (*madrasa*) that teach Sunni curricula to males and females were added. Sunni *and* Shi'i pilgrims visit to venerate *their* saint. Jami mystics still practice *'irfan* (gnosticism).

Analyzed are Ahmad-i Jam's biography and hagiography; marketing to sultans of Ahmad as the "Guardian of Kings"; history and politics of the shrine's catchment area; acquisition of patronage by shrine and shaykhs; and Sufi doctrines and practices of Jami mystics, including its Timurid-era Naqshbandi Sufis.

Shivan Mahendrarajah is Research Fellow at the Institute of Iranian Studies, School of History, University of St Andrews. He is the co-editor of *Afghanistan: The Journal of the American Institute of Afghanistan Studies*. He has traveled extensively in the Islamic world, and returns often to Afghanistan and Iran. Shivan was educated at Columbia University and the University of Cambridge, and studied Arabic at Damascus University and Persian at the University of Tehran.

Cambridge Studies in Islamic Civilization

Editorial Board
Chase F. Robinson, *Freer|Sackler, Smithsonian Institution (general editor)*
Michael Cook, *Princeton University*
Maribel Fierro, *Spanish National Research Council*
Alan Mikhail, *Yale University*
David O. Morgan, *Professor Emeritus, University of Wisconsin-Madison*
Intisar Rabb, *Harvard University*
Muhammad Qasim Zaman, *Princeton University*

Other titles in the series are listed at the back of the book.

The Sufi Saint of Jam

History, Religion, and Politics of a Sunni Shrine in Shi'i Iran

SHIVAN MAHENDRARAJAH
University of St Andrews

Shaftesbury Road, Cambridge CB2 8EA, United Kingdom

One Liberty Plaza, 20th Floor, New York, NY 10006, USA

477 Williamstown Road, Port Melbourne, VIC 3207, Australia

314–321, 3rd Floor, Plot 3, Splendor Forum, Jasola District Centre, New Delhi – 110025, India

103 Penang Road, #05–06/07, Visioncrest Commercial, Singapore 238467

Cambridge University Press is part of Cambridge University Press & Assessment, a department of the University of Cambridge.

We share the University's mission to contribute to society through the pursuit of education, learning and research at the highest international levels of excellence.

www.cambridge.org
Information on this title: www.cambridge.org/9781108813570

DOI: 10.1017/9781108884853

© Shivan Mahendrarajah 2021

This publication is in copyright. Subject to statutory exception and to the provisions of relevant collective licensing agreements, no reproduction of any part may take place without the written permission of Cambridge University Press & Assessment.

First published 2021
First paperback edition 2022

A catalogue record for this publication is available from the British Library

Library of Congress Cataloging-in-Publication data
Names: Mahendrarajah, Shivan, author.
Title: The Sufi saint of Jam : history, religion and politics of a Sunni shrine in Shi'i Iran / Shivan Mahendrarajah.
Description: New York : Cambridge University Press, 2021. | Series: Cambridge studies in Islamic civilization | Includes bibliographical references and index.
Identifiers: LCCN 2020041198 (print) | LCCN 2020041199 (ebook) | ISBN 9781108839693 (hardback) | ISBN 9781108884853 (ebook)
Subjects: LCSH: Islamic shrines – Iran – Turbat-i Jām. | Ahmad Jām, 1049 or 1050-1141 or 1142 – Shrines. | Muslim saints – Cult – Iran – Turbat-i Jām. | Sufis – Iran – Turbat-i Jām.
Classification: LCC BP187.55.I72 T876 2021 (print) | LCC BP187.55.I72 (ebook) | DDC 297.4/355592–dc23
LC record available at https://lccn.loc.gov/2020041198
LC ebook record available at https://lccn.loc.gov/2020041199

ISBN   978-1-108-83969-3   Hardback
ISBN   978-1-108-81357-0   Paperback

Cambridge University Press & Assessment has no responsibility for the persistence or accuracy of URLs for external or third-party internet websites referred to in this publication and does not guarantee that any content on such websites is, or will remain, accurate or appropriate.

*To my Mum,
Maureen Clare,
with love*

Contents

List of Plates, Figures, and Maps	*page* ix
List of Tables	xii
Preface	xiii
Acknowledgments	xv
Notes on the Text	xvii
List of Abbreviations	xviii
Introduction	1

Part I The Saint
1 Biography and Hagiography	9
2 Saintdom and Patronage	32

Part II The Successors
3 Ilkhanid/Kartid Eras to the Timurid Age	55
4 Safavid/Mughal Eras to the Islamic Republic	73

Part III The Shrine
5 Setting, Architecture, and Administration	93
6 Agro- and Hydro-management	124
7 Public Service in the Catchment Area	143
8 Sacred Topography and Islamic Learning	149

Part IV The Sufis
9 Doctrines and Practices	189
Conclusion	216

Appendices	223
Bibliography	241
Index	261

The plate section can be found between pp. 90 and 91

Plates, Figures, and Maps

PLATES

1 Shrine at the cusp of the Iranian Revolution, 1977
2 Shrine at the cusp of the Iranian Revolution, 1977
3 L–R: Kirmani Mosque, *iwan*, and Firuzshah's Dome. Ahmad-i Jam is buried immediately before the portal
4 Ahmad-i Jam's tomb, at entrance to portico (autumn 2017)
5 Ahmad-i Jam's tomb, pictured from above (winter 2011/12)
6 Squinch in corner of the *gunbad*. The inscription praising Kart *malik* Muʿizz al-Din runs around the entire chamber
7 Further views of the inscription and artwork inside the *gunbad*
8 Crown of the *gunbad*
9 Interior of the Masjid-i ʿatiq. Restored sections can be seen. Lines from the Victory verse (Q48:1–6) are on stucco frieze, but badly damaged. Lines refer to *malik* Ghiyath al-Din Kart's victory over the Chaghatay Mongols
10 Interior of Masjid-i ʿatiq. Closer view of the damaged inscription
11 Interior of Masjid-i ʿatiq. One of the original arches that survived is to the left; a restored arch is to its right
12 Section of interior of Gunbad-i Safid
13 Prayer niche (*mihrab*) inside the Masjid-i Kirmani
14 Safavid-era inscription to the *iwan* (funded by Shah ʿAbbas I, Safavi)
15 Gunbad-i Firuzshah and classic Timurid tilework

x   List of Plates, Figures, and Maps

16 Gunbad-i Firuzshah. The ladder is against the Hawza-yi ʿilmiyya Ahmadiyya. The seminary is situated where the Madrasa-i Firuzshah would have been
17 Section of interior of Masjid-i jamiʿ-i naw
18 Hawza-yi ʿilmiyya Ahmadiyya, its courtyard, and top of Gunbad-i Firuzshah, seen from atop the *iwan*
19 Ahmad-i Jam (the Furious Elephant) watching over young Akbar the Great
20 Hamida Banu Bigum bt. ʿAli Akbar Jami

FIGURES

2.1   Ahmad-i Jam (the Furious Elephant) watching over young Akbar the Great   50
4.1   Hamida Banu Bigum bt. ʿAli Akbar Jami   80
5.1   Schematic of the shrine complex and Ahmad-i Jam Park   99
5.2   Early twenty-first-century 3D image of the shrine complex   103
5.3   Schematic of the shrine complex, *ca.* 1938   104
5.4   Schematic of front of the shrine (L–R): Kirmani Mosque, *iwan* and entrance portal (*riwaq*), Gunbad-i Safid, and Gunbad-i Firuzshah   105
5.5   Schematic of east side of the shrine (L–R): New Mosque, courtyard, *gunbad*, *iwan*, Kirmani Mosque, and Gunbad-i Firuzshah   105
5.6   Lisa Golombek's reconstruction of the Old Mosque (Masjid-i ʿatiq)   107
5.7   Schematic of (L–R) Kirmani Mosque, entrance portal, and Gunbad-i Safid   108
5.8   Schematic of Firuzshah's Dome (Gunbad-i Firuzshah) and Firuzshah's Seminary (Madrasa-yi Firuzshah)   110
5.9   Schematic of the New Mosque (Masjid-i jamiʿ-i naw)   111
8.1   A "corner-catcher" (*gusha-gir*) at the shrine of ʿAbdallah Ansari, Herat, 2019   159
8.2   Principal, staff, and students at the Hawza-yi ʿilmiyya Ahmadiyya   185
9.1   The new hospice, Khanaqah-yi Masjid-i Nur   199
A1.1a Ahmad-i Jam's immediate descendants (part 1 of 2)   226
A1.1b Ahmad-i Jam's immediate descendants (part 2 of 2)   227

List of Plates, Figures, and Maps

A1.2 Qutb al-Din Muhammad Jami's descendants   228
A1.3 Shihab al-Din Isma'il Jami's descendants   229
A1.4 Tentative reconstruction of Transoxiana branch
       of Jami family   230
A1.5 Jami family marriage ties to the Kart dynasty
       of Herat   231
A2.1 Kashghari's novitiates   233

MAPS

1 Greater Iran and its neighbors   xix
2 Turbat-i Jam and its surroundings   xx

Tables

5.1 Major architectural components of the shrine complex   100
5.2 Administrators (*ra'is* or *mutawalli*) of the shrine   118
8.1 Administrators of the shrine's hospices (*khanaqah*)   169
8.2 Shrine's seminary (*madrasa*) curriculum in the Timurid era   174
8.3 Shrine's seminary curriculum for academic year AHS 1396–97/2017–18   179

Preface

The genesis for this book lies with a doctoral thesis written at Cambridge. The idea for shaping the book into a history of an Islamic institution over its entire life, 900 years – a daunting project – was inspired, however, by the observation of Dr. Tony Street of the University's Divinity Faculty, who commented about "the extraordinary spectacle of an institution dealing with pressures arising from changing dynasties and sectarian division, adopting strategies that allowed it to flourish through nine centuries." There is a need for histories of religious institutions, especially of Sufi shrines that continue to thrive and to fill spiritual voids. There is a need, relatedly, to understand the yearnings of Muslims who seek nearness to God through His "Friends" (saints), and the orthopraxes of Muslims who make pilgrimages (*ziyarat*) to sacred spaces (*haram*, *hima*).

Shrines, saints, and relic/tomb venerations are beliefs and rituals common to the Abrahamic faiths; a cursory review of the sundry pilgrimage guides to Jerusalem suffice to illustrate the point. Shrines and saints have been important not just to global Muslims, but to Iranians. Sunni and Shi'a often share shrines in Iran. Since Iran began its journey from majority Sunni to majority Shi'a in 1501, several shrines have acquired distinctively Shi'i hues; but those sites are neither closed to, nor shunned by, Sunnis; for instance, the magnificent Gawhar-Shad Mosque inside the shrine complex of Imam Riza. The saint cult of Ahmad-i Jam, still distinctively Sunni in a predominantly Sunni region, has a Shi'i following, including among Afghan Hazaras. A Shi'i following is fascinating considering that the saint was a bigoted Sunni who fulminated against the Shi'a, especially the Isma'ilis – the "Assassins" of lore.

The Shi'i Government of the Islamic Republic of Iran, allegedly "fundamentalist" and "sectarian," provides material financial and technical support to the administrators of the Sunni shrine. The saint cult and complex have been revitalized, but not entirely due to Tehran's efforts. A nebulous regional "Sunni revival" is ongoing.

In presenting this study, which spans historical periods and academic fields, I have tried to balance the needs of specialists from Islamic studies, Sufi studies, Iranian studies, Afghanistan studies, and Mongol studies, with the needs of nonspecialists who may find the subject matter to be of interest, possibly even of value, to their own work. It is unlikely that I will meet this balance to the satisfaction of everyone. I have dispensed with macrons and diacritics in transliterations: the Arabist or Persianist will know the correct word, but nonspecialists will be irritated by the dots and dashes.

The sources for a study spanning 900 years are unevenly distributed: sources are abundant for the centuries when Ahmad-i Jam's shrine and saint cult were in political, social, and economic bloom; but with the Shi'i ascendancy (1501), the indubitably Sunni shrine and saint cult withered in Iran. The cult even lost its Indian foothold when the Mughal emperor Akbar the Great – a descendant of Ahmad-i Jam – became a devotee of a Chishtiyya saint. Consequently, primary sources dwindled. But with the renaissance of Ahmad-i Jam's shrine and cult under the Islamic Republic of Iran, old and new sources are surfacing – a trend that includes this book.

Acknowledgments

This book began life as a doctoral thesis at the University of Cambridge – although little of the thesis survives in this book. At Cambridge, I benefited from assistance from Saqib Baburi, Farhad Daftary, Hamidreza Ghelichkhani, Geoffrey Khan, Charles Melville, Jürgen Paul, and Lloyd Ridgeon. At Herat University, I received assistance from Behzad Hakkak, Behzood Hakkak, and Ghulam Haydar Kabiri Harawi.

The monograph was materially transformed by keen insights from Hamid Algar, Muhammad Riza Shafiʻi Kadkani, Leonard Lewisohn,[†] Beatrice Forbes Manz, David O. Morgan,[†] Bernard O' Kane, Jürgen Paul, and Tony Street. Robert D. McChesney read the quasi-final manuscript. Their comments immeasurably improved the book. Errors of fact or understanding that stubbornly persist are my unqualified preserve. I benefited also from sources, photographs, schematics, or comments from Kamyar Abedi, Denise Aigle, Warwick Ball, Saqib Baburi, Thomas J. Barfield, Arthur Buehler, Lisa Golombek, Masoud Jafari Jazi, Rohullah Amin Mojadiddi, Zahra Talaee, and Christoph Werner. I am very grateful for their courtesies and assistance.

I have numerous friends and interlocutors at Turbat-i Jam to thank, although I will not list every name. Haji Qazi Sharaf al-Din Jami al-Ahmadi – the shrine's custodian (*mutawalli*) and Turbat-i Jam's Sunni Friday prayer leader (*imam-jumʻa*) – is thanked for hosting me on several occasions and for facilitating my research and making my visits memorable. Special thanks are due to Nasir al-Din Qiwam Ahmadi, ʻAbd al-Latif ʻArab-Timuri, and Yaghoob Nedaie – all of whom are Ahmad-i Jam's

---

[†] Died August 6, 2018.   [†] Died October 23, 2019.

progeny. I have enjoyed and benefited from their friendship, kindness, hospitality, humor, and patience.

The British Institute of Persian Studies, British Academy, Royal Historical Society, Gibb Memorial Trust, E. G. Browne Memorial Research Fund, and Soudavar Fund for Persian Studies are profusely thanked for generously financing my academic endeavors. The trustees and staff of the American Institute of Afghanistan Studies (Kabul and Boston) and Afghanistan Institute for Strategic Studies (Kabul and Herat) are warmly thanked for facilitating sojourns in Kabul, Herat, and Mazar-i Sharif. Senior colleagues at the University of St Andrews – Ali Ansari, Andrew Peacock, and Tim Greenwood – are warmly thanked for their moral and intellectual support.

The Ministry of Foreign Affairs of the Islamic Republic of Iran helped facilitate my research. The MFA (Tehran) and its embassies in London and Colombo (Sri Lanka), and the Iranian Cultural Center and Library in Colombo, are thanked for their courtesies and assistance.

Abdalrahim Taj-Muhammadi, Director of Sazman-i Miras-i Farhangi for Taybad and Turbat-i Jam, made available the architectural schematics reproduced in Chapter 5. I am indebted to Miras-i Farhangi, which does an outstanding job of preserving Iran's superlative cultural heritages. I appreciate Mr. Taj-Muhammadi's patience with the myriad of questions I hurled at him via Telegram.

Professor Chase Robinson, General Editor of CSIC, and CSIC's editorial board, and CUP's Dan Brown, Atifa Jiwa, Stephanie Taylor and her production staff in Cambridge; and the copyeditor, Muhammad Ridwaan, must be thanked for patiently working with a difficult manuscript, and for helping to bring this project to fruition. Authors perfunctorily thank reviewers while privately wanting to strangle the blighters, but I am genuinely grateful for the helpful guidance from reviewers, which helped improve the manuscript.

I appreciate the courtesies extended by the entities and individuals holding copyright to the photographs reproduced herein. I have to single out Staatsbibliothek zu Berlin with effusive praise and thanks for allowing me to use, without fuss or cost, a folio from *Jahangir Album* (Libr. Pict. A117). I was unable to include an image from *Akbarnama* (IS.2:77–1896), which is held by the Victoria and Albert Museum. The V&A refused to issue a perpetual license: a non-expiring license is indispensable in a technological age where books are available in e-book formats, "print on demand," and thus never out of print. Unless indicated, copyright to maps and photographs belongs to me. If I have failed to acknowledge someone, please forgive the oversight. It is unintentional.

Notes on the Text

QUR'AN AND HADITH

Quotes from the Qur'an are from 'Abdallah Yusuf 'Ali's translation. Qur'an citations are given in the form "Q12:15," that is, chapter (*sura*) 12, verse (*aya*) 15. Hadith refer to the six authentic (*sahih*) collections available online at https://sunnah.com (in Arabic and English). They are given here in the form "*Sahih al-Bukhari* # 1198."

TRANSLITERATION

The *IJMES* systems for Arabic and Persian are followed but without the macrons (ā/ī/ū) and diacritics (ḍ/ḫ/ṣ/ş/ṭ/ẓ/ż/ẓ). 'Ayn (') and *hamza* (') represent letters of the alphabet and are retained. The letter *waw* is rendered *w* throughout; diphthongs are *aw* and *ay*; doubled final form of the vowel *i* is -*iyy*.

Spelling follows options in dictionaries by Hans Wehr and Francis Steingass. Arabic, Turkish, Persian, and Mongol words accepted into English and included in *Webster's* or the *OED* are not transliterated; hence, ulama, darwish, waqf, and so on.

Abbreviations

BSOAS	Bulletin of the School of Oriental and African Studies
CAJ	Central Asiatic Journal
CHI	Cambridge History of Iran
EI^2	Encyclopedia of Islam (2nd ed.)
EI^3	Encyclopedia of Islam (3rd ed.)
EIr	Encyclopædia Iranica
EQ	Encyclopaedia of the Qur'an
HJAS	Harvard Journal of Asiatic Studies
IJMES	International Journal of Middle East Studies
JAH	Journal of Asian History
JESHO	Journal of the Economic and Social History of the Orient
JOAS	Journal of the American Oriental Society
JRAS	Journal of the Royal Asiatic Society
PIHC	Proceedings of the Indian History Congress
ZDMG	Zeitschrift der Deutschen Morgenländischen Gesellschaft

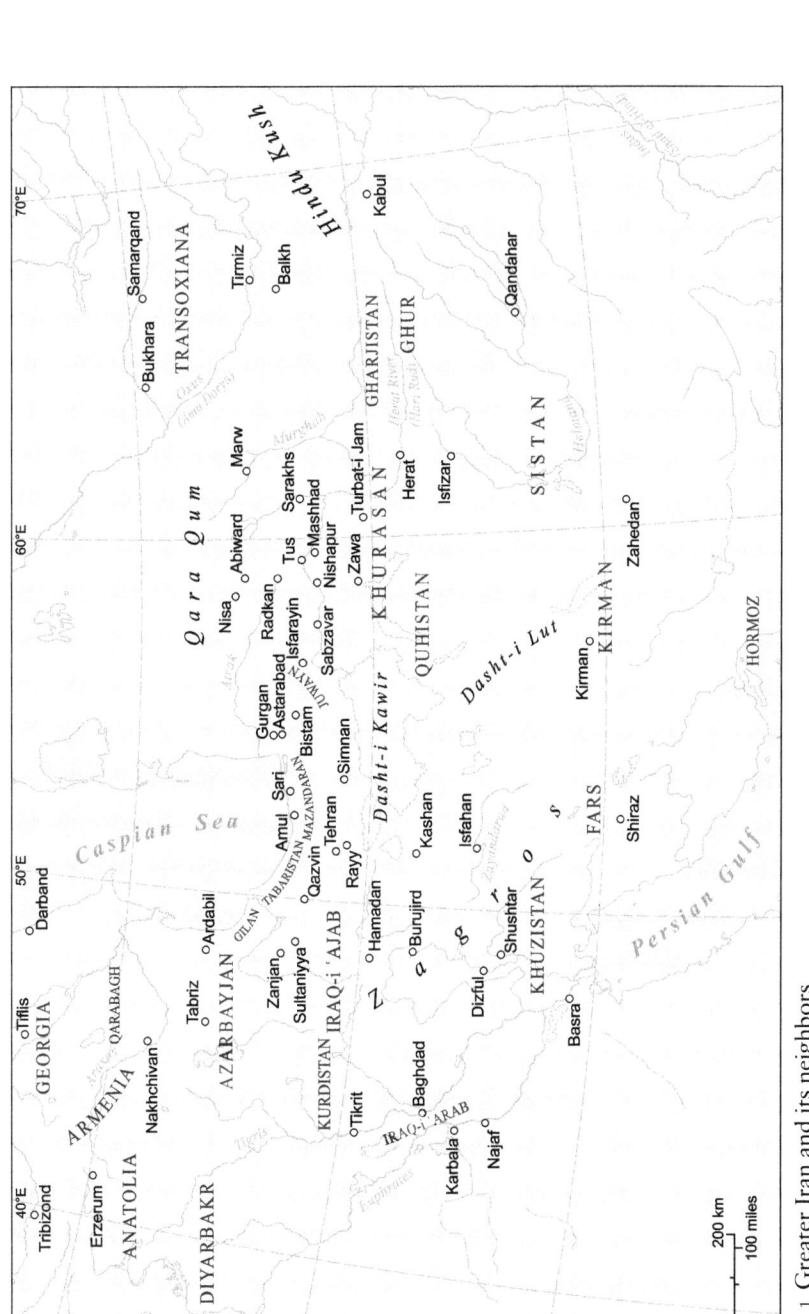

MAP 1 Greater Iran and its neighbors

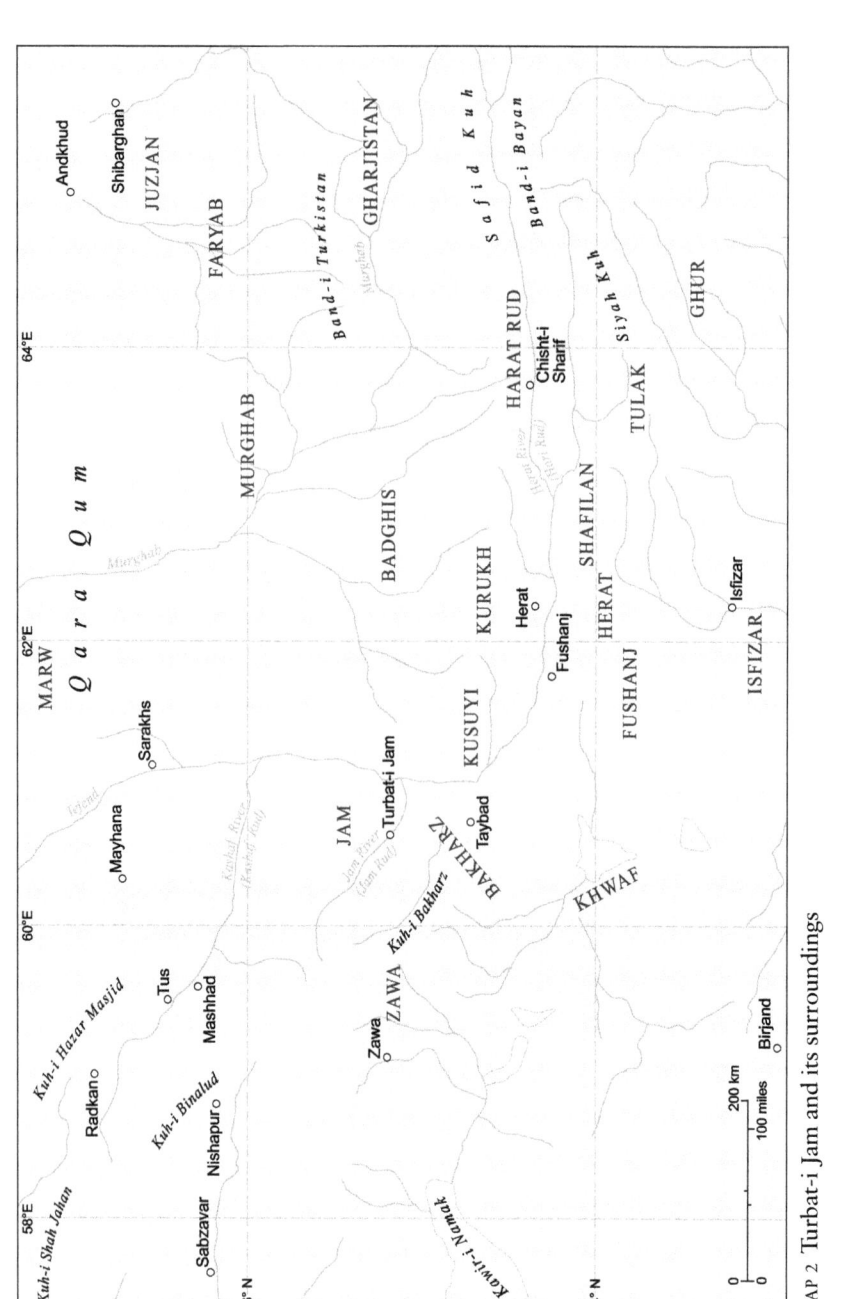

MAP 2 Turbat-i Jam and its surroundings

Introduction

This is a history of a 900-year-old Sunni shrine in the Islamic Republic of Iran and the Sufi shaykhs who propagated the legacy of the Muslim saint buried thereat.

I first visited Turbat-i Jam in eastern Iran, the seat of the mausoleum of Shaykh al-Islam Ahmad-i Jam, in spring 2010. While traveling from Mashhad to Jam by bus, the fecundity of the province of Jam became evident: distant snowcapped mountains on both sides of Jam's plains fed rivulets, rivers, channels, and subterranean waterways, which nourished agricultural and pastoral activities. Jam was as the fourteenth-century traveler Ibn Battuta had described it: "pretty, with orchards and trees, abundance of springs, and flowing streams." My fellow passengers were dressed suspiciously like their neighbors in Afghanistan. The majority of the region's residents are Sunni, with a burgeoning Shi'i minority. The passengers were mostly Iranians, with a smattering of Afghan Hazaras and Tajiks. Traditional dress – turbans and shalwar – is not uncommon, although the burqa, ubiquitous across the border in nearby Herat, is rarely seen in the city of Jam or its purlieus. Jam is a prosperous region. It profits from a sensible balance of Iranian tradition and modernity; and Iran's Sunni and Shi'i cultural heritages.

Turbat-i Jam is a charming burg of around 100,000 souls. It is typically Iranian, with broad, tree-lined boulevards and manicured plazas. The shrine of the premier saint of this section of Khurasan – a storied region with a surfeit of saints – is in the northeast corner of Turbat-i Jam ("the sepulcher of [Shaykh al-Islam Ahmad of] Jam"). Before storing my shoes and venturing past the entrance, I enjoyed the sights of the walled shrine: the ornately decorated portal arch (*iwan*) towered 88 ft/26.8 m, framed by unblemished blue sky. The Firuzshah Dome (Gunbad-i Firuzshahi) reflected the spring sunlight off its turquoise dome, partly obscuring the awful gash that had characterized it in photographs taken over decades past. The shrine complex is warm and welcoming. The daily traffic of pilgrims ebbs and flows, but is substantial on Fridays and holy days. Under Iranian law, a city can hold Friday (*jumʿa*) prayers at only one location. Ahmad-i Jam's shrine is the locus for *jumʿa* services and Eid celebrations for Sunnis (the Shiʿa of Jam hold *jumʿa* services across town). The shrine's custodian is the prayer leader (*imam-jumʿa*) for the Sunnis of Turbat-i Jam and its environs.

The shrine complex now has two flourishing Islamic seminaries (sing. madrasa) – one for males and one for females – a public library, and landscaped gardens. Ahmad-i Jam's shrine stood in contrast to more famous shrines visited by this writer on travels in the Islamic world; for example, ʿAbdallah Ansari's shrine in Herat (renovated by the Aga Khan Trust for Culture (AKTC); last visited in October 2019), Abu Nasr Parsa's in Balkh (crumbling in 2007; but reconstruction by AKTC was almost complete in October 2015 when I last visited), and Ibn al-ʿArabi's in Damascus (last visited in 2008).[1]

Why has Ahmad-i Jam's shrine flourished while other Sufi shrines throughout the Islamic world have gone to ruin?

How did this unapologetically Sunni community survive for 900 years, and come to thrive in the (Shiʿi) Islamic Republic of Iran? The Shiʿi shrines of Iraq and Iran receive official patronage. The shrine of Imam ʿAli b. Abi Talib (fourth caliph) in Mazar-i Sharif, Balkh, obtains support from Afghanistan's Tajik, Turk, Pashtun, Baluch, Hazara, Sunni, Twelver Shiʿa, and Ismaʿili Shiʿa peoples. Interlocutors at Turbat-i Jam, unwilling to credit the Islamic Republic of Iran for anything positive, claimed the complex had fared better under the *ancien régime* (Pahlawis, 1925–79); but this is contradicted by Qajar- and Pahlawi-era photographs, travelogues, and architectural studies. The shrine complex was crumbling but sparkles today. The aforementioned gash on the Gunbad-i Firuzshahi has since been repaired: the dome is resplendent. The damaged *iwan* was refurbished. The 700-year-old "Old Mosque" (Masjid-i ʿatiq), reduced to fragments of brickwork and stucco, has been masterfully restored to nearly its Ilkhanid-era condition.

---

[1] AKTC, an Ismaʿili Shiʿa nonprofit, was praised by Afghan officials for restoring Sunni and Shiʿa cultural heritages in Balkh and Herat (fifty-two projects in Herat alone).

Introduction

The reason the shrine thrives is because Ahmad-i Jam – who fathered forty-two children – is blessed to have thousands of descendants who continue to venerate his memory and to protect his legacy. The contemporary shaykhs of Jam interact with the Islamic Republic of Iran just as their ancestors did with the Seljuqs, Mongols, Timurids, Safavids, Afshars, Qajars, and Pahlawis: they adapt and shift strategy. The community's focus is singular: it is always about Ahmad-i Jam: *this, too, shall pass but Ahmad is forever*. Beatrice Manz observed that "[t]he emphasis on the founder Ahmad-i Jam [...] may help to account for the family's receptiveness to a variety of teachings and its continuing adaptability to changes of political power."

This monograph demonstrates the truth of Manz's keen insight. Ahmad-i Jam's successors protect his shrine when they must, and extract benefits from their overlords when they can. This institution's longevity is testament to the resilience and diplomacy of a shifting coalition of shaykhs – primarily males but also females – who have lovingly tendered their saint's grave and managed the complex, generation to generation, from century to century. Decisions are ordinarily based on consensus. A rash act could cost lives and lead to the confiscation of assets and the shuttering of the shrine.

To the credit of the Islamic Republic of Iran,[2] it does not view Islamic institutions such as Ahmad-i Jam's shrine through a sectarian lens, but rather, through the prism of national heritage. The institution may be Sunni, but the complex's eclectic architectural ensemble is testament to Iran's superlative cultural tapestry, and therefore deserving of public funds and technical expertise from the Sazman-i Miras-i Farhangi (Cultural Heritage Organization). The mausoleum of Zayn al-Din (Abu Bakr) Taybadi in nearby Taybad was also reconstructed by Miras-i Farhangi with public and private funds. This, too, is a Sunni institution. The Islamic Republic's outlook toward the preservation of Iranian heritages extends to major faiths: the Zoroastrian fire temple (*atishkada*) in Yazd; the mausoleum for Judaism's Esther and Mordecai in Hamadan; and Catholic and Armenian churches. Persepolis, Pasargadae, Christian monasteries, and other pre-Islamic and Islamic sites among the twenty-four

---

[2] It is apparently bad form to say anything positive about the Shiʻa state; but it is worth comparing Shiʻa Iran's approach toward its national heritages with the demolition of Islamic and non-Islamic spiritual and sepulchral edifices in Mecca, Medina, Karbala, Qatif, and elsewhere by the Wahhabi Kingdom of Saudi Arabia. Moreover, the Shiʻa minority of Saudi Arabia suffer persecutions and indignities. See Toby Matthiesen, *The Other Saudis: Shiism, Dissent and Sectarianism* (Cambridge: Cambridge University Press, 2015).

4   Introduction

recognized and fifty-six tentative UNESCO World Heritage sites in Iran[3] are preserved and protected.[4]

STRUCTURE AND THEMES OF THE BOOK

Part I covers the saint's activities in Seljuq Iran. It reveals for the first time (in Western scholarship) aspects of Ahmad-i Jam's biography that were redacted by Jami hagiographers. His initial training was with the Karrami sect (*madhhab*), but once they were branded "heretics," Ahmad's biography was revised.

The saint cult and the "branding and marketing" of Ahmad's saintly talents are addressed next. Thoughts on sainthood by Hakim al-Tirmidhi (in *Sirat al-awliya'*) offer analytical frameworks. I aim to place the formation of Ahmad-i Jam's saint cult within Islamic tradition. Sometime around 649/1251, about a century after his death, shaykhs of Jam started promoting Ahmad-i Jam as the "protector of the realm," that is, Ahmad-i Jam, "the patron saint of kings." The first king to seek Ahmad-i Jam's protection was Shams al-Din Muhammad Kart, the founder of the Kartid dynasty of Herat (1245–1381), vassals of Iran's Mongol overlords (Ilkhanids, 1254–1335). The branding of Ahmad-i Jam as a saint who protects kings attracted royal support and patronage.

Part II describes how Ahmad-i Jam's successors accumulated wealth for the shrine and propagated his legacy. Marriage between the Karts and Jamis brought financial and architectural bounties to the shrine. A Jami Sufi shaykh and his royal acolyte, the Kart king, Ghiyath al-Din, transformed Ahmad's shrine into a *complex*. The shrine continued to prosper under the Timurids. Tamerlane visited Turbat-i Jam to pay homage at Ahmad's tomb. Temür's son, Shah-Rukh, became a devotee of Ahmad-i Jam, and visited the shrine to associate with his Sufi shaykh, the shrine's custodian, and chief of its Sufi hospices. Mosques, domes, and madrasas were sponsored by Timurid officials, and charitable endowments (waqf) were established. Shah-Rukh and his munificent spouse, Gawhar-Shad, included benefits for Ahmad's shrine in their waqf deed for the Gawhar-Shad Mosque in Mashhad.

[3] See list at https://whc.unesco.org/en/statesparties/ir.
[4] In spring 2019, I again visited the archaeological sites at Persepolis and Pasargadae; and Christian, Jewish, Zoroastrian, and Islamic heritage sites in Yazd, Shiraz, Isfahan, Kashan, Natanz, and Qum. This tour (as with earlier tours) included visits to churches, synagogues, fire temples, mosques, and shrines, where I met with staff and clerics. Observations and statements are documented, and the sites are photographed.

Structure and Themes of the Book 5

The dawn of the Safavid/Shi'a age signalled the decline of the shrine's fortunes. Safavid-Uzbek wars were painful for Khurasanians. Prolonged and intense sectarian violence was visited on Khurasan. Jami shaykhs fled to India, where they found succor with their kinsman, the Mughal emperor Humayun, and his son, Akbar the Great. Shi'i policies toward the shrine were flexible. Shah Isma'il I, Safavi renewed fiscal immunities for the shrine's custodian; and Shah 'Abbas I sponsored major restorative work on the *iwan*. Nonetheless, the shrine declined as conversion to Shi'ism advanced. When Robert Byron (author of *Road to Oxiana*) visited in 1934, the shrine was in decay: "[t]he shrine there was disappointing. So was our lunch."

In Part III, Chapter 5 describes the physical setting of the shrine and its architectural developments. Included are new schematics that were graciously made available by Sazman-i Miras-i Farhangi; photographs of the shrine in decay, from 1977 – the cusp of the Iranian Revolution – courtesy of Warwick Ball; and photographs of its present state. A discussion on the shrine's administration and waqfs follows. A list of known administrators (sing. *ra'is* or *mutawalli*) is included.

In Chapters 6 and 7, the shrine's accumulation of wealth and influence through control of hydrological systems and agricultural estates is analyzed. Acquisition was principally through imperial benefices under the Ilkhanids, Kartids, and Timurids. However, with wealth and influence there existed sociopolitical obligations, namely, service to community: shaykhs had to "feed the people" (*takafful-i umur*).

In Chapter 8, the sacred topography of the shrine, and the diverse spiritual and intellectual activities that blossom within sacred topography, are considered. "Spiritual blessings" (*baraka*) and "divine effusions" (*fayz*) are believed to emanate from the saint's grave. This attracted flows of pilgrims who sought to acquire *baraka* through their venerations, and believers who wanted to be entombed near their saint to secure his blessings until the Day of Judgment. Classes were held inside the shrine: Islamic learning, it was believed, acquired "special merit" if conducted in sacred spaces; hence the erection of seminaries and hospices in sacred spaces. Islamic curricula at the shrine's seminaries (with tables of medieval and contemporary literary works studied), and putative Sufi regimens at the shrine's hospices, are analyzed. A list of known chiefs of the shrine's *khanaqah*s is included.

Part IV describes the mystical doctrines and practices of the Sufis, the core of the saint cult. Ahmad-i Jam did not bequeath a method (*tariq*, *suluk*) for gnosis (*'irfan*). The absence of binding rules proved beneficial:

Sufis were allowed freedom to explore. Jami Sufis borrowed doctrines from the Naqshbandiyya, who had become prominent in Timurid Herat. Some Jamis preferred the silent recollection of God (*dhikr-i khafi*) to the vocal method (*dhikr-i jahri*). Gnostic preferences did not degenerate into factionalism as elsewhere. Irrespective of preferred Sufi current, Jamis bonded their hearts (*rabita*) to their shaykh, Ahmad-i Jam, and focused their love on a mental image of Ahmad, the unifying figure around whom revolved sundry Sufi practices.

Critical Sufi practices, *dhikr* (recollection of God), *samaʿ* (auditory stimulation), *khalwa* (seclusion), and *rabita* (bonding the heart) are closely analyzed. The study of the *hybrid* mystical practices of the Sufis of Jam include a case study of a Jami-Naqshbandi shaykh, ʿAziz-Allah Jami, a novitiate of Saʿd al-Din Kashghari, who also initiated ʿAbd al-Rahman Jami, the last great bard of Herat, a man fondly remembered in his native land as the "seal of the poets" (*khatm al-shuʿaraʾ*), which is emblazoned on road signs pointing to his birthplace in the province of Jam.

We turn now to a biography of our protagonist, Ahmad-i Jam.

Part I
The Saint

I

Biography and Hagiography

Ahmad-i Jam's family and education are examined below. Separating biography (putative fact) from hagiography (embellishment or fabrication), however, is challenging. His background includes elements that were whitewashed when political winds shifted, namely, Ahmad's putative training in Karrami *khanaqah*s. His spiritual genealogy (*silsila*) was modified to interpolate a nexus to Imam Riza, the Eighth Imam for the Twelver Shiʻa. Ahmad-i Jam's intellectual journey is captivating, and reflective of the fluidity of Khurasanian Sufism during his long life: Ahmad-i Jam, the son of a Shafiʻi scholar, transitioned to Karrami ascetic (*zahid*) and then to Hanafi mystic (*sufi*).

THE SHAYKH

Ahmad-i Jam was born in 441/1049 in the village of Namaq, which is located south of Nishapur. He died 10 Muharram 536/15 August 1141. The conventional narrative is that Ahmad-i Jam's youth was spent in dissipation. After a "road to Damascus" moment, Ahmad repented (*tawba*) and retired to the mountains of Khurasan, where he remained in seclusion for eighteen years, meditating and praying until God commanded him to rejoin society. He was then about forty years of age. Ahmad settled in the Maʻd-Abad section of the province of Jam and embarked on a life of preaching, miracle-making (*karamat*), and enforcing of the Shariʻa. He built a congregational mosque (*masjid-i jamiʻ*) and a Sufi convent (*khanaqah*) in Maʻd-Abad village. His interpretation of the Shariʻa was uncompromising; he is depicted as a pitiless enforcer of *al-amr bi-l-maʻruf wa-l-nahy ʻan al-munkar*, an Islamic obligation whereby every Muslim is (theoretically) expected to "enjoin the good and forbid the reprehensible,"[1] or stated differently, the obligation of every Muslim to chastise their neighbors for perceived violations of God's laws. Ahmad-i Jam earned himself a reputation as a frightful busybody who harassed his neighbors and destroyed musical instruments and wine casks in the name of God.[2] He was exceptionally mean to Zoroastrians. Ahmad's circle of devotees burgeoned into a significant Sufi community in Khurasan.[3] Ahmad-i Jam's most famous loyalist was the Seljuq sultan, Ahmad Sanjar (r. 511–52/1118–57) b. Malikshah (d. 485/1092) b. Alp Arslan (d. 465/1072).[4]

Ahmad thrived in Ma'd-Abad village, which adjoined the town of Jam. In the years following Ahmad's death, village and town merged, coming to be called Turbat-i Jam, "the sepulcher of [Shaykh al-Islam Ahmad of] Jam." A Sufi community revolved around a shrine that was initially a simple tumulus. About a century after his death, a funerary building was erected behind the tumulus. Additional edifices were sponsored during the Kartid (r. 643–783/1245–1381) and Timurid (r. 783–911/1381–1506) periods by royal or other high-ranking patrons. The sacred space transformed into a sparkling shrine complex.

---

[1] Michael Cook, *Commanding Right and Forbidding Wrong in Islamic Thought* (Cambridge: Cambridge University Press, 2000); Michael Cook, *Forbidding Wrong in Islam* (Cambridge: Cambridge University Press, 2003). The second title is a superb introduction to an intricate topic.

[2] A popular activity under the rubric of "*al-amr bi-l-ma'ruf wa-l-nahy 'an al-munkar.*"

[3] Fritz Meier, "Ahmad-i Jam," *EI*², 1:283a; Omid Safi, "Ahmad-i Jam," *EI*³ (online); Heshmat Moayyad, "Ahmad-i Jam," *EIr*, 1:648a; Fritz Meier, "Zur Biographie Ahmad-i Gam's und zur Quellenkunde von Gami's Nafahat'l-uns," *ZDMG* 97 (1943): 47–67; Vladimir Ivanow, "A Biography of Shaykh Ahmad-i-Jam," *JRAS* (1917): 291–365 (Meier and Ivanow are dated but useful); Heshmat Moayyad and Franklin Lewis (trans.), *The Colossal Elephant and His Spiritual Feats: Shaykh Ahmad-e Jam. The Life and Legend of a Popular Sufi Saint of 12th Century Iran* (Costa Mesa, CA: Mazda, 2004), 8–12, 21–28; Ibrahim Zanganah, *Sarzamin-i Jam wa rijalan* (Turbat-i Jam: Intisharat-i Shaykh al-Islam Ahmad-i Jam, 1384/2006), 68–69, 71–72; 'Ali Fazl, *Karnama-yi Ahmad-i Jam* (Tehran: Intisharat-i Tus, 1382/2003), 37, 51–53.

[4] On this Central Asian Turkish dynasty, which ruled Iran, see A. C. S. Peacock, *The Great Seljuq Empire* (Edinburgh: Edinburgh University Press, 2015). On their religious outlooks, including Sanjar's association with Ahmad-i Jam, see D. G. Tor, "'Sovereign and Pious': The Religious Life of the Great Seljuq Sultans," in *The Seljuqs: Politics, Society, and Culture*, ed. Christian Lange and Songül Mecit (Edinburgh: Edinburgh University Press, 2011), 39–62.

AHMAD'S "ORIGINAL" SPIRITUAL CHAIN (*SILSILA*)

Ahmad-i Jam's spiritual pedigree, or initiatic chain (*silsila*), is problematic.[5] Firstly, a Sufi's *silsila* was not emphasized in his epoch, although in later centuries the *silsila* was to become prominent. The eponym of the Naqshbandi Sufi brotherhood (*tariqa*), Baha' al-Din Naqshband (d. 791/1389), famously retorted to an inquiry about his spiritual lineage, that "nobody gets anywhere through a *silsila*."[6] However, in later years, specifically, the Timurid period, emphasis on Sufi *silsila*s became manifest.[7] The earliest *silsila* proffered for Ahmad-i Jam is by his youngest son, Shihab al-Din Isma'il Jami (d. *ca*. 617/1220f.), in his *A Treatise on Proving the Greatness of the Shaykh of Jam*:[8]

This *silsila* is Ahmad → his preceptor, Abu Tahir Kurd → his preceptor, Abu Sa'id b. Abu al-Khayr → (and so on), Abu al-Fazl Hasan [of Sarakhs] → Abu Nasr Sarraj → Murta'ish [of Baghdad] → Junayd [of Baghdad] → Sari Saqati → Ma'ruf Karkhi → Dawud Ta'i → Habib 'Ajami → Hasan Basri → Hazrat Imam 'Ali b. Abi Talib → the Prophet of Islam.

This spiritual pedigree happens to match the *silsila* extended for Abu Sa'id b. Abu al-Khayr (d. 4 Sha'ban 440/12 January 1049) by his hagiologist, Muhammad ibn Munawwar.[9] We shall return to Abu Sa'id momentarily.

Abu Tahir Kurd is virtually unknown. Over generations, hagiographers excluded filaments of Kurd's spiritual legacy from hagiologies, leaving us with scattered fragments by the time we arrive at the biographical entry for Abu Tahir Kurd in Nur al-Din 'Abd al-Rahman Jami's *Breaths of Intimacy* (*Nafahat al-uns*).[10] There was evidently something in his background that required whitewashing – just as the first forty years of Ahmad's life were diligently sanitized and embellished (as shall be explained). What can be

---

[5] On hagiologies and interpretive paradigms, see Shahzad Bashir, "Naqshband's Lives: Sufi Hagiography between Manuscripts and Genre," in *Sufism in Central Asia*, ed. Devin DeWeese and Jo-Ann Gross (Leiden: Brill, 2018), 75–97.

[6] 'Abd al-Rahman Jami, *Nafahat al-uns min hazarat al-quds*, ed. Mehdi Tawhidi–Pur (Tehran: Intisharat-i kitabfurushi-i Mahmudi, 1336/1957), 386.

[7] See Devin DeWeese, *An "Uvaysi" Sufi in Timurid Mawarannahr* (Bloomington, IN: Research Institute for Inner Asian Studies, 1993), 6 and n14.

[8] Shihab al-Din Isma'il b. Ahmad-i Jam Namaqi, *Risala dar isbat-i buzurgi-yi Shaykh-i Jam*, ed. Hasan Nasiri Jami (Tehran: Pizhuhishgah-i 'ulum-i insani wa mutala'at-i farhangi, 1391/2012), 24.

[9] Muhammad Ibn Munawwar, *Asrar al-tawhid fi maqamat-i Shaykh Abi Sa'id*, 2 vols., ed. Muhammad Riza Shafi'i Kadkani (Tehran: Agah, 1366–67/1987–88), 1:26, 32, 48–49; Reynold A. Nicholson, *Studies in Islamic Mysticism* (Cambridge: Cambridge University Press, 1921), 10.

[10] Jami, *Nafahat*, 366–68.

12   Biography and Hagiography

gleaned is that Kurd and Ahmad had had a tense relationship.[11] They parted company.

Ahmad (or his acolytes) propagated a spiritual connection to Abu Saʿid b. Abu al-Khayr, a famous Sufi master who had died shortly before Ahmad was born.[12] "It is said that on his deathbed [Abu Saʿid] had bestowed his *khirqa* to Ahmad-i Jam ... who was just about to be born."[13] The claim is asserted in a hagiography on Ahmad-i Jam, *The Spiritual Feats of the Furious Elephant*,[14] composed *ca.* 570/1175 by Sadid al-Din Ghaznawi, one of Ahmad-i Jam's younger contemporaries.[15] This is a classic hagiographical topos: the *khirqa*, a Sufi's mantle, is handed from master to chosen disciple;[16] but a *khirqa*'s conveyance of spiritual authority does not always involve the physical transfer of the object.[17] The symbolism of the *khirqa*'s conveyance is that Ahmad-i Jam was the heir to Abu Saʿid's spiritual legacy.

Hagiologists tweaked Ahmad's birth year of 441/1049 to comport with the purported spiritual link to Abu Saʿid: they claimed Ahmad was born in Muharram 440/June–July 1048, six months before Abu Saʿid's *rihlat* – journey to Paradise.[18] The assertion of a bond with Abu Saʿid has no basis

---

[11] Muhammad Riza Shafiʿi Kadkani, *Darwish-i sitihandah: az miras-i ʿirfani-yi Shaykh-i Jam* (Tehran: Intisharat-i sukhan, 1393/2014), 51–56.

[12] On Abu Saʿid, see Muhammad Riza Shafiʿi Kadkani, *Chashidan-i taʾm-i waqt: az miras-i ʿirfani-yi Abu Saʿid Abu al-Khayr* (Tehran: Intisharat-i sukhan, 1385/2006), 15–64; Nicholson, *Islamic Mysticism*, 1–76; Fritz Meier, *Abu Saʿid-i Abu lʾHayr (357–440/1049): Wirklichkeit und Legende* (Leiden: Brill, 1976).

[13] Annemarie Schimmel, *Mystical Dimensions of Islam* (Chapel Hill, NC: University of North Carolina Press, 1975), 244; Jami, *Nafahat*, 357–66 (biographical entry on Ahmad-i Jam).

[14] Sadid al-Din Ghaznawi, *Maqamat-i Zhanda–Pil*, ed. Heshmat Moayyad (Tehran: Intisharat-i ʿilmi wa farhangi, 1388/2009 [reprint of 1340/1960 edition by Bungah-i tarjuma wa nashr-i kitab]), 193–95 (narrative no. 166).

[15] Jürgen Paul, "Constructing the Friends of God: Sadid al-Din Ghaznavi's *Maqamat-i Zinda-Pil* (with Some Remarks on Ibn Munawwar's *Asrar al-tawhid*)," in *Narrative Pattern and Genre in Hagiographic Life Writing*, ed. Stephan Conermann (Berlin: E.B.-Verlag, 2014), 205–26.

[16] See Schimmel, *Dimensions*, 102–3.

[17] Jamal J. Elias, "The Sufi Robe (*Khirqa*) as a Vehicle of Spiritual Authority," in *Robes and Honor: The Medieval World of Investiture*, ed. Stewart Gordon (New York: Palgrave, 2001), 275–89; on *khirqa*s as sacred objects, see Robert D. McChesney, "Reliquary Sufism: Sacred Fiber in Afghanistan," in *Sufism in Central Asia*, ed. Devin DeWeese and Jo-Ann Gross (Leiden: Brill, 2018), 192–237.

[18] Kadkani, *Darwish*, 189 (*Khulasat al-maqamat*); Shihab al-Din Abu al-Makarim b. ʿAlaʾ al-Mulk Jami, *Khulasat al-maqamat-i hazrat-i fil subhan*, ed. Hasan Nasiri Jami (Tehran: Pizhuhishgah-i ʿulum-i insani wa mutalaʿat-i farhangi, 1396/2018), 33. *Khulasat al-maqamat* is reproduced in the second part of Kadkani, *Darwish* (see discussion in Appendix 3 on the Kadkani edition; and the 1396/2017f. edition by Hasan Nasiri Jami).

in fact. Moreover, Ahmad-i Jam was the opposite of Abu Saʿid b. Abu al-Khayr "in almost every respect":[19] Ahmad-i Jam was haughty, belligerent, vindictive, and miserly; whereas Abu Saʿid was generous, gregarious, and tolerant. The Sufis of Jam insist that Abu Saʿid's *khirqa* remained with Ahmad-i Jam's progeny in Kusuyi (west of Herat);[20] however, Abu Saʿid's *khirqa*s were retained by his progeny in Mayhana (Turkmenistan).[21] A hagiography about Abu Saʿid, *Asrar al-tawhid* (*The Secrets of [God's] Oneness*), written between 574/1179 and 588/1192 by Abu Saʿid's fifth-generation descendant, Ibn Munawwar, does not mention the purported connection to Ahmad-i Jam.

AHMAD-I JAM'S *UWAYSI* INITIATION BY KHIZR

During Ahmad's mountain seclusion, he is alleged to have received a *khirqa* from Khizr,[22] one of God's immortal servants and the companion of Moses/Musa in the Qurʾan (Q18:60–82).[23] Khizr is a guide for mystics and a versatile source of inspiration for Sufis;[24] for instance, the topos where Khizr directs the Mongol hordes to kill evildoers,[25] thus offering spiritual justification for the Mongol carnage.

The conveyance of a *khirqa* from Khizr to Ahmad-i Jam implies the transference of exoteric (*zahir*) and esoteric (*batin*) knowledge of Revelation, in effect, *uwaysi* infusion or initiation. The term *uwaysi* is utilized here with caution because the concept and term only came into prominence in the eighth/fourteenth century. But first, the *uwaysi* concept.

Muharram is a blessed month. Ahmad-i Jam allegedly made his *rihlat* on Ashura (10 Muharram).

[19] Schimmel, *Dimensions*, 244.

[20] ʿAli Buzjani, *Rawzat al-riyahin*, ed. Heshmat Moayyad (Tehran: Bungah-i tarjuma wa nashr-i kitab, 1345/1966), 67; ʿAli Buzjani, *Rawzat al-riyahin*, ed. Hasan Nasiri Jami (Tehran: Pizhuhishgah-i ʿulum-i insani wa mutalaʿat-i farhangi, 1396/2017f) (on the new edition, see Appendix 3). On the Kusuyi Jami lineage, see Figure A1.1b # 8.

[21] Kadkani, *Darwish*, 56–63. A Sufi can aquire *khirqa*s from different masters. See, e.g., Elias, "Sufi Robe," 278ff.

[22] Kadkani, *Darwish*, 176 (his edition of *Khulasat al-maqamat*); ʿAlaʾ al-Mulk Jami/Jami (ed.), *Khulasat al-maqamat*, 19.

[23] John Renard, "Khadr/Khidr," *EQ*, 3:81–84; ʿAbdullah Yusuf ʿAli, *The Meaning of the Holy Qurʾan*, 11th ed. (Beltsville, MD: Amana, 2004), n2411 (commentary).

[24] Schimmel, *Dimensions*, 105–6; see also, Carl Ernst, *The Shambhala Guide to Sufism* (Boston, MA: Shambhala, 1997), 38–39.

[25] Devin DeWeese, "'Stuck in the Throat of Chingiz Khan,'" in *History and Historiography of Post-Mongol Central Asia and the Middle East*, ed. Judith Pfeiffer and S. Quinn (Wiesbaden: Harrassowitz, 2006), 23–60.

The *uwaysiyya* are Sufis said to have been infused with knowledge by the spiritual presence (*ruhaniyyat*) of a deceased prophet or shaykh. The term is from Uways al-Qarani (d. 37/657),[26] killed at the Battle of Siffin fighting for Imam ʿAli b. Abi Talib (d. 40/661), the fourth "rightly guided caliph" and the first imam for all Shiʿa communities. Legend has it that the Prophet and Uways had communicated telepathically; hence the popularity of the term.[27] Support for the transference of knowledge by divine presence is found in the Qurʾan: "So they found one of Our servants, on whom We had bestowed Mercy from Ourselves and whom We had taught knowledge from Our own Presence" (Q18:65). Prominent Sufis of the eastern Islamic world for whom *uwaysi* claims have been proffered include ʿAli b. Ahmad al-Kharaqani (d. 425/1033); Bahaʾ al-Din Naqshband; and Ahmad Sirhindi (d. 1034/1624), the Indian "renewer of the faith" (*mujaddidi*).

The *uwaysi* claim made for Ahmad-i Jam manifests in the *Concise Spiritual Feats*, a book dedicated in 840/1436–37 to Shah-Rukh, Tamerlane's son:

[when Ahmad-i Jam was engaged in spiritual exercises] in the mountain [Bizd, in Jam province], he received a *khirqa* from the hand of Khizr (PBUH); Abu Tahir Kurd was his [Ahmad's] directing shaykh (*pir-i suhbat*), and [Kurd] was a disciple of Shaykh Abu al-ʿAbbas [Ahmad b. Muhammad] Qassab [from Amul]. Once he [Ahmad] rejoined society, he donned the *khirqa* of Sultan Abu Saʿid b. Abu al-Khayr, and was entrusted with his legacy (*hawalih wa wasiyyat*) by his son, Abu Tahir[-i Saʿid].[28]

The *uwaysi* concept, in circulation by 840/1436f., is implied in this narrative. The narrative implicates another Sufi concept: that a Sufi can be initiated in the *uwaysi* way by someone from the unseen world (*rijal al-ghayb*), while concurrently having a living shaykh who is responsible for his mystical (gnostic or Sufi) training (see Chapter 9).

AHMAD-I JAM'S AMENDED *SILSILA*: THE GOLDEN CHAIN

Ahmad's modified *silsila* has two facets. Firstly, *uwaysi* entrée via members of the unseen world (i.e., Khizr, a servant of God; but also Abu Saʿid b. Abu

---

[26] K. Zakaria, "Uways al-Qarani: Visages d'une Légende," *Arabica* 46 (1999): 230–58.

[27] On the *uwaysiyya*, see A. S. Hussaini, "Uways al-Qarani and the Uwaysi Sufis," *Muslim World* 57/2 (1967):103–13; DeWeese, *An "Uvaysi" Sufi*; Julian Baldick, *Imaginary Muslims: The Uwaysi Sufis of Central Asia* (London: I.B. Tauris, 1993), esp. 15–21.

[28] Kadkani, *Darwish*, 176; ʿAlaʾ al-Mulk Jami/Jami (ed.), *Khulasat al-maqamat*, 19. On Qassab, see Ibn Munawwar/Kadkani (ed.), *Asrar al-tawhid*, 1:48–49.

al-Khayr);[29] secondly, the *silsila* that passes through living persons up to the Prophet. The *silsila* for Abu Saʻid and Ahmad-i Jam proffered by Shihab al-Din Ismaʻil b. Ahmad-i Jam connected Ahmad to the Prophet through Imam ʻAli.[30] The manipulated Timurid-era *silsila* interpolates the "golden chain" (*silsilat al-dhahab*), from Imam Riza (the Eighth Imam for the Twelver Shiʻa), through his exalted ancestors, to Muhammad – the Prophet of Islam.

The gateway is Abu Saʻid b. Abu al-Khayr's son, Abu Tahir-i Saʻid (d. 479/1086f.): Ahmad → Abu Tahir-i Saʻid → Abu Saʻid b. Abu al-Khayr → Muhammad al-Sulami → Abu al-Qasim Nasrabadi → Abu Bakr Shibli → Junayd Baghdadi → Sari Saqati → Maʻruf Karkhi → Imam Riza → [the six other Imams] → Imam ʻAli → the Prophet.[31]

The golden chain is not merely a Shiʻi/ʻAlid bridge to the Prophet, but implies that Muhammad's charisma, which was passed down by him to Imam ʻAli, thence through the other Imams,[32] also touches Ahmad-i Jam. The above *silsila* is markedly different from the *silsila* for Abu Saʻid in *Asrar al-tawhid*.[33] Abu Saʻid's "original" *silsila* comprised certain of the familiar names in Sufism that Hamid Algar elegantly termed "the common patrimony of Sufism,"[34] such as Hasan Basri, the link to Imam ʻAli, and thence the Prophet – the ultimate wellspring for all Sufis.

The Jamis were evidently conscious of the importance of their saint's *silsila*; hence the excisions and interpolations to Ahmad-i Jam's *silsila*. The golden chain was published in 840/1436–7: Imam Riza, the "Sultan of

---

[29] The connection to Abu Saʻid b. Abu al-Khayr is twofold: firstly, as initiator from among the *rijal al-ghayb*, when Abu Tahir-i Saʻid hands Abu Saʻid's *khirqa* to Ahmad-i Jam; secondly, through Abu Tahir-i Saʻid as the living nexus to Abu Saʻid's *silsila*.

[30] Jami, *Risala dar isbat*, 24 (the *silsila* given by him was reproduced above).

[31] Kadkani, *Darwish*, 178; see also Buzjani/Moayyad (ed.), *Rawzat*, 85–86. Names should be taken cum grano salis. Sulami, for instance, is silent on his alleged association with Nasrabadi. Abu ʻAbd al-Rahman Muhammad b. al-Husayn al-Sulami, *Tabaqat al-Sufiyya*, ed. Mustafa ʻAbd al-Qadir ʻAta (Beirut: Dar al-kutub al-ʻilmiyya, 2010), 362–65.

[32] On Muhammad's charisma, see discussion in Hamid Dabashi, *Authority in Islam* (New Brunswick, NJ: Transaction Publishers, 1989), 33–45, 95–120.

[33] Ibn Munawwar/ Kadkani (ed.), *Asrar al-tawhid*, 1:26, 32, 48–49; Nicholson, *Mysticism*, 10. According to ʻAttar, Abu Saʻid received a *khirqa* from Sulami (d. 412/1021). Farid al-Din ʻAttar, *Tadhkirat al-awliya*ʻ, ed. R. A. Nicholson (Tehran: Intisharat-i asatir, 1379/2000), 834. This connection is doubted in Ahmet T. Karamustafa, "Reading Medieval Persian Hagiography through the Prism of *Adab*: The Case of *Asrar al-Tawhid*," in F. Chiabotti et al. (eds.), *Ethics and Spirituality in Islam: Sufi Adab* (Leiden: Brill, 2017), 131–41, 131 n3; and Ahmet T. Karamustafa, *Sufism: The Formative Period* (Edinburgh: Edinburgh University Press, 2007), 78 n35.

[34] Hamid Algar, "A Brief History of the Naqshbandi Order," in *Naqshbandis: Cheminements et situation actuelle d'un ordre mystique musulman*, ed. Marc Gaborieau et al. (Paris: ISIS, 1990), 3–44, 6.

Khurasan," is entombed in a resplendent shrine complex at Mashhad. His shrine had a meaningful place in Shah-Rukh's heart and spiritual Weltanschauung: Shah-Rukh made multiple pilgrimages (*ziyarat*) to Imam Riza's shrine;[35] and his magnanimous wife, Gawhar-Shad Bigum (d. 9 Ramazan 861/31 July 1457), sponsored the superlative Gawhar-Shad Mosque inside the Imam Riza shrine complex (erected 1414–18). In the 829/1426 endowment for Gawhar-Shad's mosque, the benefactors included emoluments for Ahmad-i Jam's shrine.[36] Timurid officials followed the royal family's lead and patronized and protected the shrine.[37] In short, it was crucial for Jamis to spiritually connect Ahmad-i Jam to Imam Riza, which is what they did by interpolating the golden chain.

Just as the Jami claim of Ahmad having received a *khirqa* from Abu Saʿid is false, his link to Abu Tahir-i Saʿid may be spurious. We must entertain the likelihood that Ahmad had received training in the *zahiri* and *batini* facets of Islamic studies (*ʿulum al-din*) at hospices or seminaries not identified in hagiologies. This is a suitable point to transition to a discussion on Ahmad's education and literary oeuvre.

We do not know precisely where Ahmad had studied. His writings make manifest that he had acquired proficiency in Arabic and Persian literature, and the Islamic sciences – although his hagiographers insist he was illiterate (*ummi*), but had acquired learning via the *uwaysi* process, and autodidactically. Ahmad's theological and theosophical locutions are scattered throughout his books, which do not reveal a gnostic methodology (*tariq*, *suluk*) for acolytes. A systematic approach to stages (*maqamat*) and mystical states (*ahwal*) on the Sufi Path is absent (see Chapter 9).[38] Muhammad Riza Shafiʿi Kadkani, an eminent Iranian scholar and native of Kadkan (located between Turbat-i Haydariyya and Nishapur), identified Karrami influences in Ahmad-i Jam's writings.

AHMAD-I JAM'S INTELLECTUAL HERITAGE: THE KARRAMIYYA

A primer on the Karramiyya, a potent intellectual and political force in Khurasan, is indispensable. The Karramiyya were embroiled in the

---

[35] C. P. Melville, "The Itineraries of Shahrukh b. Timur (1405–47)," in *Turko-Mongol Rulers, Cities and City Life*, ed. David Durand-Guédy (Leiden: Brill, 2013), 285–315.
[36] Shivan Mahendrarajah, "The Gawhar Shad Waqf: Public Works and the Commonweal," *JAOS* 137/4 (2018): 821–57.
[37] Shivan Mahendrarajah, "A Revised History of Mongol, Kart, and Timurid Patronage of the Shrine of Shaykh al-Islam Ahmad-i Jam," *Iran* 54/2 (2016): 107–28.
[38] On the Sufi Path, see Schimmel, *Dimensions*, 99–186.

religious politics of Khurasan, which were frequently violent. They were activists and inquisitors who enjoyed Ghaznavid support and protection. However, when the Ghaznavids lost Khurasan to the Seljuqs after the Battle of Dandanqan (1040), the Karramiyya were persecuted and branded as heretics. The Seljuq sultan, Ahmad Sanjar, took to Ahmad-i Jam; hence the imperative for Ahmad's hagiologists to obscure the saint's connections to the Karramiyya.

Origins of the Karramiyya

The Karramiyya sect emerged under Muhammad (Abu ʿAbdallah) ibn Karram of Zaranj, in Sistan (b. *ca.* 190/806; d. 255/869 in Jerusalem). Ibn Karram studied the Islamic sciences at Herat, Nishapur, and Marw. After living in Mecca for five years, he returned to Sistan and discarded his possessions, donned the coarse garb of renunciants, and began to proselytize. A hellfire preacher, Ibn Karram's message resonated with the downtrodden and attracted crowds. The Tahirids (r. 205–59/821–73), the Iranian rulers of Khurasan and Sistan, were perturbed by his activities, which included polemics against Shiʿa and Sunni. After an inquiry before the governor, where Abu ʿAbdallah disclaimed formal learning, and claimed divine inspiration, he was incarcerated.[39] As Edmund Bosworth noted, the Tahirid rulers had a right to be apprehensive about Abu ʿAbdallah's agitations given that Khurasan had an illustrious history as the incubator and nursery of multifarious political-religious currents that had shaped (and would continue to shape) Iranian and Islamic histories. The revolutionary fervor harnessed by Abu Muslim al-Khurasani (d. 137/755) was assuredly on Tahirid minds: ancestors of the Tahirids had served Abu Muslim. Upon his parole, Abu ʿAbdallah b. Karram quit Khurasan for Palestine.

---

[39] C. Edmund Bosworth, "Karramiyya," *EI²*, 4:667–69; C. Edmund Bosworth, "The Rise of the Karamiyyah in Khurasan," *Muslim World* 50/1 (1960): 5–14; C. Edmund Bosworth, *The Ghaznavids* (Edinburgh: Edinburgh University Press, 1963), 185–89; Louis Massignon, *Essay on the Origins of the Technical Language of Islamic Mysticism*, trans. Benjamin Clark (Notre Dame: University of Notre Dame Press, 2003), 174–83; Jacqueline Chabbi, "Remarques sur le développement historique des mouvements ascétiques et mystiques au Khurasan: IIIe/IXe siècle-iVe/Xe siècle," *Studia Islamica* 46 (1977): 5–72; Aron Zysow, "Karramiya," *EIr*, 15: 590–601; Alexander Knysh, *Islamic Mysticism* (Leiden: Brill, 2000), 88–94.

Ibn Karram's views on legal and theological Islam cannot be justly summarized.[40] According to heresiologists, his beliefs included anthropomorphism, namely, that God was a substance (*jawhar*), bringing him nearer to Christian beliefs that God had a body (*jism*).[41] Ibn Karram's treatise, *The Punishment of the Grave* (*'Adhab al-qabr*), and other works, were lost.[42] Extracts from his writings are known primarily from references by critics. The Karramiyya developed from the devotional current of Ibn Karram's time into a school of jurisprudence (*madhhab*), and became prominent for their "activist and ostensive asceticism."[43] The sect splintered, although the factions are not believed to have deviated significantly from core principles. The appealing features of the Karramiyya (with commoners if not with rulers) were their emphases on piety (*'ibada*) and asceticism (*zuhd*). They were anathemized by the majority of the authors who mention them.[44] The Palestinian geographer Muhammad al-Muqaddasi (d. *ca.* 380/990), however, is not hostile. He portrays them as pious and ascetic men who read the Qur'an, recollected God, and proselytized.[45]

Karramiyya Activism in Khurasan

The Karramiyya's problems – and subsequent categorization as heretics – stem from their political agitations in Nishapur; intrigues of their enemies; and dynastic change (from the Ghaznavids to the Seljuqs). Their main enemies were the "patricians," the upper strata of the Shafi'i and Hanafi *madhhab*s then dominating politics in Nishapur.[46] The Karramiyya

---

[40] But see Wilferd Madelung, *Religious Trends in Early Islamic Iran* (Albany, NY: Persica, 1988), 39–44, for a balanced summary.

[41] For polemical perspectives on the Karramiyya, see, e.g., 'Abd al-Qahir al-Baghdadi, *al-Farq bayn al-firaq*, ed. Muhammad 'Uthman Khisht (Cairo: Maktabat Ibn Sina, n.d. [1988]), 189–97; 'Abd al-Qahir al-Baghdadi, *Moslem Schisms and Sects* [*al-Farq bayn al-firaq*], trans. A. S. Halkin (Philadelphia, PA: Porcupine Press, 1978 [reprint of 1935 Tel Aviv ed.]), 18–30.

[42] But see Josef van Ess, *Ungenutzte Texte zur Karramiya* (Heidelberg: Sitzungsberichte der Heidelberger Akademie der Wissenschaften, 1980); and Aron Zysow, "Two Unrecognized Karrami Texts," *JAOS* 108/4 (1988): 577–87.

[43] Madelung, *Religious Trends*, 44.

[44] Margaret Malamud, "The Politics of Heresy in Medieval Khurasan: The Karramiyya in Nishapur," *Iranian Studies* 27/1 (1994): 37–51, 39 and n9.

[45] Muhammad b. Ahmad al-Muqaddasi, *Ahsan al-taqasim fi ma'rifa al-aqalim*, ed. M. J. de Goeje (Leiden: Brill, 1906), 182.

[46] Richard W. Bulliet, *The Patricians of Nishapur* (Cambridge, MA: Harvard University Press, 1972). On the Shafi'i and Hanafi of Khurasan, see Christopher Melchert, *The Formation of the Sunni Schools of Law, 9th–10th Centuries C.E.* (Leiden: Brill, 1997), esp. 132–36.

appealed to rural Khurasanians; hence the fears of the political leadership of Khurasan. The Karramiyya directed polemics against the Ash'ari (who were favored by Shafi'i), Mu'tazila (who were favored by Hanafi), the Shi'a (i.e., Isma'ilis), and Sufis (i.e., mystics).[47] In short, the Karramiyya cleverly surrounded themselves with enemies.

The Karramiyya instituted *khanaqah*s throughout Khurasan.[48] Karrami *khanaqah*s – especially in the hinterlands where the Karramiyya were the only meaningful centripetal force – functioned as frontier outposts from which they could conduct political activities and social outreach. The overt asceticism and pietism of the Karramiyya, who lived off pious endowments (waqf) and alms, and opposed certain forms of economic profit (*kasb*),[49] won for themselves support among the peasantry and the lower socioeconomic strata of Nishapur. The Karramiyya had harnessed the dialectic of wealthy and well-fed versus the destitute and hungry; however, the bitter sectarian enmity that sundered Nishapur cannot be explained in simple terms. Karramiyya power waxed and waned, but allowed them to "engage in violent riots with the adherents of the dominant religious factions."[50] Hanafi and Shafi'i also marshaled their own mobs to counter the Karramis;[51] and the Isma'ili Shi'a retaliated by assassinating Nishapur's Karrami chief.[52]

Even the venerable Abu Sa'id b. Abu al-Khayr, then sojourning in Nishapur, was not safe from Karrami inquisitions. The old Sufi had become self-indulgent and corpulent. The Karrami chief, with support from the Hanafis, reported him to the Ghaznavid sultan.[53] The opposition was not due solely to Abu Sa'id's lavish lifestyle. His presence at a rival *khanaqah* had brought out supporters in droves. They enjoyed activities that included mystical dance (*raqs*) and sacred music (*sama'*). Such events posed a threat to the Karramiyya because they revealed attractive *mystical* alternatives to the austere worldviews of the Karramiyya. Like the Shi'a, Mu'tazila, and Ash'ariyya, Abu Sa'id became

---

[47] Malamud, "Heresy," 46.
[48] Muhsin Kiyani, *Tarikh-i khanaqah dar Iran* (Tehran: Intisharat-i Tahuri, 1369/1990), 157–59. *Khanqah*s are discussed in Chapter 8.
[49] Malamud, "Heresy," 42–43; see also Michael Bonner, "The *Kitab al-kasb* Attributed to al-Shaybani: Poverty, Surplus, and the Circulation of Wealth," *JAOS* 121/3 (2001): 410–27, esp. 413–15, 423–25.
[50] Bulliet, *Patricians*, 12. [51] Ibid., 14.
[52] Bernard Lewis, *The Assassins* (New York: Basic Books, 2003), 53.
[53] Abu-Ruh Lutfallah b. Abi Sa'id, *Halat wa sukhanan-i Abu Sa'id-i Abu al-Khayr*, ed. Muhammad Riza Shafi'i Kadkani (Tehran: Intisharat-i sukhan, 1384/2005), 90–94; Ibn Munawwar/Kadkani (ed.), *Asrar al-tawhid*, 1:68–73.

just another political adversary to be attacked on charges of heresy or nonconformity with *their* idea of orthodoxy. The Karrami indictment employs the term *munkar* (wrong), which suggests the allegations fell under the rubric of *al-amr bi-l-maʿruf wa-l-nahy ʿan al-munkar*. Evil (*suʾ*) and heresy (*zandaqa*) are higher levels of wrongdoing and usually involve harsher penalties.

The Ghaznavid sultan, Mahmud b. Sebüktigin (r. 388–421/998–1030), ordered a joint inquiry by the Hanafi and the Shafiʿi leadership into the charges. The Karramiyya rejoiced and prepared the scaffold. Abu Saʿid, however, wriggled out from under the charges. The hagiographical explanation is that he defeated his enemies through his spiritual prowess, and that the Karrami leader had conceded defeat and offered blessings to Abu Saʿid.[54] The Karramiyya tied their fortunes to the Ghaznavids, and by 400/1010, the apogee of Karrami power in Nishapur, they were well-protected inquisitors. The Karramiyya, in the guise of extirpating the Ismaʿili "heresy," targeted sundry groups and individuals.[55] The Ghaznavids ultimately realized their surrogates had overreached, but Ghaznavid rule in Khurasan was nearing its expiration. They lost control of Khurasan to the Seljuqs with their defeat at the Battle of Dandanqan in 431/1040.

Seljuq Persecutions and the Karramiyya

The Seljuq vizier, ʿAmid al-Mulk al-Kunduri (d. 456/1064), a Hanafi-Muʿtazila zealot, launched an inquisition (*mihna*), *ca.* 445/1053, which initially only targeted entities like the Karramiyya, but subsequently shifted to the Shafiʿi-Ashʿari in Nishapur.[56] Eventually, "the persecution led to the splintering of the Shafiʿis into smaller factions, the annihilation of the Ashʿaris, and the suppression of the Karramiyya."[57] The primary objective of the *mihna*, Richard W. Bulliet explains, is that Kunduri sought to turn "Nishapur over to total and unquestionable Hanafi domination . . . the persecution was a complete success."[58] That the Karramiyya had been allied with the Ghaznavids was a bonus for the Seljuqs. In any event, the Karramiyya were reduced to hinterland redoubts. Kunduri fell politically and the *mihna*

---

[54] The colorful account is in Nicholson, *Mysticism*, 28–32.
[55] Bosworth, *Ghaznavids*, 185–89; Bosworth, "Karamiyyah," 8–11; Bulliet, *Patricians*, 159–160, 203–4.
[56] A. C. S. Peacock, *Early Seljuq History* (New York: Routledge, 2010), 109–14, esp. 113; Heinz Halm, "Der Wesir al-Kunduri und die *Fitna* von Nishapur," *Die Welt des Orients* 6/2 (1971): 205–33.
[57] Bulliet, *Patricians*, 210.   [58] Ibid.

became an embarrassment for Seljuq court historians.[59] Kunduri's successor, Nizam al-Mulk (d. 485/1092), restored social-political balance.

Sultan Sanjar became attracted to Ahmad-i Jam's perspectives and personality. Jami hagiographers inextricably tied Ahmad to the Seljuqs and to Abu Saʿid b. Abu al-Khayr. Abu Saʿid's hometown of Mayhana had lent their support to the Seljuqs before Dandanqan, for which they were punished by the Ghaznavids.[60] There is a hagiographical narrative that the Seljuq sultan, Tughril Beg (d. 455/1063), and his brother, Chaghri Beg (d. *ca.* 452/1060), had visited Mayhana for *ziyarat* and to meet Abu Saʿid.[61] Ahmad-i Jam's links to the Karramiyya, a "heretical" sect that had harassed Abu Saʿid and had been allied with the former regime, were discomfitures to be obscured. Fortunately, concealing mortifications and embellishing spiritual heritages are among the primary responsibilities of a competent hagiologist.

CONNECTING AHMAD-I JAM TO THE KARRAMIYYA

One category of sources on Ahmad-i Jam's intellectual heritage are the biographical dictionaries produced by writers external to the Jami community. Literary works by Jami writers (including Ahmad) referencing the Karramiyya are the second category.

Biographical Literature

Ahmad-i Jam's connections to the Karramiyya appear to run through his father, ʿAli al-Namaqi; and Ahmad's upbringing in rustic Namaq and ostensible training in Karramiyya *khanaqah*s. ʿAli al-Namaqi's academic pedigree is parsed below.

Ahmad-i Jam's hometown, Namaq (or Nama), is south of Nishapur.[62] A village and district called Namaq thrive in Khurasan, south of Kadkan,

---

[59] Peacock, *Seljuq History*, 109.
[60] The Ghaznavid sultan, Masʿud, needed funds. His men extorted Herat and its vicinities "with some severity and violence, on the pretext that the people there had colluded with the Turkmens." Abu al-Fazl Muhammad b. Husayn Bayhaqi, *The History of Beyhaqi* [*Tarikh-i Masʿudi*], 3 vols., trans. C. E. Bosworth, rev. Mohsen Ashtiany (Boston, MA, and London: Ilex, 2011), 2:275. It is possible that Mayhana's punishment (if the report is accurate) was not due to collaboration (although collaborators were severely punished. See, e.g., ibid., 2:275–76).
[61] Ibn Munawwar/Kadkani (ed.), *Asrar al-tawhid*, 1:156–58; and see Tor, "Sovereign and Pious," 49.
[62] Kadkani, *Darwish*, 25; Dorothea Krawulsky, *Ḥorasan zur Timuridenzeit*, 2 vols. (Wiesbaden: Ludwig Reichert, 1982–84), 1:58.

ca. 82 mi./130 km from Nishapur by highway. Namaq's main road is Jami Namaqi Road. Namaq was apparently a Karramiyya center.[63] Shafi'i Kadkani suggests, with respect to details on Ahmad's father, 'Ali al-Namaqi, in the biographical dictionary of 'Abd al-Karim al-Sam'ani (d. 562/1167), that 'Ali al-Namaqi had studied with Karrami scholars, or Karrami-oriented scholars.[64]

A biographical notice for Ahmad-i Jam's father is given in Abu al-Hasan al-Farisi (d. 529/1135).[65] The entry referenced by Kadkani is in 'Abd al-Karim al-Sam'ani.[66] Al-Sam'ani has one entry for "Namaqi": 'Ali (Abu al-Hasan) b. Ahmad b. Muhammad b. 'Abdallah b. al-Layth al-Namaqi, who died in Jumada I 480/August 1087. He ('Ali) was a pious and upright man from Nishapur. He heard (*sama'*) hadith[67] from Muhammad (Abu Tahir) b. Muhammad b. Muhammadish al-Ziyadi (d. 410/1019);[68] [Qadi] Ahmad (Abu Bakr) b. al-Hasan [al-Harashi] al-Hiri (d. 421/1030);[69] 'Abd al-Qahir (Abu Mansur) b. Tahir al-Baghdadi (d. 429/1037–38);[70] Zahir (Abu al-Qasim) b. Tahir al-Shahhami in Nishapur (d. 533/1139);[71]

---

[63] Kadkani, *Darwish*, 106–7.

[64] Ibid., 107 and n2. Shafi'i Kadkani is here citing his (long) unpublished *Janib-i 'irfani-yi madhhab-i Karramiyya*. In e-mail communications in December 2017 with Prof. Kadkani via an intermediary, Masoud Jafari Jazi, Kadkani clarified that he is only *proposing* a Karrami link for 'Ali al-Namaqi. Kadkani has no direct evidence of a Karrami connection.

[65] Abu al-Hasan al-Farisi, *al-Muntakhab min al-siyaq li-tarikh Naysabur*, ed. Muhammad Ahmad 'Abd al-'Aziz (Beirut: Dar al-kutub al-'ilmiyya, 1989), 388 (no. 1310: a sparse entry); but see Abu al-Hasan al-Farisi, *al-Mukhtasar min kitab al-siyaq li-tarikh Naysabur*, ed. Muhammad Kazim al-Mahmudi (Tehran: Miras-i maktub, 1384/2005), 301 (no. 2130: biographical detail).

[66] 'Abd al-Karim al-Sam'ani, *Kitab al-ansab*, 13 vols., ed. 'Abd al-Rahman al-Yamani, et al. (Hyderabad: Osmania Oriental Publications Bureau, 1962–82), 12:22–23.

[67] On orality and authority in hadith studies, see R. W. Bulliet, *Islam: The View from the Edge* (New York: Columbia University Press, 1994), 13–22.

[68] Taj al-Din 'Abd al-Wahhab b. 'Ali Subki, *Tabaqat al-Shafi'iyya al-kubra*, ed. Mahmud Muhammad Tanahi and 'Abd al-Fattah Muhammad Hulw (Cairo: 'Isa al-Babi al-Halabi, 1964), 4:198–201; Farisi, *Muntakhab*, 18; Sam'ani, *Ansab*, 6:340–44; Bulliet, *Patricians*, 119.

[69] Subki, *Shafi'iyya*, 4:6–7; Hakim Nishaburi, *Tarikh-i Nishabur*, ed. Muhammad Riza Shafi'i Kadkani (Tehran: Agah, 1375/1996), 149; Farisi, *Muntakhab*, 80–81; Sam'ani, *Ansab*, 4:108–10 (al-Harashi) and 4:287–89 (al-Hiri); Muhammad b. Ahmad al-Dhahabi, *al-'Ibar fi khabar man ghabar*, 4 vols., ed. Abu Hajar Muhammad al-Sa'id b. Basyuni Zaghlul (Beirut: Dar al-kutub al-'ilmiyya, 1985), 2:243; 'Abd al-Hayy b. Ahmad b. al-'Imad, *Shadharat al-dhahab fi akhbar man dhahab*, ed. 'Abd al-Qadir al-Arna'ut and Mahmud al-Arna'ut (Beirut: Dar Ibn Kathir, 1986), 5:103; Bulliet, *Patricians*, 99–101, 267.

[70] Subki, *Shafi'iyya*, 5:136–48; Farisi, *Muntakhab*, 360; Farisi, *Mukhtasar*, 254–55; Bulliet, *Patricians*, 167 n24.

[71] Farisi, *Muntakhab*, 229–30; Farisi, *Mukhtasar*, 82–83; al-Dhahabi, *al-'Ibar*, 2:445; Abu al-Faraj 'Abd al-Rahman b. 'Ali b. al-Jawzi, *al-Muntazam fi tarikh al-muluk wa-l-umam*, 19

and al-Husayn (Abu ʿAli) b. ʿAli b. al-Husayn [al-Shahhami al-Nishapuri] (d. 545/1150 in Marw),[72] and others. I shall circle back to these scholars momentarily.

The Tehran edition of al-Farisi has ʿAli al-Namaqi's name and death date as given in al-Samʿani. The first two names of his instructors, al-Ziyadi and al-Hiri, are expressed in a manner that suggests they had been his primary teachers; and he had then studied with al-Baghdadi "and others of his rank."[73] The Beirut edition offers no educational information.[74] Ibn al-Jawzi (d. 597/1200) and Ibn al-ʿImad (d. 1089/1679) offer nothing on Ahmad or ʿAli al-Namaqi. To confirm that the latter is indeed Ahmad's father, we turn to Ahmad's name as given in the *Khulasat al-maqamat*: Ahmad b. Abu al-Hasan b. Ahmad b. [Nasr b.] Muhammad b. Jarir b. ʿAbdallah b. Layth b. Jarir b. ʿAbdallah b. Jabar ... al-Bajali.[75] Setting aside the veracity of claims to Arab bloodlines and descent from Jarir b. ʿAbdallah al-Bajali (one of the Prophet's Companions),[76] the names match, but not perfectly. "Abu al-Hasan" is ʿAli al-Namaqi's *kunya* (agnomen).[77] Al-Samʿani missed "bin Jarir," which is not extraordinary.[78]

ʿAli al-Namaqi's first three professors, al-Ziyadi, al-Hiri, and al-Baghdadi, are robust Shafiʿi scholars. Indeed, ʿAbd al-Qahir al-Baghdadi penned a powerful polemic against the Karramiyya in his book on the sects of Islam, *al-Farq bayn al-firaq*. Works by al-Baghdadi include *Fadaʾih al-Karramiyya* and *Fadaʾih al-Muʿtazila*,[79] attacks against the respective sects. ʿAli al-Namaqi (d. 480/1087) must have lived a long life if he had studied with, or heard hadith from, al-Ziyadi (d. 410/1019) and al-Hiri (d. 421/1030). The influences of Shafiʿi scholars during a student's early

---

vols. incl. index, ed. Muhammad ʿAbd al-Qadir ʿAtaʾ and Mustafa ʿAbd al-Qadir ʿAtaʾ (Beirut: Dar al-kutub al-ʿilmiyya, 1992), 17:336–37; Ibn al-ʿImad, *Shadharat*, 6:168; Bulliet, *Patricians*, 191.

[72] al-Dhahabi, *al-ʿIbar*, 2:468; Ibn al-ʿImad, *Shadharat*, 6:229; Bulliet, *Patricians*, 191.
[73] Farisi, *Mukhtasar*, 301 (no. 2130).   [74] Farisi, *Muntakhab*, 388 (no. 1310).
[75] Kadkani, *Darwish*, 172; cf. ʿAlaʾ al-Mulk Jami/Jami (ed.), *Khulasat al-maqamat*, 16: Ahmad b. Abu al-Hasan b. Ahmad b. Muhammad b. *[Nasr b.]* Jarir b. ʿAbdallah b. Layth Bajali b. Jarir b. ʿAbdallah b. Jabar.
[76] On al-Bajali, see Patricia Crone, *Slaves on Horses* (Cambridge: Cambridge University Press, 1980), 114–15. The claim to Arab descent – from a Companion no less – is surely to hide the "scandalous" fact that Ahmad-i Jam's progenitors were Zoroastrians from Khurasan.
[77] Annemarie Schimmel, *Islamic Names* (Edinburgh: Edinburgh University Press, 1989), 4. I supply the *kunya* within parentheses, e.g., ʿAbd al-Qahir (Abu al-Najib) al-Suhrawardi.
[78] Both editors of *Khulasat al-maqamat* (Kadkani and Jami) interpolate "Nasr" at different points in the genealogical chain. If accurate, then al-Samʿani missed two generations.
[79] Subki, *Shafiʿiyya*, 5:136–48, 140.

schooling do not guarantee unswerving allegiance to the *madhhab*,[80] especially since ʿAli al-Namaqi quit Nishapur for the hinterlands of Khurasan where the Karramiyya were organized and had popular support. His last two professors, Zahir and Hasan, were from a prominent Shafiʿi clan.[81] Subki often mentions that so-and-so had studied with Zahir al-Shahhami, but does not include his biography.[82] The omission is possibly explained by this assertion: "his reputation was marred by irregular attendance at prayers."[83] We know little about Hasan. His link to the al-Shahhami clan is tentative.[84] He was a *raʾis*, a "notoriously protean" title,[85] one indicating a person holding an appointed administrative post of some importance. Absent fresh evidence, Karramiyya connections to Zahir and Hasan are conjectural.

Arguments supporting the claim of Karrami influences on Ahmad-i Jam do not rest on Shafiʿi Kadkani's proposition. Ahmad-i Jam's own words betray his upbringing.

Jami Literature

The claim propagated by ʿAbd al-Rahman Jami in *Breaths of Intimacy* that Ahmad-i Jam was unlettered (*ummi*) must be discarded as hagiographical topos.[86] The son of ʿAli al-Namaqi will assuredly have received a stellar education in Arabic and Persian literatures and the Islamic Sciences (*ʿulum al-din*) in Nishapur and/or Namaq, and probably at other centers of Islamic learning. According to Jami hagiologies, Ahmad lived dissolutely until age twenty-two, had an epiphany, quit Namaq, and became an eremite for eighteen years. The sequence of events is not known, but at some point, the *raʾis* of Buzjan (in Jam district) tried to eject Ahmad-i Jam on account of the

---

[80] At this point in space and time (Nishapur Quarter, fifth/eleventh century), it is best to consider a *madhhab* as a jurisprudential *current* unique to a specific region, and not a jurisprudential *school* – especially not a school that transcends borders. On scholars revisiting views of the *madhhab*, see commentary in Arezou Azad, *Sacred Landscape in Medieval Afghanistan: Revisiting the Fadaʾil-i Balkh* (Oxford: Oxford University Press, 2013), 114–15, 132–38.
[81] Bulliet, *Patricians*, esp. 169–72.   [82] Subki, *Shafiʿiyya*, 6:448 (index) and 7:430 (index).
[83] Bulliet, *Patricians*, 171; al-Jawzi, *Muntazam*, 17:337.   [84] Bulliet, *Patricians*, 173.
[85] Jürgen Paul, "Local Lords or Rural Notables: Some Remarks on the *Raʾis* in Twelfth-Century Eastern Iran," in *Medieval Central Asia and the Persianate World*, ed. A. C. S. Peacock and D. G. Tor (London: I.B. Tauris, 2015), 174–209.
[86] Jami, *Nafahat*, 357. There is a parallel topos, namely, that the Prophet was illiterate and thus could not have composed the Qurʾan. The term "unlettered Prophet" (*al-nabi al-ummi*) is in Surat al-Aʿraf (Q7:157).

zealotry and strife (*taʿassubi wa munazaʿat*) he engendered.[87] There may be a factual basis for this averment considering the sectarianism then prevailing in Khurasan.[88] Ahmad was settled in Maʿd-Abad village, Jam district, by *ca*. 480/1087 – the year his father died. It is unlikely that he spent eighteen years in seclusion. The number (eighteen) was contrived to coincide with his age (*ca*. forty)[89] when he settled in Maʿd-Abad. It explains the "missing" years of his life, namely, his life in Namaq (and elsewhere?). In Namaq, Ahmad had presumably honored his father until his passing, but seeing the winds shift with the Seljuqs entrenched and the Karramiyya in disarray, he wanted a fresh start. In light of Ahmad's free spirit, is it likely he wanted to be his own man and to express his own ideas freely. Expressing Karrami doctrines had not yet become taboo as evidenced by the frequency with which Ahmad-i Jam quoted Karrami leaders.

Shafiʿi Kadkani analyzed Karramiyya terms manifest in Ahmad's writings, or that are attributed to him by Jami hagiographers.[90] Kadkani's tracing of Karramiyya references in manuscripts, and their excisions or revisions in subsequent recensions, is invaluable. To illustrate, in possibly the earliest manuscript of Ahmad's *Uns al-taʾibin*, the phrase "of the sayings of [Abu] ʿAbdallah Muhammad Karram" is found; however, in later recensions, the phrase was replaced with "of the sayings of some of the great scholars of Islam" (*az qala-i baʿzi-yi buzurgan-i din*).[91] This manner of editing was not necessarily for nefarious reasons.[92] When producing manuscripts that quoted Ibn Karram's words, different approaches were employed by copyists to obscure Ibn Karram's identity. One approach was to replace his name with his *kunya* (i.e., Abu ʿAbdallah), leaving it to the discerning reader to identify the interlocutor. One such reader is Aron Zysow, who identified two Karrami texts in part by connecting Abu ʿAbdallah to Ibn Karram.[93]

The Karramiyya leaders referenced by Ahmad are Muhammad (Abu ʿAbdallah) b. Karram (d. 255/869); ʿAli al-Haysam (n.d.), presumed the son of Muhammad b. al-Haysam (d. *ca*. 409/1019); and Muhammad (Abu Bakr) b. Ishaq b. Mahmashadh (d. 421/1030); Ishaq (Abu Yaʿqub) b. Mahmashadh (d. 383/993);[94] and Ahmad b. Ibrahim al-Bajistani al-

---

[87] Ghaznawi, *Maqamat*, 116–17.   [88] Paul, "Local Lords," 181.
[89] Age forty, coincidentally or not, is when the Prophet of Islam commenced his mission.
[90] Kadkani, *Darwish*, 112–42.
[91] Ibid., 129–30. In a later edition, the editor inserted the original phrase. See Ahmad-i Jam, *Uns al-taʾibin*, ed. ʿAli Fazil (Tehran: Intisharat-i Tus, 1368/1989), 257 and n8.
[92] It was not uncommon to withhold names of scholars who did not have broad acceptance.
[93] Zysow, "Karrami," esp. 579–80.   [94] Hakim Nishaburi, *Nishabur*, 157 (no. 1842).

Maydani (d. 315/927).[95] The Haysamiyya and Ishaqiyya are two of the six subsects of the Karramiyya identified by Shahrastani (d. 548/1153) in *Sects and Creeds*.[96] The Haysamiyya were based south of Nishapur; a Haysamiyya cemetery is referenced by Hakim Nishaburi.[97] Muhammad b. al-Haysam was "recognized by friend and foe as the most capable Karrami theologian."[98] The Ishaqiyya were dominant in Nishapur and reached the zenith of their influence under Abu Bakr. It was he who had targeted Abu Sa'id b. Abu al-Khayr.

In Sadid al-Din Ghaznawi's *Spiritual Feats of the Furious Elephant*, Ahmad-i Jam quotes approvingly from Karrami doctrines, to wit, words by 'Ali al-Haysam,[99] possibly another contemporary.[100] One of Ahmad-i Jam's miracles is inducing a third party to have a vision of one of the spiritual states (*ahwal*) of the "Imam of Zahedan," Abu 'Abdallah ibn Karram. The man saw light enveloping Ibn Karram's home in Sistan and shining up to the sky. This was Ibn Karram's birthplace.[101] Light is a powerful motif in religion.[102] Light ascending from or descending onto holy sites is a potent theme in blessings (*baraka*) and in the delineation of sacred spaces: "So intimate, powerful and profound was the effect of light and holiness that writers never needed to define it."[103] In Nishapur, Ahmad-i Jam went to perform *ziyarat* at the Karrami mausolea of Ustad Imam Ishaq b. Mahmashadh (d. 383/993) and Ustad Imam Ahmad

---

[95] Ibid., 131 (no. 1335); Sam'ani, *Ansab*, 2:85; Muhammad b. Ahmad al-Dhahabi, *Tarikh al-islam*, 53 vols., ed. 'Umar Tadmuri (Beirut: Dar al-kitab al-'Arabi, 1992–2000), 23:488; Kadkani, *Darwish*, 125–26 and n1.

[96] Muhammad al-Shahrastani, *al-Milal wa-l-nihal*, 2 vols., ed. Amir 'Ali Muhanna and 'Ali Hasan Fa'ur (Beirut: Dar al-ma'rifa, 1993), 1:124.

[97] Hakim Nishaburi, *Nishabur*, 277 (no. 2798) and 300–301.

[98] Madelung, *Religious Trends*, 41.

[99] Ghaznawi, *Maqamat*, 239, 242, 248–49, 252, 266, 274. 'Ali al-Haysam is also referred to as Danishmand Imam. In Ghaznawi's *Maqamat*, "Ustad Imam" and "Danishmand Imam" appear frequently in reference to Karrami figures.

[100] Kadkani, *Darwish*, 120–121 and n3.

[101] Ghaznawi, *Maqamat*, 195–96; Moayyad and Lewis, *Colossal*, 270–71.

[102] See, e.g., Gen. 1:3: "And God said, 'Let there be light,' and there was light"; and the Sufi favorite, the "Light Verse," Surat al-Nur (Q24:35): "Allah is the Light of the heavens and the earth." "The Light" is one of His names. Shrines, including Ahmad-i Jam's, are referred to as *Rawza-yi munawwar*: "the illuminated tomb."

[103] Josef Meri, "Aspects of *Baraka* (Blessing) and Ritual Devotion among Medieval Muslims and Jews," *Medieval Encounters* 5/1 (1999): 46–69, 54. Further on emanating light, i.e., the grave of Shah-i Chiragh ("king of light") in Shiraz, see Denise Aigle, "Among Saints and Poets: The Spiritual Topography of Shiraz," in *Cities of Medieval Iran*, ed. David Durand-Guédy, et al., *Eurasian Studies* 16/1–2 (2018): 142–76, 155.

b. Ibrahim al-Bajistani (d. 315/927); however, the entrance to the tombs was locked. Upon Ahmad's command, "Danishmand Ahmad [Bajistani], if you are alive open the door!" the gate swung open.[104]

The above examples suffice to illustrate the point that Ahmad had deep affections for Karrami leaders and freely discussed them; and that Ibn Karram was a man of God and source of *baraka*. Nonetheless, as Shafi'i Kadkani has shown, there was also rivalry between Ahmad and the Karramiyya.[105] In any event, during Ahmad's lifetime, Karrami connections were not discomfitures to be hidden from critics. Ahmad treats Ibn Karram as an equal of the eponyms of other *madhhab*s: Ahmad claims the eminent jurists are "Abu Hanifa, Shafi'i, Abu 'Abdallah [ibn Karram], Malik, and ..."[106] Edmund Bosworth reproduces a saying that in my opinion reflects Ahmad-i Jam's worldviews: "the only true legal system (*fiqh*) is Abu Hanifa's, just as the only true religious system (*din*) is that of Muhammad ibn Karram."[107]

Ahmad was a zealous and belligerent man who got his way through coercion. One suspects he had been in a *futuwwa* brotherhood.[108] Ahmad's oldest son, Rashid al-Din ('Abd al-Rashid) Jami (n.d.) of Turshiz, was a member of a *futuwwa* (Per. *jawanmard*) and died fighting "deserters from God," that is, the Isma'ilis.[109] The son was assuredly following in his father's path. But Ahmad's views were evolving: he was shifting from Karrami-influenced activism to Sufi (mystical) thought. This is traced below.

AHMAD-I JAM'S INTELLECTUAL DEVELOPMENT

Ahmad-i Jam's intellectual growth is fascinating and reflects the fluidity of mystical and religious thought in Khurasan during his lifetime. Ahmad transitioned from Shafi'i to Karrami ascetic (*zahid*) and then Hanafi mystic

---

[104] Ghaznawi, *Maqamat*, 197; Moayyad and Lewis, *Colossal*, 271–72.
[105] Muhammad Riza Shafi'i Kadkani, "Rawabit-i Shaykh-i Jam ba Karramiyan-i 'asr-i khwish," *Majalla-i danishkada-i adabiyyat wa 'ulum-i insani* 2/6–8 (1374/1995): 29–50. See also the discussion in John Dechant, "The 'Colossal Elephant' Shaykh Ahmad-i Jam: Legacy and Hagiography in Islam" (unpublished PhD diss., Indiana University, 2015), 151–58.
[106] Ahmad-i Jam, *Rawzat al-muznibin wa jannat al-mushtaqin*, ed. 'Ali Fazil (Tehran: Pizhuhishgah-i 'ulum-i insani wa mutala'at-i farhangi, 1372/1993), 152.
[107] Bosworth, "Karamiyyah," 8 and n12. A law school is distinct from a theological school.
[108] C. Cahen et al. "Futuwwa," *EI*², 2:961–69; M. Zakeri, "Javanmardi," *EIr*, 14:594–601.
[109] Buzjani/Moayyad (ed.), *Rawzat*, 61–62; Zanganah, *Sarzamin*, 86–87.

(*sufi*).[110] Ahmad's intellectual changes reflect borrowing, discarding, or adapting from a shifting banquet of ideas.

Nearly a Century of Learning

Ahmad-i Jam's perspectives were shaped by fluid religious and political winds over an exceptionally long life, 441/1049 to 536/1141 (ninety-five lunar/*hijri*; ninety-two solar/Julian years). His words reveal profound shifts in dogma and politics. He was exposed to Ashʿari, Muʿtazila, Shafiʿi, Hanafi, Karrami, Malamati ("People of Blame"),[111] Qalandar ("Uncouth"),[112] and Sufi doctrines and practices. He witnessed the fall of the Ghaznavids and the establishment of the Seljuq sultanate; Shafiʿi-Hanafi and Ashʿari-Muʿtazila sectarianism; the Seljuq *mihna*; and he experienced the disquiet that rippled through Iranian society as a result of Ismaʿili political violence and proselytizing. Ahmad-i Jam's thoughts and writings were shaped by the historical events and religious currents that had swept through Khurasan.

Stories in Ghaznawi's *Spiritual Feats* expose social-political concerns about Ismaʿilis in the latter part of the Seljuq era;[113] hence narratives on Ahmad disputing with Ismaʿilis to "prove" the Shiʿi "heresy";[114] and Ahmad "saving" the Seljuq sultan from Ismaʿili assassins. The concerns unveiled by hagiographical motifs were raw: viziers Nizam al-Mulk and Muʿin al-Din Kashi were assassinated by Ismaʿili sacrificers (*fidayin*), and Sultan Sanjar lived under the threat of assassination.[115]

The manifestation of Karrami doctrines in Ahmad's writings is unremarkable. His personal intellectual journey, however, is remarkable. Ahmad's early studies, as the son of an eminent Shafiʿi scholar, will have

---

[110] Since the third to fourth/tenth to eleventh centuries, there were four powerful intellectual *currents* circulating within Khurasan: *futuwwa*, Karramiyya, Malamatiyya, and Sufi. There were no bright lines of demarcation. See Muhammad Riza Shafiʿi Kadkani, *Qalandariyya dar tarikh* (Tehran: Intisharat-i sukhan, 1386/2007), 21–36. Many tenets of Malamatism were absorbed into Sufism, which also absorbed certain tenets of Karramism.

[111] On the Malamatiyya of Khurasan (*viz.*, Nishapur), see Karamustafa, *Sufism*, 60–66; Knysh, *Islamic Mysticism*, 94–99.

[112] On the Qalandariyya, see Karamustafa, *Sufism*, 164–66; Ahmet T. Karamustafa, *God's Unruly Friends* (Oxford: Oneworld, 2006), esp. 13–38.

[113] See, e.g., Ghaznawi, *Maqamat*, 72–74; Moayyad and Lewis, *Colossal*, 144–45.

[114] Ghaznawi, *Maqamat*, 70–76; Moayyad and Lewis, *Colossal*, 141–47.

[115] See, e.g., Lewis, *Assassins*, 58–59, 64–65. But for fresh interpretations on Ismaʿili-Seljuq history, see Farhad Daftary, *Ismailis in Medieval Muslim Societies* (London: I.B. Tauris, 2005), 124–48; and for the historiography of the early Ismaʿilis of Iran, see ibid., 107–23.

been rooted in Shafi'i theological and jurisprudential fundamentals. The family was, possibly, Ash'ari. Along the way, father (probably) and son (certainly) embraced Karrami doctrines. Moreover, as Aron Zysow,[116] Wilferd Madelung,[117] and Ulrich Rudolph[118] have demonstrated, aspects of Karrami doctrines are close to Hanafi doctrines, which adds another dimension to Ahmad's intellectual journey: from Shafi'i (and possibly Ash'ari?) to Karrami ascetic and then to Hanafi mystic.

The Karramis of Nishapur held themselves apart from Sufis. Their self-image was of a *madhhab* equal or superior to the Hanafi and the Shafi'i, with their own formulations on ritual and law. The Karramiyya practiced asceticism (*zuhd*) and pietism (*'ibada*),[119] but not mysticism (*tasawwuf* or *'irfan*).[120] The rationalist Hanafi tended toward asceticism (if at all), but less so toward mysticism; however, there were noteworthy exceptions like Abu Bakr al-Kalabadhi (d. *ca*. 380/990) and 'Ali al-Hujwiri (d. 481/1089). The Shafi'i inclined to mysticism: eminent Khurasanian Sufis were Shafi'i.[121] Gnostics (*sufi*) often incorporated pietism and/or asceticism. Abu Sa'id b. Abu al-Khayr, for instance, was a pietist (*'abid*) and a mystic (*sufi* or *'arif*), but *became* the antithesis of ascetic (*zahid*).[122]

Ahmad and Sufism

Ahmad-i Jam's focus shifted to Sufism. He reached middle age when Karramism was fading and Sufism was ascending. This phase coincides with the death of his father, 'Ali, in 480/1087. In the fifth to sixth/eleventh to twelfth centuries, Sufism was infused with novel concepts and the systematization of practices into stages (*maqamat*) and states (*ahwal*) by intellectuals like 'Abd al-Rahman al-Sulami (d. 412/1021), 'Ali al-Hujwiri (d. *ca*. 465–69/1072–77), Abu al-Qasim al-Qushayri (d. 465/1072),

---

[116] Zysow, "Karrami," esp. 583–87. [117] Madelung, *Religious Trends*, 40ff.
[118] Ulrich Rudolph, *Al-Maturidi and the Development of Sunni Theology in Samarqand*, trans. Rodrigo Adem (Leiden: Brill, 2015), 75–80.
[119] "Pietism" is not used in the Lutheran sense but as scrupulous devotion to God's Word, with devotional practices like fasting, renunciation, and supererogatory prayer.
[120] *Tasawwuf* "includes pious works and devotional recitals and meditations." Knysh, *Islamic Mysticism*, 199. For a refreshing perspective on mysticism, and of the dichotomies created by Western scholars, see Omid Safi, "Bargaining with *Baraka*: Persian Sufism, 'Mysticism,' and Pre-modern Politics," *Muslim World* 90 (2000): 259–87, esp. 260–63.
[121] On Sufism's Shafi'i nexus, see Margaret Malamud, "Sufi Organizations and Structures of Authority in Medieval Nishapur," *IJMES* 26/3 (1994): 427–42, 427–31.
[122] Abu Sa'id had practiced asceticism and was not opposed to it as a training regimen. He viewed asceticism as a stage (*maqam*) on the Sufi Path, not a permanent condition.

'Abdallah al-Ansari al-Harawi (d. 481/1089), and Abu Hamid al-Ghazali (d. 505/1111), to mention just a few luminaries of the age. Abu Sa'id b. Abu al-Khayr instituted ten rules for his *khanaqahs*,[123] and "house rules" became common features of Khurasanian Sufism. 'Abd al-Qahir (Abu al-Najib) al-Suhrawardi (d. 563/1168), Ahmad's contemporary, promulgated rules for comportment, which influenced master-disciple relationships and Sufi conduct (*adab*).

Ahmad-i Jam was drawn into the mystical currents wafting through Khurasan. He freely borrowed: his words manifest a mélange of Shafi'i, Hanafi, Karrami, and Sufi ideas. Heshmat Moayyad (d. 2018), a distinguished scholar of Persian literature who did much to bring Ahmad's thoughts to readers, renders his verdict on Ahmad's literary oeuvre:

[Ahmad-i Jam's writings] are more precious for their contribution to Persian literary history than for their teachings. His style is mostly conversational, clear, flawless, rich in rare obsolescences, abounding in parables and situational examples, beautiful and truly enjoyable to read.[124]

It cannot be said that Ahmad-i Jam's mystical legacy is a continuation of Abu Sa'id's, or the legacy of any of the shaykhs in Ahmad's (fabricated) *silsila*. Instead, as Shafi'i Kadkani described it, Ahmad's mystical legacy has a "unique flavor" (*ta'm-i wizha*).[125]

Ahmad the Teaching Shaykh

Ahmad was not a *directing shaykh* (*shaykh al-tarbiyya*), that is, he did not train novices. He was instead a *teaching shaykh* (*shaykh al-ta'lim*).[126] Ahmad's interactions with disciples were confined to the equivalent of the study circle (*halqa*), where students gathered around their shaykh and engaged in

---

[123] Ibn Munawwar/Kadkani (ed.), *Asrar al-tawhid*, 1:317; Nicholson, *Islamic Mysticism*, 46. The rules are last of three sets of ten advisories for darwishes, shaykhs, and hostel residents. Ibn Munawwar/Kadkani (ed.), *Asrar al-tawhid*, 1:315–17.
[124] H. Moayyad, "Ahmad-i Jam," *EIr*, 1:648a.
[125] Kadkani, *Darwish*, 38. This is explicated in Chapter 9.
[126] On the two concepts, see Arthur Buehler, *Sufi Heirs of the Prophet* (Columbia, SC: University of South Carolina Press, 1998), 29–54; Malamud, "Sufi Organizations," 432; Kiyani, *Khanaqah*, 335–37 (Kiyani uses *pir-i suhbat* and *pir-i tarbiyyat*); Fritz Meier, "Ḫurasan und das Ende der klassichen Sufik," in *Bausteine I*, ed. Erika Glassen and Gudrun Schubert (Istanbul: Franz Steiner, 1992), 131–56; but cf. Laury Silvers, "The Teaching Relationship in Early Sufism: A Reassessment of Fritz Meier's Definition of the *Shaykh al-Tarbiya* and the *Shaykh al-Ta'lim*," *Muslim World* 97 (2003): 69–97.

discussions on an array of topics from jurisprudence, theology, and theosophy. The discourses in *Rawzat al-muznibin*, *Siraj al-sa'irin*, and *Uns al-ta'ibin* show that Ahmad-i Jam reveled in the role of lecturer/orator; hence the "mostly conversational" style and the "situational examples" referenced by Heshmat Moayyad. A teaching shaykh, like his counterpart in a madrasa, established rules of conduct (*adab*) and devised curricula. Ahmad did not establish rules for his *khanaqah*.[127]

The directing shaykh model was assuredly known to Ahmad-i Jam because it had originated in Nishapur about 150 years before he was born, and had become entrenched in Khurasan by the time his vocation was in bloom. Students traveled in search of shaykhs with whom to study; however, they sought out established shaykhs. A renowned shaykh, like a renowned hadith transmitter (*muhaddith*) or seminary professor (*mudarris*), enhanced a student's status. It was undoubtedly difficult for Ahmad-i Jam to become established as a director because he had no publicized connections to eminent shaykhs. His domineering personality, suitable for drilling novitiates,[128] lacked the essential qualities for a spiritual director: patience and compassion. Ahmad enjoyed disputations and activism (*tabligh*); hence the title for Kadkani's biography, *The Bellicose Mystic*, and Ahmad-i Jam's sobriquet, "Zhanda-Pil," the "Terrible Elephant" or "Furious Elephant."

In sum, although Ahmad-i Jam was intellectually progressing from Karrami ascetic to Hanafi mystic – reflecting trends in Sufism in Khurasan – his mystical concepts had not yet matured into a discernible methodology. As a mystic at Turbat-i Jam put it, "there was no [gnostic] framework" (*chahar-chub nadarih*).[129] Ahmad's concepts were still overlaid with Karrami religious-political imperatives: (1) proselytism (*da'wa*); (2) activism (*tabligh*); (3) pietism (*'ibada*); and (4) asceticism (*zuhd*).

---

[127] But see Ahmad-i Jam, *Uns al-ta'ibin*, 328–42: Ahmad expressed decorum (*adab*) guidelines on approaching God (*haqq*) and Man (*khalq*).
[128] See Buehler, *Sufi Heirs*, 32–33 (on the training of novices).
[129] Conversation with Muhammad Nasr Jami, 25 December 2011.

2

Saintdom and Patronage

Ahmad-i Jam was better known at the time of his death in 536/1141 for activism (*tabligh*) and proselytism (*da'wa*) than for gnosticism (*'irfan*). His religious ardor contributed to the formation of his saint cult; however, the initial popularity of the saint cult was doubtless limited. It is likely that Ahmad-i Jam was primarily a local saint in a region (Khurasan) with a profusion of saints. Patronage was thin; there was no construction near his tumulus until 633/1236. To develop the cult, the saint had to be rebranded. The religious activist who had tormented Zoroastrians and Isma'ilis was transformed into the "protector of the realm" (*mulk-panah*): Ahmad-i Jam, the "patron saint of kings." This enabled the saint cult to acquire "patronage and protection" (*'inayat wa himayat*) from sultans and viziers.

Ahmad-i Jam became a saint (in Islamic terms, a "Friend of God"), and his sepulcher became a sacred locale (*hima, haram, locus sanctus*). We shall examine Ahmad-i Jam's path to saintdom, with a discussion of the literature on saints; and the acquisition of patronage by the shrine and Ahmad-i Jam's legatees.

FRIENDS OF GOD

Ahmad-i Jam is revered as intercessor and protector of those who have faith in his spiritual powers. In contradistinction to the Catholic process, a Muslim can become a saint in his lifetime; there is no equivalent to beatification: "acknowledgment of extraordinary sanctity is almost entirely a result of popular acclaim."[1]

Scholars of the eastern Islamic world – Iraq, *Iranshahr* (Greater Iran, which includes "Afghanistan"), Transoxiana, and India – articulated sophisticated interpretations of Islam, which incorporated saint cults. Muhammad al-Hakim al-Tirmidhi (fl. bet. 205–210/820–30 and 295–300/905–10) was foremost in thinking about the place within Islam for sainthood (*walayat*) and saintdom (*wilayat*). Hakim al-Tirmidhi's *Sirat al-awliya'* (*Biographies of the Saints*) is a unique intellectual effort for its time.[2] It bears noting that al-Tirmidhi's formulations mainly provide an *intellectual framework* for ulama (doctors of law) and Sufis. People will decide for themselves whether someone – male or female – is a saint or not.

"Saint" (*sanctus*) is a Christian appellation. It is not in the Qur'an. *Wali* (pl. *awliya'*), "friend," however, appears repeatedly in the Qur'an and was adopted as the synonym for saint. *Wali Allah*, "Friend of God,"[3] is used in Islamic tradition to mean saint or intercessor.[4] Al-Tirmidhi's explications on *wali Allah* are extensive. A critical passage:

> The Friend of God ... is a man who stands firm in his rank and lives up to the condition set by God, just as he lived up to sincerity (towards God) while journeying to God ... He practices the religious prescriptions and pays heed to the legal punishments, and he adheres to his rank until he becomes upright, is refined, educated, purified, cleansed, rendered sweet-smelling, broadened, developed, nourished, promoted and made accustomed. Thus his Friendship with God is brought to perfection through these ten qualities. Then he is transferred from his rank to the Possessor of sovereignty (*malik al-mulk*) and he is assigned a place before God, and his intimate converse (*najwa*) with God takes place face to face. Now he is completely engaged with God to the exclusion of all else ... He is now

---

[1] John Renard, *Friends of God* (Berkeley, CA: University of California Press, 2008), 260.

[2] Al-Hakim al-Tirmidhi, *The Concept of Sainthood in Early Islamic Mysticism: Two Works by al-Hakim al-Tirmidhi*, trans. Bernd Radtke and John O'Kane (Richmond: Curzon Press, 1996). On the author and his work, see Bernd Radtke, "The Concept of *Wilaya* in Early Sufism," in *The Heritage of Sufism*, vol. 1, ed. Leonard Lewisohn (Oxford: Oneworld, 1999), 1:483–96; and Aiyub Palmer, *Sainthood and Authority in Early Islam: al-Hakim al-Tirmidhi's Theory of Wilaya and the Reenvisioning of the Sunni Caliphate* (Leiden: Brill, 2020).

[3] The phrase appears in the Shi'i profession of faith (*shahada*): "There is no god but God, Muhammad is His messenger and 'Ali is a Friend of God." M. Radscheit, "Witnessing and Testifying," *EQ*, 5:492–506.

[4] On the distinctions in the relationships of saints with God, see al-Tirmidhi, *Sainthood*, 43, 91.

like a fully authorized deputy who does not need permission, for whenever he undertakes one of his tasks, he is in the grasp of God.[5]

On the visible signs of "Friends of God," al-Tirmidhi offers eight proofs:[6]

(1) In God's words, "They are those who when one thinks of Me, one thinks of them; and when one thinks of them, one thinks of Me"
(2) "No one can oppose them without being overwhelmed by the power of that which is due unto God"
(3) "They are endowed with clairvoyance (*firasa/firasat*)"[7]
(4) "They receive divine inspiration" (*ilham*)
(5) "Whoever contends with them is cast down and comes to an evil end"
(6) "All tongues agree in praising them" except for the jealous
(7) "Their prayers are answered and they are manifestly capable of miracles" (*karama/karamat*)
(8) The Friends of God "converse with Khadir [= Khizr], who wanders across the earth, on land and sea, in the plains and in the mountains, searching for someone like himself out of passionate longing for him"

The saint, as a Friend of God, is believed to be capable of obtaining favors from Him – such as healing the infirm or helping a family conceive a child – because "God loves his friends and they love him" (Q5:54–55);[8] and saints' "prayers are answered and they are manifestly capable of miracles." Performing miracles is important for saintdom, although miracles are not indispensable. A saint who has not performed any miracles, however, is rare. The writer Hujwiri noted, "[a] miracle is a token of a saint's veracity, and it cannot be manifested to an impostor except as a sign that his pretensions are false."[9]

SAINTS AND MIRACLES

There are tiers of miracle-makers who are not necessarily saints: (1) the prophets who are represented in the Qur'an and Hebrew Bible and/or New Testament, and shared by Islam and Judaism and/or Christianity: Moses/Musa, Abraham/Ibrahim, Jesus/'Isa, John (the Baptist)/Yahya, and others;

---

[5] Ibid., 91.   [6] Ibid., 124–25.
[7] *Firasa* is mind-reading, soul-reading, telepathy, telepathic clairvoyance, and clairvoyance of the past, present, and future. See Hans J. Kissling, "Die Wunder der Derwische," *ZDMG* 107 (1957): 348–61, 354–55; and Schimmel, *Dimensions*, 205.
[8] See Berndt Radtke, "Saint," *EQ*, 4:520–21; and Louise Marlow, "Friends and Friendship," *EQ*, 2:273–75. Further on saints, see Renard, *Friends*, et passim.
[9] 'Ali al-Hujwiri, *Kashf al-mahjub*, trans. R. A. Nicholson (London: Luzac, 1911), 218.

Saints and Miracles 35

and then (2) the "historical saints" (Sufis, ulama, martyrs) whose biographies are in hagiologies that attest to their "miracles and pious deeds."[10] Another thinker on the roles of saints and prophets was Ruzbihan Baqli (522–606/1128–1209),[11] who hypothesized that the seas (*darya*) of prophethood (*nabuwat*) and sainthood (*walayat*) course into one another,[12] an allusion from the Qur'an: "He has let free the two bodies of flowing water (*al-bahrayn*), meeting together" (Q55:19). The miracles (*mu'jizat*) of God's prophets, however, are distinct from the miracles (*karamat*) of His Friends.[13]

Ahmad-i Jam's thoughts on miracles (attributed to him by Sadid al-Din Ghaznawi) do not deviate from the distinctions between *mu'jizat* and *karamat*. Ahmad emphasizes two phenomena that accidentally may be characterized as miracles: "divine deception" (*istidraj*) and an "act of fraud" (*makhraqa*). *Mu'jizat, karamat*, and *istidraj* are God's deeds; but where *istidraj* "is God leading His servant step by step closer to his punishment."[14] Moayyad and Lewis parsed Ahmad's discourses on miracles, which demonstrate the influences on him of al-Ghazali, al-Qushayri, al-Sarraj, and others, and in particular, al-Kalabadhi.[15] In *Uns al-ta'ibin*,[16] Ahmad-i Jam "demonstrat[es] his discursive power by assessing the theological implications of miraculous events."[17] Ahmad's discursive discourses shall not detain us.[18]

Advocates of al-Tirmidhi's perspectives believe "there is no difficulty in reconciling the two classes of miracles ... the saint, by the miracles which he performs, establishes both the prophecy of the apostle and his own

---

[10] Josef Meri, *The Cult of Saints among Muslims and Jews in Medieval Syria* (Oxford: Oxford University Press, 2002), 60.
[11] On him, see Carl Ernst, *Ruzbihan Baqli* (Richmond: Curzon Press, 1996).
[12] Ruzbihan Baqli, *Kashf al-asrar wa mukashafat al-anwar*, ed. Maryam Husayni (Tehran: Intisharat-i sukhan, 1393/2014), ¶ 5 (pp. 102–3 of edition); Ruzbihan Baqli, *The Unveiling of Secrets*, trans. Carl Ernst (Chapel Hill, NC: Parvardigar Press, 1997), ¶ 5 (pp. 7–8).
[13] al-Hujwiri, *Kashf*, 219–24; discourse in Amir Hasan Sijzi, *Nizam ad-Din Awliya: Morals for the Heart* [*Fawa'id al-fu'ad*], trans. Bruce Lawrence (New York: Paulist Press, 1992), 160; Schimmel, *Dimensions*, 206; and see Richard Gramlich, *Die Wunder der Freunde Gottes* (Stuttgart: Steiner, 1987), et passim.
[14] Ghaznawi, *Maqamat*, 7, 10–11; Moayyad and Lewis, *Colossal*, 74, 79.
[15] Ghaznawi, *Maqamat*, 7–12; Moayyad and Lewis, *Colossal*, 74–81 and nn18–23; Abu Bakr Muhammad b. Ishaq al-Kalabadhi, *Kitab al-ta'arruf li-madhhab ahl al-tasawwuf*, ed. Ahmad Shams al-Din (Beirut: Dar al-kutub al-'ilmiyya, 1993), 79–88; and Abu Bakr Muhammad b. Ishaq al-Kalabadhi, *The Doctrine of the Sufis*, trans. A. J. Arberry (Cambridge: Cambridge University Press, 1935), 57–66 (the translation by Arberry is based on an earlier edition).
[16] Ahmad-i Jam, *Uns al-ta'ibin*, 119–34 (on classes and subclasses of miracles).
[17] Dechant, "'Colossal Elephant,'" 73.   [18] But see discussion in ibid., 73–86.

saintship."[19] Furthermore, "saints are not preserved from sin (*ma'sum*), for sinlessness belongs to the prophets, but they are protected (*mahfuz*) from any evil that involves the denial of their saintship."[20] Sufis were divided on the issues of whether a saint even knows that he is a saint, and how a saint should comport himself.[21] Carl Ernst's vivid descriptions of Baqli's writings conjure images of God's Friends sitting around the Prophet, like attendants. Muhammad is "the highest of authorities" and the "intercessor for humanity." Only the Prophet can see the Beloved.[22]

Sainthood (*walayat*) is distinct from saintdom (*wilayat*).[23] A saint possesses both concurrently. Nizam al-Din Awliya (d. 725/1325), an Indian saint of the Chishtiyya, explains: *walayat* is what a shaykh imparts to his disciples about God, and also in his interactions with people; whereas *wilayat* is between the shaykh and God. When a saint dies, he takes with him his *wilayat*, but his *walayat* can be conferred by him on another person.[24] When Abu Sa'id b. Abu al-Khayr died, Sufi legend recounts, inquiries were conducted to identify the recipient of his *walayat*. The answer came back that it was one "Shams al-'Arifin" ("the Sun of the Gnostics"), but since there are many Sufis bearing that sobriquet (*laqab*),[25] there are (conveniently) a slew of claimants for Abu Sa'id's *walayat*.

The miracles of Ahmad-i Jam are abundant and variegated.[26] He healed ailments, cured infertility, saved crops, punished enemies, disputed with Isma'ilis, saved kings from assassins, and so on. Al-Tirmidhi's signs of saintdom – *firasat*, *ilham*, *karamat*, his punishment of enemies, jealous tongues wagging against Ahmad-i Jam – are plentiful in the *Spiritual Feats*. "[S]tories on transsubstantiation are very frequent in this book [*Spiritual*

---

[19] al-Hujwiri, *Kashf*, 220.   [20] Ibid., 225.
[21] Abu al-Qasim al-Qushayri, *Al-Qushayri's Epistle on Sufism*, trans. Alexander Knysh (Reading: Garnet, 2007), 268–73.
[22] Ernst, *Ruzbihan Baqli*, 58–59. Regarding the relationship of saints to prophets, see Jawid Mojaddedi, *Beyond Dogma* (Oxford: Oxford University Press, 2012), esp. 28–62.
[23] For more on the theological formulations of *awliya'*, *wilayat*, *walayat*, *firasat*, *karamat*, *mu'jizat*, etc., and opposing viewpoints, see Renard, *Friends*, 259–81, and his bibliography for chapter 11; Meri, *Cult*, 66–82; Gramlich, *Wunder*, et passim.
[24] Sijzi, *Morals*, 95–96. Further on *walayat*, see Hermann Landolt, "Walayah," *Encyclopedia of Religion*, 2nd ed., ed. L. Jones (Farmington Hills, MI: Thomson-Gale, 2005), 9656–9662, esp. 9660ff. (vol. 14).
[25] Sijzi, *Morals*, 95–96.
[26] See "Motif Index of Miracles" in Moayyad and Lewis, *Colossal Elephant*, 444–49. See esp. Paul, "Constructing the Friends of God," 214–26 (Jürgen Paul analyzes Ghaznawi's stories on Ahmad, their genre, structure, and intended audience); Dechant, "'Colossal Elephant,'" 29–58 (John Dechant analyzes, inter alia, the import of miracles).

Feats], to the point that they may be considered one of its characteristic features."[27] Stories identify miracles by Ahmad in life and posthumously. Ahmad, in his lifetime (probably) and posthumously (certainly), was believed to possess *wilayat* and *walayat*. According to Ghaznawi, a challenge to Ahmad's sainthood came from the leading scholars of Nishapur's *madhhab*s, including the Shiʿa and Karramiyya. Representatives of each *madhhab* journeyed to Maʿd-Abad to test Ahmad. Needless to say, our hero won over his skeptics by performing a miracle.[28]

The Timurid-era embellishment of Ahmad-i Jam's mountain congress with God's servant, Khizr, from whom he received *uwaysi* initiation (a *khirqa*), is a critical interpolation that burnishes Ahmad's *wilayat* and *walayat*. Belief in Ahmad-i Jam's spiritual authority and abilities to heal, cure, save, punish, and protect attracted pilgrims to his tomb.

SAINT CULTS

To those whose perspectives are molded by the Enlightenment and Protestantism, Ghaznawi's miracle stories are rubbish peddled to superstitious folk: "miraculous legends appealing to the primitive masses";[29] however, Islamic saint cults do not emerge because simple minds are in awe of miracles. "Orientalists"[30] focused on the superficial element – folk practices – and categorized Islamic beliefs as "orthodox" or "popular." As Carl Ernst bluntly put it, "miracles are a very important part of the religious outlook of hundreds of millions of people ... If we wish to understand their point of view, it is necessary to take miracles seriously."[31] Furthermore, as Omid Safi observed, hagiographical stories "connect the saint to his community," pass along a tradition, and shape behaviors.[32]

Saint cults are multilayered expressions of devotion. Participation by unlettered folk is one layer, certainly, but this surface element must not detract from our appreciation of the profound spiritual experiences transpiring at multiple levels: emotional, physical, psychological, and

---

[27] Paul, "Constructing the Friends of God," 217–18.
[28] Ghaznawi, *Maqamat*, 63–66; Moayyad and Lewis, *Colossal*, 133–36.
[29] Meier, "Ahmad-i Jam." Fritz Meier dismissed Ghaznawi's *Spiritual Feats* as "almost worthless for Ahmad's real biography and thought, being full of miraculous legends appealing to the primitive masses."
[30] To adopt a term saturated with negativity.   [31] Ernst, *Shambala Guide*, 69.
[32] Safi, "Bargaining with *Baraka*," 267.

metaphysical. The intellectual underpinnings of cults – the scholarship of al-Tirmidhi, al-Ghazali, al-Hujwiri, et al. – demonstrate that phenomena more momentous than superstition; phenomena, both intellectual and spiritual, are nourishing saint cults and contributing to their manifestation and persistence over time and space.

Peter Brown, historian of Christian saint cults, rejects the two-tier model (popular v. orthodox): "[i]n modern scholarship, these attitudes take the form of a 'two-tiered' model. The views of the potentially enlightened few are thought of as being subject to continuous upward pressure from habitual ways of thinking current among 'the vulgar.'" Acceptance of saint cults, therefore, "must have been the result of the capitulation by the enlightened elites of the Christian church to modes of thought previously current only among the 'vulgar.'"[33] This attitude is evident in scholarship on Muslim saints.

Augustine of Hippo initially disfavored saints and miracles, but eventually embraced them.[34] St. Augustine's intellectual evolution was not viewed (by some) as an "intellectual breakthrough," but rather, as another concession to "popular belief."[35] The sophisticated thoughts of al-Tirmidhi, al-Ghazali, al-Hujwiri, and others are not concessions to popular Islamic beliefs, but represent intellectual frameworks intended at understanding the phenomena of saints. Islamic cults are no more "vulgar" than are Christian saint cults.

Select Islamic saint cults of the East were continuations of pre-Islamic cults, namely, Buddhist, Vedic, Christian, or Zoroastrian, which were Islamicized over the course of time; however, most Islamic cults were original expressions of devotion. Louis Dupree offers a typology of the saint shrines of Afghanistan. This includes pre-Islamic shrines that were Islamicized;[36] however, most shrine cults were organically Islamic. Dupree's typology can be *cautiously* applied to other regions of the Persianate world.

Commoners and ulama participated in saint cults, sometimes reservedly, sometimes exuberantly. Ulama reserved to themselves the duty to condemn "excesses," which they have historically done (often

---

[33] Peter Brown, *The Cult of the Saints* (Chicago, IL: University of Chicago Press, 1981), 17.
[34] Ibid., 77–78; Peter Brown, *Augustine of Hippo: A Biography* (Berkeley, CA: University of California Press, 2000), 416–22.
[35] Brown, *Cult of the Saints*, 78.
[36] Louis Dupree, "Saint Cults in Afghanistan," *South Asia Series* 20/1 (Hanover: American Universities Field Staff Reports, 1976): 1–21, 4–5. See also Meri, *Cult*, 79–82, for another useful typology of saints.

vociferously). The dichotomy of "popular" versus "orthodox," and the theory that beliefs and practices by "illiterate and ignorant" Muslims exert upward pressures that corrupt "correct" beliefs and practices must be rejected. The real dichotomy is between ortho*doxy* and ortho*praxy*: *textual* Islam versus Islamic *praxis*.

The focus on book Islam does nothing to elucidate how Muslims in any given corner of Islamdom *interpret* the Prophet's message, and how they *practice* their faith (orthopraxy). Wahhabis carp about unswerving adherence to hadith during ritual prayers (Ar. *salat*; Per. *namaz*), but how Muslims actually pray may differ from the literal language of the hadith (but which/whose hadith?). A reason for this is that people learn to pray through imitation: children learn the *rak'a* sequence (stand, bow, prostrate, sit) of *namaz* by mimicking their parents. People tend also not to follow manuals – assuming they are literate. Islamic rituals, like Islamic law, should be uniform from Morocco to Indonesia. This is the theory: God's law is the same throughout His universe. In reality, divergences exist and are sanctioned by the consensus (*ijma'*) of Muslims.

The anthropologist Ernest Gellner views *ijma'* as the harmonizing factor between textual Islam (Qur'an and hadith) and Islamic praxis.[37] In the restrictive sense, he is incorrect because *ijma'* is an aspect of law-making and it is reserved for ulama.[38] However, in the expansive sense, Gellner is correct. As a celebrated hadith attributed to the Prophet says, "my community shall never agree on an error."[39] The ulama are a subset of the Muslim community; in any given region of Islam's expanses, the ulama are generally a minority. If, hypothetically, the majority of the residents in Jam province consider Ahmad-i Jam a saint and make pilgrimages to his tomb, but the ulama of Nishapur disagree, who is right? Are the masses nullifying the views of the ulama? And what if most ulama in Herat agree with the masses that there are Muslim saints, but most ulama in Cairo reject saints? *Ikhtilaf*, differences between scholars on interpretations of God's Message, which impacts on ideas of orthodoxy (but whose orthodoxy?) and orthopraxy, will not be resolved in these pages, but bears mentioning. Saint cults, to sum, are legitimate expressions of Muslim piety and devotion to God. Innumerable ulama and laymen throughout

---

[37] Ernest Gellner, *Muslim Society* (Cambridge: Cambridge University Press, 1981), 116.
[38] Mohammad Hashim Kamali, *Principles of Islamic Jurisprudence* (Cambridge: The Islamic Texts Society, 2003), 228–63; Knut S. Vikør, *Between God and the Sultan: A History of Islamic Law* (New York: Oxford University Press, 2005), 73–88.
[39] *Sunan Ibn Majah*, hadith # 3950.

the eastern Islamic world continue to participate (to some degree) in the venerations of saints.

The sanctification of Ahmad-i Jam and the institution of his cult can be fitted within Islam's mainstream. Ahmad became *wali Allah* to Sunni *and* to Shiʿa: the majority of the cult is Sunni, with a Shiʿi minority (this was the case in bygone times, too). The case of putative Shiʿi Qasim-i Anwar (d. 838/1434f.) is illustrative. Qasim was ejected from Timurid Herat, eventually settling in Jam province. The spirit (*ruhaniyyat*) of Ahmad-i Jam appeared to him one night and infused him with his divine energy (*fayz*).[40] Qasim-i Anwar became attached to him. The Sufis of Jam still respect Qasim and pay homage at his tomb at Khargird,[41] near Jam, because they believe he was selected by Ahmad (for some purpose). As demographics of Iranian Khurasan continue their relentless march to Shiʿi dominance,[42] the Shiʿi element in Ahmad's cult has increased (see typology of pilgrims, Chapter 8).

THE PATRON SAINT OF KINGS

Ahmad and his early acolytes and descendants cultivated for him the image of miracle-maker, able to heal the sick and smite his enemies with God's assistance. He was given the nickname Zhanda-Pil, which has been translated by Heshmat Moayyad, and others, as "the colossal elephant." *Pil* (Ar. *fil*) is elephant; *zhanda* could mean "terrible" or "furious";[43] hence Ahmad-i Jam, the "terrible elephant" or "furious elephant," a droll and clever play on his belligerent personality and commanding physique. Shafiʿi Kadkani appositely titled his book on Ahmad-i Jam, *The Bellicose Mystic*. John Dechant hypothesized that the sobriquet originated with Zoroastrians.[44] Ahmad was unsparingly hateful toward Zoroastrians: he despised the path of Zoroaster and tormented adherents for enjoying wine and music.

Returning to the *Spiritual Feats*. The miracles narrated by Ghaznawi contributed to the formation of Ahmad's cult – at the folk level: "[t]here is ample evidence," for instance, that Ghaznawi had made a "conscious

---

[40] Dawlatshah al-Samarqandi, *Tadhkirat al-shuʿaraʾ*, ed. E. G. Browne (Leiden: Brill, 1900), 348.
[41] On 9 September 2017, I joined Jami friends who were visiting Qasim's tomb at Khargird.
[42] Jam's demographics are discussed in Chapter 5.
[43] Wheeler Thackston renders Zhanda-Pil as "Furious Elephant" and Nile Green renders it as "Terrible Elephant." Both are agreeable translations.
[44] Dechant, "'Colossal Elephant,'" 86.

attempt" to appeal to a "lay" audience.[45] The signs of sainthood itemized by al-Tirmidhi are manifest in Ghaznawi's stories. They helped Ahmad become established as a saint in his preserve of Khurasan.

Ahmad-i Jam's miracles did not elevate his standing in certain corners of the Sufi world that espoused sophisticated ideas. Farid al-Din ʿAttar Nishapuri (540–618/1145–1221) does not include Ahmad-i Jam in his biographical anthology, *Tazkirat al-awliyaʾ* (*Memorial of the Saints*). Heshmat Moayyad surmises that ʿAttar, although cognizant of Ahmad's activities in Khurasan, found unappealing "a populist miracle worker who was interested only in strict enforcement of religious law and not in metaphysical speculation."[46] Ahmad-i Jam was a man of uncertain intellectual pedigree and lacked a prominent directing shaykh. His spiritual pedigree (i.e., his link to Abu Saʿid) was palpably contrived, and possibly rejected outright by Sufi masters like ʿAttar. Ahmad's miracles resonated with folk and family, but otherwise had limited appeal.

Ahmad-i Jam's doctrines did not help him achieve fame. Even now, outside of Jami circles – Jamis and scholars who study Jamis – Ahmad's surviving writings, all in print, are rarely referenced. Shafiʿi Kadkani scoured early writings and found no evidence of Ahmad's imprint on religious discourses except for a solitary reference, *ca*. 597/1200f., in Mahmud b. Ahmad al-Faryabi's *Khalisat al-haqaʾiq*.[47] Ahmad's intellectual appeal was limited to family, darwishes, a handful of others. His cult did not break out of those confines until the Mongol period. Once Ahmad-i Jam's fame increased (in the seventh/thirteenth century), we find references to him in eighth/fourteenth-century Sufi circles; for instance, Bahaʾ al-Din Naqshband's quotation of a concept articulated by Ahmad.[48] But this is a situation of established prominence causing a Sufi to examine Ahmad's works, or more likely, to quote lines from Ahmad that someone brought to his attention.[49] Ahmad-i Jam finds immense popularity with the Chishtiyya – not for his expositions on Sufism, but for a couplet, which caused the verse and its author to be "celebrated in the subcontinent":[50]

---

[45] Ibid., 42; see also Paul, "Constructing the Friends of God," 214–17, on "audience."
[46] Moayyad and Lewis, *Colossal*, 58.
[47] Kadkani, *Darwish*, 65–71. *Khalisat al-haqaʾiq* is on piety, ethics, and moral conduct. Ahmad-i Jam's *Uns al-taʾibin* is referenced.
[48] Salah b. Mubarak al-Bukhari, *Anis al-talibin wa ʿuddat al-salikin*, ed. Khalil Ibrahim Sari-Ughli (Tehran: Sazman-i intisharat-i kayhan, 1371/1993), 218–19.
[49] Probably learned from Zayn al-Din Taybadi when Naqshbandi sojourned with him.
[50] Sijzi, *Morals*, 72. The Chishtiyya, now identified with Indian Sufism, originated in Chisht-i Sharif in Ghur, the mountainous region east of Herat.

Kushtagan-i khanjar-i taslim ra / har zaman az ghayb jan-i digar ast.

All those by the knife of submission killed,
Each moment from God with new life are filled.[51]

These lines undoubtedly thrilled Sufis. Submission to divine will and the promise of new life are integral not just to Islam, but to Sufi thought. Ahmad's couplet has auxiliary meanings in Sufism, namely, its relationship to *fana'* and *baqa'*, two stages on the Path to God. The terms are paired in Sufi thought (*baqa' wa-fana'*: "subsistence and passing away"), and mirror a pairing in Revelation: "All that is on earth will perish (*fanin*), but will abide (*yabqa*) forever the Face of thy Lord, full of Majesty, Bounty, and Honor" (Q55:26–27).[52] *Baqa' wa-fana'* have layered meanings to Sufis: the ascetic (*zahid*) who annihilates (*fana'*) his carnal soul (*nafs*) and replaces it with the attributes of God; the mystic (*sufi*) who effaces (*fana'*) his self-consciousness and becomes conscious only of God and subsists (*baqa'*) in Him.[53]

Returning to the immediate point, devotees of Ahmad faced a quandary. Their saint, precious to them, did not have support that extended beyond Maʿd-Abad-i Jam; and until 633/1236, nearly one century after his death, there were no sepulchral or spiritual edifices near Ahmad's tomb.[54] In order to expand Ahmad's support base and garner patronage that would enhance shrine and cult, his Sufi trademark had to be repackaged and marketed to a new audience – one with financial resources. Appeals to common folk were de-emphasized in favor of appeals to sultans. The initiative, or the idea, to transform Ahmad-i Jam's Sufi hallmark was triggered by a pilgrimage to Turbat-i Jam in 649/1251f.

The event was the visit to Turbat-i Jam by Shams al-Din Muhammad Kart for *ziyarat* at Ahmad-i Jam's grave. Shams al-Din was the founder of the Kart dynasty (*Al-i Kart*), which ruled a contiguous tract of eastern Iran and Afghanistan to India and the Hindu Kush until Tamerlane's capture of Herat in 783/1381. In 649/1251, at an investiture ceremony at the court of the Grand Qaʾan of the Mongol empire, Möngke (r. 1251–58), Shams al-Din received a diploma (*yarligh*) and "seed money" for the nascent Kartid state.[55] One of the new king's first acts after

---

[51] Ibid., 72. There is no further information on Ahmad-i Jam's impact on the Chishtiyya. E-mail communication with Bruce B. Lawrence, 9 December 2016.
[52] Logically, *fana'* follows *baqa'*, but is paired thusly in literature.
[53] Schimmel, *Dimensions*, 142ff; G. Böwering, "Baqaʾ wa fanaʾ," EIr, 3:722–24.
[54] Lisa Golombek, "The Chronology of Turbat-i Shaykh Jam," *Iran* 9 (1971): 27–44.
[55] On the investiture and Mongol policy in Iran, see Thomas R. Allsen, *Mongol Imperialism: The Policies of the Grand Qan Möngke in China, Russia, and the Islamic Lands, 1251–1259*

crossing the Oxus and attending to imperial business at the Mongol camp in Badghis (north of Herat) was to visit Ahmad's shrine for pilgrimage. He would have been hosted then by Ahmad-i Jam's grandson, Qutb al-Din Muhammad Jami (d. 10 Rabi' I 667/17 November 1268).[56] The Kart *malik* remained at Jam for two days.[57]

Shams al-Din Muhammad Kart was not collecting *baraka* at multiple shrines, that is, Jam was his primary destination. He stopped at Ribat-i Pay in Fushanj (west of Herat), made *ziyarat* there – where marks in the rocks are believed to be Abraham's/Ibrahim's footsteps – and decamped the next day for Turbat-i Jam.[58] The visit to Jam was to express his gratitude for the benefits and blessings he had received, and to obtain fresh *baraka* for his embryonic state. Fresh *baraka* was vital: although Shams al-Din Kart held the *yarligh*, he did not control the territories itemized in it. He was to spend the next two decades bringing to heel minor lords from Herat to the Indus. In any event, after concluding his pilgrimage at Turbat-i Jam, he left for the Mongol viceroy's (i.e., Arghun Aga's) headquarters in Tus to attend to further imperial business. When Shams al-Din Muhammad Kart died in Tabriz in 676/1278, his body was conveyed to Jam for interment near Ahmad-i Jam's grave.[59]

Shams al-Din Kart either had a preexisting connection to Ahmad's shrine or had learned that the shrine was the ideal place at which to offer his prayers of gratitude and to make supplications. The choice is intriguing because the *malik* (vassal king) was from Ghur in the western Hindu Kush. The *malik*'s progenitors had served the Ghurids (the Shansabani dynasty; r. from before *ca*. 401/1011 to *ca*. 610/1213). Zahir al-Din 'Isa b. Ahmad-i Jam (n.d.), a Sufi and shaykh to Qutb al-Din Muhammad Jami, had been a confidant of sultan Ghiyath al-Din Muhammad Ghuri (r. 558–99/1163–1203).[60] Another possible connection is the Chishti Sufi community of Ghur. In any event, the visit inaugurated a bond between

(Berkeley, CA: University of California Press, 1987), 70–71; and George Lane, *Early Mongol Rule in Thirteenth-Century Iran* (London: RoutledgeCurzon, 2003), 161–63.

[56] He was the patriarch of the Sufi community. See Figures A1.1b #10, A1.2, and A1.3.
[57] Sayf al-Harawi, *Tarikhnamah-yi Harat*, ed. Ghulam-Riza Tabataba'i-Majd (Tehran: Intisharat-i asatir, 1383/2004), 204–5.
[58] On the *ribat*, see Christine Noelle-Karimi, *The Pearl in Its Midst: Herat and the Mapping of Khurasan (15th–19th Centuries)* (Vienna: Österreichischen Akademie der Wissenschaften, 2014), 39. On saintly footprints (*qadamgah*) and sacred relics, i.e., *khirqa*, see McChesney, "Reliquary Sufism."
[59] Zamchi Isfizari, *Rawzat al-jannat fi awsaf-i madinat-i Harat*, 2 vols., ed. Muhammad Kazim Imam (Tehran: Danishgah-i Tehran, 1338/1959), 1:422.
[60] Buzjani/Moayyad (ed.), *Rawzat*, 75.

Jami shaykhs and Kartid kings that led to marriages and the interlocking of family fortunes.

Ahmad-i Jam was marketed to sultans as a Friend of God who helped kings achieve maximum potential. He was the "protector of the realm" (*mulk-panah*), or "protector of the king" (*malik-panah*), or "the refuge of kings"/"protector of kings" (*salatin-panah*),[61] the man who sustained kings on the Straight Path and protected them from enemies. Stated another way, Ahmad-i Jam's new hallmark was patron saint of kings.

Motifs in Jami propaganda advance the "protector of the king/realm" theme.

The Isma'ili threat in Khurasan persisted into the early Mongol period in Iran. They threatened Möngke Qa'an – not an astute action because it contributed to his decision to dispatch his brother, Hülegü Khan, to destroy Iran's Isma'ili redoubts. The fear of Isma'ili assassins lurking in markets and bedrooms waiting to pounce on their unsuspecting targets lingered in minds. The hagiographical motifs employed by Ghaznawi resonated because they are based on facts and palpable fears. Isma'ilis committed numerous assassinations with the blade; Seljuq officials had taken to wearing protective armor beneath their robes. Isma'ilis threatened Sanjar by secreting a knife under his pillow.[62] This is reported in 'Ata'-Malik Juwayni's *History of the World Conqueror*.[63] The hagiography departs at this juncture from Juwayni's report, with Ahmad-i Jam berating Sanjar for his moral laxity and failure to suppress the Isma'ili "heretics." He exhorts the sultan and the ulama to fight the Isma'ilis. Sanjar acquiesces.[64] The account will have resonated with Iranian audiences frustrated by the Seljuq state's inability to neutralize the threat. In the hagiographical telling, Ahmad saves the Seljuq state from the Isma'ili menace, which is far from reality.

---

[61] *Malik-panah*, or *mulk-panah*, is used to describe Ahmad in Jalal al-Din Yusuf-i Ahl [Jami], *Fara'id-i Ghiyasi*, ed. Heshmat Moayyad (Tehran: Intisharat-i bunyad-i farhang-i Iran, vol. I, 1356/1977; vol. II, 1358/1979), 1:173–81. The unvowelled consonants *m–l–k* can be rendered in various ways: *mulk* (kingdom); *malik* (king); *mullak* (kings; sing. *mālik*, *malīk*). F. J. Steingass, *The Student's Arabic–English Dictionary* (London: Crosby Lockwood & Son, 1884), 1057.

[62] Ghaznawi, *Maqamat*, 70–72; Moayyad and Lewis, *Colossal*, 141–43.

[63] 'Ala' al-Din 'Ata'-Malik Juvaini [Juwayni], *The History of the World-Conqueror*, 2 vols., trans. J. A. Boyle (Manchester: Manchester University Press, 1958), 2:681–82. The knife beneath the pillow is probably a topos.

[64] Ghaznawi, *Maqamat*, 72–74; Moayyad and Lewis, *Colossal*, 144–45.

In yet another story, Ahmad-i Jam discovers a plot by one Qarajih al-Saqi to poison Sanjar.⁶⁵ He leaps into action and saves the Seljuq sultan. The would-be assassin, seeing that his plot has been foiled, flees, and is pursued by Sanjar and his army. But Sanjar is defeated and his forces scattered. Ahmad intervenes, rallies the troops, and Sanjar is victorious, with Qarajih al-Saqi in shackles.⁶⁶ To Sanjar's query about the identity of his protector, Ahmad-i Jam responds, "You were *entrusted to my care* some years ago [by God] and I pray for you and *watch over you*."⁶⁷

The morals of the motifs in the above stories are that Ahmad is the spiritual guide who keeps kings from straying from the Straight Path. He exhorts them when they are lax in their obligation to uphold the Shariʻa and fight heresies (Sanjar's case). Ahmad-i Jam is the guardian *appointed by Heaven* to keep kings safe from their covert enemies – poisoners being the timeless anxiety of kings. He is the warden from the spiritual world who stands beside a king on the battlefield and guarantees victory for his ward.

The kings had to patronize the shrine in exchange for Heaven's favors. The words whispered to the Kart *malik*s on the greatness of Ahmad and his role as *mulk-panah* are not known; however, the results are clear. The Karts, namely, Shams al-Din Muhammad's grandson, Ghiyath al-Din Muhammad, transformed the shrine into a shrine complex.

MARKETING THE SAINT: THE TIMURIDS

When Jami shaykhs approached Temür/Tamerlane, they promoted Ahmad-i Jam's role as a divinely appointed guardian of kings. In a letter, *ca.* 782/1380, Muʻin al-Din Jami (702–83/1302–82), the Kartid vizier (see Chapter 3), wraps Ahmad's relationship with Sanjar in hagiological embroidery. The Seljuq sultan, Sanjar, was Ahmad-i Jam's "child and disciple" (*farzand wa murid*).⁶⁸ Sanjar became the king of the whole

---

[65] Qarajih's role in a rebellion against Sanjar, and his defeat and capture, are historical; but the remaining details are hagiographical. See Ibn Athir, *al-Kamil fi al-tarikh*, 10 vols., ed. Abu al-Fidaʼ ʻAbdallah Qadi (Beirut: Dar al-kutub al-ʻilmiyya, 1987), 9:263–65 (events of AH 526); and Moayyad and Lewis, *Colossal*, 18–19.

[66] Ghaznawi, *Maqamat*, 35–39; Moayyad and Lewis, *Colossal*, 105–9.

[67] Ghaznawi, *Maqamat*, 38; Moayyad and Lewis, *Colossal*, 108–9 (emphasis added). For further analysis on the hagiological narratives on Ahmad-i Jam and Sanjar, see Omid Safi, *The Politics of Knowledge in Premodern Islam* (Chapel Hill, NC: University of North Carolina Press, 2006), 149–53; see also Tor, "'Sovereign and Pious," 49–50.

[68] Yusuf-i Ahl/Moayyad (ed.), *Faraʼid*, 1:173–81, 175. On addressing emperors as "child," with reference to Temür, Sultan Sanjar, and the instant letter, see Safi, *Politics*, 155.

world (*padishah-i hama-yi jahan*) and the Khusraw of his age. Sanjar's imperial grandeur and longevity were Heaven's favors for his devotion to Ahmad-i Jam. Sanjar, the Kartid vizier continues, visited Ahmad-i Jam's *khanaqah*, and with his own hands, kneaded clay to the roof of "the hospice of the guardian of the realm" (*khanaqah-yi mulk-panah*).[69] A couplet proclaims that "When he was with the Furious Elephant, the Presence of God (*hazrat-i haqq*), Sanjar was but a slave (*ghulam*) kneading clay [for his shaykh]."[70] For demonstrating faith in one of God's Friends (*wali*), God bestowed His blessings and favors on Sanjar.[71]

Temür was invited to follow Sanjar's path, which he did. Temür made *ziyarat* at Ahmad's shrine. Reciprocity for blessings was patronage of the shrine and its cult. As the vizier writes in his letter to Temür, when Ahmad-i Jam inquired of Sanjar as to why he was engaged in menial labor, the Seljuq sultan replied, "if tomorrow God were to ask me, 'We made you king of the whole world [but] what have you done for Us?'" Sanjar can reply to having toiled at the blessed place of one of His Friends.[72] Sanjar kneaded clay to the roof of Ahmad-i Jam's *khanaqah*; whereas Temür, not to be outdone by anyone (even a dead king), donated two *khanaqah*s. He instituted a relationship between his royal house and the Jami shaykhs that lasted until Timurid dominance in Khurasan expired in 911/1506.

Abu Sa'id and Ahmad were promoted to Temür and his Timurid dynasty as twins: inseparable in life and in the Hereafter. This is manifest in a brief, eloquent letter to Temür, ca. 782/1380,[73] by the Kartid-era Sufi Zayn al-Din Taybadi (d. 791/1389). The two saints (Abu Sa'id and Ahmad-i Jam) are masterfully intertwined through the use of Qur'anic verses and allusions. Taybadi capitalizes on the bond he had forged with Temür during their meeting.[74] He beseeches Temür for "patronage and protection" ('*inayat wa himayat*) for the progeny of both saints because kings must honor and favor those who are pure of spirit. He adds that whoever places faith in Ahmad-i Jam shall find salvation. Temür and his heirs patronized and protected both families. Shah-Rukh visited Abu Sa'id's shrine in

---

[69] Or *khanaqah-yi malik-panah*: "the hospice of the king's guardian."
[70] Yusuf-i Ahl/Moayyad (ed.), *Fara'id*, 1:176. See also Safi, *Politics*, 156.
[71] Yusuf-i Ahl/Moayyad (ed.), *Fara'id*, 1:175–76. In Ghaznawi's telling, the subject is not Sanjar but a prince of Ghazna. See Ghaznawi, *Maqamat*, 193; Moayyad and Lewis, *Colossal*, 267–68.
[72] Yusuf-i Ahl/Moayyad (ed.), *Fara'id*, 1:176.
[73] 'Abd al-Husayn Nawa'i (ed.), *Asnad wa mukatibat-i tarikh-i Iran: az Timur ta Shah Isma'il* (Tehran: Bungah-i tarjuma wa nashr-i kitab, 1341/1963), 1–3.
[74] On their meeting, and for analysis of the letter, see Shivan Mahendrarajah, "Tamerlane's Conquest of Herat and the 'Politics of Notables,'" *Studia Iranica* 46/1 (2017): 49–76.

Mayhana for *ziyarat*,[75] but less often than he did Turbat-i Jam.[76] Temür's heirs, chiefly his son and successor, Shah-Rukh, patronized and protected the shrine. Shah-Rukh joined the cult and accepted a Jami shaykh as his preceptor (see Chapter 3). Shah-Rukh's successors, Sultan-Abu Saʻid Mirza and Sultan-Husayn Bayqara, are not known to have been devotees of Ahmad,[77] but both extended protections and benefits to shrine and shaykhs (see Chapters 3 and 6).

The "capture" of Temür by Ahmad-i Jam's cult is a case of exploiting one man's superstitions. Temür said he had prophetic visions, and that he communed with angels ("dit que Dieu lui révèle toutes choses par l'ange").[78] When Temür entered Khurasan, an eccentric (a certain Baba Sangu) "threw before Temür a piece of raw meat from the breast of an animal." Temür "declared that this was a favorable omen and that God was evidently delivering into his hands Khurasan, 'the breast of the surface of the world'"![79] Temür was susceptible to Jami propaganda, but the Jami Sufis were not manipulating a simple mind. Temür was exceptionally intelligent and politically astute; he appreciated the importance of patronizing Sufis, developing temporal support in occupied areas, and collecting *baraka*. He therefore allowed himself to be captured by the cult of Ahmad-i Jam. The Sufis of Jam offered Temür spiritual and temporal support; Temür offered the Sufis patronage and protection (*ʻinayat wa himayat*). It was a mutually profitable marriage that prospered for 125 years and shaped Iranian history.

MARKETING THE SAINT: THE TIMURIDS OF INDIA ("MUGHALS")

The passing of the Timurids of Khurasan and the ascendancy of the Safavids ended Jami bonds to the ruling house. Never again were the shaykhs to have significant political influence in Iran. India, however, offered fresh opportunities. The early Mughal emperors were Ahmad-i Jam's descendants. Humayun (r. 1530–40; 1555–56), son of Zahir al-Din

---

[75] On the shrine at Mayhana/Mihna, see Leonard Harrow, "The Tomb Complex of Abu Saʻid Fadl Allah b. Abiʼl-Khair at Mihna," *Iran* 43 (2005): 197–215.
[76] Melville, "Shahrukh" (Shah-Rukh's *recorded* visits to Mayhana and Jam).
[77] Sultan is often a component in proper names; thus, sultan Sultan-Husayn Bayqara; shah Shah-Rukh, and sultan Shah-Rukh.
[78] Jean Aubin, "Comment Tamerlan prenait les villes," *Studia Islamica* 19 (1963): 83–122, esp. 88–89 (quote p. 88). See also Jürgen Paul, "Scheiche und Herrscher im Khanat Čaġatay," *Der Islam* 67/2 (1990): 278–321, esp. 296–313.
[79] V. V. Barthold, *Four Studies on the History of Central Asia: Ulugh Beg*, trans. Vladimir and T. Minorsky (Brill: Leiden, 1958), 2:20. Baba Sangu was considered "a saintly personage."

Babur (886–937/1483–1530), the founder of the Mughal Empire (1526–1857), was of Timurid and Jami blood: Babur had married Maham Bigum, a Jami shaykh's daughter. Humayun's son, Jalal al-Din Muhammad Akbar (1542–1605), was the product of a *second* infusion of Jami blood, this through Humayun's marriage to Hamida Banu Bigum (1527–1604) bt. ʿAli Akbar Jami (n.d.),[80] preceptor to Babur's son, Hindal (d. 1551).[81]

Humayun succeeded his celebrated father, Babur, but lost his kingdom to Afghans under Shir Khan, and to his (Humayun's) stepbrother, Kamran Mirza (d. 1557).[82] After suffering defeat, Humayun decamped for Lahore to await his enemy's ambassador. In his darkest and deepest melancholy, with his kingdom now gone, Humayun drifted into sleep. He was visited in his dreams by a man clad in green and bearing a staff that he placed in Humayun's hand, urging him to "be courageous ... and do not grieve," because "God will give you a son. Name him Jalal al-Din Muhammad Akbar." To Humayun's query as to his night visitor's identity, the man identified himself as "Zhanda-Pil, Ahmad of Jam," adding, "that child will be of my lineage."[83] Jalal al-Din Muhammad Akbar b. Humayan b. Babur was born on 5 Rajab 949/15 October 1542 to Hamida Banu Bigum bt. ʿAli Akbar Jami, and named as directed by Ahmad-i Jam.[84] Akbar earned the sobriquet "Akbar the Great."[85] Returning to the story of his father, Humayun, the deposed emperor wandered India and Afghanistan, and then fled to Iran in 950/1544 with Hamida to lobby for Safavid support.

Humayun's political fortunes changed with his entry to Iran, where he was feted in gracious and opulent Persian style, and esteemed by his Shiʿi

---

[80] ʿAli Akbar is identified as her father in Sayyid Muhammad Maʿsum Bakri, *Tarikh-i Sind*, ed. ʿUmar b. Muhammad Daʾudputah (Tehran: Intisharat-i asatir, 1382/2003), 171.

[81] Annemarie Schimmel, *The Empire of the Great Mughals* (London: Reaktion Books, 2004), 144–46; on Jami marriages to two Mughal emperors, see Laura Parodi, "Of Shaykhs, Bibis and Begims: Sources on Early Mughal Marriage Connections and the Patronage of Babur's tomb," in *Mediaeval and Modern Iranian Studies: Proceedings of the 6th European Conference of Iranian Studies (Vienna, 2007)*, ed. Maria Szuppe, et al., *Cahiers de Studia Iranica* 45 (2011): 121–38; Abu al-Fazl, *The History of Akbar*, 3 vols., ed. and trans. Wheeler Thackston (Cambridge, MA: Harvard University Press, 2015), 1:388–89.

[82] Gul-Badan Begam, *The History of Humayun*, trans. Annette S. Beveridge (London: Royal Asiatic Society, 1902), 89–90 (fol. 6b-7a); Zahir al-Din Babur, *Babur-nama in English*, 2 vols., trans. Annette S. Beveridge (London: Luzac, 1922), 1:358 and 2:712. Kamran was not of Ahmad's blood.

[83] Begam/Beveridge (trans.), *Humayun*, 145 (fol. 39b); new translation by Wheeler Thackston of Gulbadan Begim, *Humayunnama*, in *Three Memoirs of Homayun* (Costa Mesa, CA: Mazda, 2009), 34 (fol. 39b).

[84] Begim/Thackston (trans.), *Humayunnama*, 41–42 (fol. 48b). Three different birth dates are given in the primary sources: 4 Rajab, 5 Rajab, and 14 Shaʿban.

[85] Andre Wink, *Akbar* (Oxford: Oneworld, 2009).

hosts – although they irked him with requests that he convert to Shi'ism.[86] From Herat, he traveled to Turbat-i Jam for *ziyarat*, arriving there on 5 Dhu al-Hijja 950/29 February 1544.[87] Hamida was present, but not their son, Akbar: he had been kidnapped on 16 December 1543 by his uncle, 'Askari (who had allied with his full brother, Kamran, against Humayun). Akbar's parents were forced to flee to Iran without him. He was not reunited with his parents until 1545.[88] Humayun may have returned to Ahmad's shrine if the 14 Shawwal 951/29 December 1544 inscription in paint or ink on a slab of white stone is by him.[89] Humayun and Hamida were undoubtedly anxious about their son who remained a hostage of 'Askari and Kamran.[90]

Humayun's reversed fortunes and eventual reconquest of India are almost entirely due to the support extended to him by Shah Tahmasp (r. 930–84/1524–76). Nonetheless, it is evident that Humayun's luck had seminally changed. Luck, or "chance and probability" as the Prussian military strategist Carl von Clausewitz termed it in *On War* (*Vom Kriege*), is one of the indispensable legs in the trinity of war.[91] Napoleon Bonaparte famously observed that one of the most important qualities in a general is luck.

Literary sources are silent about Humayun's spiritual encounters at Jam. However, it is evident from Humayun's later actions that he believed Ahmad-i Jam's intercession had improved his political fortunes; and that

---

[86] Abraham Eraly, *Emperors of the Peacock Throne* (New Delhi: Penguin, 1997), 104–8; Begim/Thackston (trans.), *Humayunnama*, 48–49 (fol. 57b–59b); Bayazid Bayat, *Tarikh-i Humayun*, in Thackston, *Three Memoirs*, 3–13 (fol. 2b–13a); Abu al-Fazl, *Akbar*, 2:71–77; Hasan Rumlu, *Ahsan al-tawarikh*, 3 vols., ed. 'Abd al-Husayn Nawa'i (Tehran: Intisharat-i asatir, 1384/2005), 3:1289–95 (events of AH 951). A copy of Shah Tahmasp's edict instructing Safavid officials on how to honor Humayun is in Bayat, *Humayun*, 4–9; and Abu al-Fazl, *Akbar*, 2:51–71.

[87] The date is in Abu al-Fazl, *Akbar*, 2:75. A date closer to late Dhu al-Hijja/early Muharram is implied in Rumlu, *Ahsan*, who does not report the visit to Turbat-i Jam. Jawhar Aftabachi, Humayun's "ewer bearer" (akin valet or batman), also does not report the visit in *Tazkirat al-waqi'at* (full citation is given in n88 below).

[88] Begim/Thackston (trans.), *Humayunnama*, 46–48 (fol. 55a–57b); Jawhar Aftabachi, *Tazkirat al-waqi'at*, in Thackston, *Three Memoirs*, 116–17 (fol. 62b–64b); Bayat, *Humayun*, 2 (fol. 2ba–2b); and Wink, *Akbar*, 8–9.

[89] Ney Elias, "Notice of an Inscription at Turbat-i-Jam, in Khorasan, about Half-way between Meshed [Mashhad] and Herat," *JRAS* (1897): 47–48.

[90] Bamber Gascoigne, *The Great Moghuls* (London: Robinson, 1971), 47, observes that under European norms at the period, an heir in the hands of his father's enemy will have perished. Unwritten rules appear to have controlled conduct between Humayun and Kamran, and thereby saved Akbar from being murdered.

[91] "Primordial violence, hatred, and enmity" is one leg; "chance and probability" the second leg; the third leg is well-known: "war as an instrument of policy."

50 Saintdom and Patronage

FIGURE 2.1 Ahmad-i Jam (the Furious Elephant) watching over young Akbar the Great. (A black and white version of this figure will appear in some formats. For the color version, please refer to the plate section.)
Courtesy of Staatsbibliothek zu Berlin, Preussischer Kulturbesitz, Libr. Pict. A117, fol. 15a

Ahmad-i Jam had become Humayun's and Akbar's protector and intercessor. Akbar was safely returned to his parents, which was "proof" of Ahmad's spiritual prowess. A painting commissioned by Humayun of Akbar's circumcision ceremony held in 953/1546 is rich in iconography (see Figure 2.1).[92] The figure of an elephant, "a metaphor for Ahmad-i Jam," watches the children at play. The interpretation that the "elephant in the painting ... seems to be protecting the group of children immediately below"[93] is supported by the evidence. It shows that Humayun believed the propaganda that Ahmad-i Jam was the guardian of kings.

Humayun was a charming dilettante who, as Stanley Lane-Poole said of Humayun's death consequent to a fall down a stairway, had "stumbled out of life as he had stumbled through it." The Mughal emperor had, however, secured Akbar's patrimony with Safavid logistical support and improved fortunes. Akbar initially ruled the empire with a regent (Bayram Khan), but blossomed, and governed independently, justly earning for himself the sobriquet Akbar "the Great."

Akbar's biographer, Abu al-Fazl, does not expound on the role of Ahmad-i Jam in his emperor's outlook, but in his panegyrics on Akbar's heritage and birth, he lavishes praise on "Her Highness, Maryam-Makani, chastity of the world and the religion, Hamida Banu Bigum – may God cause the shadow of her magnificence to last forever – the true coin of the leader of noble saints [nine lines of praise and honorifics *plus* two couplets], the Furious Elephant, Ahmad of Jam."[94] "Maryam Makani" is Hamida Banu Bigum's posthumous title. Akbar's saintly pedigree is emphasized, while his royal pedigree (from Tamerlane) is not noted. Discussed in Chapter 4 is how Akbar pivoted to the Chishtiyya when one of its saints trumped Ahmad's miracles with a miracle of his own, thereby ending any hopes the shrine cult at Jam had of Mughal financial assistance and political support.

The Jami shaykhs were successful with their propaganda. We do not know how they finessed the inglorious finales to Sanjar's and Shams al-Din Kart's careers. Sanjar permitted himself a fate worse than a warrior's death in battle: defeat, captivity, and humiliation. The Kart king came to a sticky end, literally, eating a poisoned watermelon.

---

[92] See *Jahangir Album* (Berlin: Staatsbibliothek zu Berlin, Libr. Pict. A117), fol. 15a (Figure 2.1). On the ceremony, see Bayat, *Humayun*, 23–24 (21b–22a); and Begim/Thackston (trans.), *Humayunnama*, 54 (66a–66b).
[93] Laura Parodi and B. Wannell, "The Earliest Datable Mughal Painting," *Asianart* (18 November 2011), www.asianart.com/articles/parodi/ (accessed 13 June 2020).
[94] Abu al-Fazl, *Akbar*, 1:60–65 (English and Persian text).

Part II
The Successors

3

Ilkhanid/Kartid Eras to the Timurid Age

Shrine and cult survived the Mongols. The saint cult blossomed politically and financially under the Ilkhanids and Kartids. Qutb al-Din Muhammad Jami, and his son, Shihab al-Din Isma'il, were the first accumulators of wealth and power. Qutb al-Din had opaque connections to a wealthy Indian benefactor, and hosted Shams al-Din Muhammad Kart, instituting a bond between the families. Shihab al-Din married a son to a Kartid princess, and accepted a Kart king (*malik*) as his acolyte, thereby garnering tangible and intangible benefits for shrine and cult. The apogee of the shrine's affluence and influence was under the Timurids.

THE FIRST GUARDIANS

Writing a history of the progeny of Ahmad-i Jam is a daunting task. The man married (at least) eight times and fathered (at least) three daughters and thirty-nine sons. When Ahmad died at the ripe age of ninety-five lunar years/ninety-two solar years, he was survived by fourteen sons and one daughter. The sources record only those fifteen names;[1] the names of two daughters and twenty-five sons are lacunae. Ahmad's unnamed progeny may have predeceased him as implied, or perhaps had relocated from their birthplaces in Namaq or Jam, and are thus not known to historians and hagiographers. If certain unhappy truths have inadvertently crept into Ghaznawi's *Spiritual Feats*, Ahmad-i Jam was a fractious and vindictive husband and father, which may account for the lacunae about his progeny.

---

[1] See Appendix 1, commentary and genealogical charts (Figures A1.1–A1.5).

Medieval historians also practiced their craft differently; they did not consider it obligatory to report every date and genealogical detail. Furthermore, hagiographical narratives often exclude dates, which allows the spiritual message to resonate over generations. Further confusing the picture is that once Ahmad came to be recognized as a saint, there will have been claimants to his bloodline from the "lost" children that could not be connected to any specific lineage, but which an enterprising soul (including the present author) will have hazarded to ascribe. Some generations after Ahmad's death, his descendants "numbered in the thousands" and thrived in Khurasan, Transoxiana, and India. In 840/1436, "about 1,000 of them" were living in Jam, Nishapur, Herat, and neighboring locales.[2]

We are therefore lucky in some ways that the sources report just a relatively small set of biographies, or this enterprise would be encyclopedic. Nonetheless, from the sixth/twelfth century to the ninth/fifteenth century, about 200 names connect to Ahmad, although not every name can be connected to a specific lineage. From the tenth/sixteenth century forward, with the Safavid (Shi'i) ascendancy and the decline of Sunnism and Sufism in Khurasan, biographical data becomes sparser. Jamis migrated east, to what is now called Afghanistan, while other Jamis migrated farther east, to Mughal India.

Three of Ahmad's sons and one grandson should be mentioned. Shams al-Din Mutahhar (Abu al-Ma'ali) b. Ahmad was the father of Qutb al-Din Muhammad. The latter became the first major accumulator of wealth for the shrine; and he authored a guide for mystics. Most of Ahmad's progeny are of Shams al-Din's lineage.[3] Zahir al-Din 'Isa (Abu al-Mufakhar) b. Ahmad was the intellectual force of his generation,[4] and the directing shaykh for Qutb al-Din Muhammad.[5] Ziya al-Din Yusuf b. Ahmad inherited his father's mantle (the *khirqa* supposedly bequeathed by Abu Sa'id).[6] An active Sufi, he trained darwishes and was the shaykh for the villages of Jam. Shihab al-Din Isma'il (Abu al-Mu'ayyad) b. Ahmad was the "baby" in the family and Ahmad-i Jam's favorite.[7] His fondness for Shihab al-Din may explain the regrettable Jami penchant for naming males "Shihab al-Din," creating ineffable difficulties for historians. Shihab al-Din Isma'il Jami became ill fleeing the Mongol vanguards and expired *ca.* 617/1220.

---

[2] Moayyad, "Ahmad-i Jam," 1:648a; Kadkani, *Darwish*, 181.
[3] Buzjani/Moayyad (ed.), *Rawzat*, 73; Kadkani, *Darwish*, 181. Figure A1.1a #10.
[4] Figure A1.1b #13.   [5] Figures A1.2 and A1.3.   [6] Figure A1.1b #8.
[7] Figure A1.1b #14.

SURVIVING THE MONGOLS

In 617/1220, when the Mongol strike force led by Jebe (d. *ca.* 1223) and Sübedei (d. 1243) crossed the Oxus River (*Jayhun*, *Amu Darya*) in pursuit of the Turkic shah of Iran,[8] ʿAlaʾ al-Din Khwarazm-Shah (d. winter 617/1220–21), residents of Maʿd-Abad-i Jam fled to the Binalud mountain range west of Mashhad.[9] Hibat al-Rahman bt. Burhan al-Din Nasr resided at the *khanaqah*.[10] Her uncle, Shihab al-Din Ismaʿil b. Ahmad-i Jam, pleaded with her to join the exodus, but she declined, claiming to place trust in God (*tawakkul*) that she will be safe. Since his household had already departed, he joined them, which is when he took ill. According to an account in a hagiography, when the Mongols reached Maʿd-Abad-i Jam, they had with them Muslim scouts-cum-translators, two of whom came to the shrine, where they were informed about Hibat al-Rahman's faith that God will protect her from the Mongol army. They showed her respect and performed *ziyarat* at Ahmad's grave. Maʿd-Abad-i Jam was spared.[11] The reality is that Jebe and Sübedei were ordered by Chingiz Khan "to avoid the towns inhabited by Muslims, and not to interfere with the local population,"[12] and to only fight if necessary. Maʿd-Abad-i Jam was spared because the Grand Qaʾan's (inviolable) orders were to capture or kill ʿAlaʾ al-Din, and the hastily abandoned burg was not an obstacle to the mission.

Hibat al-Rahman's first cousin Sharaf al-Din (ʿAbd al-Karim) b. ʿImad al-Din[13] was less fortunate. Chingiz Khan had dispatched an army under his youngest son, Tolui (d. 1232), to exact vengeance across Khurasan following the killing (in late 617/1220) of a Mongol leader (named Toquchar) at Nishapur. Tolui posed an existential threat to the region's peoples. The capitals of Khurasan's four administrative quarters (*rubʿ*) – Balkh, Nishapur, Marv, and Herat – had experienced (or would experience) devastation and carnage. In 618/1221, Maʿd-Abad-i Jam's citadel (*hisar*) was invested. Sharaf al-Din was killed.[14] The notorious *qatl-i ʿamm*, days of unbridled rapine and murder – standard punishment for effrontery and resistance – was not ordered, possibly because residents had not returned from the mountains. There was just the usual pillaging.

---

[8] On the Mongols' westward advance, from 1219 to 1253, see Peter Jackson, *The Mongols and the Islamic World* (London and New Haven, CT: Yale University Press, 2017), 71–93.
[9] The Binalud range is northwest to southeast, between 36° and 37° N; 59° and 60° E; it has a maximum elevation of 10,535 ft/3,211 m.
[10] Figure A1.1b #7 and #8. [11] Buzjani/Moayyad (ed.), *Rawzat*, 81–82.
[12] V. V. Barthold, *Turkestan Down to the Mongol Invasion*, 4th ed. (Cambridge: E. J. W. Gibb Memorial Trust, 1977), 323.
[13] Figure A1.1b #9. [14] Buzjani/Moayyad (ed.), *Rawzat*, 82–83.

Ahmad-i Jam's tumulus, which had no sepulchral or spiritual edifices around it until a dome (*gunbad* or *gunbad-khana*) was erected in Shawwal 633/June–July 1236, survived the Mongols. His *khanaqah* was maintained by Hibat al-Rahman, the "lady of the hospice" (*khatun-i khanaqah*). It is not clear if her husband, Siraj al-Din Ahmad, was with her. The sources say fairly little about him, which leads one to suspect the lady was in charge. Their sons, Safi al-Din Mahmud and Ibn Yamin, had decamped for the Hijaz, where they remained until the Mongol menace had receded.[15] Travel was the Jami community's commonsensical approach to surviving the Mongols. Safi al-Din and Ibn Yamin returned to Maʿd-Abad-i Jam to a tumultuous welcome, although by then their parents were deceased. Safi al-Din took up residence in Ahmad's old *khanaqah*,[16] but of Ibn Yamin, we learn no more. Hibat al-Rahman is respected at Jam. A Jami seminary dedicated to educating women is named in her honor.[17]

THE JOINT ILKHANID AND KARTID ERAS (654/1256 TO 736/1335)

Qutb al-Din Muhammad Jami

The Jami community's new leader during early Mongol rule was Qutb al-Din Muhammad (577/1181f. to 667/1268).[18] He is the most important Jami survivor of the Mongols. Shihab al-Din Ismaʿil Jami (d. *ca.* 738/1338) was Qutb al-Din's second son, and evidently conceived late in life, that is, after the Mongol irruptions. Most of the hundreds of Ahmad's descendants mentioned previously run through Qutb al-Din and Shihab al-Din Ismaʿil.[19] Should Qutb al-Din have perished in the Mongol onslaughts, Jami history – indeed, Iranian history – would have been markedly different.

Qutb al-Din Muhammad's travels had taken him to India. He had been trained in the esoteric sciences (ʿ*irfan*) by his uncle and shaykh, Zahir al-Din ʿIsa b. Ahmad-i Jam (n.d.), from whom he received a *khirqa*. After completing his training locally, he went to India, then returned to Maʿd-Abad-i Jam

---

[15] Ibid., 97. [16] Ibid., 96–97. On Safi al-Din and Ibn Yamin, see Figure A1.1b #8.
[17] Hawza-yi ʿilmiyya Hibat al-Rahman, established 1392/2013. See Table 5.1.
[18] His birth year is incorrect in Buzjani/Moayyad (ed.), *Rawzat*, 85; Buzjani/Jami (ed.), *Rawzat*, 138. The more reliable birth year and date of death is in Kadkani, *Darwish*, 259; and ʿAlaʾ al-Mulk Jami/Jami (ed.), *Khulasat al-maqamat*, 95 (on this title, see Appendix 3).
[19] Figures A1.3 and A1.4.

and settled into the shrine's *khanaqah* as *locum tenens* (*qa'im-i maqam*) for his grandfather, Ahmad-i Jam. Since Qutb al-Din lived a long life, there are critical gaps in the sources. It appears that Qutb al-Din had fled to India (and elsewhere?) during the Mongol invasions. If a report claiming that he had had an encounter with Körgüz, the ill-fated Mongol governor (*basqaq*), has any basis in fact, Qutb al-Din had returned to Iran before 640/1242f., which is when Körgüz was executed. We cannot determine how long or where he had resided in India, which is regrettable because the Jamis maintained cordial relations with the Delhi Sultanate under the Khilji and Tughluq sultans (r. 1290–1398). The epistolary collection, *Fara'id-i Ghiyasi*, compiled by Jalal al-Din Yusuf-i Ahl Jami (n.d.), has numerous letters from Jami shaykhs of Herat, Nishapur, and Jam to sultans and viziers in Delhi.[20]

It is highly probable that the relationship between the Sufis and Delhi sultans was instituted by Qutb al-Din Muhammad Jami. ʿAli Buzjani's hagiography of the Jamis relates how an unidentified man ("Khwaja Fulan"), whom Qutb al-Din had encountered in India, would send him valuable gifts: "when he [Khwaja Fulan] was the vizier in India, he sent him [Qutb al-Din] 1,000 pure, red gold (*zar-i surkh*) coins (*tangcha*), commodities, and fabrics every year; he also donated real properties (*amlak*) and farmlands (*ziraʿat*)."[21] Confirmation of specifics is not possible, but since the Jamis had convivial relations with Indian sultans, and Qutb al-Din was the first major accumulator of wealth for the Sufi community, there is assuredly a kernel of truth. Qutb al-Din's son wedded the Jamis to royalty and set the Jamis on the road to wealth and political influence.

Shihab al-Din Ismaʿil Jami

Shihab al-Din Ismaʿil Jami (d. *ca.* 738/1338) b. Qutb al-Din Muhammad has made appearances in historical chronicles, but usually not under his name, just by his title, "Shaykh al-Islam." Scholars of medieval Iran or the history of the Mongol Empire know of "l'affaire Nawruz," but for others, in brief: Nawruz (d. 696/1297) b. Arghun Aga was a powerful Mongol army commander and a (bigoted) convert to Islam. The rank and file of the Turko-Mongol armies in Iran included contingents of converts to Islam, resulting in upward pressures on the Buddhist, Christian, or Shamanist Mongol rulers of Iran, the Il-Khans.[22] In 694/1295, Ghazan Khan, a contender for the

---

[20] See Yusuf-i Ahl/Moayyad (ed.), *Fara'id*, 1:vii–xiv (table of contents); and Appendix 3.
[21] Buzjani/Moayyad (ed.), *Rawzat*, 91.
[22] Il-Khan or Il-Qaʾan: a "lord" (*qaʾan*, *khān*) "subservient" (*īl*) to the Mongol Grand Qaʾan.

Mongol throne and capital at Tabriz, was persuaded by Nawruz to convert to Islam to attract support from Muslim soldiers as their "Padishah of Islam." As David Morgan pithily explained it, "Tabriz was worth a *shahada*." This was a momentous decision in Islamic and Iranian history, and transformed the relationship between Mongol lords and Iranian subjects: the infidel and alien Mongol khan became the familiar Muslim sultan.

Nawruz remained a source of vexation for the Il-Khans. After an act of rebellion, Nawruz was pursued by a Mongol expeditionary force. He was granted asylum behind Herat's walls by the Kart *malik*, Fakhr al-Din Kart (r. 695–706/1295–1307). Qutlugh-Shah, the Mongol commander, asked the (unnamed) "Shaikhu'l-islam of Jam ... to write a letter to the [Kart] *malik* [Fakhr al-Din Kart] saying, '[y]ou must do something to remedy this situation, otherwise Herat and the whole realm of Khurasan will be lost over this affair.'"[23] Shihab al-Din Isma'il was the "Shaykh al-Islam of Jam." He impressed upon Fakhr al-Din the urgency to end the siege without harm befalling Heratis. Nawruz was delivered to Qutlugh-Shah, who promptly executed him.

Shihab al-Din Isma'il's social network in Iran was extensive. Sadr al-Din Ibrahim al-Hammuya (d. 722/1322), the Sufi who had officiated at Ghazan Khan's conversion,[24] was a friend; al-Hammuya's advice letter to Il-Khan Öljeitü (r. 703–17/1304–16) – Ghazan Khan's brother and successor – is preserved in Jami *insha'*,[25] which suggests intimacy between the Sufis of Jam and Bahrabad. Sadr al-Din had ties to the Ilkhanid court and married with the Juwayni family.[26] Rukn al-Din 'Ala' al-Dawla Simnani (d. 736/1336), another Sufi master, was a member of the Jami social network. Simnani and Shihab al-Din Isma'il may have jointly met with Öljeitü.[27]

---

[23] Rashid al-Din, *Jami' al-tawarikh*, in *Classical Writings of the Medieval Islamic World: Persian Histories of the Mongol Dynasties*, 3 vols., trans. Wheeler Thackston (London: I. B. Tauris, 2012), 3:446.

[24] Jamal J. Elias, "The Sufi Lords of Bahrabad: Sa'd al-Din and Sadr al-Din Hamuwayi," *Iranian Studies* 27/1 (1994): 53–75, esp. 67–70; C. P. Melville, "*Padishah-i Islam*: The Conversion of Sultan Mahmud Ghazan Khan," *Pembroke Papers* 1 (1990): 159–77.

[25] Yusuf-i Ahl/Moayyad (ed.), *Fara'id*, 1:86–88. Letters by Sadr al-Din's grandson, Ghiyath al-Din Hibat-Allah, are in ibid., vols. 1 and 2; further correspondence with Sadr al-Din, from Simnani and Shams al-Din Juwayni, is in Yusuf-i Ahl, *Fara'id-i Ghiyasi* (Istanbul: Süleymaniye Kütüphanesi, Fatih 4012), fol. 300a–300b; Yusuf-i Ahl, *Fara'id-i Ghiyasi* (Tehran: University of Tehran, 4756), 370–71 (paginated manuscript).

[26] The Juwaynis produced 'Ala' al-Din 'Ata'-Malik Juwayni (history of Chingiz Khan), and a vizier, Shams al-Din Muhammad (chief minister to three Il-Khans).

[27] Buzjani/Moayyad (ed.), *Rawzat*, 100.

Political allies included an Ilkhanid vizier, 'Ala' al-Din Hindu (d. 722/1322f.);[28] and a governor of Khurasan, 'Ala' al-Din Muhammad Faryumadi (d. 27 Sha'ban 742/5 February 1342).[29] Faryumadi donated a madrasa to the shrine (Chapter 5). When Amir Chupan Suldus (d. 728/1327) and his army descended on Turbat-i Jam, the Shaykh al-Islam prepared an extravagant banquet, roasting cows and sheep and baking stacks of bread that reached the roof of the *khanaqah*. He opened his silo to provision Chupan's army.[30] Ibn Battuta, the eighth/fourteenth-century Moroccan globetrotter who sojourned at Jam (dates are not certain), claims the Shaykh al-Islam had hosted a magnificent banquet for Abu Sa'id b. Öljeitü.[31] 'Ali Buzjani's assertion that Öljeitü held Shihab al-Din Isma'il in high regard would ordinarily be dismissed as a hagiographical adornment but for the political connections sketched above;[32] and for a decree by Öljeitü granting to Shihab al-Din agricultural lands and an irrigation system (see Chapter 6).[33]

Ghiyath al-Din Muhammad Kart

The Shaykh al-Islam of Jam was an influential person, but his path to power and wealth was due in large part to the promotion of Ahmad-i Jam as the protector of kings, a concept to which the Kart *malik*, Ghiyath al-Din Muhammad Kart (r. 707–29/1307–29), enthusiastically subscribed. The *malik*'s grandfather, Shams al-Din Muhammad Kart (r. 643–76/1245–78), had visited the shrine following his elevation by the Mongol Grand Qa'an, Möngke (r. 1251–58).[34] Ghiyath al-Din Kart had had an uneasy relationship with Öljeitü.[35] Ghiyath al-Din, then a prince, was in Öljeitü's court when his brother, Fakhr al-Din Kart, rebelled. In

---

[28] On him, see Ahmad Fasih Khwafi, *Mujmal-i Fasihi*, 3 vols., ed. Muhammad Farrukh (Mashhad: Intisharat-i bastan, 1339/1960), 3:34.

[29] On Faryumadi, see ibid., 3:61; Muhammad b. 'Ali b. Muhammad Shabankara'i, *Majma' al-ansab*, ed. Mir-Hashim Muhaddis (Tehran: Amir Kabir, 1363/1984), 307ff. The two 'Ala' al-Dins get muddled in the sources. See, e.g., al-Samarqandi, *Tadhkirat al-shu'ara'*, 279 (lines 15–16).

[30] Buzjani/Moayyad (ed.), *Rawzat*, 102–3.

[31] Ibn Battuta, *The Travels of Ibn Battuta*, trans. H. A. R. Gibb (Cambridge: Cambridge University Press, 1971), 3:581 (Ibn Battuta jumbles names in his report on Jam).

[32] Buzjani/Moayyad (ed.), *Rawzat*, 100.

[33] Yusuf-i Ahl, *Fara'id-i Ghiyasi* (Berlin: Staatsbibliothek zu Berlin, Ms. Orient. Fol.110), fol. 317a–317b.

[34] al-Harawi, *Harat*, 204–5.

[35] Öljeitü was hostile toward the Kartids: he "devoted much time to fighting with the Kart dynasty of Herat." Michael Hope, *Power, Politics, and Tradition in the Mongol Empire and the Ilkhanate of Iran* (Oxford: Oxford University Press, 2016), 15.

707/1307, Öljeitü issued Ghiyath al-Din Kart a governing patent (*yarligh*) and dispatched him to Herat to replace Fakhr al-Din. Ghiyath al-Din sojourned at Turbat-i Jam en route to the Il-Khan's court; and he sojourned at Turbat-i Jam on his return.[36] In 711/1311f., consequent to accusations of rebelliousness, Ghiyath al-Din was recalled to Öljeitü's camp (*urdu*), where he remained hostage for four years. He stayed at Jam on his way to the *urdu*. In 715/1315, when he was returned to Herat with a fresh *yarligh*, he again sojourned at Jam.[37] Ghiyath al-Din undoubtedly viewed Ahmad-i Jam's shrine as the fount of God's favors (*ni'mah*) and *baraka*, and Shihab al-Din Isma'il Jami as the conduit for Ahmad-i Jam's blessings (*baraka*) and divine effusions (*fayz*).

While Ghiyath al-Din was a prince and distant from the throne, he had offered a daughter in marriage to any of Shihab al-Din Isma'il's five sons. The eldest, Shams al-Din Mutahhar (d. bet. 751/1350 and 767/1366), married the Kartid princess.[38] A child named Mu'in al-Din (Abu al-Makarim) Jami (702–83/1302–82) was born of this union. He went on to serve as the Kartid vizier from 735/1334–35 until the end (or nearly the end) of Kartid rule in Iran (783/1381). The Kart-Jami marital alliance, made before Ghiyath al-Din's political fortunes seminally improved, is an indication of the faith Ghiyath al-Din had in Ahmad-i Jam's spiritual message, and his embrace of Shihab al-Din Isma'il as his spiritual conduit. Ghiyath al-Din's political fortunes began ascending with the death of Öljeitü. The late Il-Khan's young son, Abu Sa'id Bahadur Khan (r. 716–36/1316–35), was twelve when he ascended the throne. He had a formidable regent, Chupan Suldus (d. 728/1327), who was the lord of the Ilkhanate.[39] The reign of Abu Sa'id and Chupan brought immense benefits to Ghiyath al-Din, Ahmad-i Jam's shrine, and Jami shaykhs.

THE INDEPENDENT KARTIDS (736/1335 TO 783/1381)

The death of the heirless Il-Khan Abu Sa'id Bahadur Khan b. Öljeitü initiated the eclipse of the Ilkhanate. Independent Iranian polities sprouted

---

[36] al-Harawi, *Harat*, 566, 570; Hafiz-i Abru, *Tarikh-i salatin-i Kart* [*The History of the Kart Kings*], ed. Mir-Hashim Muhaddis (Tehran: Markaz-i pizhuhishi-i miras-i maktub, 1389/2010), 118.
[37] al-Harawi, *Harat*, 591–92, 630; Hafiz-i Abru, *Kart*, 131.
[38] See Figure A1.5 (Jami-Kartid marriage ties).
[39] C. P. Melville, *The Fall of Amir Chupan and the Decline of the Ilkhanate, 1327–37: A Decade of Discord in Mongol Iran* (Bloomington, IN: Research Institute for Inner Asian Studies, 1999). See also Hope, *Ilkhanate of Iran*, 189–94.

from Baghdad to Herat. One of the most fascinating of these independent polities was the "Shi'i Republic" of the Sarbadar dynasty (1336–81) at Sabzavar in the Bayhaq district of Khurasan.[40] The Karts, Ilkhanid vassals whose domains stretched from Nishapur to Kabul, became unshackled Iranian *padishah*s. They thrived until 783/1381, when the last Kart king surrendered his capital, Herat, to Temür.

Mu'izz al-Din Kart and Shihab al-Din Isma'il Jami attended the congress (*quriltai*) at Sultan-Maydan (north of Nishapur) in 736/1336 where the upper echelon of notables from Khurasan gathered to select their new suzerain.[41] The Shaykh al-Islam was near the end of his life and borne upon a litter. Tagha-Temür (d. 754/1353), a descendant of Chingiz Khan's brother, was chosen as the Chinggisid suzerain. Mu'izz al-Din sealed the political union by marrying Sultan-Khatun (fl. 783/1381) bt. Tagha-Temür. Ghiyath al-Din (Pir 'Ali) Kart is the product of their union (born *ca.* 737–38/1337–38).[42]

Jami Opposition to Mu'izz al-Din Kart

Mu'in al-Din (Abu al-Makarim) Jami (702–83/1302–82), the long-term Kart vizier, was a scholar, poet, and scribe.[43] He married a daughter of his uncle, Mu'izz al-Din Kart. Mu'in al-Din Jami's wife's mother was from the Arlat tribe of the Chaghatai Mongols;[44] his wife's brother was Muhammad Kart.[45] The brothers became rivals for their father's throne. Mu'in al-Din Jami relocated from Turbat-i Jam to Herat in 735/1334f. following his appointment as vizier.[46] Mu'in al-Din was the consummate diplomat, cultivating sultans, viziers, amirs, ulama, sayyids, and Sufis in Iran, Transoxiana, and India through flowery letters interspersed with Qur'anic verses, hadith, poetry, and rhymed

---

[40] John Masson Smith, Jr., *The History of the Sarbadar Dynasty 1336–1381 A.D. and Its Sources* (The Hague: Mouton, 1970).

[41] Shabankara'i, *Majma' al-ansab*, 306–11; and Jean Aubin, "Le Quriltai de Sultan-Maydan (1336)," *Journal Asiatique* 279 (1991): 175–97.

[42] Hafiz-i Abru, *Kart*, 172; Ghiyath al-Din Khwandamir, *Habib al-siyar*, 4 vols., ed. Muhammad Dabir Siyaqi (Tehran: Intisharat-i markazi khayyam piruz, 1333/1954), 3:380; Ghiyath al-Din Khwandamir, *Habib al-siyar*, 2 vols., trans. Wheeler Thackston (Cambridge, MA: Sources of Oriental Languages and Literatures, 1994), 220. See Figure A1.5 (on Jami and Kartid marital ties).

[43] Buzjani/Moayyad (ed.), *Rawzat*, 107–8; Zanganah, *Sarzamin*, 145–48.

[44] On the pre-Temür Chaghatai, see Jean Aubin, "Le Khanat de Čaġatai et le Khorassan (1334–1380)," *Turcica* 8/2 (1970): 16–60; on the Arlat, see Beatrice Forbes Manz, *The Rise and Rule of Tamerlane* (Cambridge: Cambridge University Press, 1989), 155–56.

[45] See Figure A1.5.   [46] Yusuf-i Ahl/Moayyad (ed.), *Fara'id*, 1:241.

prose (*saj'*). He nurtured relationships with men of power and wealth who had the ability to help or to harm Jami and/or Kartid interests.

The introduction of another wife to the royal household, and favoring her son over another woman's son, bred resentments. Taking a second wife arouses the ire of the first wife, but more ominously, her brothers may coalesce into a political-military bloc to protect the rights of their sister, more specifically, her son's rights,[47] that is, their nephew's rights (Muhammad b. Mu'izz al-Din) against his half-brother's (Pir 'Ali's) claims, which included the Kartid throne.[48] Ottoman sultans' preference for siring heirs with foreign slave girls mitigated the in-law problem – but other practices often offset this advantage, leading to epidemics of fratricide. In any event, the Arlat supported the shaykhs of Jam in an attempt to depose Mu'izz al-Din Kart.

Mu'izz al-Din did not subscribe to the saint cult of Ahmad-i Jam. If anything, he viewed that particular City of God as a threat. He and Sultan-Khatun patronized Sufis in Herat.[49] Mu'izz al-Din Kart seized Jami estates.[50] Although the vizier is named in the decree, it is almost certain the estates were commingled shrine and family assets that he managed. Mu'izz al-Din, with the Ilkhanate having passed into history, and not being his father's designated heir – he was the third son to succeed Ghiyath al-Din – may have attempted to curtail the power of the Jamis, particularly in the hinterlands around his capital, Herat, where the confiscated estates were located. His fear of the potency of the Jami shaykhs was confirmed by the subsequent events.

The Jami shaykhs initiated a complicated plan to depose Mu'izz al-Din Kart and place his brother, Muhammad Baqir Kart, on the throne.[51] The Arlat Chaghatai tribes were integral to the plan. "A group of shaykhs of Jam" (*jam'i az masha'ikh-i Jam*), led by Shaykh al-Islam Razi al-Din Ahmad (d. 767/1366) b. Shihab al-Din Isma'il, the shrine's custodian

---

[47] "Turko-Mongolian tradition followed the custom of men marrying women from their mother's clan ... Anthropologists call this MBD (mother's brother's daughter) marriage pattern and the rule of exogamy was key to alliance systems that link patrilineal clans to others by repeated marriages over many generations. The Arabs (and Islamic law) favored endogamous FBD (father's brother's daughter) in which marriages stayed with the patrilineage, stressing purity of descent over the advantages of alliances between groups." Nephews from exogamous alliances "often looked to their maternal uncles as allies ... in potential succession struggles." Thomas Barfield, e-mail to author, 17 September 2017.

[48] It is not clear if Sultan-Khatun bt. Tagha-Temür was the first or second wife.

[49] For the four *khanaqah*s built by Mu'izz al-Din and Sultan-Khatun, see Terry Allen, *A Catalogue of the Toponyms and Monuments of Timurid Herat* (Cambridge: Aga Khan Program for Islamic Architecture, 1981), 150–53 (Cat. Nos. 503, 509, 513, 520).

[50] The decree is dated 23 Safar 753/10 April 1352. The estates are analyzed in Chapter 6.

[51] For a reconstruction of the scheme, see Mahendrarajah, "Revised," 116–17.

and the vizier's paternal uncle,[52] went to the Chaghatai to demand action.[53] They marched on Herat in 752/1351; the coup succeeded when local troops turned on Muʿizz al-Din Kart. Muhammad Baqir took the throne; the estates were returned to the shaykhs by decree dated 23 Safar 753/10 April 1352. Not part of the plot, but Muʿizz al-Din got the throne back in 753/1352f. He had convinced the Chaghatai leader of his fealty and continued usefulness to him. The usurper fled. Other than for a brief stay in jail – not Muʿin al-Din Jami's first or last stint – the vizier (who continued to protest his innocence) – was released.[54] Razi al-Din Ahmad Jami was not harmed.

The relationship between the Jami shrine and the Kartid court was undoubtedly frosty from then on, but the shaykhs had their camel back inside the Kartid king's tent: the vizier returned to his duties at court. This is where matters stood between Jam and Herat until relations thawed about a decade later. Muʿizz al-Din made a benefaction to the shrine; and the shaykhs reciprocated with an inscription inside the *gunbad* (dome) refurbished by him, praising the *malik*'s kingship (see Chapter 5 and Plates 6–7).

Jami Opposition to Ghiyath al-Din (Pir ʿAli) Kart

Muʿizz al-Din expired 5 Dhu al-Qaʿda 771/31 May 1370. He divided his kingdom between his two sons, but not equally: Pir ʿAli received Herat and the lion's share of the realm, and Muhammad Kart received a rump state at Sarakhs, by the Transoxiana and Iran border – adjacent to the Chaghatai tribes.[55] The reign of Pir ʿAli Kart engendered dissatisfaction in key social-political quarters of Khurasan. Multiple Kartid campaigns against the Shiʿi Sarbardars brought devastation to the Nishapur Quarter of Khurasan.[56] The threat embodied by Temür loomed across the Oxus. Upper echelon notables (*aʿyan wa ashraf*) of Khurasan were alarmed by Pir ʿAli's reinforcing of

---

[52] See Figures A1.3 and A1.4; and Table 5.2.
[53] Hafiz-i Abru, *Kart*, 179; Khwandamir, *Habib*, 3:381.
[54] The vizier was jailed (at least) twice. Two pairs of letters reveal his pleas from jail, and then expression of gratitude for clemency. See Yusuf-i Ahl/Moayyad (ed.), *Faraʾid*, 1:304–7, 308–10, 338–42, 363–67. Considering the fate that often befell viziers (at the period), jail was effectively an admonition.
[55] Hafiz-i Abru, *Kart*, 192–93.
[56] Jean Aubin, "La fin de l'État Sarbadar du Khorassan," *Journal Asiatique* 262 (1974): 95–118; Shivan Mahendrarajah, "The Sarbadars of Sabzavar: Re-examining Their 'Shiʿa' Roots and Alleged Goal to 'Destroy Khurasanian Sunnism,'" *Journal of Shiʿa Islamic Studies* 5/4 (2012): 379–402.

Herat's fortifications and determination to fight Temür, which could have resulted in the desolation of Herat as with Chingiz Khan. They resorted to sedition.[57] The condensed version of the scheme is that the vizier, Muʿin al-Din Jami, wrote to Temür's officials in Samarqand on behalf of dissenting notables, encouraging Temür to conquer a "fearful Khurasan" (*Khurasan-i hirasan*). A distich proclaimed that security for the masses (*aman-i khalq*) is to be found only as subjects within Temür's realm (*dawlat-i tu*).[58] The vizier offered Temür support in metaphorically opening the gates of Herat. Jami family in Transoxiana assuredly facilitated communications. On receiving an indication of interest, the vizier sent a second letter, this directly to Temür. The letter promoted the saint cult of Ahmad.[59] The vizier thus instituted a relationship between the Jamis and Temür that endured until the Timurid state in Iran expired in 911/1506.

Temür visited Ahmad-i Jam's shrine on his march to Herat, and was hosted by the vizier's son, Shaykh al-Islam Ziya al-Din Yusuf Jami (see Chapter 7).

THE TIMURIDS (783/1381 TO 911/1506)

The focus here is on the successors of Ahmad-i Jam and their interactions with Timurid sultans and amirs. Shrine and shaykhs secured valuable patronage.

Temür

Shaykh al-Islam Razi al-Din Ahmad (d. 767/1366) b. Shihab al-Din Ismaʿil Jami was the shrine's indefatigable custodian (*mutawalli*). His father appointed him *qaʾim-i maqam* vis-à-vis management of the shrine; his older brother, Shams al-Din Mutahhar (the vizier's father) was appointed *qaʾim-i maqam* of the *khanaqah*.[60] Razi al-Din Ahmad supervised the shrine's expansion and endowed it with great wealth.[61] Custodianship stayed in his lineage, initially with his son, Shihab al-Din Ismaʿil (d. 809/1407).

---

[57] See Mahendrarajah, "Tamerlane's Conquest."
[58] Yusuf-i Ahl/Moayyad (ed.), *Faraʾid*, 2:556–59, 558.
[59] Ibid., 1:173–81 (this letter was discussed in Chapter 2).
[60] Buzjani/Moayyad (ed.), *Rawzat*, 106–7; Zanganah, *Sarzamin*, 131. See Figure A1.3 #1 and #3, and Figure A1.4. For a list of administrators of the shrine, see Table 5.2; for chiefs of the shrine's *khanaqah*s, see Table 8.1.
[61] Buzjani/Moayyad (ed.), *Rawzat*, 107; Zanganah, *Sarzamin*, 132–33.

Shihab al-Din Isma'il Jami died in 809/1407. The custodianship switched from the Turbat-i Jam branch of Razi al-Din Ahmad's line, to the Transoxiana branch of his line through Khandzada Fakhr al-Mulk Khatun (n.d.).[62] Her progeny are undoubtedly of Razi al-Din Ahmad's blood, but her relationship to him is unclear: was she his daughter? Granddaughter? This *khandzada* (contraction of *khudawandzada* – Persian for sayyid) from Tirmiz is known principally from a 804/1401 decree by Temür confirming fiscal-legal immunities in Jam, Bakharz, and Khwaf for her and her progeny.[63] Other than for the decree (analyzed in Chapter 6), virtually nothing is known about the family.

That a decree from 804/1401 retroactively confirms immunities from 798/1396 suggests that Temür was settling a problem that had emerged while his son, Miranshah (d. 810/1408), was the governor of Khurasan (in office, 780–98/1382–96). Miranshah was succeeded by Shah-Rukh (in office, 799–809/1396–1407). Shah-Rukh (r. 807–50/1405–47) eventually succeeded Temür. The Jami shaykhs and Miranshah appear not to have had a pacific relationship, although Miranshah was fond of the vizier's other son, Shihab al-Din 'Umar (n.d.), on whose account Miranshah had made a pilgrimage to Ahmad-i Jam's shrine, where he was generously hosted by Shihab al-Din 'Umar. The presents of cash, camels, and sheep that Miranshah offered were graciously accepted, but regifted by the ascetic 'Umar to darwishes and the indigent.[64]

Shah-Rukh bin Temür

The shaykhs had instituted a congenial association with Shah-Rukh while he was governor and supported him in the succession struggles that followed Temür's death. Shah-Rukh executed a confirmation decree (*manshur*) on 12 Dhu al-Qa'da 809/20 April 1407 for Qutb al-Din Muhammad (d. 821/1418), the Khandzada's grandson, as custodian of the shrine (succeeding Shihab al-Din Isma'il; see Table 5.2).[65] Qutb al-Din Muhammad Jami was succeeded by Shihab al-Din (Abu al-Makarim)

---

[62] See Figure A1.4.
[63] She is mentioned in another decree, which confirms she is a Husayni sayyid. Nizam al-Din 'Abd al-Wasi' Nizami [Nizami Bakharzi], *Mansha' al-insha'*, ed. Rukn al-Din Humayun Farrukh (Tehran: Danishgah-i milli-i Iran, 1357/1978f.), 151–52.
[64] Buzjani/Moayyad (ed.), *Rawzat*, 111–13; Zanganah, *Sarzamin*, 149–51; Beatrice Forbes Manz, *Power, Politics and Religion in Timurid Iran* (Cambridge: Cambridge University Press, 2007), 226. A classic Sufi gesture: graciously accepted but redistributed to the needy.
[65] Yusuf-i Ahl/Berlin, *Fara'id*, fol. 311b–313a.

Jami (b. Tirmiz, 796/1393f.; d. Bengal, 847/1443f.). This Shihab al-Din Jami has been a man of mystery to historians, no doubt complicated by the surfeit of Shihab al-Dins in the Jami genealogical thickets, but also because of two notices in Khwandamir's *Habib al-siyar*, one of which is misleading or erroneous. This notice claims that a "Shihab al-Din Abu al-Makarim" (d. 833/1429f.) was an inspector of morals (*muhtasib*) in Herat.[66] There may have been such a person, but he is not known to the Jami community.

Abu al-Makarim was Shah-Rukh's spiritual guide.[67] Ordinarily, "alleged" would be added to the above sentence, but independent evidence bolsters the assertion. Firstly, Shah-Rukh visited Ahmad-i Jam's shrine on multiple occasions throughout his reign;[68] but not all of his travels were recorded by contemporary historians: Turbat-i Jam and Mayhana/Mihna (location of Abu Saʿid b. Abu al-Khayr's tomb)[69] are not distant from Herat and will not necessarily have counted as an extraordinary journey. Shah-Rukh was a pious seeker of blessings (*baraka*), and a regular visitor to sundry regional shrines. He is known to have visited Turbat-i Jam once in 823/1420 and twice in 842/1438. The shrine's custodian, from 821/1418 to *ca*. 845/1441f., was Abu al-Makarim, and confirmed in office by Shah-Rukh on 6 Safar 821/15 March 1418.[70] Abu al-Makarim's installation was due to his pedigree and the influence of the Transoxiana branch of the Jami family; Shah-Rukh's devotion to him was probably the deciding factor.

The ʿAlaʾ al-Mulk clan of Tirmiz were wealthy, and affines and/or kin to the sayyids (*khandzada*, *khudawandzada*) of Tirmiz. Abu al-Makarim's appointment, then just twenty-five years old, while distinguished candidates from the Khurasan branch were available, was a compromise due to Shah-Rukh's affection for him. Abu al-Makarim's tenure was a boon to the shrine. Magnificent edifices were sponsored by Timurid officials (Chapter 5), undoubtedly to please his majesty by sponsoring buildings at a cherished shrine. The Gawhar-Shad waqf for the eponymous mosque was executed in mid-Rajab 829/*ca*. 23 May 1426 by Gawhar-Shad and

---

[66] Khwandamir, *Habib*, 4:11–12; cf. Ghiyath al-Din Khwandamir, ed. ʿAbd al-Husayn Nawaʾi, *Rijal-i kitab-i habib al-siyar* (Tehran: Anjuman-i athar wa mafakhir-i farhang, 1379/2000), 127–28.
[67] Buzjani/Moayyad (ed.), *Rawzat*, 110–11 (biography); Buzjani/Jami (ed.), *Rawzat*, 162–63 (same). His lineage is given as "Shihab al-Din ... b. ʿAlaʾ al-Din (Abu al-Maʿali) ʿAlaʾ al-Mulk b. Qutb al-Din Muhammad" in Khwafi, *Mujmal*, 3:138; "Abu al-Makarim b. Khwajah ʿAlaʾ al-Mulk b. Khandzada Mujir al-Mulk bt. Khandzada ʿAlaʾ al-Mulk" in Khwandamir, *Habib*, 4:11. See also Figure A1.4.
[68] Melville, "Itineraries," 285–315.   [69] See Harrow, "Tomb Complex."
[70] The decree is in Yusuf-i Ahl/Berlin, *Faraʾid*, fol. 291b–294a; Yusuf-i Ahl/Tehran, *Faraʾid*, 623–26; and Yusuf-i Ahl/Fatih, *Faraʾid*, fol. 447b–448b.

Shah-Rukh. It included benefactions for shrine and shaykhs.[71] Abu al-Makarim Jami was enlisted by Shah-Rukh as his emissary to a Bengali potentate (Mahmud Shah, r. 1435–59). He resigned his post, and accompanied by a son, traveled to Bengal, where Abu al-Makarim perished.[72] The son remained in Bengal.

Loss of Patron and Protector

Shah-Rukh died on 25 Dhu al-Hijja 850/13 March 1447. Succession challenges that had been simmering during his prolonged illness boiled over. The protection and patronage that the shrine and shaykhs had enjoyed expired with him. After decades of relative peace and stability, Khurasan was sundered by conflict: between 852/1448 and 853/1450, Khurasan and Herat suffered. There was a major battle near Turbat-i Jam in 853/1449,[73] and the movement of troops displaced peasants, ruined farmlands, villages, and irrigation systems. Abu al-Qasim Babur (d. Rabiʿ II 861/March 1457) b. Baysunghur b. Shah-Rukh blinded one brother, ʿAlaʾ al-Dawla (d. 865/1460), executed another, Sultan-Muhammad (d. 855/1452), and briefly took control of Khurasan.[74]

Babur b. Baysunghur allowed his amirs to "ride roughshod over the population of Herat and its dependencies and to make intolerable exactions from it, and he made no effort whatsoever to restore the devastated condition of Khorasan."[75] In order to acquire support, Babur "liberally distributed *soyurghal* grants to" amirs.[76] A *soyurghal* (land grant) for Jam province was given to Muzaffar al-Din Khalil, but when he moved to Sistan in 859/1455, the *soyurghal* was transferred to Mirza Sultan-Sanjar.[77]

When Babur died, a fresh cycle of violence commenced in Khurasan and lasted for two years. Three ephemeral rulers compelled the people of the Herat region to pay the same taxes three times in a year.[78] One of them was Sultan-Abu Saʿid, who took the Timurid throne on 15 Safar 863/22 December 1458. Agriculture had been ruined, and a "dreadful famine" gripped the region in winter 863/1458.[79] Mirza Sultan-Sanjar was still

---

[71] Mahendrarajah, "Gawhar Shad" (includes Persian text, translation, and annotations).
[72] Khwandamir, *Habib*, 4:11; al-Samarqandi, *Matlaʿ*, 2.1:525.
[73] al-Samarqandi, *Matlaʿ*, 2.2:654–55, 676–77; Zanganah, *Sarzamin*, 32.
[74] Manz, *Timurid Iran*, 245–75.
[75] Maria Eva Subtelny, *Timurids in Transition* (Leiden: Brill, 2007), 48 (citing Khwandamir, *Habib*, 4:31).
[76] Ibid., 48. [77] al-Samarqandi, *Matlaʿ*, 2.2:757. *Soyurghal*s are discussed in Chapter 6.
[78] Subtelny, *Timurids*, 49–51. [79] Khwandamir, *Habib*, 4:76; Subtelny, *Timurids*, 56.

a threat to Sultan-Abu Saʿid, but was killed in Jumada I 863/March 1459. Six weeks later, Sultan-Abu Saʿid returned the *soyurghal* to a shaykh from Jam.

Sultan-Abu Saʿid

Sultan-Abu Saʿid (r. 855–73/1451–69) issued two decrees relating to Jam. The first is a confirmation (*manshur*) for Razi al-Din Ahmad (d. 908/ 1502f.) b. Jalal al-Din as the custodian of Ahmad's shrine;[80] the second is a *soyurghal* dated 29 Jumada II 863/3 May 1459 for Qutb al-Din Ahmad Jami (n.d.) for the provinces of Jam, Bakharz, and Khwaf.[81] The *manshur* is undated, but was almost certainly published coterminous with the *soyurghal* (the *soyurghal* is parsed in Chapter 6).

The *manshur* is illuminating. It reveals that there had been extensive damage to endowed shrine estates during the war, and the custodian was expected to improve the conditions of peasants and restore the damaged villages. It is inferred from the text that squatters had taken advantage of the lawlessness and the diminished influence of the shaykhs; hence a clause that the endowed lands had to be left entirely for occupation by the custodian; and all must obey his orders and recognize his supremacy. In a revealing departure from earlier practices vis-à-vis confirmations, he *appoints* Razi al-Din Ahmad Jami to "the office of Shaykh al-Islam of the aforementioned province [Jam]" (*mansab-i shaykh al-islami-yi wilayat-i mazkur*). Hitherto, sultans had acknowledged – explicitly or implicitly – that the person they were confirming was entering the office of custodian already the Shaykh al-Islam of Jam. The difference here is that the Shaykh al-Islam of Jam and his Sufi community had been diminished by the death of their patron, Shah-Rukh. A public statement, a "rehabilitation" by the new Timurid sultan, was warranted. The decree proclaimed reversion to the *status quo ante bellum*.

Sultan-Abu Saʿid is not known to have been devoted to Ahmad-i Jam. It is also not known if he visited the shrine. The relationship between shrine

---

[80] Anonymous, *Recueil de documents diplomatiques* (Paris: Bibliothèque nationale de France, Supplément persan 1815), fol. 29b–30b; Nawaʾi (ed.), *Asnad wa mukatibat-i tarikh-i Iran: az Timur ta Shah Ismaʿil*, 314–15 (edited text); Buzjani/Moayyad (ed.), *Rawzat*, 143–44 (edited text); Lawrence G. Potter, "The Kart Dynasty of Herat: Religion and Politics in Medieval Iran" (unpublished PhD diss., Columbia University, 1992), 208–9 (translation).

[81] *Recueil*, Supplément persan 1815, fol. 32a–33b. The date is written as *salkh-i jumada al-thani* ("the last day of Jumada II").

and sultan is hard to gauge: on the one hand, he had issued two decrees benefiting shrine and shaykhs; on the other hand, in a wild fit of paranoia stoked by malevolent tongues into believing the venerable Gawhar-Shad was conspiring against him, he ordered the execution of the eighty-year-old dowager queen. She was executed on 9 Ramazan 861/31 July 1457, an ignoble finale to an exemplary life of public service.[82] Even Timurid court apologists could not spin Sultan-Abu Saʿid's reprehensible act. The shaykhs of Jam were surely incensed by the murder of a beloved queen. Interestingly, following Sultan-Abu Saʿid's coronation on 15 Safar 863/ 22 December 1458 in Herat, the *khutba* was pronounced in his name at the Friday mosque by Shams al-Din Muhammad Kusuyi (d. 863/1459),[83] one of Ahmad-i Jam's eminent progeny.[84] Sultan-Abu Saʿid was captured by the Aq-Quyunlu ("White Sheep") Turkmen confederation during an expedition to western Iran. Gawhar-Shad's grandson, Yadgar Muhammad, was accorded the honor of beheading him.

Sultan-Husayn Bayqara

Sultan-Husayn Bayqara (r. 873–911/1469–1506), a fourth-generation descendant of Temür through his son, ʿUmar Shaykh (d. *ca.* 796/1394), established himself in Herat. He flirted with Twelver Shiʿism early in his reign, but was hurriedly shoved back onto the Sunni path by his contemporaries. He held a lively court. He was good-humored and pious, but not scrupulously devout. Sultan-Husayn was a dedicated alcoholic who began his bouts right after midday prayers; but as his cousin, Zahir al-Din Muhammad Babur – the inveterate diarist and founder of the Mughal Empire – writes in Sultan-Husayn's defense, "he never had a morning draught!"[85] The Timurid sultan's laissez-faire piety reflected the Zeitgeist of late Timurid Herat.

Sultan-Husayn Bayqara was Iran's last Timurid sultan. His accession ushered in the last grand epoch in Herat, facilitated in some measure by his guiding hand, and in part by benign neglect. Literary life in Herat thrived. Historians, painters, poets, belles-lettrists, calligraphers, and musicians bequeathed to posterity an impressive corpus of Persian art and

---

[82] al-Samarqandi, *Matlaʿ*, 2.2:810; Khwandamir, *Habib*, 4:68; Mahendrarajah, "Gawhar Shad," esp. 821–24.
[83] Khwandamir, *Habib*, 4:76; Khwandamir/Thackston (trans.), *Habib*, 392.
[84] Buzjani/Moayyad (ed.), *Rawzat*, 118–21. Kusuyi lineage is in Figure A1.1b #8.
[85] Zahir al-Din Babur, *The Baburnama*, trans. Wheeler Thackston (New York: Modern Library, 2002), 194 (fol. 164a–164b).

literature.[86] Luminaries included ʿAli Shir Nawaʾi (844–906/1441–1501) and Nur al-Din ʿAbd al-Rahman Jami (817–98/1414–92), both confidants of the sultan. Nawaʾi penned Persian and Chaghatai poetry and sponsored numerous public works. Maria Subtelny argues for a connection between the "Timurid renaissance" and the proliferation of *soyurghal*s, principally during Sultan-Husayn's reign.[87]

ʿAbd al-Rahman Jami was the superlative poet of the epoch and the last great poet of Herat. A highway sign pointing motorists to his birthplace in Jam proudly calls him "the seal of the poets" (*khatm al-shuʿaraʾ*). Jami was not descended from Ahmad, but was devoted to him; and associated with Ahmad's heirs. Jami's correspondence reveals that he leveraged his friendships with Sultan-Husayn and ʿAli Shir Nawaʾi to advocate for supplicants.[88] None of his letters include shrine-related petitions, although he will undoubtedly have raised any shrine-related petitions at court.

A renewal decree by Sultan-Husayn for the *soyurghal* by Sultan-Abu Saʿid has not survived, but in an age that "witnessed the unbridled growth of other immunities and tax privileges connected with landholding,"[89] the sultan presumably renewed the *soyurghal* and/or issued fiscal-legal immunities of his own. Sultan-Husayn confirmed Jalal al-Din (Abu al-Qasim) (d. 920/1514f.) b. Razi al-Din Ahmad Jami as custodian on 20 Jumada I 884/ 9 August 1479.[90] Jalal al-Din's stewardship extended into the Safavid era.

---

[86] See, e.g., Maria Eva Subtelny, "Scenes from the Literary Life of Timurid Herat," in *Logos Islamikos*, ed. Roger Savory and D. A. Agius (Toronto: Pontifical Institute of Mediaeval Studies, 1984), 137–55; for an extended exposition, see Hasan Nasiri Jami, *Maktab-i Harat wa shiʿr-i Farsi* (Tehran: Intisharat-i mawla, 1393/2014 f.).

[87] Subtelny, "Socioeconomic," 480.

[88] ʿAbd al-Rahman Jami, *Namaha-yi dastniwis-i Jami*, ed. ʿAsam al-Din Urunbayif and Mayil Harawi (Kabul: Matbaʿah-i dawlati, 1364/1985); ʿAbd al-Rahman Jami, *Munshaʾat-i Jami*, ed. ʿAbd al-ʿAli Nur Ahrari (Turbat-i Jam: Intisharat-i Shaykh al-Islam Ahmad-i Jam, 1383/2004).

[89] Subtelny, "Socioeconomic," 482; see also Subtelny, *Timurids*, 37–38.

[90] *Recueil*, Supplément persan 1815, fol. 30b–32a. See also Table 5.2.

4

Safavid/Mughal Eras to the Islamic Republic

The Safavid/Shi'i age dawned ominously in Khurasan, with Herat's capitulation, the execution of Herat's last Sunni Shaykh al-Islam, and violence against Sunnis. Surprisingly, however, the shrine received Safavid support, from Shah Isma'il I and Shah 'Abbas I. Nonetheless, endless Safavid-Uzbek wars and sectarian strife scarred Khurasan, leading members of the saint cult to find succor with kinsmen in Mughal India. During the succeeding centuries – late Safavid, Afsharid, Zand, Qajar, and Pahlawi rule – the shrine fell into disrepair and the cult withered. The founding of the (Shi'i) Islamic Republic of Iran (1979), paradoxically, signaled the rejuvenation of the saint cult and the revivification of the shrine complex.

DAWN OF THE SHI'I ERA IN KHURASAN

In 906/1501, the newly crowned Safavid king, Shah Isma'il I (r. 906–30/1501–24), with his capture of the Aq-Quyunlu capital of Tabriz, declared that henceforth Twelver Shi'ism (*Ithna-'ashari*) would be the official confession of his (unconsolidated) kingdom. Isma'il thus set in train Iran's slow conversion from majority Sunni to majority Twelver Shi'a – an ongoing process: five centuries after his proclamation, large communities of Zoroastrians, Jews, Christians, Isma'ili Shi'a, and (Hanafi and Shafi'i) Sunnis flourish in Iran. While Isma'il was settling into his capital, in the east, Iran was facing an ancient challenge in a new dress: Turkic tribes of Transoxiana, now calling themselves Uzbeks (Öz Beg), and led by Muhammad Shaybani Khan (d. 916/1510), a descendant of Chingiz

Khan through his oldest son, Jochi. Shaybani ousted the Timurid, Zahir al-Din Muhammad Babur (886–937/1483–1530), from his Samarqand patrimony in 912/1506, and captured Herat in 913/1507.[1] Shaybani's march westward, without a Timurid buffer between the Safavids and the (Sunni) Uzbeks, alarmed Isma'il, who pivoted to Khurasan.

Despite Isma'il's victories in Iraq, the Caspian provinces, Diyar Bakir (Anatolia), Fars, Kirman, and Shirvan, his hold on Sunni Iran remained tenuous. He took a risk in marching east. The pivot reflected not only his concerns over the permanent loss of Khurasan, but the fear of entrenched Sunni enemies – Ottomans and Uzbeks – on two flanks. In Ramazan 916/December 1510, Shah Isma'il defeated and killed Shaybani at Marw. The Safavids and their cohorts, the Qizilbash ("Redhead"),[2] entered Herat. The Qizilbash and *early* Safaviyya subscribed to a sui generis corpus of Shi'i beliefs that they believed was Twelver Shi'ism.[3] Their intolerance, matched now by the intolerance of the Uzbeks, scarred Khurasan and its peoples for many decades. Conversion to Shi'ism was demanded of the Sunni Shaykh al-Islam of Herat, Sayf al-Din Ahmad Taftazani, who refused. He was executed – horribly and slowly if the report by Zahir al-Din Babur's cousin, Haydar Dughlat,[4] is veracious – in Ramazan 916/December 1510, and ferocious persecutions were unleashed on the Sunnis of Herat.

Shortly after the execution of Taftazani, whose family had been connected with the Jami clan for over 150 years,[5] the Shaykh al-Islam of Jam came to the court of Shah Isma'il to receive a dispensation. Isma'il's decree is dated Muharram 917/31 March to 29 April 1511.[6] Presumably, the audience with the shah was around this date.[7]

Jalal al-Din (Abu al-Qasim) Jami (d. 920/1514f.) is titled Shaykh al-Islam in the decree. Despite Sayf al-Din Ahmad Taftazani's recent fate, the Sunni office of Shaykh al-Islam had not yet been abolished. The Safavids

---

[1] Babur consequently came to Afghanistan and Iran. He founded the "Mughal Empire," properly, *Gurkaniyan* (Gurkanid dynasty), after Temür Gurkan (Tamerlane).
[2] This refers to their twelve-pointed scarlet headgear, where each point represented a Shi'i Imam. Qizilbash progeny in Afghanistan form a distinct Twelver Shi'a community and self-identify as Qizilbash.
[3] See, e.g., Moojan Momen, *An Introduction to Shi'i Islam* (London: Yale University Press, 1985), 107–9; Farhad Daftary, *A History of Shi'i Islam* (London: I.B. Tauris, 2013), 81–85.
[4] Muhammad Haidar Dughlat, *Tarikh-i Rashidi*, ed. and trans. E. D. Ross (London: Sampson Low, 1895), 236; see also Rumlu, *Ahsan*, 2:1056–57.
[5] See Shivan Mahendrarajah, The Shaykh al-Islam in Medieval Khurasan," *Afghanistan* 1/2 (2018): 257–81.
[6] *Recueil*, Supplément persan 1815, fol. 135a–136a.
[7] The primary sources, unfortunately, offer no account of their meeting.

did not appoint a Shi'i Shaykh al-Islam at Herat until 928/1521f.[8] Abu al-Qasim Jami came to the court to seek redress for an error. He kissed the floor and showed faith in the exalted family of the Imamate (*surat-i i'tiqad-i uw nisbat ba khanuwada-yi dudman-i wilayat wa imamat*). Imamate refers to "the people of the house" (*ahl al-bayt*), the Prophet's family. Affection for *ahl al-bayt* is not the preserve of the Shi'a – although one could be left with this impression in light of the passionate devotions of the Shi'a (especially Ashura commemorations). Abu al-Qasim's gesture does not imply affiliation with the Shi'a, but it is a nod to the new reality. Abu al-Qasim was awarded an annual pension of 10,000 Tabrizi dinars from the agricultural revenues of Jam province irrespective of whether said revenues increase or decrease. The award was effective from the beginning of the Year of the Dragon (Luy-il),[9] which corresponds to 9 Shawwal 913/11 February 1508. The award was irrevocable (in theory). The Khwaja and his progeny are exempt from taxation, and officials had to withdraw from his lands. A renewal must not be demanded every year. Jalal al-Din Muhammad (who is not identified here) is to receive an allotment of 5,000 Tabrizi dinars from the remaining revenues.

The context for the dispensation is not known. We cannot determine if 10,000 Tabrizi dinars constituted a large claim against the annual harvests of Jam, nor can the purchasing power of the dinar be determined. It is evident that despite Shah Isma'il's frequent outbursts of bigotry and violence against Sunnis, he had perceived political advantage in honoring Abu al-Qasim. However, the character of the advantage, and for how long his favor toward the Sunnis of Jam was sustained, are not known.

SAFAVID-UZBEK WARS AND THE SHRINE'S DECLINE

Safavid control of Khurasan was not firm. Herat and Mashhad remained prizes for the Uzbeks and Safavids, not only for prestige, but for the economic resources of the region, namely, agriculture. Political control of Herat oscillated between the Safavids and the Uzbeks. It fell to the Uzbeks in 935-36/1529, and again in 942/1535, but recovered quickly both times. The Uzbeks were routed in a battle at Jam in 935/1528,[10] but were able to

---

[8] Zayn al-Din 'Ali, an Arab *'alim*, held the post for two years. Khwandamir, *Habib*, 4:610.
[9] On the "animal calendar," see C. P. Melville, "The Chinese-Uighur Animal Calendar in Persian Historiography of the Mongol Period," *Iran* 32 (1994): 83–98.
[10] Rumlu, *Ahsan*, 2:1168ff; Babur/Thackston (trans.), *Baburnama*, 429–30 (fol. 354a–355b).

briefly capture Mashhad. The loss of Herat in 996/1588,[11] for a decade, was far graver. The city became a springboard for Uzbek attacks across Khurasan, including the prolonged siege of the Shi'i holy city of Mashhad. The occupation of Herat ended in Muharram 1007/August 1598.

There are too many Uzbek incursions into Khurasan in the tenth/sixteenth century to catalog. Turbat-i Jam was captured (*fath*) or pillaged (*gharat*) in 943/1536, 977–78/1569–70, 986/1578f., 989/1581f., 995/1587f., and 1025/1616f.[12] The violence took a terrible toll on the social and economic health of Khurasan in general, and the agricultural region of Jam in particular. Jam sits on routes traversing Mashhad and Herat: the back-and-forth movement of armies and protracted warfare ruined agriculture, hydrological systems, and dwellings; displaced the population; and resulted in food shortages – including a famine in 920/1514f. Compounding human suffering was an intense cycle of sectarian violence: Shi'i extremists/Qizilbash pillaged, tortured, raped, and killed; and when the Uzbeks ejected Safavid forces, Sunnis would indiscriminately exact revenge on Shi'is. When the Uzbeks were ejected, the bloody cycle started afresh.

Uzbek-Safavid violence was not the principal propellant for mass migrations by members of the upper social strata of Ahmad's saint cult. Persecutions were unleashed by the Safavids against Sufis, especially the Naqshbandiyya. The graves of Naqshbandi luminaries, including 'Abd al-Rahman Jami, were desecrated. Anti-Sufi persecutions were often intense, and organized Sufism was largely extirpated at the expiration of the Safavid era (1722).[13] Safavid persecutions, however, were selective: a shrine custodian (Jalal al-Din Jami) received a *soyurghal* from Shah Isma'il I (above); and Shah 'Abbas I (r. 1587–1629) funded restorations to the shrine's *iwan*. Sunni and Shi'a relations were not dictated by dichotomies of Sunni equals pro-Uzbek/anti-Safavid and Shi'a equals pro-Safavid/anti-Uzbek. In the first half of the tenth/sixteenth century at least, social relations between the Sunni and Shi'a were fashioned by complex variables.[14] Complex social,

---

[11] Audrey Burton, "The Fall of Herat to the Uzbegs in 1588," *Iran* 26 (1988): 119–23; R. D. McChesney, "The Conquest of Herat 995–6/1587–8," in *Etudes safavides*, ed. J. Calmard (Paris: Institut français de recherche en Iran, 1993), 69–107.

[12] Zanganah, *Sarzamin*, 33–34.

[13] Said Amir Arjomand, *The Shadow of God and the Hidden Imam* (Chicago, IL: University of Chicago Press, 1984), 112–13; Said Amir Arjomand, "Religious Extremism (*Ghuluww*), Sufism and Sunnism in Safavid Iran: 1501–1722," *JAH* 15/1 (1981): 1–35. "Sufi" had been a respected appellation, but after centuries of anti-Sufi polemics, "Sufi" acquired disrepute and lost adherents.

[14] Maria Szuppe, *Entre Timourides, Uzbeks et Safavides* (Paris: Association pour l'Avancement des Études Iraniennes, 1992), esp. 121–32.

political, and economic dynamics, not bigotry, tended more often to shape relations between *non*-Muslims and the Safavid/Shi'a state than did religious bigotry.[15]

SHAH 'ABBAS I, SAFAVI, AND AHMAD-I JAM'S SHRINE

The nascent Safavid state was sundered by civil wars (1524ff. and 1576ff.), Nuqtawi uprisings (1574 and 1592), and political strife.[16] When Isma'il's heir, Tahmasp (r. 1524–76) died, the supremacy of Shi'ism was not assured. Isma'il II, Safavi (r. 1576–77), initiated a "Sunni interlude," but he was killed and Shi'ism was once again proclaimed the official confession of Iran.[17] The point impressed here is that Ahmad-i Jam's shrine's fate as a Sunni institution trapped inside a Shi'i state was still not sealed by the close of the tenth/sixteenth century. The accession of Shah 'Abbas I firmly rooted Twelver Shi'ism in Iran.[18] Hitherto, the Safavids and Mughals had found common cause against the Uzbeks, but with the Uzbek threat diminishing, and two resolute monarchs – Emperor Akbar the Great and Shah 'Abbas the Great – leading their respective kingdoms, Mughal-Safavid tensions escalated.[19] Both empires abutted in "Afghanistan" and competed for valuable real estate, like Qandahar.

The religious-political stances of Shah 'Abbas I are illustrative. He had interest in Nuqtawi doctrines but subsequently persecuted the Nuqtawiyya,[20] who fled to India.[21] Sunnis were persecuted by Shah

---

[15] In *central* Iran, the treatment of Zoroastrians "had little to do with religious bigotry" than it did with bureaucratic infighting. Kioumars Ghereghlou, "On the Margins of Minority Life: Zoroastrians and the State in Safavid Iran," *BSOAS* 80/1 (2017): 45–71, 69. On non-Muslims in Safavid Iran, in general, see Aptin Khanbaghi, *The Fire, the Star and the Cross: Minority Religions in Medieval and Early Modern Iran* (London: I.B. Tauris, 2006), 93–163.

[16] See Andrew Newman, *Safavid Iran* (London: I.B. Tauris, 2006), esp. 26–28, 41–49, 50–52; Roger Savory, *Iran under the Safavids* (Cambridge: Cambridge University Press, 1980), 50–75; Abbas Amanat, *Apocalyptic Islam and Iranian Shi'ism* (London: I.B. Tauris, 2009), 83–89.

[17] Newman, *Safavid*, 45–47.

[18] On 'Abbas's legacy, see David Blow, *Shah Abbas* (London: I.B. Tauris, 2009).

[19] On Akbar's legacy, see Wink, *Akbar*.

[20] Eskander Beg Monshi, *History of Shah 'Abbas the Great* [*Tarikh-i 'Alamara-yi 'Abbasi*], 2 vols., trans. Roger Savory (Boulder, CO: Westview, 1978), 2:646–50; Arjomand, *Shadow*, 198–99; Newman, *Safavid*, 50–52, 68–69.

[21] Karim Barzegar, "The Nuqtavi Movement and the Question of Its Exodus during the Safavid Period (Sixteenth Century AD): A Historical Survey," *Indian Historical Review* 40/1 (2013): 41–66, esp. 49–65.

'Abbas: Khwaf, which had social and economic ties to Jam, was the scene of a massacre of Sunni notables (*ashraf wa a'yan*):

> When Shah 'Abbas Safavi came to Khwaf early in his reign, he compelled (*taklif*) the cursing (*sabb*) of the [Prophet's] Companions (*sahabat*), which [Sunnis] refused to do. He had seventy of their *ashraf wa a'yan* flung down from the mosque, so that each had his neck broken.[22]

Violence against Sunnis on the scale described by Shah Nawaz Khan will have frightened Ahmad-i Jam's shrine's leadership since their necks had a reasonable chance of being broken. Jami oral history claims that Jami Sufis participated in anti-Nuqtawi activities, which is plausible: they may have attempted to curry favor with Shah 'Abbas. The relationship between the shrine and the Safavid court was cordial in the middle of Shah 'Abbas's reign: in 1010/1601f., one of the shah's officials, Firuz-Jang b. Husayn (d. 1025/1616f.), donated a cistern to the shrine;[23] and Shah 'Abbas funded restorations to the shrine's *iwan*. Legends abound at Turbat-i Jam as to why a bigoted Shi'i shah would donate funds to a Sunni shrine. One tale is that it was a posthumous miracle by Ahmad, who had convinced the shah that the saint (Ahmad) entombed at Jam was Shi'i!

MIGRATIONS FROM JAM AND CONVERSION TO SHI'ISM

A century of violence ruined Khurasan's agricultural and pastoral economies, displaced peasants and pastoralists, and spurred migrations by high- and lowborn to India and stabler areas of Iran. The exodus of Jamis is reflected in Ibrahim Zanganah's prosopography. Biographical notices decline precipitously with the Safavid age: for the eleventh/seventeenth century, there are seventeen entries (not all Jamis); the twelfth/eighteenth century, five notices. Other men with the "Jami" *nisba* (adjective of place of origin or adopted land) are known to have migrated to Gilan, Tabriz, Ardabil, and other Iranian cities. It is likely that most will have discarded their original *nisba*, particularly so if they had taken to Shi'ism and/or did not wish to publicize their dissolved – or perhaps their

---

[22] Shah Nawaz Khan, *Ma'athir al-umara'*, 4 vols., ed. 'Abd al-Rahim and Ashraf 'Ali (Calcutta: Royal Asiatic Society, 1888–95), 1:668–69; Shah Nawaz Khan, *Ma'athir al-umara'*, 3 vols., trans. Henry Beveridge and B. Prashad (Calcutta: Royal Asiatic Society, 1941–64), 2:807 (my translation is materially different from Henry Beveridge's rendition).

[23] Firuz-Jang served as governor of Sarakhs. Monshi, *Shah 'Abbas*, 1:227, 2:1129–30.

enduring – association with Ahmad-i Jam's saint cult.[24] The Jamis' Transoxiana branch is not heard from other than for a scattered notice.[25] A measure of the decline of the saint cult is the precipitous decline in publications about Ahmad-i Jam, the shrine, Sufism, and the saint cult; hence the unevenness of the primary sources.

Ibrahim Zanganah's biographical entries suggest Jami conversions to Shi'ism; for example, one Riyazi (d. 921/1515f.), a poet with the court of Sultan-Husayn Bayqara, penned verses praising Imam 'Ali and Shah Isma'il's victory.[26] A poet with the nom de plume (*takhallus*) "Jami" resided at Ardabil,[27] but whether he served the Safavid spiritual center is not expressed. A master weaver, Ghiyath al-Din Jami, worked at Tabriz. Arthur Upham Pope suggested that Ghiyath al-Din or his family were "'probably one of the group of superior artists who left Khurasan at the beginning of the sixteenth century to profit by the new and exciting opportunities opened up by the Safavid renaissance, just beginning at the court of Shah Isma'il at Tabriz."[28]

Jami Sufis, doubtless, discarded their Sufi and/or Sunni allegiances and walked the Shi'i path. Conversion to Shi'ism offered political, social, and economic advantages, which will have enticed Sunnis. The Shi'a majority of modern Iran had to have come from conversions from other faiths; but it is important to recognize that Iran's border regions remain dominantly Sunni, that is, conversion at the peripheries was at a slower pace than elsewhere. Certain of Ahmad-i Jam's descendants converted to Shi'ism, but the extent of Jami conversions to Shi'ism is uncertain.

MUGHAL INDIA

Elements of the upper strata of the Jami community migrated to Mughal India. Litterateurs are not readily forgotten as their writings tend to survive even if – possibly because – their oeuvre is prosaic. The number of litterateurs of Mughal India bearing the *nisba* and/or *takhallus* "Jami," a subset of whom are known progeny of Ahmad-i Jam, is quite remarkable.[29] Some litterateurs

---

[24] *Taqiyya* (dissimulation) is not the preserve of Shi'a. Sufis (both Shi'i and Sunni) have found reasons to practice *taqiyya*; for instance, in Mao's China and the USSR. The term employed in Iran to refer to Sunni attitudes is *ihtiyat*: caution or circumspection.
[25] Zanganah, *Sarzamin*, 216–17, 223–24, 233–35.   [26] Ibid., 215.   [27] Ibid., 217.
[28] Savory, *Safavids*, 138, quoting A. U. Pope (ed.), *A Survey of Persian Art*, 6 vols. (Oxford: Oxford University Press, 1938–58), 6:2296.
[29] Zanganah, *Sarzamin*, 223, 225, 228, 231, 236, 237, 238, 239, 240, 241–42, 242–43, 244, 245, 247.

FIGURE 4.1 Hamida Banu Bigum bt. ʿAli Akbar Jami. (A black and white version of this figure will appear in some formats. For the color version, please refer to the plate section.)
Wikipedia Commons

used the *takhallus* "Jami" to capitalize on ʿAbd al-Rahman Jami's fame. Safavids and Mughals competed for artistic talent; Jami litterateurs and artisans heard the call and decamped Iran for India. A promoter of Persian arts in India was Humayun's wife,[30] Hamida Banu Bigum bt. ʿAli Akbar Jami (Figure 4.1).

When Humayun (r. 1530–40; 1555–56) and Hamida Banu Bigum (1527–1604) were in Herat (late 950/early 1544), inhabitants of Jam came to visit.[31] The pair were invited to visit Turbat-i Jam, which they did. Humayun's mother, Maham Bigum, was related to Sultan-Husayn and Ahmad-i Jam.[32] Despite these royal and spiritual heritages, and the proliferation of Iranians and Central Asian Turks in the courts of Humayun and

[30] Abolala Soudavar, "Between the Safavids and the Mughals: Art and Artists in Transition," *Iran* 37 (1999): 49–66.
[31] Abu al-Fazl, *Akbar*, 2:71.   [32] Ibid., 1:389.

Akbar;[33] and Annette Beveridge's tantalizing remark that "the saint's [Ahmad-i Jam's] posterity was numerous in Akbar's court,"[34] Jami shaykhs appear not to have wielded power in Mughal India.[35] Jami litterateurs were plentiful, but not Jamis in administrative posts that would have allowed them access to state funds with which to enhance their power and patronize Ahmad's shrine.

An onomastic analysis of the *nisba* "Khwafi" yielded profitable results;[36] but a parallel approach for the Jami *nisba* is not possible because the *nisba* is rarely found in the sources on Mughal officials. The Jami *nisba*, to hazard a guess, although respected in Persian literary circles, was discarded by men who accepted employment in the Mughal *diwan* because Jam district (*wilayat-i Jam*) in Gujarat province was "infidel" territory: the Mughals conquered Jam in 1590. Nawanagar, Jam's capital, was renamed Islamnagar (= Islamabad: "the place where Islam thrives").[37]

Initially, Ahmad-i Jam's shrine cult had hope that their longstanding association with India's Muslim rulers, datable to the Delhi Sultanate; kinship with Humayun and Jalal al-Din Muhammad Akbar (1542–1605), and Akbar's mother, Hamida Banu Bigum, would generate support and patronage for the shrine; but a Chishti miracle trumped Ahmad-i Jam's spiritual prowess.

Akbar was nearing thirty and had no male heir. Shaykh Salim Chishti (d. 1572) predicted the birth of *three* boys. The future emperor, Jahangir (d. 1627), was born on 31 August 1569 and named Salim to honor the shaykh.[38] To demonstrate gratitude, Akbar set forth on pilgrimage to the mausoleum of the Chishtiyya's primary saint, Mu'in al-Din Chishti (d. 633/

---

[33] Ibid., 2:437–39 (list of notables); Bayat, *Tarikh-i Humayun*, 79–90 (longer list); Afzal Husain, "Provincial Governors under Akbar (1580–1605)," *PIHC* 32 (1970): 269–77; Afzal Husain, "Growth of Irani Element in Akbar's Nobility," *PIHC* 36 (1975): 166–79; Iqtidar Khan, "The Nobility under Akbar and the Development of His Religious Policy, 1560–80," *JRAS* 1/2 (1968): 29–36; Richard Foltz, "Central Asians in the Administration of Mughal India," *JAH* 31/2 (1997): 139–54.

[34] Gul-Badan, *Humayun*, 239 (this is the translator's, i.e., Beveridge's, commentary).

[35] A thorough investigation of Jamis in Mughal India is outside the scope of this book.

[36] Afzal Khan, "Iranis in the Mughal nobility: A Case Study of the Khawafis," *PIHC* 41 (1980): 248–64. The bulk of the study covers the reigns of Shah Jahan and Awrangzib.

[37] Munshi Muhammad Kazim b. Muhammad Amin, *'Alamgir Nama*, ed. Khadim Husayn and 'Abd al-Hayy (Calcutta: Royal Asiatic Society, 1868), 768–75; and Khan/Beveridge (trans.), *Ma'athir al-umara'*, 2:549. After 1707 Muslims lost control of Islamnagar and the town's name was changed to Jamnagar, which it retains. Jam district is now Halar.

[38] Nur al-Din Muhammad Jahangir, *Jahangir Nama*, ed. Muhammad Hashim (Tehran: Intisharat-i bunyad-i farhang-i Iran, 1359/1980), 442–43; Munis D. Faruqui, *The Princes of the Mughal Empire, 1504–1719* (Cambridge: Cambridge University Press, 2012), 145–46.

1236), walking the 220 miles from Agra to Ajmer.[39] Sons Murad (b. 1570) and Daniyal (b. 1572) were born (Daniyal was named after a Chishti saint). Akbar was impressed by the fulfillment of Salim's prophecy. His new capital at Sikri, a village near Agra where Salim had lived, burgeoned near the saint's tomb. Akbar's decision was shaped by politics, too: he had picked Agra over its rival, Delhi;[40] the prophecy offered him cover. It was inevitable that the emperor of India would honor an Indian saint cult. Jahangir's mother was a Rajput princess. Hindu and Sikh influences increased in Akbar's court. Akbar repealed the poll tax (jizya) on non-Muslims and adopted local cultural trappings. The Hindufication of the Persianized Timurids of India was the trend.

THE QAJARS

The Safavids passed into history in 1722, precipitated by the invasion of Iran by the Ghilzai Pashtuns of Qandahar.[41] The fall of the Safavids was followed by years of turmoil, raiding by predatory bands, Ottoman invasions, and struggles for supremacy. Information on the shrine's status, and Ahmad's devotees, in the two eras sandwiched between the Safavids and the Qajars – the Afsharids (r. 1736–47) and Zand (r. 1751–94) – is scant. Consequent to the turmoil in Iran, and the weakening of Mughal rule by Nadir Shah Afshar (d. 1747), is the cleaving of eastern Iran into "Afghanistan" by Ahmad Shah Durrani of the Abdali Pashtuns (r. 1747–73).[42] This was to have major ramifications for the shrine, specifically, the dismemberment of the shrine's catchment area.

The Qajar-era (1796–1925) offered little hope to weary Khurasanians. Although the Qajar government was present outside Tehran, there was hardly any governing or delivering of services. Offices were sold or stayed with elite Iranian families and tribes. The state depended heavily on agricultural, land, and customs taxes, but possessed "a most meager knowledge either of the revenues which it could expect to receive, or of the

---

[39] Jahangir, *Jahangir*, 444. An image from *Akbarnama* (IS.2:77–1896), held by the V&A in London, depicts Akbar's walk, but could not be reproduced here for copyright reasons.

[40] Carl W. Ernst and Bruce B. Lawrence, *Sufi Martyrs of Love: Chishti Sufism in South Asia and Beyond* (New York: Palgrave, 2002), 98–101.

[41] A sweep of 500 years of Iranian history, from the Safavids to the Islamic Republic, is in Abbas Amanat, *Iran: A Modern History* (New Haven, CT: Yale University Press, 2017).

[42] On the emergence of Afghanistan, see B. D. Hopkins, *The Making of Modern Afghanistan* (New York: Palgrave, 2008); Thomas Barfield, *Afghanistan: A Cultural and Political History* (Princeton, NJ: Princeton University Press, 2010).

The Qajars

justice or injustice of the apportionment of the taxes."[43] Taxation was farmed and offered opportunities for graft and extortion. The famine of 1869–73 killed countless Iranians; the impact in the vicinities of Jam was severe.[44] The Qajars turned over Iran's industries and mines in the notorious *Reuter Concession* (1872),[45] which even the fervent imperialist Lord Curzon found astounding: "the most complete and extraordinary surrender of the entire industrial resources of a kingdom into foreign hands."[46] The *Tobacco Concession* (1891), whereby an Englishman acquired a monopoly on the sale and export of Iranian-grown tobacco,[47] sparked opposition throughout Iran, a prelude to the Constitutional Revolution (1905–11).[48] When an assassin felled the Qajar shah, Nasir al-Din Shah, in 1896, "Iran was in a condition of anarchy, corruption, and poverty."[49]

Apart from mismanaging Iran's economy, finances, and natural resources, the Qajars initiated military adventures that cost Iran dearly. They attempted to retrieve Herat in 1837–38 and 1856–57,[50] but failed to appreciate the depth of Britain's anxiety over the defense of colonial India in the context of Tsarist Russia's advances in Central Asia.[51] Britain ended both occupations of Herat and imposed on Iran humiliating terms in the *Treaty of Paris* (4 March 1857), whereby the Qajars renounced Iran's inalienable right to Herat, "the Pearl of Khurasan." Wars, raids by Uzbek and Pashtun nomads, Turcoman slave raiding,[52] and the Second Anglo-

---

[43] W. Morgan Shuster, *The Strangling of Persia* (New York: Century, 1912), 282. On the economic picture, see Ervand Abrahamian, *Iran between Two Revolutions* (Princeton, NJ: Princeton University Press, 1982), 55–61, 69–80; and Ervand Abrahamian, *A History of Modern Iran* (Cambridge: Cambridge University Press, 2008), 8–41.

[44] Mohammad Gholi Majd, *A Victorian Holocaust: Iran in the Great Famine of 1869–1873* (London: Hamilton, 2018), 53–68; C. P. Melville, "Persian Famine of 1870–1872: Prices and Politics," *Disasters* 12/4 (1988): 309–25, esp. 315–17 and table 3 (Khurasan); Henry Walter Bellew, *The Indus to the Tigris* (London: Trubner & Co., 1874), 343–44, 349–50, 356, 364; F. J. Goldsmid (ed.), *Journeys of the Persian Boundary Commission*, 2 vols. (London: Macmillan, 1876), 1:94–95 (origins of the famine), 1:98 (Khurasan), 1:368–70 (the situation west of Jam).

[45] Abrahamian, *Two Revolutions*, 55; Abrahamian, *Modern Iran*, 38.

[46] George Curzon, *Persia and the Persian Question*, 2 vols. (London: Longmans, 1892), 1:480.

[47] Abrahamian, *Modern Iran*, 38–39.

[48] On the first Iranian revolution, see ibid., 34–62; and E. G. Browne, *The Persian Revolution of 1905–1909* (Cambridge: Cambridge University Press, 1910).

[49] Hamid Algar, *Religion and State in Iran, 1785–1906* (Berkeley, CA: University of California Press, 1969), 221.

[50] Peter Hopkirk, *The Great Game* (New York: Kodansha, 1994), 175–87, 287ff.; cf. Hopkins, *Afghanistan*, esp. 34–60.

[51] Hopkirk, *Great Game*, esp. 59–62 (on the Russian bogey).

[52] Fear of "Toorkmun" slave raiding in the vicinities of Sarakhs, Mashhad, Herat, Jam, and Khwaf is recorded in C. M. MacGregor, *Narrative of a Journey through the Province of*

Afghan War (1878–80) destabilized the borderlands. The crisscrossing of armies reverberated at Jam.[53] The catchment area of Ahmad-i Jam's shrine was dismembered. Unequal portions of the catchment area were divided between Iran and Afghanistan. In due course, most of the saint cult's Sufi and non-Sufi members in Afghanistan found it difficult to pay homage at the sepulcher of their saint. The frontier between Iran and Afghanistan became a border – a border that was hardened by Afghanistan's xenophobic, barbarous, and virulently anti-Shi'a ruler, Amir Abdur Rahman (r. 1880–1901).[54] The amir was financed and supported by Britain, which expected him to seal his country from foreign incursions and influences; hence the status of Afghanistan as a buffer between British India and Russia.

The reign of the Qajars was not conducive for economic growth,[55] Iran's national interests, or the acquisition of political patronage for a Sunni shrine far from Tehran. It is possible to discern from travelogues that the peoples of Jam were doing exactly what other Iranians were doing: subsisting. The region's peoples engaged with agriculture, pastoralism, trades, and crafts. A prominent feature of the Qajar period were the self-contained socioeconomic units that operated in the hinterlands, and characterized by personal socioeconomic interactions and autonomy from the government.[56]

THE PAHLAWIS

The Pahlawi period (1925–79) brought great social and economic improvements. As Ervand Abrahamian explained, "Iran entered the twentieth century with oxen and wooden ploughs. It exited with steel

---

Khorassan, 2 vols. (London: W.H. Allen, 1879), 1:234–77. The "man-stealing" Turcomen were hated: the Russians punished them when Geok-Tepe fell in 1881; but Iranians had to suffer their depradations until the accession of Riza Shah Pahlawi.

[53] See, e.g., Zanganah, *Sarzamin*, 34; J. F. Standish, "The Persian War of 1856–1857," *Middle East Studies* 3/1 (1966): 18–45.

[54] A 1299/1882 *"manshur of admonition and reproof"* by the amir to an officer who let a traveler pass is informative: "We have sent you letters numerous times telling you not to give anyone the opportunity to cross the border unless they are bearers of letters." Robert D. McChesney and M. M. Khorrami (trans.), *The History of Afghanistan: Fayz Muhammad Katib Hazarah's Siraj al-tawarikh*, 6 vols. (Leiden: Brill, 2013–16), 400–401.

[55] See, generally, Charles Issawi (ed.), *The Economic History of Iran, 1800–1914* (Chicago, IL: University of Chicago Press, 1971).

[56] On de facto autonomous rule in rural Iran, see Abrahamian, *Two Revolutions*, 11–14; Abrahamian, *Modern Iran*, 12–13, 20–27.

mills [and] a nuclear program."[57] Riza Shah (khan, r. 1921–25; shah, r. 1925–41), an astute and resolute Cossack, was Iran's modernizer.[58] He also delivered security to regions that had been lawless, including the Iran-Afghanistan borderlands.[59] However, Riza Shah was deposed in 1941 by the USA, UK, and USSR.[60] The Allied Powers invaded and divided Iran into zones of occupation. They then installed Riza Shah's pusillanimous and maladroit son, Muhammad Riza Shah (1941–79).[61] The occupation had negative socioeconomic impacts, including famine and epidemic.[62]

Socioeconomic conditions throughout Iran improved measurably after World War Two. However, better socioeconomic conditions and improved physical security offered little in the way of tangible improvements at Ahmad-i Jam's shrine, although as Bernard O'Kane noted, when he visited Turbat-i Jam several time in the 1970s, *Sazman-i Hifazat* (a precursor of *Miras-i Farhangi*), "had already begun restorations in the early 70s."[63] The shrine's continued disrepair at the expiration of the Pahlawi era is attested in photographs taken by Warwick Ball in 1977 – the cusp of the Iranian Revolution.

THE ISLAMIC REPUBLIC

The 1978–79 Revolution in Iran, which elevated Ayatollah Rohullah Khomeini (d. 1989) to power and instituted the Islamic Republic of Iran, sent shockwaves around the world. The establishment of the "Islamic Republic" unsettled Iran's religious minorities. Zoroastrians, Christians, Jews, and Sunnis emigrated to Australia, Europe, and North America. The war imposed on Iran by Saddam Hussein on 22 September 1980 further destabilized Iran and exacerbated outflows of Iranian talent. Sanctions regimes, and destabilization activities by the United States, Israel, and Saudi Arabia – including material support for terrorist organizations operating along

---

[57] Abrahamian, *Modern Iran*, 1.
[58] Ibid., 63–96; Ali M. Ansari, *Modern Iran since 1921* (Edinburgh: Pearson, 2003), 40–74, esp. 73–74 (assessment of Riza Shah).
[59] On Iran's "tribal problem," see Stephanie Cronin, *Tribal Politics in Iran: Rural Conflict and the New State, 1921–1941* (London: Routledge, 2007), 16–39.
[60] Abrahamian, *Modern Iran*, 97–99; Ansari, *Modern Iran*, 72–73.
[61] On the events leading to his fall in 1979, see Ansari, *Modern Iran*, 195–211.
[62] Mohammad Gholi Majd, *Iran under Allied Occupation in World War II* (Lanham, MD: University Press of America, 2016), 473–76 (Khurasan), 689–91 (estimate of deaths; but note that Majd's figures appear to be excessive and based on extrapolations).
[63] E-mail to author, 5 March 2018.

Iran's borders,[64] *Mujahidin-i Khalq* (MEK) in the west,[65] a terrorist group supported first by Saddam Hussein, and presently supported by the United States; and *Jundallah*, "Army of God," in Pakistani Baluchistan[66] – are reminders of the political vulnerabilities of the Shi'i republic.

Once the twin crises of the Shi'i republic's tumultuous birth and the "Imposed War" (Iran-Iraq War; 1980–88) receded, the government focused on pressing internal problems. Non-Shi'a Iranians (Zoroastrians, Christians, Jews, and Sunnis) had loyally served alongside their Shi'i brethren in the "sacred defense" (*difa'-i muqaddas*), a fact proudly emphasized by interlocutors at Jam. Indeed, in a 2015/16 journal interview, Haji Qazi Sharaf al-Din Jami al-Ahmadi, the administrator of Ahmad-i Jam's shrine and the prayer leader (*imam-jum'a*) for the Sunnis of Turbat-i Jam (and environs), extolled the sacrifices of the region's Sunnis.[67]

As Ali Ansari has demonstrated, the construction of Iranian nationalism predates the founding of the Islamic Republic, which extended or modified Pahlawi-era nationalist rhetoric. Reviving memories of Iranian empire (*Iranshahr*), and replacing Shi'a narratives with Iranian narratives, proved useful to the Islamic Republic.[68] Loyalty to the Shi'i republic by religious minorities is not extraordinary.[69] Nonsubscribers to Ayatollah Khomeini's vision of Islamic government participated in Iran's Revolution.[70] Jews, for instance, joined the 1979 Revolution; many Iranian Jews (today) harbor firm anti-Zionist views and insist they would support Iran over Israel in

---

[64] William Lowther and C. Freeman, "US Funds Terror Groups to Sow Chaos in Iran," *Daily Telegraph* (25 February 2007); Shireen Hunter, *Iran's Foreign Policy in the Post-Soviet Era* (Santa Barbara, CA: Praeger, 2010), 148–51.

[65] Designated as "Foreign Terrorist Organization" (FTO), 8 October 1997. U.S. State Department, *Country Reports on Terrorism 2011* (Washington, DC, July 2012), 248–50. MEK was delisted as a FTO in 2012 by anti-Iran fanatics in the Republican Party *and* Democratic Party seeking to use MEK's terrorists against the Islamic Republic of Iran. On Donald Trump and Muhammad bin Salman exacerbating Shi'i-Sunni relations and Saudi-Iran rivalries, see Dilip Hiro, *Cold War in the Islamic World: Saudi Arabia, Iran, and the Struggle for Supremacy* (Oxford: Oxford University Press, 2018), 313–49.

[66] On *Jundallah*, see R. C. Elling, *Minorities in Iran* (New York: Palgrave, 2013), et passim.

[67] Anonymous, "Musahaba ba [Interview with] Mawlana Sharaf al-Din Jami al-Ahmadi," *Faslnamah-yi Habl al-matin* 4 (Winter 1394/2015f.): 8–16, 10.

[68] Ali M. Ansari, *The Politics of Nationalism in Modern Iran* (Cambridge: Cambridge University Press, 2012), esp. 230–49 and 295–300.

[69] Sunnis (as Muslims) are not legally a "religious minority." Many Sunnis support the Government of the Islamic Republic of Iran because they fear instability and upheaval as in Afghanistan, Iraq, Syria, Libya, and Egypt. Lessons learned: "Arab Springs" and "preemptive wars" by the USA inevitably lead to social and political catastrophes.

[70] Said Amir Arjomand, *The Turban for the Crown* (New York: Oxford University Press, 1988), 103–14.

The Islamic Republic

a war.[71] Iranian national identities and political allegiances cannot be readily pigeonholed.

Rewarding Sunnis became a critical political imperative for the Islamic Republic, and connected to initiatives to stabilize Iran's borderlands in the face of Wahhabi and CIA aggressions. A preponderance of Iran's Sunnis live on Iran's peripheries. Sistan and Baluchistan province is restive. It has socioeconomic infirmities that are exploited by Wahhabi terrorist entities operating from Pakistan. The most radicalized madrasas of Pakistan are still funded by Saudi Arabia – feeders for *Lashkar-i Tayba*, *Tehrik-i Taliban-i Pakistan*, etc. – and strategically emplaced along Iran's borders, bricks in Saudi Arabia's "Sunni Wall."[72] With bloody insurgencies raging concurrently in Iraq and Afghanistan, the United States "opted for regime change through destabilization and began, among other things, encouraging Iran's ethnic and religious minorities, especially in Kurdistan, Sistan, and Baluchistan, to rebel against Tehran. In this effort, the United States was supported by Saudi Arabia and Pakistan."[73] State-sponsored terrorist groups committed heinous acts of violence against Iranian civilians and soldiers.

The Jam region is stable and protected by the Islamic Revolutionary Guard Corps. But Tehran frets that the Wahhabi malady prevalent in Afghanistan and Pakistan will cross Iran's borders and infect its Sunni population.[74] Rasmus Elling has shown that destabilization activities by foreign powers, which Tehran calls "the dirty hands of disorder" (stoking divisions within ethnic communities on Iran's borders),

---

[71] Daniel Tsadik, "Identity among the Jews of Iran," in *Iran Facing Others*, ed. Abbas Amanat and Farzin Vejdani (New York: Palgrave, 2012), 221–44. On the legal statuses and treatments of religious communities, see Eliz Sanasarian, *Religious Minorities in Iran* (Cambridge: Cambridge University Press, 2004).

[72] Vali Nasr, "The Rise of Sunni Militancy in Pakistan: The Changing Role of Islamism and the Ulama in Society and Politics," *Modern Asian Studies* 34/1 (2000): 139–80, 157; on madrasas in Baluchistan, see Stéphane Dudoignon, *The Baluch, Sunnism and the State in Iran: From Tribal to Global* (Oxford: Oxford University Press, 2017), et passim.

[73] Hunter, *Iran's Foreign Policy*, 149. On Saudi and Pakistani support for Baluch militants, see Dudoignon, *Baluch*, 1–3.

[74] On 8 September 2017, at Turbat-i Jam, I spoke with a visitor from Rahmat-Abad, an Iranian village near the Afghan border. My informant's strident views on Sufi shrines, pilgrimages, and the Shiʻa were closer to the views I had heard in Afghanistan, Pakistan, and Syria from radicals than from Iranian Sunnis. Even Mutasim Agha Jan, the former Taliban minister and Quetta Shura member with whom I met on 18 October 2019 in Herat, offered nuanced views on *ziyarat*. I saw him on 20 October 2019 at the shrine of ʻAbdullah Ansari when he visited for *ziyarat* – putting words to practice. The Wahhabi plague is a clear and present danger along Iran's eastern borders.

spurred the government to strengthen Islamic and nationalistic bonds of unity.[75]

A central pillar in strengthening nationalistic bonds of unity (and in "pacifying" restive Sunni regions like Sistan and Baluchistan) is the lavishing of state funds on Sunni communities and Sunni institutions. Regions like Jam, Taybad, and Khwaf benefited from Tehran's largesse. State patronage for Islamic institutions (Sunni and Shiʻi), and Iran's accepted non-Muslim faiths – Judaism, Christianity, and Zoroastrianism – makes sense to an ancient civilization that is justifiably proud of its rich cultural heritages.[76] Financial and technical support from Tehran for Sunni institutions, and by extension to the Sunni communities that depend on, study at, utilize, and respect those institutions (mosques, shrines, and seminaries), makes for sensible security policy. Furthermore, it is sensible to funnel Iranian students into Sunni madrasas in Iran that are supervised by the Islamic Republic's educational bureaucracies, rather than allowing them to travel overseas to study, where they will become radicalized by Wahhabi ideologies.

It is from this context that official support for Ahmad-i Jam's shrine emerged. While "the dirty hands of disorder" contributed to the renaissance at Ahmad-i Jam's shrine, financial support also comes from Ahmad-i Jam's descendants and residents of Jam province.[77] There has been a renaissance of Ahmad's saint cult, which is possibly tied to a nebulous "Sunni revival" around the Islamic world. It is certainly connected to improved prosperity in Khurasan, specifically, Turbat-i Jam. Despite the just complaints of Iranians about the abysmal state of the Iranian economy – exacerbated today by the unilateral imposition of sanctions by the Trump administration – the economy of Jam (city and district) has improved considerably since 1979. Jam district's prosperity is manifest; its bazaars are stocked with locally produced comestibles.[78]

---

[75] Elling, *Minorities*, 101–7.

[76] I have visited pre-Islamic, Zoroastrian, Jewish, Christian, Shiʻa, and Sunni spiritual and sepulchral sites throughout Iran since 1388/2009. In spring 1398/2019, I visited Qum, Kashan, Isfahan, Shiraz, Persepolis, Pasargadae, and Yazd – and photographed and documented conditions at sites. *Miras-i Farangi* is responsible for protecting national heritages (www.mcth.ir/, accessed 13 June 2020).

[77] Interlocutors insist the private-to-public funds ratio is strongly in favor of donations by Sunnis, but refused to offer proof. In fairness, *Miras-i Farangi* also refused to reveal their expenditures, which are assuredly considerable.

[78] Even during the long drought – alleviated by the rainfalls and snowfalls of 2018/19 and 2019/20 – agricultural production in Jam was stellar.

The Islamic Republic

Five Sunni seminaries operate in Turbat-i Jam: the Hawza-yi ʿilmiyya Ahmadiyya (for males) is integral to the shrine (see Table 5.1, § XI); the Hawza-yi ʿilmiyya Hibat al-Rahman (for females) is sponsored by the Jami shrine but located outside the shrine's confines (Table 5.1, § XII); Hawza-yi ʿilmiyya Fakhr al-Mudarris, Hawza-yi ʿilmiyya Imam Abu Hanifa, and Hawza-yi ʿilmiyya Sadiqiyya. Sadiqiyya, founded 1380/2001, is the largest Sunni college in Turbat-i Jam, but it is small relative to the seminaries at Khwaf, Taybad, and Zahedan. Zahedan, the capital of Baluchistan and Sistan province, has been the epicenter of Baluch nationalist agitation since the Pahlawi period.[79]

Sharaf al-Din Jami al-Ahmadi, popularly called Haji Qazi, was born in Turbat-i Jam in 1319/1940. He was the principal for the Hawza-yi ʿilmiyya Ahmadiyya until his son, Husayn Jami, assumed the post in Autumn 1396/2017. Haji Qazi inherited posts that had been held by his father and grandfather.[80] He is an intermediary between the shrine and local, provincial, and national governments. Haji Qazi, as Friday prayer leader for the Sunnis of Jam, represents the city and its vicinities in an indeterminable manner. This possibly conflicts with the responsibilities of the elected mayor (*shahardar*).[81] The Jamis have previously held the mayoralty. The political activism of the shrine's leadership is limited to making the indispensable public utterances in support of the government and common decency; for example, the Sunnis of Jam unite with their Shiʿi brethren in condemning outrages by al-Qaʿida, ISIS, and Baluchi terrorists, as evinced by the joint statements published by Shiʿi and Sunni leaders of Iranian Khurasan.

---

[79] Elling, *Minorities*, 41, 49.   [80] "Musahaba ba," 8–16.
[81] The current mayor, Sayyid ʿAli Husayni, is a Twelver Shiʿa, elected in 1396/2017 with robust Sunni support.

PLATE 1 Shrine at the cusp of the Iranian Revolution, 1977.
Courtesy of Warwick Ball

PLATE 2 Shrine at the cusp of the Iranian Revolution, 1977.
Courtesy of Warwick Ball

PLATE 3 L–R: Kirmani Mosque, *iwan*, and Firuzshah's Dome. Ahmad-i Jam is buried immediately before the portal

PLATE 4 Ahmad-i Jam's tomb, at entrance to portico (autumn 2017)

PLATE 5 Ahmad-i Jam's tomb, pictured from above (winter 2011/12)

PLATE 6 Squinch in corner of the *gunbad*. The inscription praising Kart *malik* Muʿizz al-Din runs around the entire chamber

PLATE 7 Further views of the inscription and artwork inside the *gunbad*

PLATE 8 Crown of the *gunbad*

PLATE 9 Interior of the Masjid-i ʿatiq. Restored sections can be seen. Lines from the Victory verse (Q48:1–6) are on stucco frieze, but badly damaged. Lines refer to *malik* Ghiyath al-Din Kart's victory over the Chaghatay Mongols

PLATE 10 Interior of Masjid-i ʿatiq. Closer view of the damaged inscription

PLATE 11 Interior of Masjid-i ʿatiq. One of the original arches that survived is to the left; a restored arch is to its right

PLATE 12 Section of interior of Gunbad-i Safid. Courtesy of Bernard O'Kane

PLATE 13 Prayer niche (*mihrab*) inside the Masjid-i Kirmani

PLATE 14 Safavid-era inscription to the *iwan* (funded by Shah ʿAbbas I, Safavi)

PLATE 15 Gunbad-i Firuzshah and classic Timurid tilework

PLATE 16 Gunbad-i Firuzshah. The ladder is against the Hawza-yi 'ilmiyya Ahmadiyya. The seminary is situated where the Madrasa-i Firuzshah would have been

PLATE 17 Section of interior of Masjid-i jamiʿ-i naw. Courtesy of Bernard O'Kane

PLATE 18 Hawza-yi 'ilmiyya Ahmadiyya, its courtyard, and top of Gunbad-i Firuzshah, seen from atop the *iwan*

PLATE 19 Ahmad-i Jam (the Furious Elephant) watching over young Akbar the Great. Courtesy of Staatsbibliothek zu Berlin, Preussischer Kulturbesitz, Libr. Pict. A117, fol. 15a

PLATE 20 Hamida Banu Bigum bt. 'Ali Akbar Jami. Wikipedia Commons

Part III

The Shrine

5

Setting, Architecture, and Administration

The physical setting for Ahmad-i Jam's shrine is sketched. The shrine lay in the middle of a perilous tract of Greater Iran (*Iranshahr*), one that witnessed the crisscrossing of armies from Europe and Asia. Paradoxically, while post-Mongol Khurasan lay in ruins, the shrine's first major edifice was erected in 633/1236. Consequent to Ilkhanid-, Kartid-, and Timurid-period benefactions, an eclectic architectural ensemble characterized the shrine, which became a shrine *complex*. The architectural contours were frozen (*ca.* 844–46/1440–43). Recent developments – facilitated partly by the Islamic Republic of Iran – have unfrozen the architectural contours. The architectural ensemble and the administration of Ahmad-i Jam's shrine are described.

KHURASAN

The histories of Ahmad-i Jam's shrine and saint cult, and the doctrines and practices of Jami Sufis (a subset of the cult – and there are subsets of mystical groups; see Chapter 9), were shaped by the religious and political currents that wafted through the shrine's/cult's catchment area: Khurasan, broadly; but specifically, the tract situated between Nishapur and Balkh. The shrine, in its turn, shaped the social, political, and economic histories of its catchment area (see also Chapter 6).

Geographical Khurasan is a narrow band whose ill-defined boundaries stretch from the southeastern littoral of the Caspian Sea to the Hindu Kush. Cultural Khurasan, which was shaped by Iranian languages and cultures, extended into Transoxiana (Turkmenistan and Uzbekistan). The tract is bounded in the north by the River Oxus (Amu Darya, Jayhun) and the Black Sands desert (Qara-Qum); and in the southwest and south by the Dasht-i Kawir and Dasht-i Lut salt deserts; with Quhistan, Sistan, Ghur, and Bamiyan forming the south and the southeast (see Maps 1 and 2). Khurasan is an arid region, yet water originating in mountain ranges is plentiful. Water tables are ingeniously tapped through subterranean canals (*qanat, kariz*) that deliver water miles away from the source. Irrigation networks comprising *qanat*s, channels (*juy*), canals (*nahr*), dams (*band*), sluices (*qulb, juy-bar*), and timers (*natarah*) control and direct waters from underground reservoirs; and from arterial waterways like the Herat River (Hari Rud), Bird River (Murghab), and the Oxus before they debouch in the deserts of Iran or Central Asia. Absent sensible management of Khurasan's waters, food insecurity will prevail. Famines, a by-product of war, have ravaged the region. Khurasan's reputation as one of Iran's granaries is testament to the resourcefulness of the region's multifarious peoples.[1]

Armies from East and West have for ages crisscrossed Khurasan on marches to conquer India, China, or Persia. Furthermore, Khurasan's agricultural, commercial, and pastoral wealth – stored gold, silver, pelts, textiles, grains, fruits, vegetables, dairy, and meats – attracted predators. Migrations of Turkic peoples from Inner Asia, with their four-footers, frequently brought socioeconomic instabilities and violence. The Mongols were the most ruthless military to have marched through Khurasan. Lord Curzon's observation, "[m]ore persons have probably died a violent death in Khorasan than in any other territory of equal size in Asia,"[2] is a fair assessment.

DISTRICT OF JAM AND CITY OF TURBAT-I JAM

Turbat-i Jam, "the sepulcher of [Shaykh Ahmad of] Jam," is approximately 100 mi./160 km equidistant from the Shi'a shrine city of Mashhad; and the medieval capital of Khurasan, Herat. The northern border between Iran and Afghanistan is demarcated by the Hari Rud, roughly 25 mi/40 km east of Turbat-i Jam. The town is situated on the plains (*dasht*) of Jam district

---

[1] For stellar descriptions of Khurasan's geography and peoples, see Bosworth, *Ghaznavids*, 145–52; and Elton Daniel, *The Political and Social History of Khurasan under Abbasid Rule, 747–820* (Minneapolis, MN, and Chicago, IL: Bibliotheca Islamica, 1979), 13–24.

[2] Curzon, *Persia*, 1:8.

(*shahristan*).³ The Shah Nishin mountain range traverses north and northeast of the plains; and the Miyan-i Jam mountain range, which boasts four snowcapped peaks, runs west and northwest. The Jam River (Jam Rud), which is nourished by multiple sources in the northwest, passes north and east of Turbat-i Jam on its hasteless journey to merge with the Hari Rud. Streams from the Shah Nishin mountains debouch into the Jam Rud. A network of springs, channels, subterranean canals, deep wells, and shallow wells combine to form an irrigation network. The network has enabled the region to withstand the droughts to which Khurasan is prone. Severe drought gripped the land until winter 2018/19, when rainfalls and snowfalls offered relief. Winter 2019/20 was also quite wet.

Fariman, Taybad, Khwaf, and Turbat-i Haydariyya are four major towns encircling Turbat-i Jam, and closely connected to it historically and economically. Thirteen village agglomerations (*dihistan*s) and hundreds of villages (*dih, abad*) sprinkle the piedmonts and plains. There are many abandoned settlements, reflecting shifts in agricultural practices and water resources. Jam is an administrative subdivision of Khurasan-i Rizawi province (*ustan*); the province is one of the three provinces carved out of historical Khurasan. The balance of Khurasan was lost to Afghanistan and Turkmenistan.

TRAVEL REPORTS ON JAM

Hamdallah Mustawfi described Turbat-i Jam (*ca.* 1340) as a "medium-sized town, with nearly 200 villages of its dependencies. There are many gardens, with much fruit. Water, for both the town and district, is got from underground channels."⁴ The eighth/fourteenth-century globetrotter, Ibn Battuta, says of Jam: "a place of middling size, pretty, with orchards and trees, abundance of springs, and flowing streams ... Most of its trees are mulberries, and silk is to be had there in quantities."⁵ The descriptions, in the main, hold true. Rice, wheat, barley, potatoes, vegetables, fruits – apricots, apples, pomegranates, melons (*kharbuza*), and watermelons (*hinduwana*) – and cotton (*pamba*) are cultivated in Jam.

---

[3] In medieval times, Jam region was termed province (*wilayat*), but today it is called a sub-province or district (*shahristan*). In modern terminology, *ustan* means province.
[4] Hamd-Allah Mustawfi, *Nuzhat al-Qulub* (London: Brill, 1915), 153–54; Hamd-Allah Mustawfi, *The Geographical Part of the Nuzhat al-Qulub*, trans. Guy Le Strange (Leiden: Brill, 1919), 151–52.
[5] Ibn Battuta, *Travels*, 3:580.

James B. Fraser, traveling through Khurasan in 1821 and 1822, describes the Jam region as "fertile and well peopled."[6] The Russian consul, Nicholas de Khanikoff (Nikolai Khanykov; 1819–78), writing of his travels in 1858 and 1859, discusses components of the shrine, but offers little information about the Jam region, noticing only the continuing influence of Ahmad-i Jam's heirs.[7] Joseph Ferrier (1811–86), a French officer traveling in Khurasan in the 1840s, describes Turbat-i Jam as a small town with 800 houses "surrounded by gardens and cultivation."[8] The British political agent, Sir Charles Yate (1849–1940), who traveled through Khurasan between 1893 and 1896, claims that Jam comprised 250 houses and 4,000 families of the "tribe" of Jami who were "all cultivators." The region had many gardens and produced fruits. The Jami families had no power because "the tribe were under the control of the governor."[9] A scribe accompanying a Qajar princeling claims that only 20 villages of Jam province's 350 villages were flourishing in Shawwal 1299/June 1882 and its irrigation canals were in disrepair. Turbat-i Jam's citadel (*qal'a*) then stood (but no longer); it housed shops and was surrounded by thriving orchards and vineyards.[10]

Estimates by Ferrier and Yate of around 800 and 250 houses, respectively, reveal a huge decline in Jam's population in the half-century between 1845 and 1895. The travel report of 20 villages, if accurate, indicates that the socioeconomic deterioration of this section of Khurasan had become severe. Under the Qajars, lands remained in the hands of tribes and large landholders, and exploitation of peasants was the norm.[11] Titles to private lands, even estates held in trusts (waqf), were usurped. When socioeconomic conditions deteriorated in a particular region, peasants migrated to cities or other agricultural regions in search of labor or share-cropping opportunities. In 1821/22, the Imam Riza shrine (now the largest estate holder in Khurasan) saw its rental and agricultural revenues from waqfs

---

[6] J. B. Fraser, *Narrative of a Journey into Khorasan* (New Delhi: Oxford University Press, 1984 [reprint of 1825 ed.]), appendix B, p. 39.

[7] Nicholas de Khanikoff, *Mémoire sur la partie méridionale de l'Asie centrale* (Paris: Imprimerie de L. Martinet, 1861), 116–19.

[8] J. P. Ferrier, *Caravan Journeys and Wanderings in Persia, Afghanistan, Turkistan and Beloochistan*, trans. W. Jesse (London: John Murray, 1856), 137.

[9] C. E. Yate, *Khurasan and Sistan* (Edinburgh: William Blackwood, 1900), 36–37.

[10] Muhammad 'Ali Munshi, *Safarnamah-yi Rukn al-Dawla*, ed. Muhammad Gulban (Tehran: Intisharat-i sahr, 1977), 100.

[11] See, generally, A. K. S. Lambton, *Landlord and Peasant in Persia: A Study of Land Tenure and Revenue Administration* (London: I.B. Tauris, 1991), 129–77.

decline by around 80 percent,[12] but by approximately 1892, its revenues had measurably improved,[13] reflecting the social and economic vicissitudes of this section of Khurasan. Physical security – from Turcoman slave raiders and predatory tribes – did not to improve in the Iran-Afghanistan borderlands until Riza Shah Pahlawi (r. 1924–41) harshly suppressed recalcitrant tribes. According to Donald Wilber, Turbat-i Jam in 1937 was a "small village."[14]

DEMOGRAPHICS

The first census of the Pahlawi era (1924–79), held 1335/1956, shows 99,464 people in the Jam *region*. Between 1345/1966 and 1395/2016, Turbat-i Jam's population increased from 13,958 to 100,449. The ethnically diverse population of the *shahristan* of Jam is said to divide equally between Twelver Shi'a and Sunnis (dominantly Hanafi, with possibly some Shafi'i). Census data record only confessional minorities, that is, Zoroastrians, Christians, and Jews.[15] Iran's Sunnis are lumped together with Shi'a under "Muslim." Local newspapers and interlocutors aver that *ahl-i sunnat* ("people of the traditional path") are the majority, and proffer estimates of the Sunni population from 60 to 70 percent. Sunni-Shi'a sectarianism is not pronounced. In 1396/2017, Turbat-i Jam elected the current mayor, who is Twelver Shi'a, which will not have happened without robust Sunni support.

The population of the district (*shahristan*) of Jam is 267,671. Turbat-i Jam has 100,449 denizens.[16] The population of Khurasan-i Rizawi is 6,434,501.[17] Jam *shahristan*'s population was dominantly Sunni until the Iran-Iraq War (1980–88), when Iranians migrated from the frontline provinces of Azarbayjan, Ilam, Kermanshah, Khuzistan, and Kurdistan to regions farthest from Iraqi bombings, missiles, and chemical attacks. The Soviet occupation of Afghanistan (1979–89) generated influxes of refugees: mostly (Sunni) Tajiks and Turks, and (mostly Twelver Shi'a but some Isma'ili Shi'a)

---

[12] Fraser, *Khorasan*, 454–55. The Mashhad shrine owns properties across Iran; its annual revenues are therefore not reflective of economic conditions in Khurasan alone.
[13] Curzon, *Persia*, 2:489. Same caveat as above.
[14] Donald Wilber, *The Architecture of Islamic Iran: The Il Khanid Period* (Princeton, NJ: Princeton University Press, 1955), 174.
[15] *Iran Statistical Yearbook 1395 [2016–17]* (Tehran: Statistical Center of Iran, 1398/2019), p. 163, table 3.17, www.amar.org.ir/english (accessed 13 June 2020).
[16] Ibid., 155, table 3.10.   [17] Ibid., 172, table 3.24.

98   Setting, Architecture, and Administration

Hazaras; whereas most Pashtuns migrated to Pakistan to merge with its indigenous (Sunni) Pashtuns.

Baluchs and Hazaras had lived in this section of Khurasan from before the Soviet invasion.[18] Charles Yate recorded the presence of Turkic peoples called "Timuris" who had been forcibly settled in Khurasan by Temür.[19] Most Afghans were repatriated consequent to bilateral agreements between Iran and Hamid Karzai's government; nonetheless, Afghans continue to arrive or to remain in Iran, legally or illegally. Iran's Afghan population swelled from 1,211,171 (1385/2006 census) to 1,452,513 (1390/2011 census), and is presently given as 1,583,979 (1395/2016 census).[20] Afghans comprise around 90 percent of all noncitizen residents in Iran (there are 1,759,448 noncitizens in an overall population of 79,926,270). Khurasan-i Rizawi is home to 219,442 Afghan citizens, most of whom live in urban areas.[21]

THE SHRINE

The shrine complex's magnificent landscaped features demarcated in Figure 5.1 were analyzed by Vahid Nattaj and Zohreh Sanaati.[22] Roman numerals VII, X, and XI were added to Figure 5.1 by this author. They comport with edifices identified in Table 5.1, a summary of building developments at the shrine complex. "Section" in Table 5.1 (e.g., § IIIa, § VII, etc.) refers to components of the complex. Roman numerals correspond with those in Figure 5.1 and/or Figure 5.3. The latter is a schematic from 1938 that was utilized by Lisa Golombek in her article in *Iran* (1971).[23] Roman numerals I to VIII correspond to the numerals she used in her discussions on shrine edifices; and in my article in *Iran* (2016),[24] where Golombek's chronology of architectural developments was updated.

The components are discussed below.

Ahmad-i Jam's shrine complex is located in the northeast quadrant of Turbat-i Jam. Developments at the shrine in the Kartid and Timurid eras,

---

[18] Ferrier, *Caravan*, 137.
[19] Yate, *Khurasan*, 38. "Timuri" and "'Arab-Timuri" persist in Iran as distinct peoples.
[20] *Iran Statistical Yearbook 1395*, p. 171, table 3.22.   [21] Ibid., 172, table 3.24.
[22] V. H. Nattaj and Z. Sanaati, "Recognition of the Persian Garden Plan in Sheikh Ahmad-e Jam Complex," *Manzar* 11/46 (Spring 2019): 6–13.
[23] See Golombek, "The Chronology of Turbat-i Shaykh Jam." As Lisa Golombek reminded this author (email of 5 November 2019), the original 1938 map by John McCool has "many errors." Figure 5.1, drawn by Miras-i Farhangi, should be precise.
[24] See Mahendrarajah, "Revised."

The Shrine

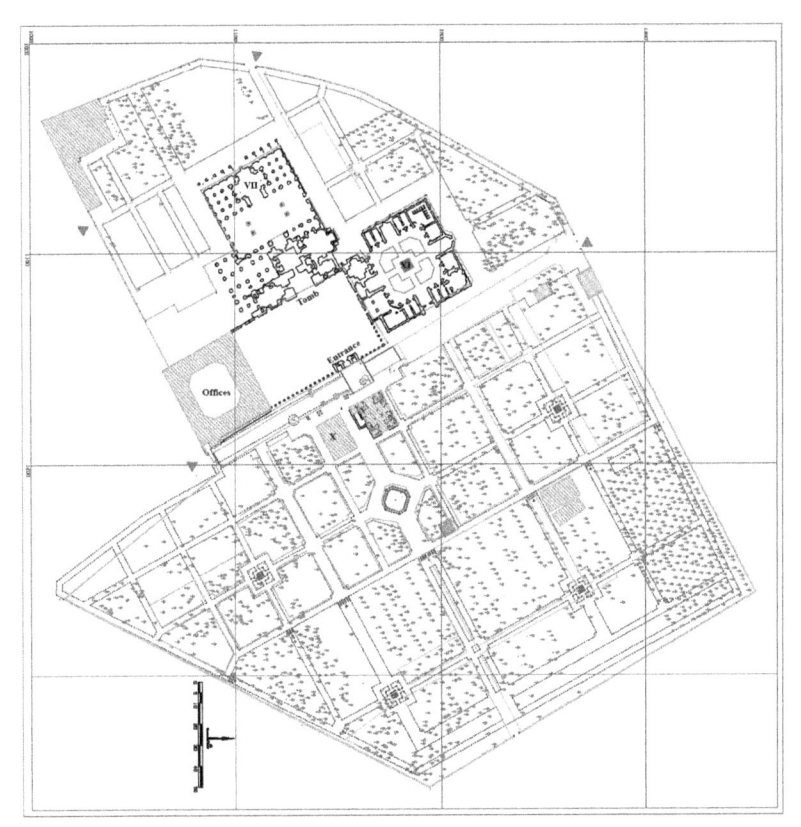

FIGURE 5.1 Schematic of the shrine complex and Ahmad-i Jam Park
Courtesy of Miras-i Farhangi, Islamic Republic of Iran

and increased pilgrim traffic, shaped the shrine's immediate vicinities. Vendors, tailors, smiths, carters, guesthouses, and eateries burgeoned. The village of Maʿd-Abad was transformed into an important and sizeable town as the shrine morphed into a shrine complex, and Maʿd-Abad and Turbat-i Jam merged and became a waystation between Herat and Mashhad.

The shrine of Shaykh al-Islam Ahmad-i Jam "has a complex building history,"[25] an understatement considering the layers still being uncovered by Iranian preservationists. From humble origins – a bare tumulus – burgeoned a resplendent shrine complex of eclectic architectural and artistic

---

[25] Bernard O'Kane, *Timurid Architecture in Khurusan* (Costa Mesa, CA: Mazda Publishers), 219.

TABLE 5.1 Major architectural components of the shrine complex

Section	Component	Date	Sponsor/comments
§ I	*Gunbad* (dome-chamber) • Decorations and inscriptions	Built 633/1236 Added 763/1361f.	Original sponsor: unknown Muʿizz al-Din Kart
§ II	Masjid-i ʿatiq (Old Mosque) • Being rebuilt from ruins	Work initiated *ca.* 720/1320f.; concluded 733/1333 Restoration in advanced stage in AHS 1396/2017–18	Ghiyath al-Din Kart • Private and public funds
§ IIIa	*Iwan* (portal) • Mosaic faience decoration	Work initiated *ca.* 751/1350f.; ended *ca.* 763/1361f. Sponsored in 1022/1613f.	Self-funded Shah ʿAbbas I (Safavid)
§ IIIb-c	Khanaqah-i saracha (Small Hospice)	Built before 736/1335f. (not extant)	Unknown
§ IIIb-c	Madrasa-i Faryumadi (Faryumadi College)	Built between 706/1316 and 736/1336 (probably between 729/1329 and 736/1336; not extant)	ʿAlaʾ al-Din Faryumadi (Ilkhanid vizier)
§ IVa	Gunbad-i Safid (White Dome)	Built in 728/1328	Ghiyath al-Din Kart
§ IVb	Masjid-i Kirmani (Kirmani Mosque)	Built in 728/1328	Ghiyath al-Din Kart
§ V	Two unnamed *khanaqah*s	Built *ca.* 783/1381 (operated until at least 929/1523, but are no longer extant)	Temür (Tamerlane)
§ VIa	Gunbad-i Firuzshahi (Firuzshah's Dome)	Built between 844–46/1440–43	Jalal al-Din Firuzshah (Timurid amir)
§ VIb	Vestibule	N/A	Small oratory for prayer?

§ VIc	Madrasa-i Firuzshahi (seminary)	Built between 844–46/1440–43 (not extant)	Jalal al-Din Firuzshah (The new seminary, § XI, is where Firuzshah's Seminary was located)
§ VII	Masjid-i jami'-i naw (New Mosque)	Built between 844–46/1440–43	Jalal al-Din Firuzshah
§ VIII	Madrasa-i Amir Shah-Malik (seminary)	Built before 822/1419f. (not extant)	Amir Shah-Malik (Timurid amir)
§ IX	Ab-i anbar (cistern)	Built in 1010/1601f. (extant, but no longer in use)	Firuz-Jang b. Husayn (Safavid)
§ X	Masjid-i zir-i zamin (aka Masjid-i zamistan) (Underground Mosque, aka Winter Mosque); prayer space (musalla) on roof of mosque is called the Masjid-i tabistan (Summer Mosque)	Built in AHS 1357/1978	Self-funded (Pahlawi-era)
§ XI	Hawza-yi 'Ilmiyya Ahmadiyya (seminary for males)	Built in AHS 1389/2010	Self-funded. Colloquially called "Madrasa-yi Firuzshahi"
§ XII	Hawza-yi 'ilmiyya Hibat al-Rahman (seminary for females)	Founded AHS 1392/2013	Self-funded. In the southwest corner of the shrine (not depicted in Figure 5.1)
§ XIII	Kitabkhana-yi Mazar-i Shaykh al-Islam Ahmad-i Jam (public library)	In operation at current location since 2018	Self-funded. Located south of the shrine (not depicted)

styles, which range from Ilkhanid-era technologies and designs, to Safavid-period decorative flourishes.[26]

At its political zenith in the medieval period, the shrine complex was honored by sultans, viziers, amirs, and officials: Shams al-Din Kart, Ghiyath al-Din Kart, Temür, Shah-Rukh b. Temür, Miranshah b. Temür, and Mughals Humayun and his wife, Hamida Banu Bigum. When Charles Yates visited, however, "the whole place looked dirty and deserted, and the musjid [mosque], corridors, and buildings around were mostly in a state of ruin."[27] Robert Byron's remarks encapsulate the decline of town and shrine: "The shrine there was disappointing. So was our lunch."[28] Warwick Ball's photographs of 7 July 1977 memorialize the shrine's condition at the cusp of the 1978–79 Iranian Revolution (Plates 1–2).

No structures have been built above or immediately near Ahmad's grave (see Plate 3),[29] which remains exposed to the elements, shaded by a pistachio tree, and protected by a paneled fence (Plates 4–5). There were no developments around Ahmad-i Jam's tumulus for one century, but there was a Sufi hospice (*khanaqah*) nearby, occupied initially by Ahmad's son, Shams al-Din Mutahhar, and subsequently by Ahmad-i Jam's granddaughter, Hibat al-Rahman bt. Burhan al-Din Nasr b. Ahmad, and grandson, Qutb al-Din Muhammad b. Shams al-Din Mutahhar. Hibat al-Rahman was a continuator of Ahmad's legacy and rests beside him. A madrasa at the shrine dedicated to educating women is named in her honor.

---

[26] Wilber, *Architecture*, 174; Lisa Golombek and Donald Wilber, *The Timurid Architecture of Iran and Turan*, 2 vols. (Princeton, NJ: Princeton University Press, 1988); Golombek, "Chronology"; O'Kane, *Timurid Architecture*; Bernard O'Kane, "Timurid Architecture in Khurasan" (PhD diss., University of Edinburgh, 1982); Bernard O'Kane, "Taybad, Turbat-i Jam and Timurid Vaulting," *Iran* 17 (1979): 87–104; Bernard O'Kane, "Natanz and Turbat-i Jam: New Light on Fourteenth-Century Iranian Stucco," *Studia Iranica* 21 (1992): 85–92; and Faramarz Sabr Muqaddam, *Mazar-i Shaykh Ahmad-i Jam* (Turbat-i Jam: Nashr-i sunbalah, 1383/2004).

[27] Yate, *Khurasan*, 37.

[28] Robert Byron, *The Road to Oxiana* (London: Pimlico, 2004), 282. Byron's photographs are at Archnet (https://archnet.org/), a partnership of the Aga Khan Trust for Culture and Aga Khan Documentation Center, MIT Libraries.

[29] This could be responsive to a hadith proscribing construction: "The Messenger of Allah prohibited plastering graves, writing on them, building over them, and treading on them." *Jami' al-Tirmidhi*, hadith # 1052. On the perceived origins of Islamic funerary architecture, see Oleg Grabar, "The Earliest Islamic Commemorative Structures, Notes and Documents," *Ars Orientalis* 6 (1966): 7–46; but cf. Christopher S. Taylor, "Reevaluating the Shi'i Role in the Development of Monumental Islamic Funerary," *Muqarnas* 9 (1992): 1–10.

The Architectural Ensemble

THE ARCHITECTURAL ENSEMBLE

The figures below should orientate the reader. Figure 5.2 is a computer-generated overview prepared by Miras-i Farhangi. To the right is the madrasa, the Hawza-yi ʿilmiyya Ahmadiyya. The grand *iwan* behind Ahmad's tomb and the *gunbad* were not included in the overview as both would have obscured views of the Masjid-i ʿatiq and Masjid-i jamiʿ-i naw. The columns to the left indicate remnants of the Masjid-i ʿatiq, which has now mostly been reconstructed. The overview shows how the new seminary, Hawza-yi ʿilmiyya Ahmadiyya, is integrated with the historical structures.

The first building erected at the shrine is the *gunbad* (dome-chamber). It sits atop a square-walled room (Table 5.1, § I). Construction began in Shawwal 633/June–July 1236; the building's sponsor's identity is unclear.[30] The dust-colored and unimposing exterior belies the *gunbad*'s later centrality to the shrine complex, where it was connected on four sides to other edifices. The center of the *gunbad* is approximately twenty yards behind the tumulus. The *gunbad* is visible in Figure 5.5, a schematic of the complex's length as seen from the east. It shows, left to right, the New Mosque and courtyard, the "hump" of the *gunbad* behind the *iwan*, outline of the Kirmani Mosque, and the Firuzshah Dome in the far background.

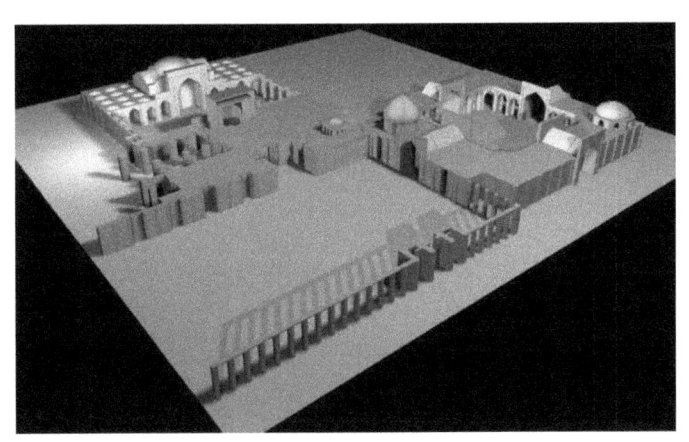

FIGURE 5.2 Early twenty-first-century 3D image of the shrine complex
Courtesy of Miras-i Farhangi, Islamic Republic of Iran

---

[30] See discussion in Mahendrarajah, "Revised," 119–22.

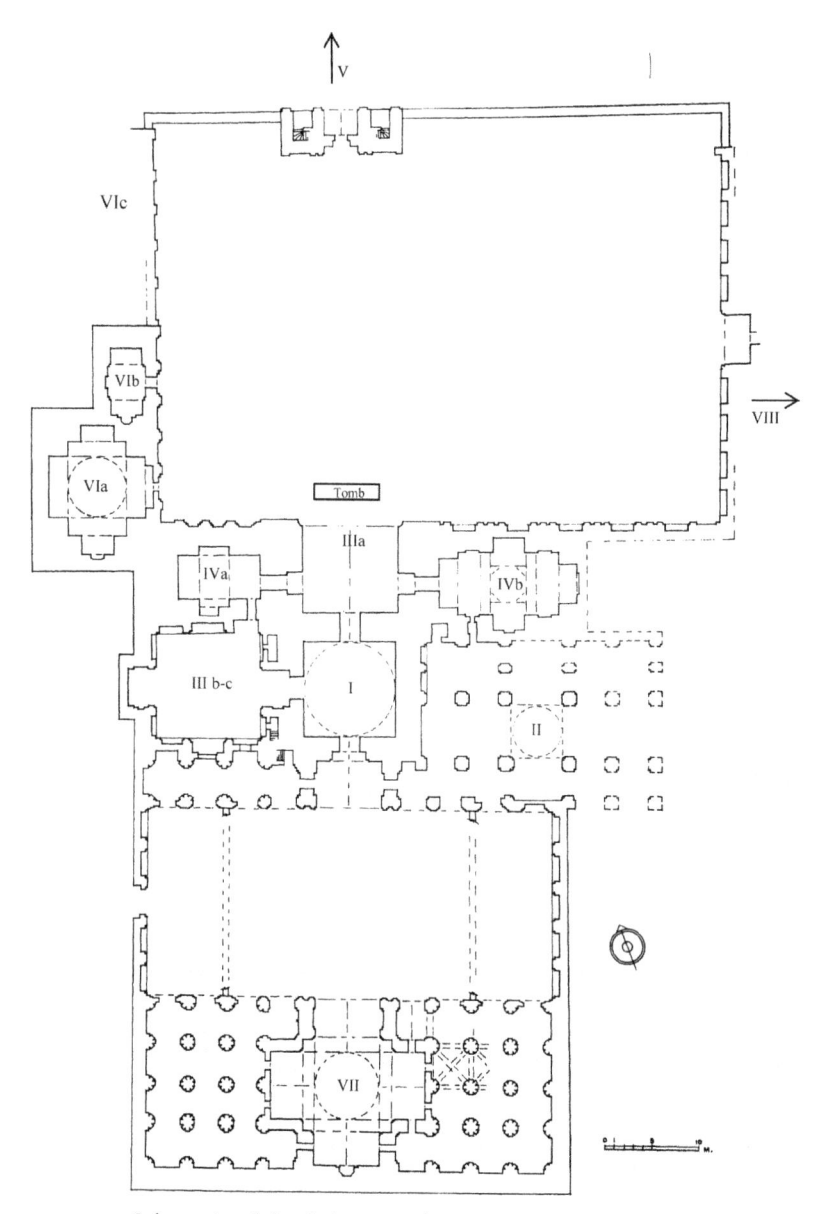

FIGURE 5.3 Schematic of the shrine complex, *ca.* 1938
Courtesy of the Asia Institute, Shiraz, Iran

The Architectural Ensemble

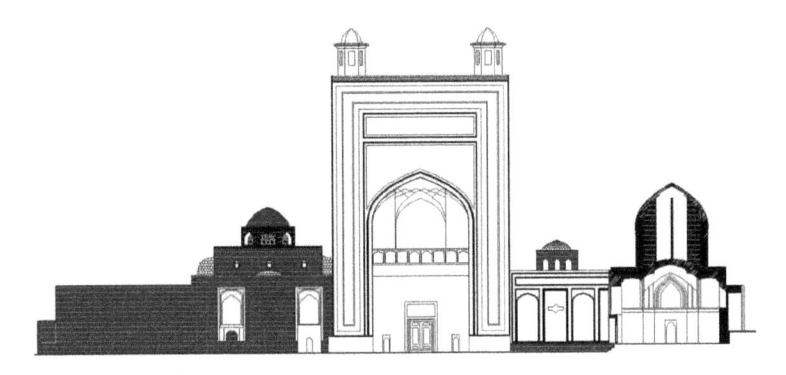

FIGURE 5.4 Schematic of front of the shrine (L–R): Kirmani Mosque, *iwan* and entrance portal (*riwaq*), Gunbad-i Safid, and Gunbad-i Firuzshah
Courtesy of Miras-i Farhangi, Islamic Republic of Iran

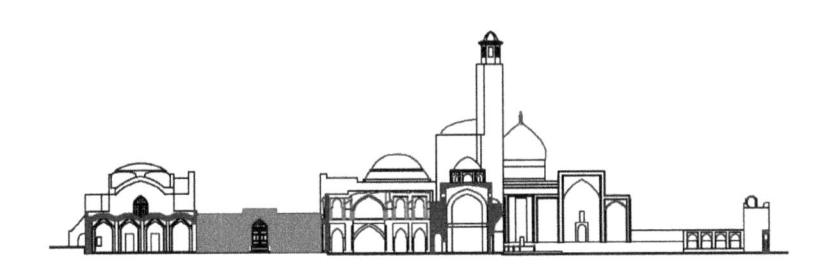

FIGURE 5.5 Schematic of east side of the shrine (L–R): New Mosque, courtyard, *gunbad*, *iwan*, Kirmani Mosque, and Gunbad-i Firuzshah
Courtesy of Miras-i Farhangi, Islamic Republic of Iran

The *gunbad*'s interior is welcoming. The chamber's four walls – mostly concealed now by components that were subsequently added – rise up about ten yards to an octagonal "zone of transition," which supports the dome. The transition zone has four squinches and four arched panels.[31] In the course of nearly 800 years, the *gunbad* has undergone multiple

[31] See Lisa Golombek, "A Thirteenth-Century Funerary Mosque at Turbat-i Shaykh Jam," *Bulletin of the Asia Institute* 1 (Shiraz, 1969): 13–26, 14.

restorations and enhancements. The chamber was redecorated in the eighth/fourteenth century, and panels and inscriptions were added.[32] The interior is exquisitely detailed in red, white, yellow, and blue tones, with floral motifs (Plates 6–8).

The *gunbad*'s functions are open to interpretation. It is not a mosque (*masjid*) in the sense it does not have a prayer niche (*mihrab*) directed toward Mecca, although the absence of a *mihrab* does not preclude it from being utilized as a mosque. Lisa Golombek theorizes that the *gunbad* "functioned as a small funerary chapel, primarily for recitation from the Qurʾan."[33] The chamber is ordinarily not accessible to the public.

In 763/1361–62, Muʿizz al-Din Kart paid for some or all costs for the refurbishment of the *gunbad*. His donation served to thaw relations between him and the Jami shaykhs, which had deteriorated with their instigation of his ouster (Chapter 3). They reciprocated with an inscription inside the *gunbad* (see Plate 7; section of the inscription):

> The Prophet, upon him be peace, said: "At the beginning of every 100 years, He sends to this people someone to restore its religious edifice." Since in accordance with these two authentic Traditions [hadith] and the Clear Text [the Qurʾan] the opportunity of reviving the rites (due) the shrines of men of great virtue and miracles fell upon the weak slave [Muʿizz al-Din Kart] – may Allah the Exalted cause him to prosper in what he wishes and pleases – to repair this dome which competes with the firmament and has the worth of Suha (i.e. a star), the strengthening of the foundations and the construction of which was in the name of him who resides in its tomb [Ahmad-i Jam].[34]

Nearly a century passed before another major component was added to the shrine. The new addition was an imposing mosque (Table 5.1, § II; Figure 5.6; and Plates 9–11). It was sponsored by *malik* Ghiyath al-Din Kart; work began in 720/1320f., and was finalized around 733/1333. It was dubbed the "Old Mosque" (*masjid-i ʿatiq*) following the construction of the "New Mosque" (*masjid-i naw*) in 844–46/1440–43. It was two stories, with aisles, arches, bays, and a central dome (see Figure 5.6).[35] "Soffits, spandrels, angle colonnettes and other elements," writes Wilber, "are covered with extraordinarily fine plaster relief decoration bearing traces of blue and yellow pigment."[36] The first six lines of Surat al-Fath (The Victory

---

[32] Golombek, "Chronology," 30–32.   [33] Golombek, "Funerary," 16.

[34] Golombek, "Chronology," 31 (the parentheses are Golombek's; the square brackets are mine. The translation and transcribed text are given in full in her article).

[35] Ibid., 32–34; and Golombek's diagram 3.   [36] Wilber, *Architecture*, 174 (Cat. No. 81).

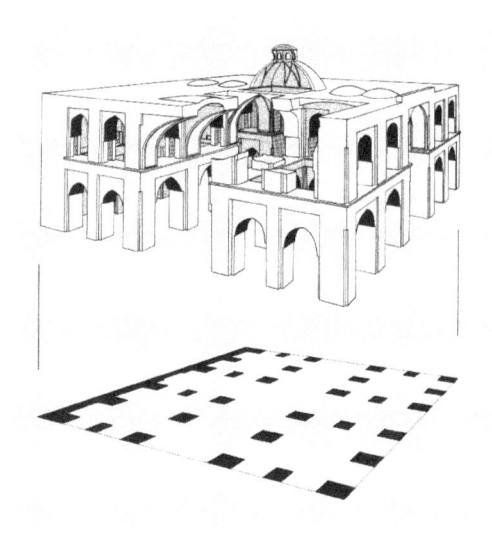

FIGURE 5.6 Lisa Golombek's reconstruction of the Old Mosque (Masjid-i ʿatiq) Courtesy of Lisa Golombek and the Timurid Research Archive, Aga Khan Documentation Center at MIT

Chapter: Q48:1–6) are inscribed on stucco frieze, although a large section has been effaced.[37] The verse glorifies Ghiyath al-Din Kart's victory over the Chaghatai.[38]

Most of the original work was lost when the mosque fell into ruin.[39] In 1937, the Archaeological Service of Iran, then led by the eminent French archaeologist André Godard, engaged in prophylactic repairs "to protect the plaster from the weather."[40] Reconstruction of the Masjid-i ʿatiq began many years ago; major work is now complete.[41] Ruined sections have been masterfully filled in, although the original work could not be easily replicated, particularly sections of ruined frieze and decorative brickwork. Restored sections comprise a substantial surface area of the mosque (Plates 9–11).

[37] Golombek, "Chronology," 32.
[38] On the Kartid-Chaghataid conflict, see Mahendrarajah, "Revised," 113–14.
[39] For images dated 1937, see Wilber, *Architecture*, plates 172–76.
[40] Wilber, *Architecture*, 174 and plate 172 (work on ruined mosque).
[41] Work on the vestibule and artworks remain according to the director of Miras-i Farhangi (for Jam and Taybad), Mr. Taj-Muhammadi (communications via WhatsApp, 11 June 2020).

108 Setting, Architecture, and Administration

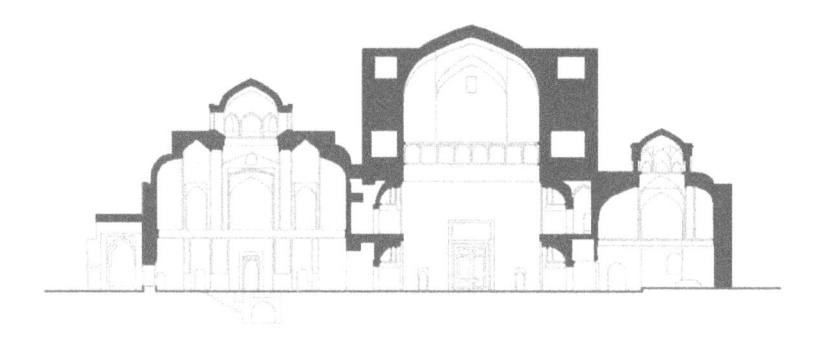

FIGURE 5.7 Schematic of (L–R) Kirmani Mosque, entrance portal, and Gunbad-i Safid
Courtesy of Miras-i Farhangi, Islamic Republic of Iran

The years 720–29/1320–29 were stellar for the shrine and its Sufis. Ghiyath al-Din Kart's political and economic fortunes had soared with his successes against the Chaghatai, for which he, and the citizens of Herat, were rewarded by the Ilkhanids.[42] The *malik* put part of this new wealth toward charitable projects at Herat and Turbat-i Jam. He commissioned renovations to the *gunbad* and sponsored the Gunbad-i Safid (White Dome; Table 5.1, § IVa; schematic, Figure 5.7; Plate 12) and Kirmani Mosque (Table 5.1, § IVb; schematic, Figure 5.7; Plate 13).[43] Access to the Kirmani Mosque and White Dome is now by escort because both house valuable property like ancient Qur'ans, manuscripts, and artifacts. One artifact is a pitcher and basin set (allegedly) donated by the Seljuq Sultan Sanjar.

Erected sometime before 736/1336 is an edifice known as the Khanaqah-i saracha (small hospice), and the Madrasa-i Faryumadi (Table 5.1, § IIIb and § IIIc). The seminary was sponsored by 'Ala' al-Din Muhammad Faryumadi (d. 27 Sha'ban 742/5 February 1342), an Ilkhanid vizier. Faryumadi was appointed financial vizier in 729/1329. The madrasa was erected during the reign of Faryumadi's master, the last Il-Khan of Iraq and Iran, Abu Sa'id Bahadur Khan, between 706/1316 and

---

[42] Mahendrarajah, "Revised," 113–16.
[43] The Gunbad-i Safid (White Dome) is also called the Portal Mosque (*masjid-i riwaq*); the Kirmani Mosque is named after the architect.

736/1336; but it was most likely built between 729/1329 and 736/1336, which is when the vizier had access to funds with which to sponsor pious constructions. Neither edifice is extant.

With the death of Shihab al-Din Isma'il Jami (*ca.* 738/1338) and his patrons Chupan Suldus in 728/1327, Ghiyath al-Din Kart in 729/1329, and Il-Khan Abu Sa'id in 735/1336, the shrine entered a wilderness period of forty-five years when patronage from the Kart ruler tapered. Ghiyath al-Din's successor, Mu'izz al-Din, was not devoted to Ahmad; moreover, his relations with Jami shaykhs were undoubtedly strained.[44]

The resplendent and ornately decorated *iwan* (Table 5.1, § IIIa; Figure 5.4; Plate 3) looms 88 ft./26.8 m over Ahmad-i Jam's tomb.[45] André Godard observed, "in contrast to the tradition in the west where the dome was the dominant feature, the immense and magnificent *iwan* ... proclaims from afar the funerary mosques and the *musalla* mosques of Khurasan."[46] The construction of the *iwan* commenced around 751/1350f. under Shams al-Din Mutahhar Jami (d. *ca.* 751–67/1350–66), the chief of the *khanaqah* and the eldest son of Shihab al-Din Isma'il Jami (d. *ca.* 738/1338). Shams al-Din's brother, Razi al-Din Ahmad Jami (d. 767/1366), was then the custodian. Funding for the *iwan* came from Jami sources because funding by the Kartids had evaporated as a consequence of the 752/1351 coup. Shams al-Din's son, Ghiyath al-Din Jami (n.d.), finalized the work on the *iwan* (*ca.* 763/1361–62). In 1022/1613f., Shah 'Abbas I, Safavi, sponsored a mosaic faience decoration to the *iwan* (Plate 14); his generosity is recognized in a "large horizontal frieze over the spandrels of the arch."[47]

The invasion of Khurasan by Temür/Tamerlane commenced in 782/1380f. In Dhu al-Hijja 782/February–March 1381, Temür stopped at Turbat-i Jam en route to Herat.[48] Temür paid homage to Ahmad-i Jam and donated two *khanaqah*s (Table 5.1, § V; Figure 5.3, § V).

Gunbad-i Firuzshah (Table 5.1, § VIa); vestibule (Table 5.1, § VIb);[49] Madrasa-i Firuzshah (Table 5.1, § VIc).[50] Figure 5.3 shows the location of

---

[44] Mahendrarajah, "Revised," 115–17. Discussed in Chapter 3.
[45] On the *iwan*, see Golombek, "Chronology," 34–35. On the *iwan*'s Khurasanian origins, and the *iwan-masjid* style, see André Godard, *The Art of Iran* (New York: Praeger, 1965), 279–84.
[46] Godard, *Art of Iran*, 282. [47] Golombek, "Chronology," 35. Discussed in Chapter 4.
[48] Mahendrarajah, "Revised," 118–19. Discussed in Chapter 3.
[49] Rather than functioning as a passageway, the vestibule could possibly be "a small oratory for quiet contemplative prayer." O'Kane, *Timurid Architecture*, 220.
[50] Further on the three components, see ibid., 219–22; and Golombek, "Chronology," 39–40.

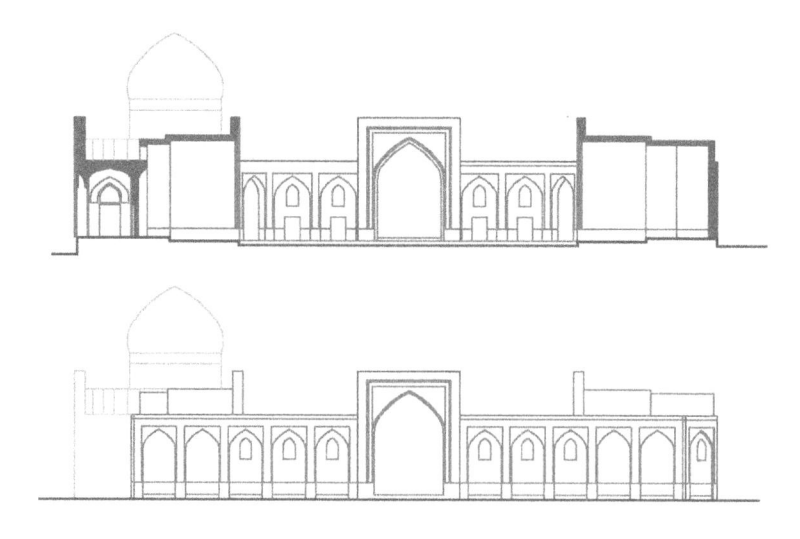

FIGURE 5.8 Schematic of Firuzshah's Dome (Gunbad-i Firuzshah) and Firuzshah's Seminary (Madrasa-yi Firuzshah)
Courtesy of Miras-i Farhangi, Islamic Republic of Iran

these three components (note that § VIc in Figure 5.3 shows the putative location of the Madrasa-i Firuzshah). Figure 5.8 and Plates 15–16 are of the above components. They were sponsored by Jalal al-Din Firuzshah (d. 848/1444f.), an army commander who served Temür and Shah-Rukh (see following section, "The Shrine's Political and Financial Benefactors"). The Masjid-i jami'-i naw (Table 5.1, § VII; schematic, Figure 5.9; Plate 17) was also sponsored by Firuzshah.[51] The New Mosque is attractive but unimpressive.

The Madrasa-i Amir Shah-Malik (Table 5.1, § VIII) was sponsored by Amir Ghiyath al-Din Shah-Malik (d. 829/1426; see also the following section, "The Shrine's Political and Financial Benefactors").[52] The building is not extant (but see Figure 5.3, § VIII); vestiges were perhaps captured in photographs.[53] Yusuf-i Ahl (the compiler of the *Fara'id-i Ghiyasi*) studied at Amir Shah-Malik's seminary and received his teaching license (*ijaza*) from Jalal al-Din al-Qayini in 822/1419f. (the *ijaza* is analyzed in Table 8.2). The expiration of Timurid rule in Khurasan in 911/1506

---

[51] See also Golombek, "Chronology," 40–41.
[52] See ibid., 41; and O'Kane, *Timurid Architecture*, 217.
[53] O'Kane, *Timurid Architecture*, 217.

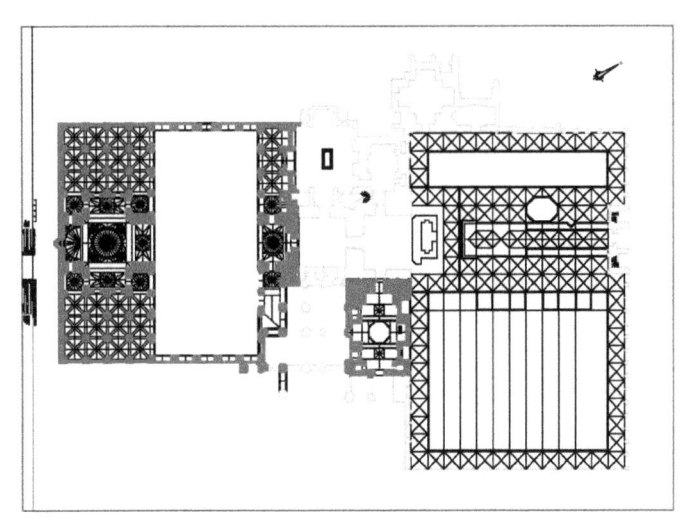

FIGURE 5.9 Schematic of the New Mosque (Masjid-i jami'-i naw) Courtesy of Miras-i Farhangi, Islamic Republic of Iran

terminated the shrine's glorious age. There were no major architectural additions at the shrine complex following Shah-Rukh's death in 850/1447.

In 1010/1601f., a Safavid official donated a cistern (*ab-i anbar*) (Table 5.1, § IX). Around AHS 1357/1978, a utility mosque was constructed (Table 5.1, § X),[54] about where Temür's *khanaqah*s had once stood. The mosque has two distinct sections: an Underground Mosque (Masjid-i zir-i zamin), which is also called the Winter Mosque (Masjid-i zamistan); and the flat roof, called the Summer Mosque (Masjid-i tabistan) – although it is actually a *musalla* (open prayer space). The utility mosque is used continually: the faithful do not have to traipse across the courtyard without footwear in inclement weather.

In AHS 1389/2010, the Hawza-yi 'ilmiyya Ahmadiyya, a seminary, was erected in the space where Firuzshah's Seminary would have been (Table 5.1, § XI; Figure 5.2; Plate 18).[55] The seminary's construction was initiated by Haji Qazi Sharaf al-Din Jami al-Ahmadi, the shrine's custodian. Haji Qazi was the college's first principal. The seminary's construction is utilitarian, and blends with the existing architecture. There is a small courtyard (*hujra*) in the

---

[54] § IX and § X are not depicted in Figure 5.3.
[55] The new madrasa is where Firuzshah's madrasa would have stood. This space is visible in Plate 2 (left of the dome toward the greenery).

center. The college, which is integrated with Iran's educational bureaucracies, received from the "Office for Sunni Affairs for the [Three] Provinces of Khurasan" (Daftar-i umur-i ahl-i sunnat-i ustanha-yi Khurasan) a donation of Islamic texts.

The Hawza-yi ʿilmiyya Hibat al-Rahman, the shrine's college for ladies, was founded in AHS 1392/2013 as a seminary integrated with Iran's educational bureaucracies. It now occupies quarters in a refurbished Pahlawi-era building in the southwest corner of the shrine.[56] The new public library (funded by the shrine) is located south of the shrine complex.[57]

THE SHRINE'S POLITICAL AND FINANCIAL BENEFACTORS

Notes on the shrine's principal benefactors may prove useful.

Ghiyath al-Din Kart's affection for his in-law and preceptor, Shihab al-Din Ismaʿil Jami, was discussed. Political supporters in late Ilkhanid Iran included viziers Taj al-Din ʿAli Shah (in office, 711–24/1312–24), who assumed control of the vizierate with Rashid al-Din's execution in 718/1318.[58] Rashid al-Din's son, Ghiyath al-Din Muhammad (d. 736/1336),[59] who was elevated to office with the fall of Amir Chupan's clique;[60] ʿAlaʾ al-Din Hindu,[61] and ʿAlaʾ al-Din Faryumadi. Although there is no documentary evidence of political or financial favors by ʿAlaʾ al-Din Hindu, Rashid al-Din, his son, and Taj al-Din ʿAli Shah in the direction of the shrine, the Ilkhanate's bureaucrats will have ensured the fulfillment of Öljeitü's and Abu Saʿid Bahadur Khan's benefactions to the shrine and/or shaykhs.

Jami shaykhs maintained ties with the financial viziers of the Timurid era, mainly, Ghiyath al-Din Pir Ahmad Khwafi (in office,

---

[56] Not depicted in Figure 5.1. The shrine's administrator secured the building from Miras-i Farhangi (communications with Mr. Taj-Muhammadi, Director of Miras-i Farhangi, 4–5 November 2019, via Telegram; status update received 11 June 2020).

[57] A website for the shrine that was not sanctioned by the shrine's administration was taken down a few years ago; however, the information (in Persian) and images were preserved at the Internet Archive: https://tinyurl.com/Ahmad-Jami (accessed 13 June 2020).

[58] There is correspondence between Jamis and Ilkhanid bureaucrats. See, e.g., letter from Shihab al-Din Ismaʿil to Taj al-Din, in Yusuf-i Ahl/Fatih, *Faraʾid*, fol. 222a–223a.

[59] Letters from Qutb al-Din Yahya Nishapuri Jami (d. 740/1339) to the vizier in Yusuf-i Ahl, *Faraʾid*, 2:23–24, 25–30. Nishapuri is said to have been Khurasan's chief judge (*qadi al-qudat*). On him, see Buzjani/Moayyad (ed.), *Rawzat*, 115–18; Zanganah, *Sarzamin*, 137–39.

[60] On these individuals and the fading Ilkhanate, see Melville, *Amir Chupan*.

[61] Letter from Yahya Nishapuri to the vizier in Yusuf-i Ahl, *Faraʾid*, 2:53–55.

820–50/1417–47; d. 857/1453),[62] then his son, Majd al-Din Muhammad (in office, 876–83/1472–78; 892–95/1487–90).[63] There is no evidence of benefactions from the two viziers,[64] but as with Ilkhanid viziers, they will have helped implement the wishes of powerful benefactors.

The community's relationships with Ghiyath al-Din Shah-Malik (d. 829/1426),[65] and Jalal al-Din Firuzshah (d. 848/1444f.),[66] were fruitful. The former was a military commander who served Temür and Shah-Rukh. He was *atabeg* (Turkish: father-chief, guardian-tutor) to Shah-Rukh's and Gawhar-Shad's first son, Muhammad Taraghay (d. 853/1449), more famous as the astronomer and mathematician "Ulugh Beg" than as Transoxiana's governor for four decades.[67] Shah-Malik involved himself in Ulugh Beg's affairs, which made the young prince resentful. In 815/1413f., Shah-Malik was shunted to Khwarazm as governor. He sponsored public projects, which he endowed with waqfs. Shah-Malik is interred at the shrine of Imam Riza. Shah-Malik's son, Ibrahim-Sultan (r. 829–39/1426–35), inherited the governorship of Khwarazm.[68] Jamis maintained convivial relations with Ibrahim-Sultan.

Jalal al-Din Firuzshah rose to high rank with Temür and Shah-Rukh, and like Amir Shah-Malik, supported Shah-Rukh in the post-Temür internecine struggles for supremacy. Firuzshah "clearly had a serious interest in both exoteric religion and Sufism."[69] In addition to his benefactions at Ahmad-i Jam's shrine, he sponsored restorations and constructions in and around Herat, including an eponymous madrasa.[70] Moreover, he patronized shaykhs and sayyids in the Mamluk territories of the Hijaz, Syria, and Egypt.

---

[62] The *Fara'id* was dedicated to Pir Ahmad. See Yusuf-i Ahl, *Fara'id*, 1:xx–xxi. On Pir Ahmad, see Manz, *Timurid Iran*, et passim.

[63] On Majd al-Din, see Subtelny, *Timurids*, et passim.

[64] Viziers have access to state funds; they are valuable friends. Pir Ahmad funded the shrine for Ahmad's devotee Zayn al-Din Taybadi (d. 791/1389). See O'Kane, "Taybad."

[65] On him, see Khwafi, *Mujmal*, 3:259; Hafiz-i Abru, *Zubdat*, 2:898–901; Khwandamir, *Habib*, 3:613–14; Khwandamir/Thackston (trans.), *Habib*, 339; Taj al-Salmani, *Tarikhnamah: Shams al-husn*, ed. Akbar Saburi (Tehran: Intisharat-i Duktur Mahmud Afshar, 1393/2014f.), 21–24; Manz, *Tamerlane*, et passim; Manz, *Timurid Iran*, et passim; Shiro Ando, *Timuridische Emire nach dem Mu'izz al-ansab* (Berlin: Klaus Schwarz, 1992), 166–67.

[66] On him, see Khwandamir, *Habib*, 3:630–33; Khwandamir/Thackston (trans.), *Habib*, 347–48; al-Salmani, *Shams al-husn*, 312, 546 n84; al-Samarqandi, *Matla'-i sa'dayn*, 2.1:565–67; Manz, *Timurid Iran*, et passim; Ando, *Timuridische*, 150–52.

[67] On Ulugh Beg, see Barthold, *Four Studies*, 2:43–177; Manz, *Timurid Iran*, et passim.

[68] Ando, *Timuridische Emire*, 167, 242, 244. [69] Manz, *Timurid Iran*, 221.

[70] Allen, *Catalogue*, 102, 132, 222 (Cat. Nos. 407, 465, 663).

In 847–48/1444, when Shah-Rukh's health deteriorated and his death appeared to be imminent, Firuzshah supported Gawhar-Shad's choice of successor, her favorite grandson, ʿAlaʾ al-Dawla (d. 865/1460) b. Baysunghur. Firuzshah swore fealty to ʿAlaʾ al-Dawla. Shah-Rukh, however, recovered. His choice was his son, Muhammad Juki (but who predeceased him later that same year, 848/1444f.). Muhammad Juki, meanwhile, had been investigating irregularities at the *diwan*. His findings disfavored Firuzshah, who suffered disgrace, which precipitated his death.[71] Bernard O'Kane suggests that Firuzshah had intended to be buried at Turbat-i Jam, "to obtain the greater *baraka* (blessings) possible from interment in the vicinity of Shaikh Ahmad, but that his disgrace before his demise obliged his relatives to bury him in the nearest convenient location,"[72] that is, his madrasa in Herat.

Firuzshah's endowments at Turbat-i Jam went beyond the financial: he contracted with architect Haji Zayn b. Mahmud Shirazi (n.d.), protégé of renowned architect Qiwam al-Din Shirazi (d. 842/1438).[73] Qiwam al-Din had designed the Gawhar-Shad Mosque inside the Imam Riza complex (one of the most magnificent mosques in Iran),[74] and Gawhar-Shad's mosque-madrasa complex in Herat.[75]

Haji Zayn b. Mahmud Shirazi designed the Madrasa-i Firuzshah, Gunbad-i Firuzshah, and Masjid-i jamiʿ-i naw.[76] Other architects with the cognomen "Shirazi" designed edifices at nearby Khargird (Khwaf district),[77] and Taybad (the shrine of Zayn al-Din Taybadi).[78] Since three "Shirazi" architects shared time and space, Wilber and Golombek have argued, "it is fair to suggest that there existed a 'school' of architecture."[79] The "Shirazi school" designed exceptional buildings in Khurasan: the Gawhar-Shad Mosque in Mashhad; the Gawhar-Shad madrasa and mosque complex in Herat;[80] Shah-Rukh's madrasa and Sufi convent in

---

[71] Manz, *Timurid Iran*, 47–48. [72] O'Kane, *Timurid Architecture*, 220.
[73] See Donald Wilber, "Qavam al-Din ibn Zayn al-Din Shirazi: A Fifteenth-Century Timurid Architect," *Architectural History* 30 (1987): 31–44.
[74] O'Kane, *Timurid Architecture*, 119–30.
[75] Ibid., 167–77; Allen, *Catalogue*, 113–15, 122–29 (Cat. Nos. 431 and 457).
[76] An inscription reads: "The work of the weak slave Haji Zayn b. Mahmud of the peoples of Shiraz, the year 846/1442f." See also O'Kane, *Timurid Architecture*, 219.
[77] Bernard O'Kane, "The Madrasa al-Ghiyasiyya at Khargird, *Iran* 14 (1976): 79–92.
[78] O'Kane, "Taybad." [79] Wilber and Golombek, *Timurid Architecture*, 193.
[80] The complex was mostly destroyed in 1885 by the British army in order for their artillery to have unimpeded lines of fire against the "invading" Russian army. Abdur Rahman Khan (r. 1880–1901), Afghanistan's British-sponsored tyrant, gave approval for this act of cultural vandalism. On the Gawhar-Shad complex, see Warwick Ball, *The Monuments of Afghanistan* (London: I.B. Tauris, 2008), 206–9, plates 120–22, and figure 32.

Herat; and the shrine of ʿAbdullah Ansari in Herat.[81] The structures sponsored at Turbat-i Jam by Firuzshah testify to architectural concepts that have implications far beyond Jam, namely, to other regions of Iran, Bidar (India), Istanbul, and Central Asia, where derivatives of Shirazi technologies and artistic styles were recorded by specialists.[82]

THE SHRINE'S ENDOWMENTS (WAQF)

An Islamic institution needs income for its daily operations. If an institution wants to expand its operations and/or offer public services, it needs substantial levels of income. Alms ordinarily collected from the pious, while beneficial, are presumably insufficient. As Maria Subtelny observed, waqfs are of insuperable importance for the viability of Islamic institutions. The sponsorship of edifices by sultans, princes, princesses, amirs, and viziers in the medieval period was facilitated by their wealth, power, and access to labor (including corvée), but "it was the endowment established for their maintenance and for the support of the activities they housed that guaranteed their permanence and ensured their viability as social institutions."[83]

An Islamic institution's trustee is responsible for the sound fiscal administration of the income-producing assets endowed to it. Secondarily, he has to efficiently administer the institution, which includes upkeep and renovations, maintenance of accounting ledgers (*daftar-i hisab*), supervision of sundry "secular" staff – accountants, engineers, hydrologists, agronomists – and imams, sermonizers (*khatib, waʿiz*), lecturers (*mudarris*), and such. And he must interact with *diwan* officials and the judiciary.

A succinct recapitulation of waqf will be helpful. A waqf involves the "voluntary conveyance of private property" by a settlor (male: *waqif*; female: *waqifah*) to "the status of mortmain, or permanent inalienability, and the assignment of the revenue or usufruct from that property to a charitable purpose."[84] In common usage this means immovable property, but Hanafi law allows for the conveyance of movable property, "including cash and income-producing instruments such as the *soyurghal*."[85] The

---

[81] Ibid., 211–12, plates 125–27, and figure 34.
[82] Wilber and Golombek, *Timurid Architecture*, 193–94.
[83] Maria Eva Subtelny, "A Timurid Educational and Charitable Foundation: The Ikhlasiyya Complex of ʿAli Shir Navaʾi in 15th-Century Herat and Its Endowment," *JAOS* 111/1 (1991): 38–61, 38.
[84] Subtelny, *Timurids*, 148.   [85] Ibid., 148–49.

116 Setting, Architecture, and Administration

settlor memorializes the transfer in a deed (*waqfiyya*; Per: *waqfnamah*) and describes the immobilized properties in a *mawqufat* section of the deed. This is the waqf's principal (*asl*), which ordinarily cannot be sold or transferred.[86] The settlor designates the waqf's conditions (*shart*; pl. *shurut*); names the trustee (*mutawalli*) and protocols of succession for trustees (in *theory*, waqf is perpetual); the settlor assigns the waqf's usufruct (*manfa'a*) to specified beneficiaries per a prescribed formula; for example, 20 percent (after taxes) is paid to the trustee for administrative expenses; 50 percent to a specified madrasa (public beneficiary); the balance to the settlor's heirs (private beneficiaries), to be divided among them according to a prescribed formula.

The trustee could even be the settlor, and his heirs the primary beneficiaries, with a public institution (mosque or hospital) as the secondary beneficiary. The deed is signed by witnesses (*shahid*), seals (*muhr*) are affixed, and the deed is probated before a judge (*qadi*). A "mixed waqf," with commonweal (*maslaha*) and private benefit facets, was not uncommon in the premodern period. By designating an Islamic institution as beneficiary of the waqf's income, a settlor made it discomfiting for rulers to seize his waqf; however, the avaricious were not easily embarrassed. Seizure of waqfs with change of ruler was commonplace. This is precisely what happened to the Jami shrine's waqfs in the Safavid and Qajar periods. The trend in post-Mongol Iran, especially with the Timurids and Safavids, was to bring waqfs under government control. Waqfs in Khurasan-i Rizawi province are now supervised by the office for waqf administration and charitable affairs (Idara-yi kull-i awqaf wa umur khayriyya-yi Astan-i Quds-i Rizawi) based in Mashhad.[87]

Specific details on the shrine's waqf assets are unknown. Only a handful of legal documents on the shrine's endowments and appointments of trustees have survived. Waqfs are subject to judicial review,[88] but judicial documents relating to waqfs at the shrine have not survived. Robert McChesney explained this pervasive problem:

Ideally, every waqf foundation would leave a trail of legal documents beginning with the waqf deed. Periodic changes in the administration, subsequent court

---

[86] Exceptions apply. Certain assets are subject to depletion (e.g., oil, minerals, grain), while others are subject to depreciation (e.g., buildings, hydrological systems). In order to protect the waqf, the trustee has discretion and may dispose of assets.
[87] https://razavi.oghaf.ir/ (accessed 13 June 2020).
[88] On waqfs and legal documents, see R. D. McChesney, *Waqf in Central Asia* (Princeton, NJ: Princeton University Press, 1991), 170–97.

resolutions of litigation, government decrees defining the prerogatives of a waqf administration, and additions to the endowments of the original foundation all meant filing evidence establishing proof of claims and, consequently, generating records. For a full understanding of how any given foundation fared in its "natural milieu," we need the entire record. Single documents, however illuminating on particular economic issues, are records of specific moments in time.[89]

A near complete record of a major waqf foundation in the Persianate world would be an anomaly.[90] The Balkh ʿAlid shrine examined by McChesney has a bare archive; Herat's Friday mosque (another venerable 900-year-old institution) has a bare archive. The Gawhar-Shad Mosque has a number of legal documents, several of which have been published.[91] It is not surprising that only a handful of waqf legal documents for Ahmad-i Jam's shrine have survived – or if they have survived, they are not being publicized by Ahmad's shrine or the government of the Islamic Republic of Iran. Both jealously shield waqf documents.[92]

SHRINE ADMINISTRATION

The lineage of Qutb al-Din Muhammad Jami (577–667/1181–1268) retained the shrine's trusteeship into the early Safavid period (Table 5.2). This reflects the accumulation of wealth by Qutb al-Din Muhammad, his son Shihab al-Din Ismaʿil, then his son, Razi al-Din Ahmad, and then his son, Shihab al-Din Ismaʿil b. Razi al-Din Ahmad; and then the shift in the Timurid period to Razi al-Din Ahmad's descendants from Transoxiana.[93] As originators of wealth, Qutb al-Din Muhammad's descendants had the "right" to the custodianship.

---

[89] Ibid., 20.
[90] This assessment is based on multiple visits between 2007 and 2019 to archives in Kabul, Balkh, Herat, Tehran, Turbat-i Jam, and Mashhad. On the survival of documents, generally, see Jürgen Paul, "Archival Practices in the Muslim World prior to 1500," in *Manuscripts and Archives: Comparative Views on Record-Keeping*, ed. Alessandro Bausi et al. (Berlin: de Gruyter, 2018), 339–60.
[91] See Mehdi Sayyidi (ed.), *Masjid wa mawqufat-i Gawhar Shad* (Tehran: Bunyad-i pizhuhish wa tawsiʿa-yi farhang-i waqf, 1386/2007); Zahra Talaee and Ilahi Mahbub Farimani, *Guzida-yi asnad-i masjid-i Gawhar Shad az Safaviyya ta Qajariyya* (Mashhad: Sazman-i kitabkhana-ha, muzi-ha, wa markaz-i asnad-i Quds-i Rizawi, 1396/2017).
[92] I researched at Mashhad's Idara-yi kull-i awqaf wa umur khayriyya-yi Astan-i Quds-i Rizawi in May 2016. Approval for access is tedious despite introductions from influential colleagues at the University of Tehran.
[93] See Figures A1.3 and A1.4.

TABLE 5.2 Administrators (ra'is or mutawallī) of the shrine

Administrator	Dates of tenure	Primary sources	Comments
Burhan al-Din Nasr b. Ahmad (n.d.) See Figure A1.1b #7	Unknown	Buzjani/Moayyad (ed.), *Rawzat*, 52	Seventh son and father to Hibat al-Rahman. *Locum tenens* (*qā'im-i maqām*) to Ahmad; lived in Kariz-i Sa'ad (near Turbat-i Jam).
Shihab al-Din Isma'il (d. *ca.* 617/1220) b. Ahmad See Figure A1.1b #14	From ? to death ?	His role is inferred	Ahmad's fourteenth son
Razi al-Din Ahmad b. Qutb al-Din Muhammad b. Ahmad-i Jam See Figure A1.1a #4	From ? to ?	Buzjani/Moayyad (ed.), *Rawzat*, 79–80	Ahmad's grandson. Designated *qā'im-i maqām*
Qutb al-Din Muhammad (d. 667/1268) b. Shams al-Din Mutahhar b. Ahmad-i Jam See Figures A1.1b and A1.2	From ? to death in 667/1268	Buzjani/Moayyad (ed.), *Rawzat*, 85–97; Kadkani, *Darwish*, 259–67 (*Khulasat al-maqamat*)	Appears to have served as custodian for decades. Birth date given by Buzjani (*Rawzat*) is incorrect; *Khulsat al-Maqamat* has correct dates
Not known	?	?	Another custodian may have been in office given the age of Qutb al-Din's son (see below)

Shihab al-Din Ismaʿil (d. ca. 738/1338) b. Qutb al-Din Muhammad b. Ahmad-i Jam See Figures A1.3 and A1.4	From ? to ? (handoff to son, Razi al-Din Ahmad; see below)	Buzjani/Moayyad (ed.), Rawzat, 99–106 (biography); Zanganah, Sarzamin, 155–60	He was born late in his father's life; hence the comment above
Razi al-Din Ahmad (d. 767/1366) b. Shihab al-Din Ismaʿil See Figures A1.3 and A1.4	From ? (assumed office during father's lifetime) to his death in 767/1366	Buzjani/Moayyad (ed.), Rawzat, 105	He developed shrine and endowed it with wealth. Custodianship stayed with his lineage.
Shihab al-Din Ismaʿil (d. 809/1407) b. Razi al-Din Ahmad See Figure A1.4	From before 5 Dhu al-Qaʿda 771/ 31 May 1370 to death in 809/ 1407	Buzjani/Moayyad (ed.), Rawzat, 109 (biography); al-Samarqandi, Matlaʿ, 1.2:642 (with Temür); Yusuf-i Ahl/Berlin, Faraʾid, fol. 315b–316b (Kart decree); ibid., fol. 314a–315b (Miranshah decree)	Confirmation decree (manshur) issued by Muʿizz al-Din Kart. Rights confirmed by Miranshah b. Temür in a decree dated 7 Dhu al-Hijja 796/ 3 October 1394
Qutb al-Din Muhammad (d. 821/1418) b. ʿAlaʾ al-Mulk al-Tirmizi b. Fakhr al-Mulk Khatun See Figure A1.4	From 12 Dhu al-Qaʿda 809/ 20 April 1407 to death in 821/ 1418	Yusuf-i Ahl/Berlin, Faraʾid, fol. 311b–313a	Confirmation decree issued by Shah-Rukh b. Temür

TABLE 5.2 Continued

Administrator	Dates of tenure	Primary sources	Comments
Shihab al-Din (Abu al-Makarim) Tirmizi Jami (d. 847/1443f., in Bengal) See Figure A1.4	From 6 Safar 821/ 15 March 1418 to ca. 845/1441f.	Buzjani/Moayyad (ed.), *Rawzat*, 110–11, 147–49; Khwafi, *Mujmal*, 3:138; Khwandamir, *Habib*, 5:11–12; Yusuf-i Ahl/Berlin, *Fara'id*, fol. 291b–294a; Yusuf-i Ahl/Tehran, *Fara'id*, pp. 623–26; Yusuf-i Ahl/Fatih, *Fara'id*, fol. 447b–448b	Confirmation decree issued by Shah-Rukh b. Temür (in three recensions of Yusuf-i Ahl, *Fara'id*) Resigned post to travel to Bengal as a royal emissary
Abu al-Fath b. Shihab al-Din (Abu al-Makarim) See Figure A1.4	From *ca.* 845/1441f. to ?	Khwandamir, *Habib*, 4:11–12	Assumed office when his father resigned to travel to Bengal
Razi al-Din Ahmad b. Jalal al-Din (d. *ca.* 884/1479) (Jami genealogical connection is unclear)	From *ca.* 29 Jumada II 863/ 3 May 1459 to death in 884/1479	Khwandamir, *Habib*, 4:338–39; Supp. persan 1815/Paris, fol. 29b–30b	Confirmation issued by Sultan-Abu Sa'id Mirza. Date of death in Khwandamir is incorrect
Jalal al-Din (Abu al-Qasim) b. Razi al-Din Ahmad (d. 920/1514f.)	From 20 Jumada I 884/ 9 August 1479 to	Khwandamir, *Habib*, 4:338–39;	Confirmation decree by Sultan-Husayn Bayqara. Received a *soyurghal* from Shah Isma'il I,

(Jami genealogical connection is unclear)	death in 920/1514f.	Supp. persan 1815/Paris, fol. 30b–32a	Safavi (see Supp. persan 1815, fol. 135a–136a)
—	—	—	Safavid era to Qajar era. See discussion above regarding the absence of reliable information
Haji Muhammad Yusuf Jami al-Ahmadi	Unclear	Miras-i Farhangi	Confirmed in writing on 8 March 2018. Pahlawi-era to Islamic Republic-era records are available
Haji Qazi Muhammad Naʿim Jami al-Ahmadi	Unclear	Miras-i Farhangi	See above
Haji Qazi Muhammad Jami al-Ahmadi	Unclear	Miras-i Farhangi	See above
Haji Qazi Sharaf al-Din Jami al-Ahmadi (b. 1319/1940)	From ? to present	Miras-i Farhangi	See above; he is also the town's *imam-jumʿa*

122   Setting, Architecture, and Administration

Table 5.2 is a list of administrators. Safavid to Qajar periods are incomplete because reliable information is unavailable. On 22 December 2011, the shrine's custodian, Haji Qazi, gave me copies of some legal documents.[94] One document, dated Rabi' II 1281/September–October 1864 (but copied on 15 Tir 1330/2 Shawwal 1370/7 July 1951), is a list of custodians, purportedly from Ahmad-i Jam to around 1281/1864. The list is responsive to some bureaucratic demand. It lists a number of names without identifying information. Reproduction of those names would reify unreliable information.[95]

Administrators of the Shrine

An administrator/trustee had to be a man of rectitude and learning. The threat of "the wrath of God" was insufficient to thwart embezzlers. Mismanagement was a problem. In these respects, a Timurid-era document describing protocols for the succession for waqf trustees at Ahmad's shrine is illuminating. This is the only known document of its type for the shrine. The protocols were executed in Herat in Shawwal 809/March–April 1407, but the copy is dated 28 Ramazan 1295/25 September 1878;[96] however, the handwritten copy given to me is datable to the Pahlawi era.[97] The protocols were attached to a *waqfiyya* that has not survived. Problems of provenance and illicit emendations notwithstanding, a broad but judicious reading of the seven conditions is edifying:

(1) Whoever assumes the office of trustee/custodian (*mutawalli*) becomes the manager of the aforementioned estates (*amlak*). He may use them as he chooses.
(2) The estates cannot be bought, sold, or leased.[98]
(3) He should make the endowed villages (*raqabat*) and the surrounding areas (i.e., farmlands) flourish (*ma'mur wa abadan*). In every activity, expenditure, and

---

[94] Reported in Shivan Mahendrarajah, "The Shrine of Shaykh Ahmad-i Jam: Notes on a Revised Chronology and a *Waqfiyya*," *Iran* 50 (2012): 145–48, 146.
[95] A certified copy and translation are in Shivan Mahendrarajah, "The Sufi Shaykhs of Jam: A History, from the Il-Khans to the Timurids" (PhD diss., University of Cambridge, 2014), appendix 2, part A (certified copy) and part B (translation). The thesis is accessible at the Cambridge University Library, West Road, Cambridge, CB3 9DR, United Kingdom.
[96] It was given to me by Haji Qazi Sharaf al-Din Jami al-Ahmadi. A copy of the document (certified in Iran by the appropriate authority), with a preliminary transcription, are in appendix 1 to Mahendrarajah, "Sufi Shaykhs of Jam."
[97] I am grateful to Christoph Werner for sharing his expertise on Persian documents.
[98] Only short-term rentals and share-cropping contracts are permitted.

annual payment to the state (*dawlat*),[99] care must be taken to ensure permanent sustainability and to avoid losses to the properties.

(4) Whoever assumes the custodianship (*tawliyat*) should be trustworthy (*amin*), the most proper (*aslah*), the most ascetic (*azhad*), the most devout (*atqa*), and the most learned (*a'lam*), and he must surrender himself to the conditions (*sharayit*). Not a single one of the descendants (*farzandan*) [of the settlor] should engage in any disputation with him about the conduct of his duties. His preeminence (*muqaddam*) must be recognized. His errors and transgressions should not be publicized.

(5) No government official shall enter the aforementioned properties.

(6) The custodians's administrative fee (*haqq al-tawliya*) is 20 percent (*khums*) of the (agricultural) revenue (*mahsulat*). The custodian should not take in excess of the *khums* and (thereby) transgress the conditions of the custodianship (*tawliya*). Any excess taken for virtuous affairs should be properly explained.

(7) The income from the estates, after the *diwan*'s taxes have been taken, is for the settlor's descendants, males and females, to be divided according to their ranks as God has ordained: the males will receive shares equivalent to that of two females without there being any disagreement or debate about the shares. Funds should be allocated for the construction of subterranean canals (*qanats*); and efforts should be expended to increase the *haqq al-tawliya* (by increasing revenues).

The conditions are illustrative. The protocols were presumably annexed to a mixed waqf, that is, public and private beneficiaries: in other words, the shrine and the settlor's heirs. The conditions are applicable to any trustee at Turbat-i Jam, which is why the document is illuminating despite the possibility of illicit emendations. Condition 3 shows that he had to help develop the endowed regions and maintain sustainability (read: environmental and economic sustainability). Condition 4 relates to the question of skill and probity. Since the trustee's fee (Condition 6) is a percentage of agricultural revenues, he has the incentive to increase revenues by developing agriculture and increasing harvests.

Apropos of this, we next examine the source of the shrine's wealth: agriculture.

---

[99] A waqf is not automatically tax exempt; hence the importance of tax immunities. See discussion in Chapter 6.

6

Agro- and Hydro-management

The greatest source of wealth for Ahmad-i Jam's progeny and shrine was their control of hydrological systems (aqueducts, canals, dams, water mills, sluices, etc.) and agricultural production in the provinces of Bakharz, Fushanj, Harat-Rud, Jam, Khwaf, and Kusuyi. In the wake of the Mongol irruptions, peasants not murdered or deported, or fleeced by rapacious Mongol viceroys, fled to safer locales. The Ilkhanids and Kartids recognized the urgency of rebuilding ruined hydrological systems and revitalizing fallow lands (*ihya' al-mawat*); and enticing wary peasants to return and to farm. Responsibility for managing irrigation and improving food production was shifted to Islamic institutions (e.g., shrines and mosques), which consequently became wealthy and influential. Timurids built on Kartid and Ilkhanid socioeconomic policies. Jamis received fiscal and legal immunities (*mu'afi*) and land grants (*soyurghal*) from the Timurids.

The shrine and the shaykhs administering it were extraordinarily wealthy by the end of the Timurid-era. However, much (or most) of the combined institutional and personal wealth, in agricultural, pastoral, and hydrological assets, was undoubtedly the result of royal patronage, namely, land grants (*soyurghal*) and fiscal and legal immunities (*mu'afi*). Ibn Battuta's claim that Jam "is exempted from paying taxes to the [Ilkhanid] sultan [Abu Sa'id Bahadur Khan]" rings true.[1] It is unlikely that shaykhs and the shrine became affluent landlords and waterlords on pious donations alone, that is, waqfs and alms. The bulk of their wealth had to have come from royal patronage.

---

[1] Ibn Battuta, *Travels*, 3:581.

Ahmad-i Jam's shrine complex's acquisition of wealth was not merely a situation of Il-Khans and sultans patronizing Sufis in exchange for blessings. Shrines located in agricultural sections of Khurasan were entrusted with the management of agricultural estates and hydrological systems. Consequently, in addition to the myriads of small-to-medium-scale agro- and hydro-managers that came to dot the landscapes of Khurasan, four shrines – Ahmad-i Jam's (influential in Bakharz, Fushanj, Jam, Khwaf, and Kusuyi); ʿAbdallah Ansari's (Herat and vicinities); Imam Riza's (Mashhad-Tus and vicinities); and Imam ʿAli's (Balkh and vicinities) – were transformed into large-scale agro- and hydro–managers. With imperial favors, including low-to-zero taxation of incomes and capital assets, and immunity from interference by *diwan* officials and governors, the regions economically dominated by these shrine complexes became *semiautonomous enclaves*: ruled (in effect) by the institution's administrator (*raʾis* or *mutawalli*). This man usually held the title of Shaykh al-Islam.[2]

Ahmad-i Jam's shrine complex became the paramount manager of agricultural estates and hydrological systems in Bakharz, Fushanj, Jam, Khwaf, and Kusuyi. In order to appreciate how this came to be, the following four aspects are discussed.

First, a sketch of the socioeconomic harm inflicted in the Mongol irruptions and by Mongol viceroys, and how irrigation systems decayed and agricultural lands fell fallow. Second, Ilkhanid legal and fiscal reforms that offered incentives to investors to expend their capital to overhaul hydrological systems and revivify fallow lands. Third, Kartid policy imperatives to repair irrigation networks and improve food production in the vicinities of Herat (the Kartid capital). Fourth, Timurid initiatives that expanded on Kartid initiatives. Volleys of waqfs, land grants, and tax immunities by the Timurids transformed local shrines into *regional* economic powerhouses. Ahmad-i Jam's shrine lost most of its wealth, including waqf assets, under the Safavids and Qajars.

THE MONGOL INVASIONS OF KHURASAN

The Mongol invasions of Iran beginning in 617/1220 were unprecedented. Iran had suffered invaders before, but never invaders who bore with them the psychological and technological capacities to kill peoples

---

[2] Mahendrarajah, "Shaykh al-Islam," 270–73.

and destroy burgs with extreme violence.[3] Cities, from Balkh in the east to Ardabil in the west, suffered devastations. Villages and towns ceased to exist. Balkh, a vibrant center for trade and Perso-Islamic culture, did not fully recover. Although medieval historians inflated statistics on casualties, sizeable majorities of metropolises like Balkh, Marw, Herat, Nishapur, Hamadan, and Qazvin were massacred or deported to Inner Asia. Iranians fled to other parts of Iran: Yazd and Kirman (hot, dry regions, with poor pasturing for the Mongols' horses), and the Caspian Sea littoral (hot, humid, dense jungle regions that the steppe peoples loathed). Iranians also fled to Anatolia, India, Egypt, the Hijaz, the Yemen, and Levant. Agricultural lands fell fallow; and economic and social activities declined. After the Mongol hordes came their viceroys, who abused survivors through capricious rules and imposts. Peasants who emerged from hiding found it expedient to hastily decamp for viceroy-free regions of Iran (chiefly, central Iran, south/Persian Gulf, and the Caspian littoral).

Social and Economic Decline in Post-Mongol Khurasan

An Iranian peasant's lot was not a happy one. The majority of Iranian peasants were tenant farmers who farmed under a share-cropping contract (*muzara'a*) with the landlord. At harvest time, the peasant paid an agreed percentage of the crop as rent; he then repaid any outstanding interest-free advances (*taqawi*), and interest-bearing loans (*musa'ada*), for cash, seed, or tools; and pursuant to Hanafi legal *theory*, he paid the *'ushr* tax (10 percent) and the *kharaj* tax (20 percent) on the crop. The landlord usually paid the *kharaj* on the land.[4] Tax practices and rates varied across Khurasan and over time, but generally, landlords shifted financial burdens to the peasant. The share-cropping family subsisted until the next harvest on the remainder (if any) of the crop. Between Mongol pillagers and Mongol viceroys, Iranian peasants had little left, especially the incentive to sharecrop. Fallow lands in Khurasan stayed fallow.

Hydrological systems (subterranean channels, aqueducts, dams, sluices, water-timers, water mills, etc.) were wrecked by the Mongols,

---

[3] For a sober reappraisal of the Mongols' employment of violence, see Jackson, *Mongols and the Islamic World*, 153–73.
[4] The *kharaj muqasama* (tax on the crop) is generally 20 per cent and paid by the tenant; the *kharaj wazifa* (variable tax on the land) is paid by the landlord. Baber Johansen, *The Islamic Law on Land Tax and Rent* (London: Croom Helm, 1988), 15–17.

or fell into disrepair through disuse (siltation is a pervasive problem). The restoration or construction of hydrological systems, especially dams and subterranean channels (*qanat, kariz*), is capital and labor intensive. Investors were reluctant to assume risks while the political climate remained stormy, and while the legal framework under the Mongols remained unsettled. Labor supply was tight. There was little socioeconomic improvement in Khurasan even after the age of viceroys was terminated by Möngke Qaʾan (a son of Tolui), who dispatched his brother, Hülegü Khan (r. 1256–65), to initiate direct rule over Iran and Iraq; hence the Ilkhanate (654–736/1256–1335). Another brother, Qubilai Khan (r. 1260–94), was dispatched to China; he founded the Yuan dynasty (1260–1368).

ILKHANID EFFORTS TO REVIVE FALLOW LANDS AND REPAIR HYDROLOGICAL SYSTEMS

Enter now Sultan Mahmud Ghazan Khan (r. 694–703/1295–1304), heir to the throne of Hülegü, and his Iranian vizier, Rashid al-Din Fazlallah (645–718/1247–1318), himself a convert to Islam, albeit from Judaism. The revitalization of fallow lands (*ihyaʾ al-mawat*) became a pillar of Ilkhanid policy. This was, of course, seventy-five years after the Mongol invasions, meaning prodigious levels of damage had been inflicted by the hordes; by the actions or inactions of Mongol administrators (*basqaq, darugha, shahna*); and through the neglect of hydrological assets. Socioeconomic conditions in Iran were dreadful, particularly with respect to agriculture,[5] the source not only of nutrition but of wealth in preindustrial times. Rashid al-Din Fazlallah, in his *Compendium of Histories*, laments that "there has never been a realm more devastated than this one";[6] and that uncertainty resulting from arbitrary rules and taxes was thwarting investments in agriculture and irrigation: "If anyone wants to make improvements, he doesn't even begin for fear .... If we make it so that those fallow lands can be improved, and one portion goes to the owner if it is private property and another portion goes to the divan and

---

[5] I. P. Petrushevsky [Petrushevskiĭ], *Kishawarzi wa munasabat-i arzi dar Iran-i ʿahd-i Mughul* [*Agriculture and Land [Use] in Iran: the Mongol Era*], 2 vols., trans. Karim Kishawarz (Tehran: Intisharat-i nil, 1347/1968), 1:125–34; and I. P. Petrushevsky [Petrushevskiĭ], "The Socio-economic Conditions of Iran under the Il-Khans," in *CHI* 5:483–537, esp. 483–91.

[6] Rashid al-Din, *Jamiʿ*, 3:528.

the people who make improvements."[7] A critical concern for any investor was that if he revitalized an irrigation system with his own capital, absent legal safeguards, a local "warlord" could seize the developed asset or lay claim to its revenues.

Sultan and vizier implemented wide-ranging fiscal, legal, and administrative reforms. They amended, inter alia, land-tenure laws; rates and modes of taxation; and offered incentives for the restoration of hydrological systems and the revivification of fallow lands. Their policies included a three-tier "triage" for bringing fallow lands and irrigation systems into operation in the shortest and cheapest manner. Their reasoning was impeccable: "when fallow lands are made to flourish, grain will be cheap; and when [military] expeditions are mounted ... provisions will be readily available. Money will also flow into the treasury and increase."[8]

Rashid al-Din describes three classes of lands subject to revivification projects: *Tier 1*: lands that had "water and irrigation canals and did not entail great expense or outlay of labor to be cultivated and irrigated," that is, they did not require the construction of subterranean channels, dams, or aqueducts. *Tier 2*: "lands that needed moderate improvement, where irrigation canals had to be repaired or dug." *Tier 3*: lands that required "difficult" improvements, where "dams had to be made for irrigation, and the underground water channels [sing. *qanat*] were ruined and had to be repaired."

For Tier 1 lands, the *diwan* receives no tax revenues from the first harvest. From the second harvest, revenue equal to one-third of the prevailing rate went to the *diwan*, and two-thirds to the investor. For the third harvest, 75 percent of the rate "customary in each province" was paid to the *diwan*; 25 percent to the investor. "Over and above that, any money realized by the cultivator was his." And so on for Tiers 2 and 3. In recognition of the difficulties in improving Tier 2 lands, in Year 3, the *diwan* received 66.67 percent; whereas the investor received 33.33 percent. For Tier 3 lands, where substantial improvements were made, by Year 3, the *diwan* rate was 50 percent, with 50 percent to the investor. Ownership transferred to the investor and his progeny "in perpetuity."[9]

---

[7] Ibid., 3:529.
[8] Ibid. It is worth appreciating Adam Smith's analyses on the importance of agriculture for the well-being of nations; the interdependencies of (1) landowners; (2) farmers and laborers; and (3) craftsmen, manufacturers, and merchants. Adam Smith, *An Inquiry into the Nature and Causes of the Wealth of Nations*, ed. Edwin Cannan (Chicago, IL: University of Chicago Press, 1976 [2012 reprint]), 882 et seq.
[9] Rashid al-Din, *Jami'*, 3:529–30.

Ilkhanid Efforts to Revive Agriculture

This comports, by the by, with Hanafi law, which prevailed in Khurasan: Hanafi law rewards investment in fallow (*mawat*) lands.[10] To stimulate investment, the Il-Khan decreed that crown lands (*injü*) untended for years, and farms uncultivated for extended periods, were henceforth deemed fallow, thereby freeing said lands for investment. That said, the Ilkhanid vizier's words reveal political *intent*. They do not illuminate on practices.

An investor's outlays for the revivification of fallow lands are prohibitive; for example, he has to supply cash, oxen, fodder, tools, supplies, and shelter.[11] In Year 1, he must advance (*taqawi*) seed for planting, and cereals for farmers and their families since there is no stored surplus from previous harvests.[12]

If the investor has to overhaul or excavate a subterranean canal before fallow lands can be tilled and seeded, costs will skyrocket.[13] It could take a series of good harvests to recover even the outlays for restoring Tier 1 *juy*s and *qanat*s, which Rashid al-Din and Ghazan recognized through their revenue formulae for Tier 1, 2, and 3 lands. Investors prefer cash crops (e.g., saffron and cotton), but hungry burgers and peasants need rice, wheat, barley, corn, and vegetables.

In weighing costs against benefits, private investors were undoubtedly hesitant. Indeed, even Islamic institutions will have hesitated. However, Islamic institutions are (in theory), long-term (or perpetual) enterprises (i.e., shrines expect to thrive until the end of days); and such institutions already controlled farms, pastures, and hydrological systems obtained as pious endowments (waqf). Islamic institutions frequently possessed (or will have acquired) the technical expertise to manage agriculture and

---

[10] See *Kitab ihya' al-mawat* in Burhan al-Marghinani's *al-Hidaya* (various editions).
[11] On these "ground expenses (*dépenses foncières*)," see Smith, *Wealth of Nations*, 882–83.
[12] British farmers contributed certain "original and annual expenses (*dépenses primitives et dépenses annuelles*)," not unlike medieval Iranian sharecroppers. All startup expenses *plus* annual expenses for Year 1 were borne by investors in fallow lands.

The *original expenses* consist in the instruments of husbandry, in the stock of cattle, in the seed, and in the maintenance of the farmer's family, servants, and cattle during at least a great part of the first year of his occupancy, or till he can receive some return from the land. The *annual expenses* consist in the seed, in the wear and tear of the instruments of husbandry, and in the annual maintenance of the farmer's servants and cattle, and of his family too (ibid., 883).

[13] On *qanat*s, see H. E. Wulff, "The Qanats of Iran," *Scientific American* 218/4 (1968): 94–105; Mohammad Kamiar, "The Qanat system in Iran," *Ekistics* 50/303 (1983): 467–72. See also Anthony Smith, *Blind White Fish in Persia* (New York: E. P. Dutton, 1953), esp. 56–60, 79–86, 97–101, 110–14, and 151–54, for explorations of *qanat*s, and for socioeconomic insights. Smith's sketches and photographs (plates 19–24) are illuminating.

irrigation.[14] Islamic institutions have to consider long-term needs – a waqf is (in theory) perpetual – and to plan accordingly, and be willing to accept lower profits (or losses), and low (even negative) cash flows in the early years in exchange for tax abatements, legal and fiscal immunities, and ownership of the asset free of legal encumbrances.

Waqfs are not inherently tax exempt. Fiscal-legal immunities and abatements were incentives for custodians to make investments. Short-term imperial favors, namely, the *soyurghal*, *iqta'*, and *tiyul*,[15] encourage short-term mentalities: a grantee exploits the asset irrespective of the commonweal and environmental sustainability before he is compelled to relinquish the asset to another short-termer, who continues the cycle of exploitation. Although we cannot know how Ghazan's and Rashid al-Din's fiscal-legal reforms and initiatives unfolded in eighth/fourteenth-century Khurasan, and precisely how they contributed to agricultural development and economic growth,[16] we know from Kartid initiatives to develop agriculture and irrigation, and pious donations to mosques and shrines, that Islamic institutions in the Herat Quarter became small-to-medium-scale agro- and hydro-managers (see below).

Ilkhanid Initiatives and the Shrine

How did the Ilkhanid reforms impact Ahmad's shrine, if at all? Öljeitü (r. 703–17/1304–16) held Shihab al-Din Isma'il Jami in high regard.[17] The Il-Khan granted him agricultural lands and an irrigation system. The imperial decree (*yarligh*) was issued on 29 Safar 706/9 September 1306, in Tabriz.[18] It is directed to the vizier, 'Ala' al-Din Hindu; the governor, 'Ala' al-Din

---

[14] Medieval manuals on agriculture and hydrology were authored by Qasim Harawi (fl. ca. 921/1515), an accountant with 'Abdallah Ansari's shrine. Qasim b. Yusuf Abu Nasr al-Harawi, *Risala-i tariq-i qismat-i ab-i qulb* [*Treatise on Apportioning Waters through Sluice-gates*], ed. Mayil Harawi (Tehran: Intisharat-i bunyad-i farhang-i Iran, 1347/1969); and Qasim b. Yusuf Abu Nasr al-Harawi, *Irshad al-zira'a* [*Guidance on Agriculture*], ed. Muhammad Mushiri (Tehran: Danishgah-yi Tehran, 1346/1968); see Maria Eva Subtelny, "A Persian Agricultural Manual in Context: The *Irshad al-zira'a* in Late Timurid and Early Safavid Khorasan," *Studia Iranica* 22 (1993): 167–217.
[15] See Lambton, *Landlord and Peasant*, 53ff; A. K. S. Lambton, "The Evolution of the *Iqta'* in Medieval Iran," *Iran* 5 (1967): 41–50.
[16] But see evaluations by Petrushevsky, "Socio-economic Conditions," 494–500 (analysis of data), and 500–505 (state of agriculture). The data for Khurasan, however, is weak.
[17] Buzjani/Moayyad (ed.), *Rawzat*, 102–3.
[18] Yusuf-i Ahl/Berlin, *Fara'id-i Ghiyasi*, fol. 317a–317b.

Muhammad [Faryumadi];[19] the Kartid ruler at Herat [Fakhr al-Din Kart]; and [Ilkhanid and Kartid] functionaries in Zir-i Pul.[20]

Shihab al-Din Isma'il Jami's virtues are extolled in the preamble. He is described as an advisor (*nasih*) to the Il-Khans of Iran and Iraq. The Ilkhanid state grants to Shihab al-Din Isma'il Jami until the end of time, with favor, affection, and kindness, the Juy-yi Baghand.[21] Öljeitü's *yarligh* is authorized with the "golden seal" (*altun tamgha*), which was utilized to validate chancery documents of economic import.[22] At the time (the decree informs) there were thirty farmers cultivating the tract straddling Taybad and Zandjan; their shares of the harvest shall continue under the existing agreement, but the balance of the harvest is to be delivered to the Shaykh al-Islam's agents (instead of to the state under current policy). Functionaries shall not interfere in any aspect of his legal rights (*bih hich wajh min al-wujuh dar kar-i ishan madkhal na-sazand*), however major, minor, infinitesimal, or insignificant (*qalil wa kathir wa naqir wa qitmir*). Officials are not entitled to payments/allocations (*hawala*), and must not try to apply any levies, tolls, or taxes on his income (*wa bih jihat-hu ikhrajat wa 'awarizat wa sayir-i takalif-i diwani muzahim wa muta'arriz-i ishan na-gardand*).[23] The Shaykh al-Islam should be permitted to cultivate the lands in peace and tranquility (*sar faragh-i bal wa rifagh-i hal bi-'imarat wa zira'at an ishti'al tawanand namud*).[24] The proscriptions are not unusual:[25] tax collectors and state functionaries were officious and rapacious; the decree blocks them from interfering with the Shaykh al-Islam's agents and hindering the objectives of the grant.

The Shaykh al-Islam and his shrine community benefitted from Ilkhanid fiscal reforms. The grant to Shihab al-Din Isma'il Jami of the Juy-yi Baghand was an element in the Ilkhanid program to revitalize fallow lands. A *juy* is a channel; a *juy-bar* is a feeder channel. The *juy* at Baghand was a *juy-bar*,[26] a regulator for a network of channels and rivulets

---

[19] The MS has *hukkam* (sing. *hakim*), a copying error (by a bygone scribe).
[20] *Zir-i Pul*: localism for the agricultural region lying south of Herat's Malan Bridge. On this ancient bridge, see Ball, *Monuments*, 210, and plate 124.
[21] The MS has *Baghiyand*, a scribal error.
[22] The manuscript has *alyun*. "The golden seal [*altun tamgha*] was used almost exclusively for financial or fiscal edicts. The red seal [*al tamgha*] was used for documents with broader administrative import." G. Doerfer, "Al Tamga," *EIr*, 1:766–68.
[23] On the terms *ikhrajat*, *'awarizat*, *hawala*, and *takalif-i diwani*, see Vladimir Minorsky, "A 'Soyurghal' of Qasim b. Jahangir Aq-qoyunlu (903/1498)," *BSOAS* 9/4 (1939): 927–60.
[24] See also Mahendrarajah, "Shaykh al-Islam."
[25] See, e.g., Mahendrarajah, "Gawhar Shad Waqf," 849 (proscriptions in a waqf).
[26] In modern usage, *juy-bar* refers to a mechanical water-distribution system.

that distributed water to farmlands. The Shaykh al-Islam had to maintain the *juy* and develop farmlands. The preexisting farmers became his tenants.

One Ilkhanid land grant does not a revitalization program make. Ilkhanid efforts vis-à-vis Khurasan are opaque. I. P. Petrushevsky claims that there were improvements in agricultural production in the districts of Khurasan that he itemizes, including Herat and Jam, with waters flowing in overground and underground canals, and cereals and fruits in abundance after Ghazan's/Rashid al-Din's reforms;[27] but whether the economic improvements were the result of Ilkhanid fiscal-legal reforms or of Kartid endeavors is unclear. Ilkhanid legal-fiscal reforms, and Kartid initiatives, undoubtedly combined to improve land use and irrigation systems and to increase agricultural production, which consequently will have boosted the economy of Khurasan.

KARTID EFFORTS TO REVIVE FALLOW LANDS AND REPAIR HYDROLOGICAL SYSTEMS

Ghiyath al-Din Kart (r. 707–29/1307–29) and his successor, Muʿizz al-Din Kart (r. 732–71/1332–70),[28] were closely engaged with agricultural and hydrological projects. The Kartid state's fisc, economy, and security depended on agriculture and irrigation. Flows of comestibles and potable waters into Herat were indispensable to its survival. Herat's inner city, which contains the citadel, stored grain to safeguard against famines and sieges, but city cisterns (sing. *hawz*) held limited supplies of potable water. The Injil district (*buluk-i Injil*) supplied inner Herat with fresh water, which entered inner Herat through an aqueduct to the north.[29] By blocking water flows, besiegers could subjugate Herat. One of the first acts in the revitalization of Herat, ruined in 619/1222, was the reopening of *juy*s in 635/1237f., especially the *Juy-i Injil*.[30] This was consequent to an order by the Mongol Grand Qaʾan, Ögödei (r. 1229–41). Maintenance of

---

[27] Petrushevsky, *Kishawarzi*, 1:174–75. See also descriptions for Khurasan (from *ca*. 1340) in Mustawfi, *Nuzhat al-Qulub*, 181–96; Mustawfi/Le Strange (trans.), *Nuzhat al-Qulub*, 146–56.

[28] Muʿizz al-Din succeeded his brothers Shams al-Din Muhammad (d. *ca*. 730/1330) and Hafiz (d. *ca*. 732/1332), each of whom reigned briefly.

[29] On Injil, see Krawulsky, *Ḫorasan*, 1:23–24; and Allen, *Catalogue*, 10–24, esp. Cat. Nos. 18 and 46.

[30] al-Harawi, *Harat*, 145–49.

hydrological systems sustaining Herat and its environs was an indispensable duty for Herat's rulers.

Ghiyath al-Din Kart invested in public works in Herat and its purlieus.[31] Mu'izz al-Din devised a system for the equitable distribution of canal waters: water-managers (*mard-i juy* or *mirab*), sluices (*qulb*), barrages (*band*), and timers (*natarah*) diverted flows from major to minor channels, thence to farmlands. A distribution schedule determined flows, with each parcel being irrigated every five days at minimum. Barrage-keepers and water-managers were compensated through shares of the harvest.[32]

The agricultural and hydrological holdings of the shrines, mosques, *khanaqah*s, and madrasas of Kartid Herat are indeterminable. Prominent local Islamic institutions are known (or reasonably presumed) to have held agricultural and hydrological assets in the region. To illustrate: Herat's Friday mosque, Madrasa-i Ghiyasiyya, Khanaqah-i Jadid, Khanaqah-i Mu'izz al-Din Husayn Kart, Khanaqah-i Sabz-i Khiyaban, Khanaqah-i Sultan-Khatun, Gunbad-i Khwaja Abu al-Walid, and 'Abdallah Ansari's shrine at Gazurgah were patronized by Fakhr al-Din Kart (r. 695–706/1295–1307) and brother, Ghiyath al-Din; and Mu'izz al-Din Kart and one of his wives, Sultan-Khatun bt. Tagha-Temür.[33] Kartid benefactions (explicitly or implicitly) included waqfs of agricultural and hydrological assets. Ghiyath al-Din Kart overhauled and enlarged the Juy-i Sabaqar (it then acquired the appellation Juy-i Naw: New Canal), which irrigates an extensive tract (north and east of Herat); and conveyed farmlands and seven water mills situated along the course as waqf for a *khanaqah*.[34] Other benefactors endowed their favorite institution(s) with farms and waterways, and built cisterns (*hawz*) and water mills (*juy-i tahuna*).

The agricultural regions of Bakharz, Fushanj, Harat-Rud, Isfizar, Jam, Khwaf, Kusuyi, Kurukh, and Shafilan, which encircle Herat, depended on Herat for economic exchanges; and Herat depended on them for comestibles, potables, pelts, textiles, crafts, and agricultural and commercial

---

[31] Ibid., 742–45; al-Harawi, *Risala-i tariq*, 6–7; Isfizari, *Rawzat al-jannat*, 1:505–7. Allen, *Catalogue*, 105, 131, 149, 229–30.

[32] al-Harawi, *Risala-i tariq*, 1–2, 12–16. The Kartid system was reinstated by the Timurid Sultan-Abu Sa'id (r. 855–73/1451–69).

[33] al-Harawi, *Harat*, 462–63, 742–45; Isfizari, *Rawzat al-jannat*, 1:437–38, 1:505–7; Harawi, *Risala-i tariq*, 6–12; Allen, *Catalogue*, 105–6, 131, 137, 148, 149, 150, 151, 152, 153, 174, 177 (Cat. Nos. 428, 460, 484, 493, 499, 501, 502, 503, 508, 509, 513, 520, 573, 580).

[34] al-Harawi, *Harat*, 745; Allen, *Catalogue*, 149 (Cat. No. 501); al-Harawi, *Risala-i tariq*, 10–11.

taxes. Sayf al-Harawi's *History of Herat* (which ends *ca.* 722/1322 with his death) offers clues to the prosperity of Herat and its environs; for example, the recovery by the Kartids of 10,000 *kharwars* (3 mil. kg/6.6 mil. lb) of wheat (*gandum*) plundered by Chaghatai raiders.[35] This was only part of the stocks plundered from regions lying beyond Herat's protection. Herat and its frontier outposts held food stocks of their own. The weight given by Sayfi, even allowing for hyperbole, is revealing of a high degree of agricultural production, around 720/1320. The prosperity of the region attracted raids by a Chaghataid princeling, Yasa'ur (d. 720/1320).

Kartid Initiatives and the Shrine

How did Kartid initiatives impact Ahmad-i Jam's shrine? The impact is found in Jami wealth from Ghiyath al-Din Kart's reign to the passing of the Kartid age. Hitherto, the shrine was not wealthy, although Ahmad-i Jam's grandson, Qutb al-Din Muhammad (d. 667/1268), had set the shrine and Jami progeny on the road to affluence.

Shihab al-Din Isma'il Jami (d. *ca.* 738/1338) exemplifies the family's and shrine's situation after around 700/1300. Buzjani states that the Shaykh al-Islam of Jam commanded immense wealth: "he held an exalted position, great wealth, extensive farmlands, and innumerable cattle. His riches were so abundant that he had no measure of it."[36] Jami wealth, and sources of income, are gleaned from anecdotes: a granary (*anbar-i ghalla*) in Baghand (where Öljeitü's grant, Juy-yi Baghand, was located);[37] farmlands (*zaya'*) in Jam province; a horse ranch in Khwaf; and estates in Zur-Abad.[38] The farmlands held in Jam were extensive: 1,000 *kharwars* - (300,000 kg/660,000 lb) of seed were endowed in a waqf for the benefit of the shrine,[39] which suggests control of extensive agricultural estates capable of producing a large quantity of high-grade seed. Nothing precise is known of the grainlands, vineyards, orchards, ranches, and silos in Bakharz, Fushanj, Harat-Rud, Jam, Khwaf, and Kusuyi. Considering the bonds between Ghiyath al-Din Kart and Shihab al-Din Isma'il, and the *malik*'s sponsorship of buildings at the shrine, it is likely that the Kartid was the source of much of Jami's wealth.

---

[35] al-Harawi, *Harat*, 764–67 (1 Khurasani *kharwar* = 100 Herati *mann* 297 kg/653.4 lb).
[36] Buzjani/Moayyad (ed.), *Rawzat*, 100–101.   [37] Ibid., 102.   [38] Ibid., 103–5.
[39] Ibid., 102. Even allowing for exaggerations by Buzjani, evidence indicates that Jami shaykhs and Ahmad's shrine had acquired valuable agricultural holdings.

A Kartid decree of 23 Safar 753/10 April 1352 illustrates Jami family and shrine holdings.[40] It lists properties (1) in the province of Harat-Rud, consisting of vineyards, orchards, and other things; (2) in (the province of) Kusuyi and (district of) Zir-i Pul; (3) in the province of Fushanj; and (4) the farm (*mazra'a*) of Karchih and Faraha. In this decree, one Kart *malik* (Muhammad Baqir) was returning estates seized by a deposed Kart *malik* (his brother, Mu'izz al-Din Kart).[41] The estates were being returned because "earlier covenants" (*'uhud-i salifa*) with "bygone kings of bypast ages" (*muluk-i maziya dar qarun-i sabiqa*) had been breached when the Jami estates were improperly seized (*bi-ta'addi girifta bashad*) by *malik* Mu'izz al-Din Kart.

The wording ("earlier covenants" with "bygone kings") suggests that the estates were land grants by the Ilkhanids and/or Kartids. The Ilkhanate collapsed when sultan Abu Sa'id Bahadur Khan died in 736/1335. Mu'izz al-Din Kart became an independent ruler. With Jami patrons Ghiyath al-Din Kart, Chupan Suldus, and Abu Sa'id deceased, and the powerful patriarch and Shaykh al-Islam of Jam, Shihab al-Din Isma'il Jami, also deceased, Mu'izz al-Din seized the estates, precipitating a crisis with the shaykhs of Jam. The decree reveals extensive agricultural holdings of indeterminate title. It is unlikely (but not impossible) that the estates included waqf assets as their confiscation would spark public opprobrium, which Mu'izz al-Din, reputably a pious king – one lauded for his piety in the hagiology of Zayn al-Din Taybadi (a devotee of Ahmad-i Jam who was fond of the Kartid)[42] – would not bring upon himself absent good cause.

TIMURID EFFORTS TO REVIVE FALLOW LANDS AND REPAIR HYDROLOGICAL SYSTEMS

In the Timurid period, 783/1381 to 911/1506, there were sustained programs originating with Temür to revitalize hydrological systems and

---

[40] Yusuf-i Ahl/Berlin, *Fara'id*, fol. 310b–311b; Buzjani/Moayyad (ed.), *Rawzat*, 146 (edited text of decree); and Mahendrarajah, "Revised," 116. The assets are not itemized as personal or corporate (shrine) holdings. My sense is that assets were commingled. Legal or accounting restrictions on the commingling of corporate and personal holdings were probably not stringently applied (or applied at all).
[41] Yusuf-i Ahl/Berlin, *Fara'id*, fol. 311b; Buzjani/Moayyad (ed.), *Rawzat*, 146.
[42] Anonymous, *Maqamat-i Taybadi*, ed. Sayyid 'Ala' al-Din Gusha-Gir (Dizful [Khuzistan]: Intisharat-i afham, 1382/2003), 86–89. Taybadi was a confidant of the Jami shaykhs. His Timurid-era hagiography speaks glowingly of Mu'izz al-Din Kart.

agriculture in Iran.[43] He ordered his high officials to build canals to convey waters from the Murghab River to the dry regions of Khurasan. Temür's officials had to bear the costs – but were allowed to name the canals.[44] In 812/1410, Shah-Rukh ordered the revitalization of the Marw oasis, ruined in 618/1221 by Tolui. The Timurid treasury paid the associated costs for oxen, fodder, construction materials, salaries, and comestibles for the Turks and Tajiks who migrated to the oasis to engage in commerce and agriculture.[45]

The approaches of Temür and Shah-Rukh – compelling amirs to construct canals or pay from the fisc for development projects – had inherent limitations, that is to say, unlike today, with liquid global capital markets underwriting bonds guaranteed by the "full faith and credit" of a state, with risks borne by a broad taxpayer base, Ilkhanid and Timurid ambitions for large-scale hydrological and agricultural projects lacked capital. Absent capital, plans for improving infrastructure and agriculture will not go far. Since non-investment (i.e., investors sitting on cash instead of putting their cash to work) was the principal problem, the Ilkhanids offered fiscal incentives for investors, along with legal and fiscal reforms and protections. Kartids had endowed or encouraged Islamic institutions to invest in agricultural and hydrological projects. The Timurids followed Ilkhanid and Kartid empowerment patterns.

Timurid sultans (from Shah-Rukh to Sultan-Husyan Bayqara) delegated to *select* shrine complexes of Khurasan the responsibilities for the management of agricultural and hydrological projects. This made economic sense since shrines had acquired such experiences in the Kartid period, and employed specialists (agronomists, hydrologists, engineers, accountants, etc.). Maria Subtelny explains:

> With their staffs of administrators, accountants, agronomists, and hydrologists, the major Timurid shrine complexes possessed the professional expertise and resources

---

[43] On Temür's intentions regarding agriculture, see Sharaf al-Din 'Ali Yazdi, *Zafarnama*, 2 vols., ed. Muhammad 'Abbasi (Tehran: Amir Kabir, 1336/1957), 2:17–18; and Ismail Aka, "The Agricultural and Commercial Activities of the Timurids in the First Half of the 15th Century," *Oriente Moderno* 15/2 (1996): 9–21, esp. 10.

[44] Krawulsky, *Ḥorasan*, 1:32; Aka, "Agricultural," 10–12.

[45] Hafiz-i Abru, *Zubdat al-tawarikh*, 2 vols., ed. Kamal Hajj Sayyid Jawadi (Tehran: Nashr-i nay, 1372/1993), 1:337–40; 'Abd al-Razzaq al-Samarqandi, *Matla'-i sa'dayn wa majma'-i bahrayn*, 4 vols., ed. 'Abd al-Husayn Nawa'i (Tehran: Pazhuhishgah-i 'ulum-i insani wa mutala'at-i farhangi, vol. I, pt. 1, 1372/1993; vol. 1, pt. 2, and vol. 2, pts. 1 and 2, 1383/2004f.), 2.1:115–16; Aka, "Agricultural," 12; Krawulsky, *Ḥorasan*, 1:60–61; Subtelny, *Timurids*, 125.

to rationalize agricultural activity and to become efficiently run large-scale agricultural enterprises.[46]

Farming was a large-scale business enterprise. Iranians' knowledge of agronomy and hydrology had improved in the Mongol age, profiting from scientific and technical knowledge from East Asia.[47] The Ilkhanid vizier Rashid al-Din was one of the principal Iranian accumulators of Asian scientific knowledge on agronomy and hydrology.[48] He published a treatise incorporating this knowledge, but only the section on agronomy has survived.[49] Agricultural and hydrological techniques were improving in Iran (on paper if not in actual practice) since the eighth/fourteenth century, and will (if implemented) have improved agricultural production (i.e., higher yields and better quality produce); and benefited the environment through improved farming techniques and avoidance of ecologically unsound practices.

In any case, Islamic institutions became wealthy as Timurid royals and officials bequeathed liquid assets, livestock, pasturelands, farmlands, and hydrological systems as waqf; and sultans issued land grants and immunities.[50] *Soyurghal*s and *mu'afi*s often benefited waqfs, which otherwise would have been liable for land or agricultural taxes; for example, a *soyurghal* for the benefit of Abu Sa'id b. Abu al-Khayr's shrine in Mayhana (Abiward province) fiscally and legally immunized "immobilized and freehold" (*waqfi wa milki*) estates,[51] thereby freeing the shrine of fiscal obligations to the state.

Soyurghal *and* Mu'afi

Brief remarks on *soyurghal*s and *mu'afi*s are overdue.

Soyurghal, benefice, is related to the Mongolian word *soyurghamishi*, "favor," and sometimes used with the Persian auxiliary verb *kardan*:

---

[46] Subtelny, *Timurids*, 199.
[47] Thomas Allsen, *Culture and Conquest in Mongol Eurasia* (Cambridge: Cambridge University Press, 2001), 115–26.
[48] Ibid., 72–80.
[49] Rashid al-Din, *Athar wa ahya'*, ed. Manuchihr Sutudah and Iraj Afshar (Tehran: McGill University and Tehran University, 1368/1989).
[50] See Maria Eva Subtelny, "Centralizing Reform and Its Opponents in the Late Timurid Period," *Iranian Studies* 21/1 (1988): 123–51; Maria Eva Subtelny, "Socioeconomic Bases of Cultural Patronage under the Later Timurids," *IJMES* 20/4 (1988): 479–505.
[51] Nawa'i (ed.), *Asnad wa mukatibat*, 299–301. The undated decree was issued by Abu al-Qasim Babur (d. Rabi' II 861/March 1457) b. Baysunghur b. Shah-Rukh. See *Recueil*, Supplément persan 1815, fol. 14a–15b (the first line is omitted in Nawa'i's edition).

soyurghamishi kardan, "to show favor." The term *soyurghal* was rare in the Ilkhanid period. Öljeitü's grant to Shihab al-Din Ismaʻil comes near through the use of *soyurghamishi*. A *soyurghal* is an exercise in royal favor and takes miscellaneous forms, from fiscal immunities to grants of estates, even entire provinces. The grantee retained the *soyurghal* as a hereditary asset, but in reality, *soyurghal*s were abrogated by incoming governments – the price for the defeat or death of a sultan. A Jami shaykh, for instance, lost a *soyurghal* following Shah-Rukh's death; however, it was returned by Sultan-Abu Saʻid (see below). Generally, a *soyurghal* was a fiscal immunity tied to land. It included judicial and administrative freedoms, and entitled the holder to collect (some or all) of the taxes within the defined territory.

Apart from "tax immunities connected with landholding and [waqfs]," there existed the *muʻafi* (or *musallami*), which "exempted the grantee from the payment of specified taxes to the central treasury and from the performance of certain duties and obligations. Although it did not involve the granting of land, the exemption could apply to a tract of land already in the possession of the grantee."[52] The *muʻafi*, needless to say, was not the extent of exemptions available to anyone close to the Timurid court. In any event, with respect to *muʻafi* grants connected to land, "the holder of the immunity had no right to collect the taxes for himself."[53]

Numerous Mongol taxes and imposts survived in Timurid guises. The Timurids, not to be outdone, concocted fresh exactions, and inflicted a dizzying array of taxes, exactions, tolls, and levies on agriculture, commerce, land, and four- and two-footers (plumed and plumeless). Franz Schurmann's exposition on Mongol exactions;[54] John M. Smith's revisions to Schurmann;[55] Vladimir Minorsky's dissection of *soyurghal*s;[56] and Ryoko Watabe's analysis of the *qubchur* taxation system[57] reveal the terrifying arsenal available to bureaucrats in state finance (*diwan-i mal, bayt al-mal*). In the century after Temür (1405–1506), fusillades of *soyurghal*s were discharged by Timurid sultans, which had the unfortunate – but not unexpected – effect of reducing cash inflows to the fisc: the

---

[52] Subtelny, "Socioeconomic Bases," 483.   [53] Ibid., 484.
[54] Franz Schurmann, "Mongolian Tributary Practices of the Thirteenth Century," *HJAS* 19/3 (1956): 304–89.
[55] John Masson Smith, Jr., "Mongol and Nomadic Taxation," *HJAS* 30 (1970): 46–89.
[56] See Minorsky, "Soyurghal."
[57] Ryoko Watabe, "Census-Taking and the *Qubchur* Taxation System in Ilkhanid Iran," *Memoirs of the Toyo Bunko* 73 (2015): 27–63.

"unbridled granting" of *soyurghal*s and tax immunities resulted in cash shortages that "jeopardized the functioning of government."[58]

A *soyurghal* or *muʿafi* was prized. A *soyurghal* was ordinarily devised to function as both sword and shield: the holder had the right to collect (some or all) of the taxes in the territory designated in the *soyurghal*; and it also inoculated him from harassments and legitimate demands by the *diwan*'s bureaucrats. Even without unqualified/absolute immunity, a *soyurghal* offered a beneficiary a degree of physical and mental peace and security not available to commoners. Terms like *muʿaf wa musallam wa marfuʿ al-qalam* (exclusions from itemized taxes, personal services, cadastral surveys, etc.); and *qalam wa qadam kutah darand* ("with their pens cut and their feet amputated),"[59] which compelled bureaucrats to withdraw their pens and feet from the beneficiary's estates, were shields against bureaucrats, including officials making legitimate demands.

Timurid Initiatives and the Shrine

How, if at all, did the shrine benefit? The documents parsed below relate to Jami elders of the Timurid era, not the shrine. The terms of one document, which appears to be a *muʿafi*, include a clause that allows the holder to bring the assets of third parties under the holder's protective umbrella (*himayat*),[60] that is, the shrine's assets. Whether this was actually done is impossible to know.

The first decree is by Temür himself, and dated 9 Rabiʿ I 804/ 17 October 1401.[61] It is directed to officials in Khurasan, specifically, functionaries in the provinces of Jam, Khwaf, and Bakharz where the estates (at issue) were located. It is unclear if the decree relates to *muʿafi* or *soyurghal* rights.

The properties of (1) Khandzada Fakhr al-Mulk Khatun; (2) her son, Shaykh al-Islam ʿAlaʾ al-Din ʿAlaʾ al-Mulk; (3) the Shaykh al-Islam's sons, Razi al-Din Ahmad and Qutb al-Din Muhammad, and their (unnamed) sister, are confirmed in their immunities, beginning in the Year of the Rat (Sichqan-il), which corresponds to 8 Jumada I 798/18 February 1396. They are exempt from taxes on incomes; and from levies on shares and properties; and from making contributions to the army. From this date forward, the

---

[58] Subtelny, *Timurids*, 38.   [59] See Minorsky, "Soyurghal," 953–54.
[60] On *himayat*, see Jürgen Paul, "Forming a Faction: The *Himayat* System of Khwaja Ahrar," *IJMES* 23 (1991): 533–48.
[61] Yusuf-i Ahl/Berlin, *Faraʾid*, fol. 313b–314a.

diwan should not demand anything further from them regarding their properties or for anything they add to their holdings. There is a clause (which may have been of value to the shrine), that if estates of third parties are brought under the Khandzada's *himayat*, they have to pay the "tax quota" (*rasad*) to the *diwan*.[62]

The second document is a *soyurghal* dated 29 Jumada II 863/3 May 1459 for Qutb al-Din Ahmad Jami (n.d.), for the provinces of Jam, Bakharz, and Khwaf.[63] It was issued by Sultan-Abu Saʿid (r. 855–73/1451–69).

The *soyurghal* commands that all properties (*amlak wa asbab*), old and new, in the provinces (*wilayat*) of Jam, Khwaf, and Bakharz, pursuant to the patents that were in force earlier (*bih dastur-i ahkam-i sabiq*),[64] are for the possession and free enjoyment of Shaykh al-Islam Qutb al-Din Ahmad, his progeny, and the heirs of Shaykh al-Islam ʿAli Asghar. Beginning in the Year of the Rooster (Takhaquy-il)[65] (corresponding to 1 Safar 857/20 February 1453), they are irrevocably and perpetually (*hudbari*) exempt from taxation (*muʿaf wa musallam wa marfuʿ al-qalam*),[66] contributions of soldiers, gifts, and other levies. There should be no interference with the valuation (*hazr*) of harvests or harvesting (*rafʿ-i mahsulat*). It is forbidden to enter their estates (*qalam wa qadam kutah darand*). They hold absolutely the *soyurghal* for the above three provinces (*jamaʿat-i soyurghal daran wilayat-i mazkura*); their estates are exempt. Do not enter their homes, nor demand of their employees and functionaries the poll tax (*sar-shumar*). This decree is irrevocable and protected from alterations and transfers. An annual renewal decree (*nishan*) or license (*parwancha*) is not necessary.

The term *bih dastur-i ahkam-i sabiq* reveals that the al-Mulk Jami clan of Tirmiz had held these three provinces as *soyurghal*, with an interruption consequent to Shah-Rukh's death. A *soyurghal* or *muʿafi* executed by Shah-Rukh has not survived, but the language above (*ahkam-i sabiq*) suggests he had issued a *soyurghal* or renewed Temür's decree. Sultan-Abu Saʿid was returning matters to the *status quo ante bellum*, that is,

---

[62] Further on this decree, see Shiro Ando, "The Shaykh al-Islam as a Timurid Office: A Preliminary Study," *Islamic Studies* 33/2 (1994): 253–80, 264; John Woods, "Turco-Iranica II: Notes on a Timurid Decree of 1396/798," *JNES* 43/4 (1984): 331–37. I am grateful to Dr. Saqib Baburi for his assistance with reading this decree.

[63] *Recueil*, Supplément persan 1815, fol. 32a–33b. The date is written as *salkh-i jumada al-thani* ("the last day of Jumada II").

[64] Cf. the term in Kartid decree (analyzed above): "earlier covenants" (*ʿuhud-i salifa*), which suggests preexisting grants and agreements.

[65] The corresponding *hijri* year is not given, but most likely the date given by me.

[66] Technically *hudbari*, but revoked or amended with the death of a benefactor.

where matters stood when Shah-Rukh died in Dhu al-Hijja 850/ March 1447.[67]

ANALYSIS AND CONCLUSIONS

Reports and anecdotes scattered in prosopographies, hagiologies, histories, and chronicles reveal that Ahmad-i Jam's shrine was wealthy.

There is a waqf from 802/1399–1400 that lists properties (*amlak*) held by Ahmad's shrine. It showed extensive holdings of villages, farms, orchards, and irrigation systems within a radius of around 50 mi./80 km of Turbat-i Jam. The original document was seized in the aftermath of the 1979 Revolution. A copy of the document was read aloud to me and an audience of elders by the custodian Haji Qazi Sharaf al-Din Jami al-Ahmadi, on 1 Dey 1390/22 December 2011. He declined to provide a photocopy on the premise that the *mawqufat* (the attachment to a waqf itemizing properties immobilized by the waqf) is politically sensitive.[68] Haji Qazi's concern is that a valid claim to the properties listed in the *mawqufat* persists under Islamic law, and publicizing the contents may displease the government of the Islamic Republic of Iran. Waqf properties of Ahmad-i Jam's shrine, to the best of my knowledge, were seized in the Safavid and Qajar eras.

The decrees above of individual Jami wealth in the Ilkhanid, Kartid, and Timurid periods cannot be dispositively connected to Ahmad-i Jam's shrine. They are snapshots taken at random points between 700/1300 and 864/1460; and cannot inform on socioeconomic histories of Jam or Ahmad's shrine. The documents reviewed (termed *muʿafi* or *soyurghal*) relate to personal assets, although the shrine's holdings could have been conveyed under the protective umbrella (*himayat*) of Temür's decree. A corresponding clause regarding *himayat* is not included in Sultan-Abu Saʿid's *soyurghal*.

The historian's lament is that we are prisoners of our sources. Timurid *muʿafi*s for the shrine of Ahmad-i Jam have not survived, so we cannot be certain any *muʿafi*s were even issued. An exemption (from the chancellery of Sultan-Husayn Bayqara) has survived for a Friday mosque at Ziyaratgah

---

[67] The accompanying *manshur* by Sultan-Abu Saʿid installed Razi al-Din Ahmad Jami in "the office of Shaykh al-Islam of the aforementioned province [of Jam]" and restored the *status quo ante bellum* (see Chapter 3).

[68] Reported in Mahendrarajah, "Shrine of Shaykh Ahmad-i Jam," 146.

(outside Herat).[69] It immunized waqf and other incomes from taxation; and prohibited officials from making demands of farmers and managers.[70] There is a similar decree for ʿAbdallah Ansari's shrine at Gazurgah.[71] As noted, waqf and private estates of Abu Saʿid b. Abu al-Khayr's shrine at Mayhana were immunized.[72] In sum, important Islamic institutions involved in agricultural production had received valuable fiscal-legal immunities. It is almost certain, but unprovable, that Ahmad-i Jam's shrine – a major agro- and hydro-manager of Timurid Iran – had received fiscal-legal immunities.

Document categories referenced here, like *soyurghal* and *muʿafi* (or *musallami*), are probably positivist and restrictive. Ad hoc tax exemptions, fiscal-legal immunities, and other royal benefices (*soyurghamishi*) will have been available to people connected to the Timurid court; for example, the ʿAlaʾ al-Mulk sayyids of Tirmiz, and Shah-Rukh's preceptor, Shihab al-Din (Abu al-Makarim) Tirmizi Jami (d. 847/1443f.). The survival of chancellery documents was a matter of chance:[73] if Yusuf-i Ahl Jami's position had not granted him access to Kartid, Timurid, and shrine archives, he will not have been able to preserve his family's epistolary heritage. Even the near 650 items in his *Faraʾid-i Ghiyasi* (see Appendix 3) represent a miniscule amount of the volume of documents produced over centuries by the shaykhs of Jam, or created by *qadi*s, *mufti*s, sultans, *malik*s, amirs, bureaucrats, and others regarding Ahmad-i Jam's shrine and progeny.

---

[69] Ziyaratgah: Allen, *Catalogue*, 85, and Cat. Nos. 391, 436; Noelle-Karimi, *Pearl*, 28.
[70] Nizami Bakharzi, *Mansha'*, 169–72.   [71] Ibid., 137–39.
[72] Nawaʾi (ed.), *Asnad wa mukatibat*, 299–301.
[73] Paul, "Archival Practices," 339: "even though millions if not billions of sheets of paper must have been involved over the years," not much has survived.

7

Public Service in the Catchment Area

In premodern times Islamic institutions (Sufi shrines, hospices, and mosques) were often responsible for the provision of social services: healthcare and food for the indigent and the infirm, schooling, and so on. During times of crises – famine, epidemic, and war – Sufis (especially) served the people. The Persianate social obligation to "feed the people" (*takafful-i umur*), still valid in Iran, Afghanistan, and South Asia (but known by sundry terms – if at all), was an imperative for the shrine's leadership in the past, and to an extent today, namely, access to the shrine's library, the construction of a new public library, and financial aid for students enrolled at the shrine's seminaries. The provision of services to the public will have intensified symbiotic bonds between shrine and community.

PUBLIC SERVICES BY ISLAMIC INSTITUTIONS

It has long been recognized that Islamic institutions, often through their waqfs, provided various services to the community. Leonor Fernandes has demonstrated how the *khanaqah* evolved in the Mamluk Sultanate, and came to provide salaries and food for religious and "secular" staff and students, and under specified conditions, food for the public for Ramazan, ʿAshura, or other high holy days (ʿid); and for the indigent, say, every Friday (*jumʿa*).[1] Literature on the use of waqfs to promote the commonweal is extensive.[2]

---

[1] Leonar Fernandes, *The Evolution of a Sufi Institution in Mamluk Egypt: The Khanqah* (Berlin: Klaus Schwarz Verlag, 1988).
[2] See, e.g., McChesney, *Waqf in Central Asia*; R. D. McChesney, "Waqf and Public Policy: The Waqfs of Shah ʿAbbas, 1011–1023/1602–1614," *Asian and African Studies* 15 (1981): 165–90;

Islamic institutions often were complexes, meaning, they had (1) seminaries, which had libraries (although the libraries may not always have been accessible to the public); (2) hospices, which included dormitories for residents and travelers, and often served hot meals to the indigent and/or infirm (if not every day, on holy days); and (3) mosques for prayer and meditation, billeting for itinerants/refugees, and the convoking of classes within its confines. Hence the "educational-charitable institution" label. Saïd Amir Arjomand notes also of educational-charitable complexes that included "teaching hospitals."[3] There is no record of medical care of any kind being offered at the shrine.[4] Ahmad-i Jam's shrine complex, too, undoubtedly, offered food, cash, and medicines to indigent and the infirm; but there are no literary references to such programs. Shihab al-Din Isma'il Jami (d. *ca.* 738/1338) had endowed 1,000 *kharwar*s (≈ 300,000 kg/ 660,000 lb) of seed from Jam province for Ahmad's shrine and its *khanaqah*s, with emoluments for family, clients (*mawali*), Qur'an readers, darwishes, laborers, neighbors, indigents (*fuqara'*), and the infirm (*za'ifan*).[5] A benefaction of this sort is not unusual (in principle if not in magnitude). It is just the sort of demonstration of goodwill that is expected by the lower socioeconomic classes from men of affluence and social prominence.

SERVICE TO COMMUNITY AND TO SULTAN

In making benefactions to shaykhs and shrines, sultans undoubtedly expected the beneficiary to demonstrate gratitude for the patronage and protection (*'inayat wa himayat*) that he received. Gratitude and respect

---

R. D. McChesney, "Economic and Social Aspects of the Public Architecture of Bukhara in the 1560's and 1570's," *Islamic Art* 2 (1987): 217–37; Subtelny, *Timurids*, esp. 148–63; Subtelny, "Timurid Foundation"; Christoph Werner, "Soziale Aspekte von Stiftungen zugunsten des Schreins von Imam Riza in Mashhad, 1527–1897," in *Islamische Stiftungen zwischen juristischer Norm und sozialer Praxis*, ed. A. Meier et al. (Berlin: Akademie Verlag, 2009), 167–89; and Mahendrarajah, "Gawhar Shad Waqf."

[3] Said Amir Arjomand, "The Law, Agency, and Policy in Medieval Islamic Society: Development of the Institutions of Learning from the Tenth to the Fifteenth Century," *Comparative Studies in Society and History* 41/2 (1999): 263–93, 272.

[4] Our knowledge of medical care in premodern Iran is wanting, principally due to the lack of records. Hormoz Ebrahimnejad, *Medicine, Public Health and the Qajar State* (Leiden: Brill, 2004), 24–26. There is a tantalizing (but unsourced) remark that "Tamerlane [had] decreed that each city of his realm was to contain at least one mosque, [etc.], and one hospital." Cyril Elgood, *A Medical History of Persia and the Eastern Caliphate* (Cambridge: Cambridge University Press, 1951), 173.

[5] Buzjani/Moayyad (ed.), *Rawzat*, 102.

will be demonstrated through service (*khidma*) and fidelity (*wafa'*) to the benefactor. The sultan expected the recipient of his largesse "to pray perpetually for the stability of our kingdom and in every way to give faithful assistance to our governance."[6] Alas, this statement is by kings Charlemagne and Carloman in decrees benefitting Benedictine abbeys. Carolingian kings were prolific sponsors of churches and monasteries which, not accidentally, became major landlords and agricultural and dairy producers in medieval Europe. The study of imperial decrees from the Mongol and Timurid periods, especially, has not occasioned discoveries with such lucid explanations.[7] Although we do not have descriptions of the quid pro quo, the sultan will undoubtedly have expected "faithful assistance to our governance." It is the character of said assistance that is opaque. Norman Jones's explanation with respect to Tudor England has applicability to the processes of governance in rural Khurasan of the Ilkhanids, Kartids, and Timurids:

> Governance took place in a world in which place, personal connection, trust, honor, and expertise were granted authority that never appeared on an organizational chart ... Largely informal [governance] depended heavily on the will, knowledge, and motivation of a few hundred gentlemen and nobles for its effectiveness. It [governance] was shaped by law and custom.[8]

Ziya al-Din Yusuf Jami (d. 797/1394f.),[9] the Kart vizier's son, was Temür's host on his visit to Jam. He was Shihab al-Din Isma'il Jami's (d. 809/1407) cousin. Both joined Temür in 793/1391 on campaign,[10] as his spiritual advisors and to help bring victory. As discussed (Chapter 3), Shihab al-Din (Abu al-Makarim) Tirmizi Jami (d. 847/1443f.) was Shah-Rukh's plenipotentiary to a Bengali sultan. These are some of the ways in which Jami leaders, most of whom held the title of Shaykh al-Islam, served their sultans.

---

[6] C. H. Lawrence, *Medieval Monasticism* (London: Longman, 1984), 61, quoting from Engelbert Mühlbacher (ed.), *Die Urkunden der Karolinger* (Hanover: Hahnsche Buchhandlung, 1906), 1: 75–76, 1:86–87.

[7] Some Mughal decrees have been identified with statements like: "[so-and-so] has been granted a piece of fallow but cultivable land ... so that he can use it for his livelihood and pray for the perpetuation of the empire." M. Z. A. Shakeb, *A Descriptive Catalogue of Miscellaneous Persian Mughal Documents from Akbar to Bahadur Shah II* (London: India Office Library and Records, 1982), 1. I am grateful to my friend and colleague Dr. Saqib Baburi for this reference, and for identifying other decrees with these types of qualifications.

[8] Norman Jones, *Governing by Virtue* (Oxford: Oxford University Press, 2015), 13.

[9] Buzjani/Moayyad (ed.), *Rawzat*, 108–9; Zanganah, *Sarzamin*, 148–49.

[10] Buzjani/Moayyad (ed.), *Rawzat*, 109; al-Samarqandi, *Matla'*, 1.2:642.

The ruler (in Herat) ordinarily appointed local judges (*qadi*) and *sadr*s. Numerous members of the Jami community served as shaykhs al-Islam, judges, lecturers/teachers (*mudarris*), preachers (*wa'iz* or *khatib*), imams, muezzins, and such. This is manifest from the Jami biographies by Ibrahim Zanganah and 'Ali Buzjani;[11] and Yusuf-i Ahl's massive collection of Jami correspondence (*insha'*), the *Fara'id-i Ghiyasi*.

Jürgen Paul's illuminating studies of notables,[12] and my own exposition on the Shaykh al-Islam,[13] have shown how de facto or de jure officeholders, and prominent persons, served their communities; for instance, the *ra'is* – a "notoriously protean" term – of a small Khurasanian town maintained "the internal peace in their town, and that meant that they tried to control who settled there ... they decided, more or less on their own, about the political allegiance of the place."[14] Indeed, the *ra'is* of Buzjan (as mentioned in Chapter 1) had tried to eject Ahmad-i Jam from Buzjan on account of the zealotry and strife (*ta'assubi wa munaza'at*) that he engendered.[15] We saw, too, how Shihab al-Din Isma'il Jami helped end the sieges of Herat. Sufi shaykhs were formidable social-political forces in the Ilkhanid, Kartid, and Timurid periods in Khurasan, and will have shaped politics and administration in town and country.

"FEED THE PEOPLE"

Ahmad-i Jam's shrine had become a major social-political institution by the late Ilkhanid period. A close-knit community (*Gemeinschaft*) – one defined by organic social relationships characterized by bonds of kinship, affinity, loyalty, and shared values – had developed around the shrine. The *Gemeinschaft* produced the preachers, imams, muezzins, scholars, judges, and merchants that comprised the upper socioeconomic strata of Jam, and who guided the lower socioeconomic strata. The upper social strata employed laborers, servants, peasants, pastoralists, artisans, and craftsmen, thereby providing housing, food, and education for them, and for their dependents. Social and economic liaisons were close and personal.

Shihab al-Din Isma'il Jami's concern for the welfare of peasants on his lands is evinced by his actions when a major famine (*qahti 'azim*) struck

---

[11] See Appendix 3.
[12] Paul, "Lords," 174–209; Jürgen Paul, "Where Did the *Dihqāns* Go?" *Eurasian Studies* XI (2013): 1–34; and Jürgen Paul, "Balkh, from the Seljuqs to the Mongol Invasion," in *Cities in Medieval Iran*, ed. David Durand-Guédy et al., *Eurasian Studies* 16/1–2 (2018): 313–51.
[13] Mahendrarajah, "Shaykh al-Islam." [14] Paul, "Lords," 183–84.
[15] Ghaznawi, *Maqamat*, 116–17; Moayyad and Lewis, *Colossal*, 187–88.

Bakharz province. He ordered his agents to distribute grain to the hungry. The agents followed his orders, but secured legal notes (*tamassukat*) that acknowledged the recipient's debt. The Shaykh al-Islam traveled to Bakharz, where his debtors gathered around. He ordered his agents to wash the debtors' notes in water (*kaghaz parihha ra farmud kih dar ab rikhtand*), thereby erasing their legal obligations.[16] His community will have expected nothing less from him. As Roy Mottahedeh noted in his magisterial study of "loyalty and leadership," men are judged by *nasab* and *hasab*: "*Nasab* is genealogy, the influence of a man's pedigree on his condition. *Hasab* is the honor acquired through deeds."[17] Someone with Shihab al-Din Isma'il Jami's pedigree was honor bound to have an open hand and open table – as when the Shaykh al-Islam provisioned Chupan's army and hosted banquets (Chapter 3) – and to help people in his homeland (*watan*) during crises. He had to "feed the people," a critical aspect of social relations in the Indo-Persian world. The phrase and its social implications remain valid. "Feed" has literal and metaphorical components.[18]

A *khan* is the lord of his tribe – not unlike a provincial Shaykh al-Islam. *Khan*s are "individuals who 'feed the people,'"[19] usually through employment and other forms of patronage, and support during times of want:

In "feeding people," *khan*s develop leadership through patronage. In effect, they convert their own surplus, mostly agricultural wealth, into social relations through hospitality, providing employment and other less clear cut patronage of their fellows ... *khan*s, in short, traffic in patronage and respect, service and influence.[20]

The expression "feed the people" is found in a decree (*farman* or *manshur*) from 771/1370 by Mu'izz al-Din Muhammad Kart confirming another Shaykh al-Islam of Jam (Shihab al-Din Isma'il's grandson, Shihab

---

[16] Buzjani/Moayyad (ed.), *Rawzat*, 101. On this legal procedure, see A. K. S. Lambton, *Continuity and Change in Medieval Persia* (London: I.B. Tauris, 1988), 92.

[17] Roy Mottahedeh, *Loyalty and Leadership in an Early Islamic Society*, 2nd ed. (New York: I. B. Tauris, 2001), 98.

[18] *Takafful-i umur* and *mutakaffil-i umur* still retain the meaning of "feed the people" in Afghanistan. "Feed" is to take responsibility for feeding, clothing, educating, sheltering, and protecting a family or group. I am grateful to my friend and colleague Dr. Rohullah Amin Mojaddidi, former country director of the American Institute of Afghanistan Studies, for his elucidations. The principle of taking care of domestics, clients, etc. is prevalent in Indo-Persian cultures, but known by sundry terms – *if at all*; for instance, a specific term is not necessary to inform an adult that his *ayah* (nanny), now elderly and infirm, has to be sponsored by him. Certain social/cultural duties are just known.

[19] Jon Anderson, "There Are No Khans Anymore: Economic Development and Social Change in Tribal Afghanistan," *Middle East Journal* 32/2 (1978): 167–83, 168–69.

[20] Ibid., 169–70.

al-Din Isma'il, d. 809/1407) as *mutawalli*. The expression "feed the people" (*takafful-i umur* and *mutakaffil-i umur*) is employed several times.[21] The Kart *malik* is not ordering the incoming custodian to feed the people; he is expressing in obiter dictum his expectations for the continued maintenance of social obligations, where the shrine's agricultural wealth is utilized to offer employment and hospitality. Visitors to, and residents of, Jam were to be treated equitably.

It is not surprising that a ruler (Kartid *malik* or Timurid sultan) would expect the beneficiary to honor social-political obligations: since the shaykhs and shrine received much (probably most) of their wealth as a direct result of the crown's grants of fiscal, legal, and political favors (see Chapter 6), they were expected to provide the "social services" that the crown was unable to offer – social services that were indispensable in quelling disquiet in society, and leveling (to some extent) economic disparities. Famines and bread riots were not uncommon in Iran. Responsibility will have fallen to wealthy Islamic institutions like the shrines of Ahmad-i Jam, 'Abdallah Ansari, Imam Riza, and Imam 'Ali, among others, to feed the people during famines. Shihab al-Din Isma'il Jami's magnanimity toward the peoples of Bakharz is illustrative.

The peoples of medieval Khurasan depended on social compacts with their local Islamic institution for employment, and for money, food, and medical attention when conflict, famine, epidemic, poverty, infirmity, and dotage struck. The poor, the infirm, and the elderly, even if they were callously allowed to die on the streets of Herat, with passersby ignoring their plight, could not be ignored or allowed to die in the streets of Turbat-i Jam. The relationship between Ahmad's shrine and people in the catchment area was symbiotic. The shrine needed laborers, peasants, and craftsmen, but the shrine was obligated with providing not only for its employees and their dependents, but for an extended community in the catchment area. Ahmad-i Jam's shrine could not operate as an inanimate entity, mechanical and cold. It was obligated to operate as a responsive, compassionate, and flexible *organism*.

---

[21] Yusuf-i Ahl/Berlin, *Fara'id*, fol. 316a. The decree was issued toward the end of the *malik*'s life (d. 5 Dhu al-Qa'da 771/31 May 1370).

8

Sacred Topography and Islamic Learning

> Blessing (*baraka*) is at the heart of hallowed ground (*haram, hima*), and pilgrimages (*ziyarat*) to sanctified mausolea (*ziyarat al-qubur*) and to reliquary sites (locations of visions, saintly footprints, fabrics, etc.). The acquisition of "divine energies" (*fayz*) is an aspect of *ziyarat*, but the modes of acquiring *fayz* are opaque. Sacred ground is a venue for oaths (*bayʻa*), vows (*nazr*), sanctuary (*bast*), and interments. Acquisition of Islamic knowledge at "sacred pastures" was believed to bring "special merit"; hence the construction of Sufi hospices (*khanaqah*) and seminaries (madrasa) near shrines; and the convening of tutorials (*nawb al-jalis*) and Sufi circles (*halqa*) on hallowed soil. Hospices and seminaries (i.e., curricula) at the Jami shrine are examined.

Denise Aigle,[1] and Arezou Azad,[2] proffer expositions on "sacred territory" (*haram*) or "sacred pasture" (*hima*), Islamdom's parallel to Christendom's "sacred space" (*locus sanctus*). Both reference Rudolf Otto's work on "the spirituality of the place": the spiritual quality or divine power that attributes a distinct sacredness to a locale.[3] Sacredness or spirituality of a place could mean, for instance, that a given *haram* has acquired prominence for alleviating a particular ailment, and attracts pilgrims seeking medical relief.[4]

---

[1] Azad, *Sacred Landscape*, 12–18.
[2] Aigle, "Spiritual Topography," 145–46. Further on sacred topography, see Harry Munt, *The Holy City of Medina: Sacred Space in Early Islamic Arabia* (Cambridge: Cambridge University Press, 2014), esp. 65–122. On the "sacred" in urban layouts, see Paul Wheatley, *The Places Where Men Pray Together* (Chicago, IL: University of Chicago Press, 2001), esp. 231–38.
[3] Rudolf Otto, *The Idea of the Holy*, 2nd ed., trans J. W. Harvey (London: Oxford University Press, 1950), esp. 5–7.
[4] My experiences traveling the Tehran-Mashhad express train show that scores of afflicted travel to Imam Riza's shrine seeking relief. On one trip, I shared a four-seater table with

Zamchi Isfizari identified springs in the Harat River Valley with curative powers;[5] and Louis Dupree identified shrines that may cure mental disorders, mad dog bites, infertility, and so on.[6] Ahmad-i Jam's shrine has no accepted "specialty," but considering the frequency with which kings of yesteryear visited his mausoleum to acquire spiritual favors and blessings, his spiritual niche was "the patron saint of kings." Furthermore, stories in Ghaznawi's *Spiritual Feats* of Ahmad-i Jam healing, curing, saving, punishing, and protecting will have attracted pilgrims seeking restoration, redemption, protection, or retribution.[7]

In general terms, however, *haram*s are "locations rendered sacred by the presence of a venerated saintly body."[8] Azad showed that medieval writers extended sacredness to the city of Balkh.[9] Shiraz, the "fortress of saints" (*burj al-awliya'*), is another sanctified city;[10] and Jerusalem, Mecca, and Medina are holy cities for Muslims.[11] Although Turbat-i Jam is not known for multiple saints, the entombment of a great saint could sanctify it; however, there are no known literary references to Turbat-i Jam as a sanctified city. The confines of Ahmad-i Jam's shrine complex are sacred; whereas residents and businesses in its vicinities engage in prosaic – and occasionally profane – activities: overcharging pilgrims. The shrine's sanctity attracts pilgrims, mystics, scholars, students, and entombments.

BARAKA AND FAYZ

The lynchpin of saint cults is *baraka*, the quintessence of devotion and prayer. "Be grateful for the favors of Allah, if it is He whom ye serve" (Q16:114). God expects man to show gratitude for His blessings (*baraka*) and favors (*ni'mah*). This is a religious duty, and failure to show gratitude

---

parents taking their afflicted young daughter from Tabriz (via Tehran) to Mashhad. I sensed that the pilgrimage was the parents' last hope.

[5] Isfizari, *Rawzat al-jannat*, 1:101–2 (cited by Aigle, "Spiritual Topography," 146).
[6] Dupree, "Saint Cults," 1; Louis Dupree, *Afghanistan* (Princeton, NJ: Princeton University Press, 1980), 105.
[7] Appendix A, the "Motif index of the miracles of Shaykh Ahmad," in Moayyad and Lewis, *Colossal*, lists nearly as many motifs under "affliction of enemies" as under "healing."
[8] Aigle, "Spiritual Topography," 146.   [9] Azad, *Sacred Landscape*, 69.
[10] See Aigle, "Spiritual Topography." Further on the sanctification of an entire city (in this instance, Qum), see Mimi Hanaoka, *Authority and Identity in Medieval Islamic Historiography* (Cambridge: Cambridge University Press, 2016), 171–203.
[11] On carving out Islamic sacred space in Jerusalem, see Jacob Lassner, *Medieval Jerusalem* (Ann Arbor, MI: University of Michigan Press, 2017).

to God "is tantamount to unbelief."[12] "*Baraka* is the stuff of faith," and "sanctified a location through the presence or the apparent presence of a saint and his personal effects, which became devotional or ritual objects."[13] Demands by man for *baraka* and *ni'mah* can often be insatiable. Man makes his supplications directly to God, or through intercessors, "the Friends of God" (*awliya' Allah*), because "God can implant an emanation of *baraka* in the person of his prophets and saints."[14]

Baraka is potent. The quest for *baraka* takes myriads of forms. Pilgrims touch, kiss, and even lick holy relics and shrines;[15] drink "holy water" found at sacred sites;[16] and eat the soil, considered (by some) to be "pure soil" (*pak-i khak*). They seek relics belonging to the subjects of their devotion, and return to their homes with soil or water collected at holy sites. Returnees from the Hajj carry waters from the Zamzam well.[17] Sunni and Shi'a of Jam returning from Mecca serve waters of the Zamzam to their guests in tumblers emblazoned with an image of the blessed Ka'ba. This to share with his/her friends God's *ni'mah*, which permitted the newly minted "Haji" to afford the Hajj pilgrimage, and allow friends unable to travel – due to financial, health, or visa constraints – to ingest *baraka*.

Clifford Geertz illustrates a believer's quest for *baraka* with a vivid tale (it is hearsay but edifying): a man approached a shaykh who was afflicted with "a loathsome disease" and offered to wash his soiled nightshirt, which the shaykh's disciples had refused to touch. The man was given the shirt, which he rinsed, and after squeezing it out, "drank the foul water." He returned to the shaykh, "his eyes aflame, not with illness, for he did not fall sick, but as though he had drunk a powerful wine."[18] Infamous videos circulating on social media show devotees licking the enclosures to Fatima Ma'sumih's shrine in Qum; and Imam Riza's shrine in Mashhad, claiming they do not fear COVID-19 because the saints' *baraka* has the power to protect, or if they become afflicted, then to cure.

---

[12] Devin Stewart, "Blessing," *EQ*, 1:236–37.   [13] Meri, *Cult of Saints*, 17.
[14] G. S. Colin, "Baraka," *EI*^{2}, 1:1032. See also Meri, *Cult of Saints*, 101–8; and Meri, "Baraka."
[15] The spread of coronavirus (COVID-19) in Qum, Iran, in 2020, is traced to pilgrims kissing and touching the shrine of Hazrat Fatima Ma'sumih (the sister of Imam Riza).
[16] The most famous source of holy water in Islam is the Zamzam well in Mecca. See G. R. Hawting, "The Disappearance and Rediscovery of Zamzam and the 'Well of the Ka'ba,'" *BSOAS* 43/1 (1980): 44–54.
[17] Bottled "Zamzam water" is made available by the Wahhabi Kingdom of Saudi Arabia. It is unlikely the well can provide the quantities of water demanded by millions of pilgrims.
[18] Clifford Geertz, *Islam Observed* (Chicago, IL: University of Chicago Press, 1968), 32.

Fayz, divine effusions or energies, is an aspect of shrine visitations. Ibn Ruzbihan, for example, touches on the acquisition of *fayz* during pilgrimages (*ziyarat*),[19] but the process of acquisition of *fayz* remains unclear. Indeed, the subject of *fayz* demands deeper exploration. One mode of transference of *fayz* is via dreams; for example, Qasim-i Anwar (d. 838/1434f.): Ahmad-i Jam's spirit (*ruhaniyyat*) appeared to him and infused him with his *fayz*.[20] *Fayz* in the Sufi context involves the transference of the shaykh's divine effusions into his darwish. *Fayz* and a corollary, *tawajjuh*, are discussed in Chapter 9.

Ahmad-i Jam's cult revolves around his sanctified remains. The nearer a person is to Ahmad-i Jam (a believer in his saintliness will insist), the nearer s/he is to Ahmad's *baraka*. A prime reason for making *ziyarat* to a shrine is to be beside the saint, to offer prayers, and to make supplications, and (a supplicant hopes) to receive the saint's *baraka*.

VISITS TO MAUSOLEA (*ZIYARAT AL-QUBUR*)

We cannot determine precisely when the idea of Ahmad-i Jam's shrine as a source of *baraka* spread beyond the limits of Jam, and who visited his shrine on pilgrimage in the first century or thereabouts after his death in 536/1141. As explained, we still do not know the identity of the sponsor of the *gunbad* erected in 633/1236.

The idea of Ahmad as the protector of kingdoms and the source of *baraka* for kings was traced to around 649/1251, when Shams al-Din Kart visited to express his gratitude for God's *ni'mah* and to seek fresh infusions of *baraka*. As the shrine's popularity among commoners, kings, and officials increased, pilgrim traffic increased. With pilgrimages to holy sites came the handbooks of etiquette (*adab*) for pilgrimages. Who can visit? When should one visit? Which activities are prescribed or proscribed?

Ziyarat means more than is suggested by "pilgrimage": it is a way of honoring the "holy dead through experiencing spiritual closeness to God at their tombs."[21] Appropriate ways and times in which to honor the dead,

---

[19] Fazl-Allah b. Ruzbihan Khunji, *Mihmannamah-yi Bukhara*, ed. Manuchihr Sutudah (Tehran: Bungah-i tarjumah wa nashr-i kitab, 1341/1962), 333–34.

[20] al-Samarqandi, *Tadhkirat*, 348. On dreams, see Nile Green, "The Religious and Cultural Roles of Dreams and Visions in Islam," *JRAS* 13/3 (2003): 287–313.

[21] Josef Meri, "The Etiquette of Devotion in the Islamic Cult of Saints," in *The Cult of Saints in Late Antiquity and the Middle Ages: Essays on the Contribution of Peter Brown*, ed. J. Howard-Johnston and P. A. Hayward (Oxford: Oxford University Press, 1999), 263–86, 286.

Visits to Mausolea (*Ziyarat al-qubur*)

and etiquette at holy sites, are dictated by local customs and traditions that are transmitted orally, or learned through the observation of elders, which is principally how children learn rituals. The Qurʾan offers sparse guidance on the rituals of the Hajj, leaving hadith, custom, and exegesis to fill in the gaps.[22] Likewise with *ziyarat*. The discussion below on the *theoretical* framework for *ziyarat* will have little connection with actual *practices*; nonetheless, the framework is worth appreciating.

The Ulama and Ziyarat

The permissibility of tomb visits is contentious even today. There are hadith that permit visits: "It was narrated from ʿAʾisha that the Messenger of Allah gave permission for visiting the graves";[23] "the Messenger of Allah said: 'I had prohibited you from visiting the graves; but Muhammad was permitted to visit the grave of his mother: so visit them, for they will remind you of the Hereafter.'"[24] There are hadith that bar worship (*ʿibada*) near tombs: "The Messenger of Allah said: 'Let there be the curse of Allah upon the Jews and the Christians for they have taken the graves of their apostles as places of worship (*masajid*)'";[25] and "Do not sit on the graves and do not pray facing toward them."[26] Women are barred from visiting: "Indeed the Messenger of Allah cursed the women who visit the graves."[27] The hadith do not elucidate permissible activities, although some forbid actions that violate decency; for example, treading, sitting, or urinating on graves.

Duʿaʾ (invocation, prayer, benediction) is distinct from *namaz* (prescribed ritual prayer, i.e., the five daily prayers), and has gradations in praxis: supplications of sundry sorts, and supererogatory prayers. *Duʿaʾ* is at the crux of the debate on *ziyarat*: what are the permissible or impermissible *duʿaʾ* at tombs? Is it licit to make petitions to the dead?

Tomb veneration is an instance of Islamic orthopraxis with ambiguous support in the Qurʾan and hadith. It is supported, however, by community consensus (*ijmaʿ*) and custom (*ʿurf, rawaj*). The most prominent critic of, inter alia, saint cults and *ziyarat*, was the Hanbali Ibn Taymiyya (d. 728/

---

[22] See, e.g., Gerald Hawting, "Pilgrimage," *EQ*, 4:91–100; Josef Meri, "Ritual and the Qurʾan," *EQ*, 4:484–98; F. E. Peters, *The Hajj* (Princeton, NJ: Princeton University Press, 1994), esp. 7–9.
[23] *Sunan Ibn Majah*, hadith # 1570.
[24] *Jamiʿ al-Tirmidhi*, hadith # 1054; see variant in *Sahih Muslim*, hadith # 977.
[25] *Sahih Muslim*, hadith # 530; see also *Sahih al-Bukhari*, hadith # 437.
[26] *Sahih Muslim*, hadith # 972.   [27] *Jamiʿ al-Tirmidhi*, hadith # 1056.

1328), "patron saint" of al-Qaʿida, ISIS, and the Wahhabi Kingdom of Saudi Arabia.[28] Ibn Taymiyya's attacks on the practice clashed with the interpretations of ulama and the social practices of his time;[29] and were refuted by his contemporaries.[30] Ibn Taymiyya was incarcerated in Damascus citadel in 726/1326 for a polemical treatise he had written against *ziyarat al-qubur*. He died in prison in 728/1328.

Despite the polemics, ulama and laymen participated in the veneration of saints. The need for an "invisible companion" or an "intimate friend" (to appropriate Brown's fitting terms)[31] can be overwhelming. Juridical imperatives, however, were not ignored. The eminent Shafiʿi scholar Muhammad (Abu Hamid) Ghazali Tusi (d. 505/1111), author of *Ihyaʾ ʿulum al-din* (*The Revivification of the Islamic Sciences*) and professor at Baghdad's premier seminary, was instrumental in formulating sophisticated defenses of *ziyarat*.[32] He affirmed the existence of saints, but did not distinguish between visiting the graves of saints or of loved ones. "The goals were one and the same: supplicating God on behalf of the dead."[33] Ghazali's defense, published two centuries before Ibn Taymiyya's polemics, or the defenses by Ibn Taymiyya's nemesis, the Shafiʿi chief justice (*qadi al-qudat*) of Damascus, Taqi al-Din Subki (d. 756/1355), "reflect [the] mainstream view within Sunni Islam on the permissibility of the *ziyara*."[34] Another Shafiʿi, Fazl-Allah b. Ruzbihan Khunji (d. 927/1521), is in accord with Ghazali. Ibn Ruzbihan reflects a consensus that had settled in Persian-speaking lands above and below the Oxus, which permitted *ziyarat*, provided unlawful innovations in the faith (*bidʿa*), or practices mimicking the Hajj, were not exercised.[35]

---

[28] On Ibn Taymiyya's role in shaping Muhammad ibn ʿAbd al-Wahhab's perspectives, see Hamid Algar, *Wahhabism* (Oneonta, NY: Islamic Publications, 2002).
[29] On juridical arguments against *ziyarat*, including Ibn Taymiyya's, see Meri, "Etiquette," 273–79; and Christopher Taylor, *In the Vicinity of the Righteous: Ziyara and the Veneration of Muslim Saints in Late Medieval Egypt* (Leiden: Brill, 1999), 168–94.
[30] Taylor, *Righteous*, 195–226 (the legal defense of *ziyarat*).
[31] Brown, *Cult of the Saints*, 50.
[32] Meri, "Etiquette," 279–86; Abu Hamid al-Ghazali, *Ihyaʾ ʿulum al-din*, 10 vols. (Jeddah: Dar al-minhaj, 2011), 9: 436–67 (chapter 6: "The Remembrance of Death and the Afterlife"); Abu Hamid al-Ghazali, *The Remembrance of Death and the Afterlife*, trans. T. J. Winter (Cambridge: The Islamic Texts Society, 1989), 97–120.
[33] Meri, "Etiquette," 280. [34] Taylor, *Righteous*, 210–11.
[35] Ruzbihan Khunji, *Mihmannamah*, 301–5; see also Subtelny, *Timurids*, 193–94.

Protocols for Pilgrims (Sing. Zaʾir)

Etiquette guides for pilgrims – the "dos and don'ts" of *ziyarat* – and guides to sacred sites in the Islamic world, bear quick examination. Here, too, is a *theoretical* framework that may have little bearing on actual practices.

An important early guidebook is ʿAli b. Abi Bakr al-Harawi's (d. 611/1215) *Guide to Knowledge of Pilgrimage Sites*, which includes select shrines from Hamadan to Imam Riza's, and to Samarqand.[36] The *Complete Pilgrimage Guide* by Ibn Qawlawaya (d. 368/978f.) is a handbook for Shiʿi sites, offering instructions on ablutions, rituals, and supplications.[37] A book from mid-ninth/fifteenth-century Iran is Asil al-Din Waʿiz's (d. 883/1478f.) guide to sites in and around Herat.[38] Descriptions of sanctified mausolea, with biographies of the occupants, follow Waʿiz's explications on etiquette. Impermissible activities warrant little commentary here: eating, sleeping, defecating, urinating, sitting, walking on graves is reprehensible (*makruh*). The performance of obligatory prayers near graves is forbidden.[39]

Waʿiz's recommended veneration protocols:[40] The four best days for *ziyarat* are Monday, Thursday, Friday, and Saturday; however, on Fridays, *ziyarat* should be after the *jumʿa* prayers; and on Thursday and Saturday, before sunrise; while the first Monday is best. It is believed that on the evening of *jumʿa* (i.e., Thursday night), the whole of Friday, Saturday, and Monday, (the spirits of) the dead are more attuned (*wuquf mi yaband*) to the spiritual condition (*hal*) of the pilgrim.[41] Holy nights, especially the fifteenth of Shaʿban (*shab-i barat*),[42] the tenth of Dhu al-Hijja (the climax of the Hajj), festival days,[43] and ʿAshura (the first to the tenth of Muharram), are especially efficacious. In preparation for *ziyarat*, it is recommended (*mustahabb*) that ritual ablutions (Ar. *wuduʾ*; Per. *wuzuʾ*)

---

[36] Josef Meri (trans.), *A Lonely Wayfarer's Guide to Pilgrimage: ʿAli ibn Abi Bakr al-Harawi's Kitab al-isharat ila maʿrifat al-ziyarat* (Princeton, NJ: Darwin, 2004), 264–69.
[37] Jaʿfar b. Muhammad b. Qawlawaya, *Kamil al-ziyarat* (Qum: Nashr al-faqahat, 1429/2009).
[38] Asil al-Din ʿAbdallah Waʿiz, *Maqsad al-iqbal al-sultaniyya*, ed. Mayil Harawi (Tehran: Pizhuhishgah-i ʿulum-i insani wa mutalaʿat-i farhangi, 1386/2007 [reprint of 1972 ed.]). The title is reproduced in Fikri Saljuqi, *Risalah-yi mazarat-i Harat: shamil-i sih hisah* (Afghanistan: Markaz-i nashrati Faruqi, 1379/2001), 28–147.
[39] Waʿiz, *Maqsad*, 6–7.   [40] Ibid., 5–6.
[41] On the efficacy of visits on Thursdays, Fridays, and Saturdays, see al-Ghazali, *Ihyaʾ*, 9:460–61; al-Ghazali/Winter (trans.), *Remembrance*, 114–15.
[42] The Shiʿa mark this as a high holy day and the birthday of Imam Mahdi.
[43] Presumably *ʿid al-fitr* and *ʿid al-adha*. These two major festivals are celebrated communally at Ahmad's shrine, with prayers led by Turbat-i Jam's Sunni prayer leader (*imam-jumʿa*).

be performed, and that the pilgrim make two *rak'a* of *namaz* inside his quarters (*dar khana-yi khud*). With each *rak'a*, he should say the "opening chapter" (Surat al-Fatiha, Q1:1–7), the "throne verse" (Ayat al-Kursi, Q2:255) one time, and the "sincerity chapter" (Surat al-Ikhlas, Q112:1–4) three times. Following the meritorious prayers, he should go to the tombs. Barefoot, without delay, move quietly and slowly to the tomb and position himself near the sanctified area (*haram*), neither too near nor too far from it. He may utter the following prayer (omitted), but if non-Muslims are present,[44] the following sequence of prayers (omitted) could be offered.

The above conveys the flavor of veneration protocols. It bears repeating that while Wa'iz is enlightening, practices will diverge, sometimes significantly, from guidelines. Ibn Ruzbihan takes the position that venerations by women are reprehensible (*makruh*),[45] but Wa'iz dismisses the claim's premise, explaining that the hadith in question was abrogated (*mansukh*) by the Prophet himself.[46] Moreover, Ibn Ruzbihan was an opinionated Sunni and bigoted toward Shi'a. He represents doctrinaire factions or perspectives. Wa'iz, however, was a political-social insider of late Timurid Iran;[47] his *Maqsad al-iqbal* is dedicated to the Timurid ruler Sultan-Abu Sa'id (r. 855–73/1451–69). Wa'iz reflects the perspectives of the upper strata of Khurasanian society. Women are not prohibited from venerating Ahmad. It is possible, but unlikely, that women had been prohibited in bygone ages. Hibat al-Rahman has a honored place in Ahmad-i Jam's cult and reposes beside him. It is certain that the Jami community had always permitted women to follow Hibat al-Rahman's stellar example and venerate their saint.

The Ziyarat *Experience*

To receive *baraka*, a pilgrim must ritually purify himself (as Wa'iz recommends), but this writer has observed on visits to Sunni and Shi'a shrines

---

[44] This suggests that shrines in Khurasan were shared by different confessions. On shared shrines in general, see Meri, *Cult of Saints*, et passim; Dupree, "Saint Cults"; Dionigi Albera and M. Couroucli (eds.), *Sharing Sacred Spaces in the Mediterranean: Christians, Muslims and Jews at Shrines and Sanctuaries* (Bloomington, IN: Indiana University Press, 2012); and F. W. Hasluck, *Christianity and Islam under the Sultans* (Oxford: Clarendon, 1929), 67–74 (Christian holy sites visited by Muslims) and 75–97 (Muslim holy sites visited by Christians).

[45] Ruzbihan Khunji, *Mihmannamah*, 332.

[46] Wa'iz, *Maqsad*, 5. He is in accord with al-Ghazali, *Ihya'*, 9:456–57; al-Ghazali/Winter (trans.), *Remembrance*, 112.

[47] Manz, *Timurid Iran*, 70–71.

Visits to Mausolea (*Ziyarat al-qubur*) 157

from India to the Levant that pilgrims often fail to perform this fundamental ritual. Many pilgrims do purify and perform *namaz* in a shrine's mosque or *musalla* before engaging in venerations; whereas others make their way directly to the tomb, and promptly commence their *ziyarat*.

Ziyarat, however, is a personal experience and spiritual journey.[48] It is not regulated by the ruminations of pedagogues on ablutions and protocols. Performance of the five daily ritual prayers is because God had commanded it, but daily prayers may not be emotionally or spiritually satisfying; and indeed, may become perfunctory and unsatisfactory. However, pilgrims visit shrines, whether to supplicate or to meditate, because they want to know God on a personal level. Being in the vicinity of one of His Friends brings the visitor emotional and spiritual fulfilment. The Friend is his/her conduit to Him: s/he speaks and supplicates with his/her invisible Friend. *Ziyarat* is a spiritual voyage that takes place *inside* a pilgrim's heart, while his/her body is physically at the *haram*. The rapture that grips some pilgrims, or the manifestation of emotions on a supplicant's face, is proof that s/he is on a personal voyage that is bringing spiritual joy and satisfaction.[49] This writer has observed devotees at Sunni and Shi'a shrines,[50] lost in rapture while reading or reciting the Qur'an out loud, or just lost in contemplation of the Divine.

A saint may have departed this world, but a pilgrim knows that a *wali* is flourishing in the world of spirits (*'alam-i arwah*). Carl Ernst's descriptions of Ruzbihan Baqli's writings (see Chapter 2) conjure images of God's Friends sitting around the Prophet like attendants, which is presumably how many pilgrims visualize Ahmad-i Jam's role in Paradise. Pilgrims make visitations to Ahmad's shrine with the expectation of reciprocity (sacred exchange). However, reciprocity is not necessarily about a simple exchange between pilgrim and saint: prayers and donatives for *baraka* and (tangible and intangible) benefits.[51] The relationship can become an intimate and intricate one.

---

[48] For anthropological insights on *ziyarat*, see Anne H. Betteridge, "*Ziarat*: Pilgrimage to the Shrines of Shiraz" (PhD diss., University of Chicago, 1985), esp. 24–43.
[49] On "experiencing the holy," see Meri, *Cult of Saints*, 120ff.
[50] In April 2019, I observed the fifteenth of Sha'ban commemorations at Shah-i Chiragh (Shiraz) honoring Imam Mahdi; thereafter, I visited the shrine in Qum for Fatima Ma'sumih, the sister of Imam Riza. Shi'i commemorations are instructive.
[51] For nuanced views of reciprocity (sacred exchange), see Pnina Werbner, "*Langar*: Pilgrimage, Sacred Exchange, and Perpetual Sacrifice in a Sufi Saint's Lodge," in *Embodying Charisma*, ed. Pnina Werbner and Helene Basu (London: Routledge, 1998), 95–116.

Seeking Help from Ahmad-i Jam

"Seek help from those dwelling in graves" (*ista'inu min ahl al-qubur*). This purported hadith is in select Timurid chancery documents from the reign of Sultan-Husayn Bayqara (r. 873–911/1469–1506).[52] The Timurids' attachment to spirits (sing. *ruh*; pl. *arwah*) in graves is traceable to Temür, whose proclivities in this direction were known (see Chapter 2). Mu'in al-Din Jami (the Kartid vizier) targeted Temür's attraction to the spiritual world in a letter to Temür: the spirits of the true (*sadiq*) and the pure (*pak*), essentially, the sanctified spirits (*arwah-i muqaddasa*) of our exalted ancestors, repose at Turbat-i Jam.[53] During Zayn al-Din Taybadi's celebrated encounter with Temür,[54] he beseeched Temür to spare Herat and its denizens from pillage and desolation because Herat is where spirits thrive (*arwah-abad*); and the lofty progenitors (i.e., spirits) of the (living) shaykhs, sayyids, and ulama of Herat could become Temür's hidden helpers: "assistance in the world of spirits ('*alam-i arwah*) is superior to all the armies, treasures, and defenses."[55]

F. W. Hasluck showed how Christians and Muslims shared sacred spaces in late nineteenth- and early twentieth-century Anatolia. Some Anatolian Muslims purchased supplemental spiritual insurance by baptizing their children.[56] In general, Muslims and Christians sought succor at shared shrines, especially during crises (e.g., epidemics and famines).[57] Therefore, despite the lack of probative evidence, it is reasonable to believe that Turbat-i Jam's Sunnis, Shi'is, Jews, Christians, and Zoroastrians shared a spiritual foxhole – Ahmad-i Jam's shrine – when drought, famine, pandemic, and conflict afflicted their patch of Khurasan. Lord Curzon's observation that "[m]ore persons have probably died a violent death in Khorasan than . . ." is a reminder that Khurasanians had endured numerous existential crises. In trying times, one purchases – to borrow from David Morgan – multiple "celestial insurance" policies.

---

[52] Nizami Bakharzi, *Mansha' al-insha'*, 141 and 144; Subtelny, *Timurids*, 197 n25.
[53] Yusuf-i Ahl/Moayyad (ed.), *Fara'id*, 1:175. The phrasing suggests cumulative *baraka*: sanctified bodies (Ahmad + other Jamis) exuding an aura of amalgamated blessings.
[54] Manz, *Timurid Iran*, 227; Barthold, *Four Studies*, 2:21–22.
[55] Anon./Gusha-Gir (ed.), *Maqamat-i Taybadi*, 73–74. The letter is analyzed in Mahendrarajah, "Tamerlane's Conquest," 68.
[56] Hasluck, *Christianity and Islam*, 63. [57] Ibid., 63ff. and 75ff.

FIGURE 8.1 A "corner-catcher" (*gusha-gir*) at the shrine of ʿAbdallah Ansari, Herat, 2019

Typology of Pilgrims to Ahmad-i Jam's Shrine

Descendants: Ahmad-i Jam's legacy has been maintained for nearly 900 years by his progeny. The majority of Ahmad's living progeny are Sunni, but some of his progeny, like other Iranian families, accepted the Shiʿi interpretation of Islam. This did not lead Ahmad's descendants to discard their devotion to Ahmad, although some (or many?) assuredly did abandon their devotion to Ahmad. Other Jamis renegotiated their spiritual ties to Ahmad to fit him within their Shiʿi beliefs.

Residents: Sunni and Shiʿa from Jam and its purlieus visit on pilgrimage, usually on Fridays and holy days. Since early times, Ahmad has been the premier saint in this section of Khurasan, and the "guardian of the province" (*wilayat-panah*). Friday prayers according to Sunni rites are held at Ahmad's shrine. The shrine's administrator is the leader of Friday prayers (*imam-jum'a*) for the Sunnis of Jam.[58]

Herat: The catchment area of the shrine once stretched from Nishapur to Tirmiz. The institution's catchment area is more limited today following the dismemberment of Khurasan. A significant "half" of the community thrives in Herat and its environs. With the anti-Soviet war (1980–89) and the rise of the Wahhabi-oriented Taliban (1996–2001), Sunni refugees and *mujahidin* from the Herat region became acquainted with Ahmad-i Jam's cult. Afghans (Shi'a Hazara and Sunni Tajiks) visit Jam for pilgrimage, but experience difficulties entering Iran due to visa regulations or security impediments.[59] There is a quasi-permanent community of Hazaras in the Jam region, some of whom find succor at Ahmad's shrine.

Elsewhere: Believers are found in other regions of Iran (especially in Tehran), but are not thought to be many.[60] The majority of the saint cult persists in Khurasan.

Turning to an examination of royal visitors to Jam. Shams al-Din Muhammad Kart was the first Kartid pilgrim to Ahmad's shrine.

Shams al-Din's grandson, Ghiyath al-Din Muhammad Kart, undoubtedly saw Ahmad-i Jam as the protector of his kingdom and his life (*mulk-panah*, *salatin-panah*). Ghiyath al-Din had an uneasy relationship with Il-Khan Öljeitü (r. 1304–16).[61] In 707/1307, Ghiyath al-Din received a patent from Öljeitü; he sojourned at Jam en route to the Il-Khan; he sojourned at Jam on his return to Herat.[62] On his way to Öljeitü, Ghiyath al-Din assuredly sought *baraka* and prayed that the Mongols would not murder him; on his return, he will have expressed gratitude for God's *ni'mah*, His *baraka*, and for his life. Around 711/1311–12, Ghiyath al-Din was back at Öljeitü's camp. He stayed at Jam on his journey to the Il-Khan, undoubtedly anxious, recalling the dastardly murder of his grandfather, Shams al-Din Muhammad Kart, after being lured to the

---

[58] Under Iranian law, there can only be one Shi'i and one Sunni prayer leader per town. The Sunnis congregate at Ahmad-i Jam's shrine; the Shi'a hold their Friday prayers across town.

[59] Due to Jam's proximity to Afghanistan and American troops entrenched there, security along the border is enforced by the Islamic Revolutionary Guard Corps.

[60] Although a small community, they can be influential. 'Ali Fazl, who wrote extensively on Ahmad-i Jam (see Appendix 3), was not of Jami blood, but was devoted to Ahmad. A street near the shrine complex is named for him.

[61] Öljeitü dedicated time to sparring with the Karts. See Hope, *Ilkhanate of Iran*, 15.

[62] al-Harawi, *Harat*, 566, 570; Hafiz-i Abru, *Kart*, 118.

The *Haram*: Oaths, Vows, Sanctuary, and Interments   161

Mongol court in Tabriz. Ghiyath al-Din was sent back to Herat in 715/ 1315 with a fresh patent. He again stayed at Jam before decamping for Herat.[63]

Temür, Shams al-Din, and Ghiyath al-Din were not the only potentates to visit for *ziyarat* or to subscribe (explicitly or implicitly) to the refuge of kings concept. Shah-Rukh b. Temür visited eight times for *ziyarat*. Shah-Rukh traveled extensively between 807/1405 to 850/1447, spending 30 percent of his reign away from Herat;[64] he visited other shrines, too, often at the onset of a campaign. Nonetheless, it is evident he favored Ahmad's shrine, which, after Imam Riza's shrine, was his most frequent *ziyarat* destination.[65]

THE *HARAM*: OATHS, VOWS, SANCTUARY, AND INTERMENTS

As a *haram*, the shrine was inviolable space and offered asylum (*bast*);[66] it was also the venue for oaths (*bay'a*) and vows (*nazr*),[67] burials, and parleys.

Nawruz (d. 696/1297) b. Arghun Aga (on him, see Chapter 3), during his final act of rebellion against the Ilkhanate, was routed in a battle near Jam.[68] There were, claims ʿAli Buzjani, inimicable relations between Nawruz and the Jamis. Nawruz had come to Turbat-i Jam to perform *ziyarat* but could not because blood spewed from his nose, apparently from a blow by the spirit of Ahmad's son, ʿImad al-Din (ʿAbd al-Rahim).[69] No dates are offered, so even if Nawruz had visited, it may not have been after his defeat. However, the narrative is (by my interpretation) a hagiographical explanation for the denial of asylum. The reason for denying entry to the shrine is placed on the spirits at Jam, when in fact, Jami Sufis (then led by Shaykh al-Islam Shihab al-Din Ismaʿil Jami) will have been afraid to cross Ghazan by sheltering a fugitive – especially *this* polarizing character. Nawruz traveled thence to Herat, where he was granted refuge by Fakhr al-Din Kart, which infuriated the Il-Khan. Shihab al-Din Ismaʿil

---

[63] al-Harawi, *Harat*, 591–92, 630; Hafiz-i Abru, *Kart*, 131.
[64] Melville, "Itineraries," 308.   [65] Ibid., 293.
[66] J. Calmard, "Bast," *EIr*, 3:856–58; R. Savory, "Bast," *EI²*, 1:1088.
[67] *Bayʿa* is in the Qurʾan (Q9:111, Q48:10, Q48:18, Q60:12) and understood to refer to pledges of allegiance. On *bayʿa* in Islamic thought, see Andrew Marsham, *Rituals of Islamic Monarchy* (Edinburgh: Edinburgh University Press, 2009), esp. 40–78. On oaths between men (with God as the witness) and vows (made by man to God), see Mottahedeh, *Loyalty*, 42–66. On making vows at shrines, see S. H. al-Houdalieh, "Visitation and Making Vows at the Shrine of Shaykh Shihab al-Din," *Journal of Islamic Studies* 21/3 (2010): 377–90.
[68] al-Harawi, *Harat*, 444; Rashid al-Din, *Jamiʿ al-tawarikh*, 3:445.
[69] Buzjani/Moayyad (ed.), *Rawzat*, 71. On ʿImad al-Din, see Figure A1.2b #9.

Jami defused the crisis when he wrote to the Kart *malik* recommending swift resolution. Nawruz was surrendered by the Kartid, executed by the Mongol commander, and the Ilkhanid siege of Herat lifted (Chapter 3).

Chupan Suldus, a protector-benefactor of the shrine, fell from grace. This story has been told in vivid detail by Charles Melville.[70] When Chupan was in Mashhad, he gathered his commanders about him at the blessed shrine of the "Sultan of Khurasan" (Imam Riza), and extracted from them oaths of loyalty.[71] Obviously not an instance of making oaths or vows at Ahmad's shrine, but nonetheless illustrative of the use of "sacred pasture" (*ḥima*) for making pledges of allegiances *before* God and vows *to* God.

The last example is of a parley held at a sacred pasture because blood should not be spilled in sacred spaces, that is, none of the parties attending need fear assassination. A parley was held at Turbat-i Jam in Muharram 768/September–October 1366 between Muʻizz al-Din Kart and a "friendly rival," Muhammad Bik (d. 774/1373) of the Jawni-Qurban,[72] to benefit the "tranquillity and security of Muslims."[73]

Interment within the sanctified confines of Ahmad-i Jam's shrine was the final step for believers in Ahmad's sainthood and ability to deliver *baraka*. If *ziyarat* to acquire *baraka* benefited body and soul, eternal rest beside Ahmad "guaranteed" decedents superfluous inflows of *baraka* until Judgment Day. There are innumerable descendants of Ahmad-i Jam buried within the shrine confines and in the adjoining Ahmad-i Jam Park. Those interred nearest to Ahmad include Hibat al-Rahman – possibly an indication of the favor in which he held his granddaughter. A necrology is not available. Shams al-Din Kart was the first major non-Jami personality known to be buried at Jam.[74] Kart *maliks* are said to be buried inside Herat's congregational mosque (*masjid-i jamiʻ*), but their graves are not known.[75] Jami lore claims that Ghiyath al-Din Kart is buried inside the

---

[70] Melville, *Amir Chupan*, 19–28.
[71] Hafiz-i Abru, *Zayl-i jamiʻ al-tawarikh-i Rashidi*, ed. Khanbaba Bayani (Tehran: Intisharat-i anjuman-i asar-i milli, 1350/1971), 174.
[72] Jürgen Paul, "Zerfall und Bestehen: Die Ğaun-i qurban im 14. Jahrhundert," *Asiatische Studien/Études Asiatiques* 65/3 (2011): 695–733. The Jawni-Qurban were rivals of the Karts, but frequently cooperated with the Kartid state; hence "friendly rival."
[73] Yusuf-i Ahl/Moayyad (ed.), *Faraʼid*, 1:275–81.
[74] Following his murder in Tabriz, his body was conveyed to Jam for interment. See Isfizari, *Rawzat al-jannat*, 1:422.
[75] On 21 October 2019, I was granted access to the tomb of Sultan Ghiyath al-Din Muhammad Ghuri (r. 558–99/1163–1203) in Herat's *masjid-i jamiʻ*. Lore claims the Kartids are buried with their Ghurid ancestors, but I found no marked Kartid tombs.

Kirmani Mosque, which is plausible but unverifiable since there are no inscriptions. Ahmad's youngest son, Shihab al-Din Isma'il, and architect, Ma'sud Kirmani, are among those interred in passages and vestibules. Khalifa Mir Yahya, a Qadiriyya shaykh, is entombed in the small courtyard where the small hospice once stood. His connection to Jam and Ahmad is unclear.

The main courtyard is a graveyard. Most of the headstones had collapsed or broken in the centuries of neglect, and could not be matched to graves. Management relocated the surviving headstones to the right side of the courtyard, in front of the Firuzshah buildings (see Plate 16). A visitor entering by the main gate and walking toward Ahmad-i Jam's tomb will inevitably tread on unmarked graves.

THE JAMI *KHANAQAH*

The Sufi hospice (*khanaqah*) was the locus for mystical endeavors.

Hospices mushroomed across the Islamic world, variously termed *duwayra*, *ribat*, *tekke*, or *zawiya*. *Khanaqah*, the term (if not the institution), originated in Persian cultural space: it is associated with the Manicheans according to a reference from around 372/982, to "the monastery of the Manicheans" (*khanagah-i Manawiyan*) at Samarqand.[76] A *khanaqah*, broadly, is a residential facility for travelers taking the Sufi Path to God. They doubled as hostels for visitors, including visitors not traveling the Sufi Path.[77] Traveler/wayfarer (*salik*) includes those persons variously termed ascetic, darwish, Sufi, and so on. *Salik*s wandered Islam's expanse for spiritual masters with whom to study Sufism, and to perform *ziyarat* at the mausolea of prophets and saints. *Khanaqah*s offered hospitality to mendicants. *Khanaqah*s were erected within or near to sacred pastures, in part to acquire *baraka*. To illustrate, beginning in the late sixth/twelfth century, seminaries and hospices were erected around Mecca's Great Mosque (*al-masjid al-haram*).[78] Even before these developments, professors had convened classes inside the Great Mosque because "the

---

[76] Anonymous, *Hudud al-'alam*, 2nd ed., trans. Vladimir Minorsky (Cambridge: E. J. W. Gibb Memorial Trust, 1982), 113 (fol. 23a).

[77] See, generally, R. Lifchez, *The Dervish Lodge* (Berkeley, CA: University of California Press, 1992).

[78] See Robert T. Mortel, "Madrasas in Mecca during the Medieval Period: A Descriptive Study Based on Literary Sources," *BSOAS* 60/2 (1997): 236–52, 236; Robert T. Mortel, "'Ribats' in Mecca during the Medieval Period: A Descriptive Study Based on Literary Sources," *BSOAS* 61/1 (1998): 29–50.

transmission of the Islamic sciences within its walls was seen to acquire special merit."[79]

The early *khanaqah*s of Khurasan, Transoxiana, and some Caspian Sea regions were the purview of the Karramiyya.[80] The early history of the *khanaqah* "cannot be properly elucidated until the early evolution of the Karramiyya and their eventual connections with the Manichaeans are examined."[81] Karrami influences on Ahmad-i Jam's *khanaqah* cannot be determined. Al-Muqaddasi's reports of Karramiyya activities within their *khanaqah*s and mosques present an image of benign piety: memorizing or reading the Qur'an, recollecting God (*dhikr*), and inviting people to piety.[82] In contrast to heresiologists, he presents a sober portrait of the Karramiyya; however, Islamic sects are fissiparous and may exhibit disparate beliefs across time and space; moreover, al-Muqaddasi died sixty years before Ahmad-i Jam was born. The validity of his insights with respect to Khurasan, specifically, the Nishapur and Herat Quarters, is unclear.

Rules for Khanaqahs

Rules for comportment (*adab*) within *khanaqah*s emerged. Abu Sa'id b. Abu al-Khayr is thought to have been the first major Sufi shaykh to promulgate *khanaqah* guidelines. The guidelines were intended to foster comity and uniformity.[83] Shihab al-Din Isma'il Jami (d. *ca.* 738/1338) instituted rules and customs (*sharut wa rusum*), which his successors continued;[84] however, even the contours of his rules are not known. Guidelines and etiquette adopted by the *khanaqah*s of Turbat-i Jam possibly included the incorporation of certain of Abu Sa'id's guidelines; and possibly advice from Abu Najib al-Suhrawardi's *Rules for Novices*.[85] Works by the Suhrawardis were studied (*ca.* 822/1419f.) at the Amir Shah-Malik madrasa (see Table 8.2). *Rules for Novices* emphasizes comportment, an imperative for Sufis. The rules are not limited to novices (despite the title), and form an ethical system for Sufis. A popular Sufi

---

[79] Mortel, "Madrasas in Mecca," 236.
[80] al-Muqaddasi, *Ahsan*, 179, 182, 238, 323, 365, 377; J. Chabbi, "Khankah," *EI*^{2}, 4:1025–26.
[81] Chabbi, "Khankah," 4:1025. See also Kiyani, *Khanaqah*, 157–59.
[82] al-Muqaddasi, *Ahsan*, 182. See also Kiyani, *Khanaqah*, 157–58.
[83] The ten rules are in Nicholson, *Islamic Mysticism*, 46.
[84] Buzjani/Moayyad (ed.), *Rawzat*, 102.
[85] ['Abd al-Qahir b. 'Abdallah] Abu Najib al-Suhrawardi, *Kitab adab al-muridin*, trans. M. Milson (Cambridge, MA: Harvard University Press, 1975).

aphorism is that "the whole of Sufism is comportment" (*al-tasawwuf kulluhu adab*).[86]

The Khanaqahs *of Jam: Curricula*

Ahmad-i Jam's successors had a less activist political agenda. Proselytizing activities by Jamis from the late Mongol period were limited to the Friday sermons (*khutba*). The zeal exhibited by Ahmad-i Jam, and his son, Rashid al-Dan ('Abd al-Rashid) Jami (n.d.), a member of a *futuwwa* who died fighting "deserters from God" (i.e., Isma'ili Shi'a),[87] is not manifest. A degree of political quietism was inevitable as shaykhs and shrine connected their political, social, and economic fortunes to the sultanate du jour. Embarrassing utterances or reckless deeds will have unsettled their patrons in Tabriz, Samarqand, or Herat.

Ahmad-i Jam's heirs incorporated Sufi training (*tarbiyya*) in their hospices. 'Ali Buzjani's biographies of Shihab al-Din Isma'il;[88] his son, Shams al-Din Mutahhar;[89] Shihab al-Din Isma'il b. Razi al-Din Ahmad;[90] and Shihab al-Din Isma'il (Abu al-Makarim) Jami[91] reveal that these Jami luminaries had received training in the esoteric (*batin*) and exoteric (*zahir*) branches of the Islamic Sciences ('*ulum al-din*), and had participated in spiritual exercises (*riyazat*). We do not know specifics about their curricula, except that it will have included the four exercises discussed in Chapter 9: *khalwat, dhikr, sama', and rabita*.

The early *khanaqah*s of Jam included training not just in Sufism (*tasawwuf*), but also in the "traditional" Islamic Sciences (hadith, Qur'an, law, etc.) The division – *if any* – in early Islamic history between *khanaqah* activities and madrasa activities is not clear. The view of *khanaqah*s and madrasas of the early Islamic period in Khurasan as dissimilar institutions, each with its own exclusive and delineated mission, must be revised.

The Jami community claims there has continuously been a teaching institution at Turbat-i Jam since the founding of a *khanaqah*-cum-madrasa by Ahmad-i Jam (with funds from a waqf established by one Khadijah Khatun), down to the Hawza-yi 'ilmiyya Ahmadiyya (the new seminary at

---

[86] Javad Nurbakhsh, *In the Tavern of Ruin* (New York: Khaniqahi Nimatullahi, 1978), 67; and Qamar ul-Huda, "The Light beyond the Shore in the Theology of Proper Sufi Moral Conduct (*Adab*)," *Journal of the American Academy of Religion* 72/2 (2004): 461–84.
[87] Buzjani/Moayyad (ed.), *Rawzat*, 61–62; Zanganah, *Sarzamin*, 86–87.
[88] Buzjani/Moayyad (ed.), *Rawzat*, 99–106. [89] Ibid., 106–7. [90] Ibid., 109.
[91] Ibid., 110–11.

the Jami shrine).[92] Ahmad-i Jam's *khanaqah* curricula are undefined, but Jami tradition claims that gnostic (*'irfan*) studies and Islamic Studies (*'ulum al-din*) were both taught side by side at Turbat-i Jam since Ahmad-i Jam's lifetime. There is no literary evidence to substantiate the claim; however, I do not dismiss the averment. The hospice-seminary combo was recorded in eighth/fourteenth-century Mamluk Egypt.[93] Moreover, as Terry Allen keenly perceived, *khanaqah*s of Kartid Herat appear to have "taken on many of the functions of the madrese."[94] He considers the Kartid *khanaqah* "the functional equivalents of the Seljuq or Timurid madrasas."[95] The Kartids collectively sponsored twelve *khanaqah*s,[96] but only three madrasas.[97]

The above emphasis on *khanaqah*s may well reflect the interests of the benefactors; however, I suggest that it reflects instead the absence of *major division* in Islamic curricula. The "jurisprudential schools" (sing. *madhhab*) of Herat, namely, the Hanafi and Shafi'i, had their own dedicated seminaries (*madrasa*) for training future judges (*qadi*), juris-consults (*mufti*), lecturers (*mudarris*), and so on.[98] However, outside of this context, there is no reason why *khanaqah*s could not offer a holistic curriculum in the "traditional" subjects that comprised *'ulum al-din*: hadith, Qur'anic exegesis (*tafsir*), jurisprudence (*fiqh*), theology (*kalam*), logic, grammar, philology, rhetoric, and so on – while concurrently teaching Sufi subjects (*tasawwuf*, *'irfan*). After all, any Sufi will aver, knowledge of God has two complementary facets: the esoteric (*batin*) and the exoteric (*zahir*). Buzjani's biographies of Jami shaykhs show that most of them had received exquisite training in both facets.

---

[92] See 'Abd al-Latif 'Arab-Timuri, "Hawza-yi 'ilmiyya Ahmadiyya," *Faslnamah-yi Habl al-matin* 4 (Autumn 1394/2015): 172–81, 175. Ahmad is said to have constructed about ten *khanaqah*s in his section of Khurasan. See Kiyani, *Khanaqah*, 191–92.

[93] See Fernandes, *Khanqah*, 33–34.

[94] See Terry Allen, *Timurid Herat* (Wiesbaden: Reichert, 1983), 47 n99; Allen, *Catalogue*, 147.

[95] Allen, *Timurid*, 47. On the popularity of *khanaqah*s in medieval Iran, see Leonard Lewisohn, "Sufism in Late Mongol and Early Timurid Persia, from 'Ala' al-Dawla Simnani (d. 736/1326) to Shah Qasim Anvar (d. 837/1434)," in *Iran after the Mongols*, ed. Sussan Babaie (London: I.B. Tauris, 2019), 177–209, esp. 186ff.

[96] The twelve hospices: Allen, *Catalogue*, 147–54 (Catalog Nos. 493, 499, 500, 501, 502, 503, 508, 509, 512, 513, 520, 521), and 228–31 (discussion of Kartid-era developments); and Allen, *Herat*, 47 and n99. Cat. No. 521 is possibly Kartid.

[97] The three colleges: Allen, *Catalogue*, 137 and 142 (Nos. 483, 484, 487), 228–31 (discussion); and Allen, *Herat*, 47 and n99. Kartids possibly patronized Cat. No. 460, a Ghurid madrasa.

[98] In Timurid Herat, ulama also served in sundry administrative positions. See, e.g., Allen, *Herat*, 38–39; and Manz, *Timurid Iran*, 208–19.

Table 8.2, on the medieval curricula at a Jami madrasa, shows that *tasawwuf* and Sufi works on ethics and etiquette (*akhlaq wa adab*) were integral to the program. The inclusion of Sufi subjects alongside "traditional" Islamic curricula is viewed by scholars as the "mainstreaming" of Sufism. Principals of madrasas – many of whom were pedagogically and socially conservative – had permitted Sufi studies to breach their scholastic ramparts. I suggest that they yielded reluctantly. Rather than any "mainstreaming" of *'ilm al-tasawwuf*, this was a strategic retreat by principals, their concession to economic realities and to popular demand, to wit, principals had to attract and retain wealthy patrons who would otherwise have sponsored the construction of *khanaqah*s in lieu of madrasas; and/or executed waqfs for the benefit of *khanaqah*s. Furthermore, seminary principals had to attract and retain students who would otherwise have enrolled at *khanaqah*s. When the Timurid period in Herat expired in 906/1511, the ratio had swung decidedly in favor of the madrasas (*ca.* 2:1).[99] But as Terry Allen observed of the *khanaqah*s and madrasas of Timurid Herat, "[t]he same men taught at both kinds of institutions," and "there seems to have been a large overlap in the pool of students and teachers interested in the two fields [*'ilm al-tasawwuf* and *'ulum al-din*]."[100]

Returning to the *khanaqah*s of Jam.

A *khanaqah* at Turbat-i Jam will have taught the Islamic Sciences also, until the first seminary at the shrine (Madrasa-i Faryumadi) was erected (bet. 729/1329 and 736/1336). Amir Shah-Malik's seminary (built before 822/1419f.) replaced Faryumadi's seminary, and operated into the early Safavid period.[101] The *khanaqah* was the only educational institution to *continuously* operate at Turbat-i Jam, from Ahmad-i Jam's lifetime (d. 1141), into the early Safavid period: 'Ali Buzjani (d. 929/1523) claims that Temür's *khanaqah*s were operating in early Safavid Iran.[102] The *khanaqah* at Turbat-i Jam will have been the premier teaching institution for *'ulum al-din* and *'ilm al-tasawwuf* until the Madrasa-i Faryumadi opened its doors. The *khanaqah* will again have been the premier teaching institution between the demolition of the Faryumadi seminary and the commencement of lectures at the Madrasa-i Amir Shah-Malik (early ninth/fifteenth century). And if we accept Buzjani's claim, then seminary and hospice continued to operate concurrently into the early Safavid era. All

---

[99] See the list of educational buildings in Allen, *Herat*, 73–76.
[100] Allen, *Catalogue*, 147.
[101] It is possible Firuzshah's seminary was not completed due to his political fall (Chapter 5).
[102] Buzjani/Moayyad (ed.), *Rawzat*, 108.

this is to say, the *khanaqah*s at Jam were in continuous operation for 400 years, from the early sixth/twelfth to early tenth/sixteenth centuries. The division of curricula between Jami seminaries and Jami hospices when both were operating concurrently cannot be determined.

The Khanaqahs of Jam: Administration

The posts of chief of *khanaqah* and *mutawalli* were frequently separated (cf. Table 5.2 and Table 8.1). The separation allowed for efficient management of two distinct activities: training darwishes versus managing the shrine, staff, assets, and public officials. As the shrine expanded, it had to employ more secular staff (gardeners, janitors, laborers, etc.) and religious staff (imams, muezzins, preachers, sermonizers, etc.). Furthermore, as the shrine's assets – agricultural and hydrological holdings – increased and sprawled over several administrative provinces (i.e., Bakharz, Fushanj, Jam, Khwaf, and Kusuyi), a staff of estate managers, water-managers, agronomists, hydrologists, and accountants had to be supervised. The custodian-administrator had other exhausting obligations: interacting with public officials, judges, vendors, and litigants.

The custodian-administrator, as the purse holder and trustee of endowments, had overall responsibility for the shrine. This is manifest from a Kartid *manshur*. The *khanaqah* remained within the trustee's compass because the (unidentified) waqfs included benefits for the hospices (*shaykhi khanaqah-i ma'arif panah wa tawliyat-i awqaf-i an*). The trustee is the leader of the *khanaqah*, its "men of God," and manager of community affairs (*uw ra shaykh-i khanaqah-i ma'arif panah [wa] panah-i ahl-i Allah wa muqtada-yi an dargah danand wa mutakaffil-i umur-i jumhur shanasand*).[103] The *khanaqah*'s chief was subordinate to the *mutawalli*.

In Timurid confirmations, too, it is manifest that the trustee has oversight of the *khanaqah*. Qutb al-Din Muhammad Jami (d. 821/1418) was confirmed by Shah-Rukh (r. 807–50/1405–47).[104] In his appointment decree, he is shown to be foremost (*muqaddam*) and the leader (*pishwa*) of the *khanaqah*. He is confirmed in the "office of Shaykh al-Islam, trustee of the waqfs of Amir-i Buzurg ['the Great Amir' = Temür?], and shaykh of the *khanaqah*s (*sahib-i mansab-i shaykh al-islami wa mutawalli-yi*

---

[103] Yusuf-i Ahl/Berlin, *Fara'id*, fol. 315b–316b. Issued before 5 Dhu al-Qa'da 771/31 May 1370.
[104] Yusuf-i Ahl/Berlin, *Fara'id*, fol. 311b–313a. Dated 12 Dhu al-Qa'da 809/20 April 1407.

TABLE 8.1 Administrators of the shrine's hospices (*khanaqah*)

Head of *khanaqah*	Dates	Sources	Comments
Ahmad-i Jam	d. 536/1141	Various	Founder
Ziya al-Din Yusuf b. Ahmad-i Jam	n.d.	Buzjani/Moayyad (ed.), *Rawzat*, 66–69	Received *khirqa* from father and is described as successor (*khalifa*), i.e., shaykh, for the villages of Jam; he had many darwishes
Zahir al-Din 'Isa b. Ahmad	n.d.	Inferred (see Buzjani/Moayyad (ed.), *Rawzat*, 78, 85ff.)	Zahir al-Din was shaykh to Qutb al-Din Muhammad (Chapter 9).
Hibat al-Rahman bt. Burhan al-Din Nasr Jami See Figure A1.1b #7	n.d. Headed hospice from before 617/1220 to ?	Buzjani/Moayyad (ed.), *Rawzat*, 81–82; Zanganah, *Sarzamin*, 108–9	"Lady of the hospice" (*khatun-i khanaqah*). Resided at the *khanaqah* in Ma'd-Abad. She developed the hospice and added a courtyard, garden, and cells (sing. *chilla-khana*) for seclusions (*khalwat*)
Qutb al-Din Muhammad b. Shams al-Din Mutahhar b. Ahmad	b. 577/1181–82; d. 667/1268	Kadkani, *Darwish*, 262f.; Buzjani/Moayyad (ed.), *Rawzat*, 88–89; Zanganah, *Sarzamin*, 112–19	Custodian and chief of *khanaqah* in Ma'd-Abad; his nephew (Safi al-Din, see below) occupied another *khanaqah*
Safi al-Din Mahmud b. Hibat al-Rahman See Figure A1.1b #8	n.d.	Buzjani/Moayyad (ed.), *Rawzat*, 97–98; Zanganah, *Sarzamin*, 120–21	Fled to Hijaz ahead of Mongols; returned and occupied the "old hospice" (*khanaqah-i qadim*). Parents were deceased and uncle led the community. It appears there were now two hospices. Safi al-Din's progeny include illustrious Sufis with the *nisba* Kusuyi

TABLE 8.1 Continued

Head of *khanaqah*	Dates	Sources	Comments
Shihab al-Din Isma'il b. Qutb al-Din Muhammad	d. *ca.* 738/1338	Buzjani/Moayyad (ed.), *Rawzat*, 99–106; Zanganah, *Sarzamin*, 155–60 Cf. Kiyani, *Khanaqah*, 323–24	*Mutawalli* and head of *khanaqah*; later he split the posts between two sons (see below). Endowed shrine and hospices (pl. *khawaniq*) with great wealth; and established rules and customs (*sharut va rusum*) Muhsin Kiyani confuses the Kartid-era Shihab al-Din Isma'il and his progeny with the Timurid-era Abu al-Makarim (on him, see below)
Shams al-Din Mutahhar b. Shihab al-Din Isma'il	d. bet. 751/1350 and 767/1366	Buzjani/Moayyad (ed.), *Rawzat*, 106–7; Zanganah, *Sarzamin*, 131	Razi al-Din Ahmad (d. 767/1366) became the *mutawalli*; and brother Shams al-Din Mutahhar headed the *khanaqah*
Ziya al-Din Yusuf b. Mu'in al-Din b. Shams al-Din Mutahhar b. Shihab al-Din Isma'il Jami	d. 797/1394 (in Tabriz)	Buzjani/Moayyad (ed.), *Rawzat*, 108–9; al-Samarqandi, *Matla'*, 1.2:642	His cousin Shihab al-Din Isma'il (d. 809/1407) was the *mutawalli*. Ziya al-Din hosted Temür at shrine, where he performed *ziyarat*
Shihab al-Din Isma'il (d. 809/1407) b. Razi al-Din Ahmad b. Shihab al-Din Isma'il Jami	From death of Ziya al-Din Yusuf to *ca.* 809/1407	Buzjani/Moayyad (ed.), *Rawzat*, 109; al-Samarqandi, *Matla'*, 1.2:642	The cousins accompanied Temür on campaign as spiritual advisors Role is inferred given his biography and relationship with Temür
Shihab al-Din Isma'il (Abu al-Makarim) al-Tirmizi Jami	From *ca.* 809/1407 to *ca.* 845/1441f.	Buzjani/Moayyad (ed.), *Rawzat*, 110–11; Khwafi, *Mujmal*, 3:138; Khwandamir, *Habib*, 5:11–12 Zanganah, *Sarzamin*, 174–75	Shah-Rukh's preceptor. Shah-Rukh (r. 807–50/1405–47) visited Jam often (see Melville, "Itineraries of Shahrukh," 285–315). The shrine was developed by Timurid amirs and benefited from Gawhar-Shad's *waqfiyya* for her mosque in Mashhad

Nasir al-Din ʿAbd al-ʿAziz Jami (d. 920/1514) (Jami genealogical link is not clear)	From ? to 920/1514	Khwandamir, *Habib*, 4:339; Zanganah, *Sarzamin*, 228–29	"In conducting wayfarers [Sufis] along the Path (*sabil*) he followed Shaykh al-Islam *Zhanda-Pil*, Ahmad of Jam." Darwishes in Temür's two *khanaqahs* (Table 5.1, § V) and *khanaqahs* inside the shrine were taught the "traditional" path; cf. path of ʿAziz-Allah Jami (below), a Khawajagan-Naqshbandi
ʿAziz-Allah Jami (d. 27 Rabiʿ II 902/2 January 1497) b. Qutb al-Din Muhammad Zahid (Jami genealogical link is not clear) Sunni *khanaqahs* go underground	From ? to his death in 902/1497	Buzjani/Moayyad (ed.), *Rawzat*, 124–33, esp. 131–32; Zanganah, *Sarzamin*, 167–71	Rebuilt *khanaqah* in Maʿd-Abad as his primary center of operation. This is where his shrine is today, *ca*. 200 yards from the northern limits of Ahmad's shrine. This was a Jami-Naqshbandi *khanaqah*. On ʿAziz-Allah and the Jamis/Naqshbandis, see Chapter 9 Safavid era. Temür's *khanaqahs* were active, *ca*. 929/1523, when Buzjani died (see Buzjani/Moayyad (ed.), *Rawzat*, 108)

tawliyat-i awqaf-i amir-i buzurg wa khanaqah-at)."[105] The *manshur* for Shihab al-Din Isma'il (Abu al-Makarim) Jami (d. 847/1443f.),[106] who succeeded Qutb al-Din Muhammad in 821/1418, installs him as trustee of waqfs and leader of the *khanaqah*. He, however, appears not to have divided the posts of trustee and *khanaqah* chief (cf. Table 5.2 and Table 8.1). He managed the *khanaqah* and shrine complex during one of the shrine's liveliest periods of growth. Abu al-Makarim Jami's successors as trustees (for whom *manshur*s have survived) are Razi al-Din Ahmad b. Jalal al-Din Jami (d. *ca*. 884/1479),[107] and Jalal al-Din (Abu al-Qasim) b. Razi al-Din Ahmad Jami (d. 920/1514f.).[108] The first was confirmed by Sultan-Abu Sa'id (r. 855–73/1451–69); the other by Sultan-Husayn Bayqara (r. 873–911/1469–1506). Both decrees stress the trustee's preeminence is social-religious and business affairs, and control of *khanaqah*s and waqfs.

Explicit terms indicate the existence of more than one *khanaqah* within the confines of the shrine. In the 12 Dhu al-Qa'da 809/20 April 1407 *manshur*, the hospice is identified as "Shaykh al-Islam Shihab al-Din Isma'il's *khanaqah*, known as Shaykh al-Islam Ahmad-i Jam's *khanaqah*" (*khanaqah-yi shaykh al-Islam Shihab al-Din Isma'il kih mashhur bih khanaqah-yi shaykh al-Islam Ahmad-i Jam*).[109] The two *khanaqah*s donated by Temür are not mentioned, but *khanaqah* is employed in the plural when referring to waqfs for the *khanaqah*s (*tawliyat-i mawqufat-i khanaqah-at*). There was a thriving *khanaqah* at Hasan-Abad village;[110] however, this *khanaqah* is known only from the above decree.

The decrees are snapshots. They reflect a sultan's wishes, which will have shaped nothing with respect to the daily decisions and activities of the administrators. The decrees proscribe state officials from interfering with shrine activities, its waqfs, and operations on its endowed farmlands and villages. Herein lies the supreme value of the *manshur*s: shields against oleaginous or avaricious minions seeking to ingratiate, harass, or extort.

---

[105] Yusuf-i Ahl/Berlin, *Fara'id*, fol. 312b.
[106] Ibid., fol. 291b–294a; Yusuf-i Ahl/Fatih, *Fara'id*, fol. 447b–448b; Yusuf-i Ahl/Tehran, *Fara'id*, 623–26. Dated 6 Safar 821/15 March 1418.
[107] Supp. persan 1815/Paris, fol. 29b–30b; Nawa'i (ed.), *Asnad wa mukatibat*, 314–15. Undated, but *ca*. 29 Jumada II 863/3 May 1459. See discussion in Chapter 3.
[108] Supp. persan 1815/Paris, fol. 30b–32a. Dated 20 Jumada I 884/9 August 1479.
[109] Yusuf-i Ahl/Berlin, *Fara'id*, fol. 312a.
[110] Ibid., fol. 312b. Hasan-Abad is a generic toponym; it is not known where the village is located, or if it is even one of the three identified by Hafiz-i Abru. See Krawulsky, *Ḥorasan*, 1:41 (Zawa), 1:77 (Yazir), 1:99 (Mashhad-Tus).

The Jami Madrasa

The Sunni *khanaqah* began waning with the Safavid triumph. The Safavids – Sufis of extremist (*ghulat*) Shi'i bent – attacked Sufi institutions. Sunni *khanaqah*s hastily took their activities underground. The Iranian *khanaqah* did not disappear, but rather, manifests today in sundry Shi'i and Sunni guises. Apropos of this, a new *khanaqah* was founded by a subset of Jami mystics. It is called a "guesthouse" (*mihman-khana*) to minimize tensions with the Shi'i state, which detests the term *khanaqah*. It is located at Kuh-yi Bizd, a mountain region west of Turbat-i Jam where Ahmad-i Jam claims to have spent part of his eremite years, and where he erected his Masjid-i Nur (see Chapter 9).

THE JAMI MADRASA

Medieval Curriculum

Maria Subtelny and Anas Khalidov analyzed the license (*ijaza*) issued to Yusuf-i Ahl Jami, the compiler of the *Fara'id-i Ghiyasi*, by Jalal al-Din al-Qayini (d. 838/1435) in Dhu al-Hijja 822/December 1419–January 1420.[111] An *ijaza* is a license from a professor (*mudarris*) to transmit learning acquired by the pedagogical means of audition (*sama'*) and/or reading (*qira'a*). The license (or an attachment to it) will itemize the academic works (or parts thereof) that the licensee is authorized to transmit, and the licensor's own authorities (i.e., his professors – a student usually studied with several teachers).[112] The *ijaza* was preserved by Yusuf-i Ahl in his *insha'* compilation.[113] His *ijaza* is the product of a specific time, place, and situation; but given its issuance at Turbat-i Jam, and the academic titles and scholars listed therein, the *ijaza* can be utilized to trace the *contours* of the curricula of higher learning at Jam from the late Kartid period to the end of the Timurid era. The core curriculum at Jam (gleaned from the *ijaza*) includes Hanafi and Shafi'i scholarship, but is weighted toward the Hanafi. The *ijaza* lists the six canonical (*musannaf*) hadith books; *musnad*s by Abu Hanifa, al-Shafi'i, Ibn Hanbal, and Malik b. Anas's *al-Muwatta*; and works on Maliki, Shafi'i, Hanafi, and Hanbali law – including by Ibn Taymiyya and Ibn al-Jawzi. Listed under Qur'anic exegesis are titles by al-Nasafi, al-Sulami, and al-Zamakhshari (a Mu'tazila scholar). In addition to mystical works taught in *khanaqah*s, books on Sufism, ethics, and etiquette were studied.

---

[111] Maria Eva Subtelny and Anas Khalidov, "The Curriculum of Islamic Higher Learning in Timurid Iran in the Light of the Sunni Revival under Shah-Rukh," *JAOS* 115 (1995): 210–36.
[112] Ibid., 214–15; S. Bonebakker, "Ijaza," *EI*², 4:1021b–1022a.
[113] Yusuf-i Ahl/Moayyad (ed.), *Fara'id*, 2:550–52.

TABLE 8.2 Shrine's seminary (*madrasa*) curriculum in the Timurid era

Category	Author	Illustrative titles (if given)	Comment
Ethics and etiquette (*akhlaq wa adab*)	Abu al-Najib al-Suhrawardi (d. 563/1168)	not specified (probably *Kitab adab al-muridin*)	N/A
	al-Qushayri (d. 465/1072)	not specified	
	al-Kalabadhi (d. 380/990)	not specified	
	al-Ghazali (d. 505/1111)	not specified	
	al-Bakharzi (d. 659/1261)	not specified	
	Najm al-Din Kubra (d. 618/1221)	not specified	
Grammar, philology, rhetoric, linguistics, literature	Isma'il al-Jawhari (d. *ca.* 398/1008)	*Taj al-lugha*	GAL I:133–34, bio. 3, ti. i
	al-Farabi (d. 350/961)	*Diwan al-adab*	GAL I:133, bio. 2
	Ahmad al-Qazwini (d. 395/1005)	*Kitab al-mujmal*	GAL I:135–36, bio. 5, ti. 1
	Muhammad al-Azhari al-Harawi (d. 370/980)	*Tahdhib al-lugha*	GAL I:134–35, bio. 4, ti. 1
	al-Sakkaki (d. 626/1229)	*Miftah al-'ulum*	GAL I:352–53, bio. 16, ti. 1
History (*tarikh*)	al-Isfahani (d. 430/1038)	All (history, biography, hadith)	GAL I:445–46, bio. 1
	al-Namari al-Qurtubi (d. 463/1071)	All (biography, literature, hadith)	GAL I:453–54, bio. 1
	al-Hakim al-Nishapuri (d. 405/1014)	All (history, biography, hadith)	GAL I:175, bio. 16
Mysticism (*tasawwuf*)	Shihab al-Din 'Umar (Abu Hafs) al-Suhrawardi (d. 632/1234)	All (includes *Kitab 'awarif al-ma'arif*)	GAL, I:218–19, bio. 11
	'Abd al-Qahir (Abu al-Najib) al-Suhrawardi (d. 563/1168)	All (includes *Kitab adab al-muridin*)	
	Muhammad al-Sulami (d. 412/1021)	All (includes *Risala al-malamatiyya*)	
	Abu Sa'id b. Abu al-Khayr (d. 440/1049)	Not identified	

Qurʾanic exegesis (*tafsir*)	al-Makki (d. 386/996)	*Qut al-qulub*	GAL, I:344–50, bio. 11
	al-Zamakhshari (d. 538/1144)	*al-Kashshaf* and *Taqrib* (Muʿtazila texts)	GAL, I:218–19, bio. 11
	Muhammad al-Sulami (d. 412/1021)	Several qualifying titles	GAL, I:465, bio. 22, ti. 2
	al-Kasani (d. 587/1191)	*Kitab al-taʾwilat*	GAL, I:429, bio. 2, ti. 3
	al-Thaʿlabi al-Nishapuri (d. 427/1035)	*Kitab al-kashf*	GAL, I:524–25, bio. 6, ti. 1
	al-Kirmani (d. *ca*. 500/1106)	*Lubab al-tafasir*	GAL, I:210–11, bio. 6, ti. 1
	al-Samarqandi al-Hanafi (d. *ca*. 373/983)	*Tafsir al-Qurʾan*	GAL, I:111–12, bio. 22, ti. 3
	al-Zajjaj (d. *ca*. 311/923)	*Maʿani al-Qurʾan* (*Iʿrab al-Qurʾan*)	GAL, I:525, bio. 10
	Muhammad al-Samarqandi (d. 556/1161)	*Kitab al-ihqaq*	
Qurʾanic readings, recitations, variations (*al-qiraʾa wa-l-ada*ʾ)	al-Sakhawi al-Hamadhani (d. *ca*. 643/1245)	All	GAL, I:522–23, bio. 14
	al-Mukhtar al-Razi (fl. *ca*. 631/1233)	All	GAL, I:527–28, bio. 16
	al-Fasawi al-Farrisi (d. 377/987)	All	GAL, I:116, bio. 29
The "roots of law" (*usul al-fiqh*) and the "branches of law" (*furuʿ al-fiqh*)	Malik b. Anas (d. 179/795)	*al-Muwatta*	GAL, I:176–77, bio. 1
	Abu Hanifa (d. 150/767)	*al-Fiqh*; *al-Wasiya*; *Kitab al-ʿalim*	GAL, I:367–73, bio. 8, ti. viii
	Ibn al-Hajib (d. 646/1249)	*Muntaha* (handbook of Maliki law)	GAL, I:466–69, bio. 24
	Burhan al-Din al-Marghinani (d. 593/1197)	*al-Hidaya* and *al-Bidayat*	GAL, I:471, bio. 27
	Zahir al-Din al-Marghinani (fl. *ca*. 600/1203)	not given (likely his fatwa collection)	GAL II:276–78, bio. 1, ti. 3, 3a
	al-Shafiʿi (d. 204/820)	All	GAL II:278–80, bio. 2, ti. 15
	Sadr al-Shariʿa (d. 747/1347)	*Tanqib al-usul* and *Tawdih al-Talwih*	GAL, I:496–501, bio. 30, ti. xix
	Saʿd al-Din Taftazani (d. *ca*. 793/1390)	*Kitab hilyat al-abrar*	GAL, I:181–82, bio. 7
	Abu Zakariyya Yahya al-Nawawi (d. 676/1278)	All	GAL, I:446–47, bio. 4
			GAL, I:434, bio. 4

TABLE 8.2 Continued

Category	Author	Illustrative titles (if given)	Comment
Theology, metaphysics, dogmatics (*ʿilm al-kalam*)	Abu Jaʿfar Ahmad al-Tahawi (d. 321/933)	All (Shafiʿi, Ashʿari)	
	al-Bayhaqi al-Khusrawjirdi	All	
	Ibn Makula al-ʿIjli (d. *ca.* 487/1094)		
	ʿAdud al-Din al-Iji (d. 756/1355)	*Kitab al-mawaqif fi ʿilm al-kalam*	GAL II:267–71, bio. 1a, ti. iv
	ʿAbdallah b. ʿUmar al-Baydawi (d. *ca.* 685/1286)	*Tawaliʿ al-anwar*	GAL I:530–34, bio. 25, ti. vi
	Shams al-Din al-Jazari (d. 833/1429)	*al-Hisn al-hasin*	GAL I:542, ti. 47
Traditions (*hadith*)	Muhammad al-Bukhari (d. 256/870)	*Sahih al-Bukhari*	GAL I:171–72, bio. 5
	Muslim ibn al-Hajjaj (d. 261/874)	*Sahih Muslim*	GAL I:447–49, bio. 6, ti. 1
	Muhammad b. ʿIsa al-Tirmidhi (d. 279/892)	*Jamiʿ al-Tirmidhi*	GAL II:249, bio. 2
	Ahmad al-Nasaʾi (d. 303/915)	*Sunan al-sughra*	GAL I:443–44, bio. 21, ti. 1
	Muhammad b. Majah al-Qazwini (d. 273/887)	*Sunan Ibn Majah*	GAL I:496–501, bio. 30, ti. x
	Abu Daʾud Sulayman al-Sistani (d. 275/888)	*Sunan Abu Daʾud*	
	ʿAbd Allah al-Samarqandi (d. 255/869)	*Kitab al-sunan*	
	Abu Hanifa (d. 150/767)	*Musnad*	
	al-Shafiʿi (d. 204/820)	*Musnad*	
	Ahmad ibn Hanbal (d. 241/855)	*Musnad*	
	al-Baghawi (d. *ca.* 516/1122)	*Kitab masabih (al-duja) al-sunna*	
	Shams al-Din M. al-Tabrizi (fl. *ca.* 737/1336)	*Mishkat al-masabih*	
	Razi al-Din al-Saghani (d. 650/1252)	*Mashariq al-anwar al-nabawiyya*	
	Abu Zakariyya Yahya al-Nawawi (d. 676/1278)	*Riyad al-salihin*	

I have utilized Khalidov's and Subtelny's study for Table 8.2,[114] the curriculum of higher learning in the medieval period.

Al-Qayini's program for Yusuf-i Ahl Jami is precisely the sort of conservative and inclusive curriculum one expects of him. He had authored a treatise, *Advice for Shah-Rukh*,[115] a didactic opus of no discernible social impact, which described a utopian program for the renewal of Sunni orthodoxy. Al-Qayini was a cudgel in Shah-Rukh's fantasy of eliminating immorality in his realm; he served as Herat's censor of public morals (*muhtasib*).[116] Shah-Rukh liked public demonstrations of "morality": shuttering taverns and pouring out good wine.[117] The Islamic obligation to "enjoin the good and forbid the reprehensible," a popular and blunt weapon of puritanical reformers,[118] was undoubtedly exercised by al-Qayini.

Al-Qayini's intellectual pedigree (*sanad*), nonetheless, is illustrious. His learning can be traced to distinguished exegetes like Sa'd al-Din Mas'ud Taftazani (722–93/1322–90) – the de facto Shaykh al-Islam of Kartid Herat, whose grandson and great-grandson were de jure shaykhs al-Islam of Timurid Herat;[119] Burhan al-Din al-Marghinani (d. 593/1197), the first in a train of shaykhs al-Islam of Transoxiana; Shams al-Din Muhammad al-Jazari (d. 833/1429); Sadr al-Din Ibrahim al-Hammuya (d. 722/1322), Sufi and theologian who officiated at the Il-Khan Ghazan's conversion ceremony in 694/1295; and Muhammad Parsa (d. 822/1419), the intellectual colossus of the Khwajagan-Naqshbandiyya. These and other scholars, and their intellectual heirs, shaped al-Qayini's education.[120]

Sa'd al-Din Taftazani is one of the most important scholars identified in the *ijaza*. He was a polymath and savant of Shafi'i and Hanafi law. He is identified as a Shafi'i, perhaps because he took theological positions favoring the Ash'ari, but he also backed criticisms of Ash'ari doctrines.

---

[114] Select titles are given. *GAL* is Carl Brockelmann's *Geschichte der arabischen Litteratur*, but refers to a translation, which corresponds to Carl Brockelmann, *History of the Arabic Written Tradition*, 2 vols. and 3 supp. vols., trans. Joep Lameer (Leiden: Brill, 2017–19); however, *GAL Supp.* refers to the three original supplements (Leiden: Brill, 1937–42).

[115] Jalal al-Din al-Qayini, *Nasa'ih-i Shah–Rukhi* (Vienna: Nationalbibliothek, Cod. A.F. 112).

[116] Manz, *Timurid Iran*, 210–12.

[117] The "elite [of Timurid Herat] were used to a culture in which large quantities of alcohol were consumed publicly, and several members of the [Timurid] dynasty were known as serious drinkers." Ibid., 212.

[118] On puritanical reformers and *al-amr bi-l-ma'ruf*, see Mercedes Garcia-Arenal, *Messianism and Puritanical Reform* (Leiden: Brill, 2006), 96ff (the case of the Almoravids); Cook, *Commanding Right*, 180ff (the Wahhabi Kingdom of Saudi Arabia).

[119] See Mahendrarajah, "Shaykh al-Islam."

[120] Subtelny and Khalidov, "Curriculum," 219–22 (on al-Qayini's authorities and oeuvre).

However, his jurisprudential path – derived from comments in *al-Talwih* – shows that he "personally adhered to the Hanafi school."[121] Taftazani's pedagogical style suited the Jami shaykhs, who straddled the Shafi'i and Hanafi *madhhab*s. Ahmad's grandson, Qutb al-Din Muhammad (d. 667/ 1268), authored a book that still informs gnostics at Jam. In Jami's chapter on the Shari'a, borrowings from Shafi'i and Hanafi *madhhab*s are manifest.[122] Sa'd al-Din's relationship with the Jamis was intimate. He resided at Jam in 752/1351 while composing a commentary, *Sharh al-shamsiyya*. As a honored guest, he delivered lectures at the shrine's madrasa or *khanaqah*. He was a confidant of the Kartid vizier Mu'in al-Din Jami, and educated his son, Ziya al-Din Yusuf Jami – Temür's host on his visit to Jam.

Preceding his education at a madrasa, a Jami shaykh will have studied at a *maktab* where he was trained in Arabic, Persian, literature, and calligraphy. The Jami community produced numerous calligraphers, litterateurs, Sufis, judges, ulama, and professors. A Jami shaykh of late Kartid to late Timurid Iran acquired a firm foundation in the Islamic sciences by reading and/or audition of diverse works on jurisprudence of the four Sunni *madhhab*s, encompassing the roots (*usul al-fiqh*) and the branches (*furu' al-fiqh*) of the law; an array of hadith collections (including the lesser known but still critical titles); Qur'anic exegeses, dogmatics, ethics, morals, etiquette, literature, history, and Sufism. Even if a student did not become a professor, he will have graduated from a Jami madrasa with a first-class education in the Islamic Sciences. If he were inclined to pursue a career in law, academia, or ministry, he will have traveled to Herat, Samarqand, Bukhara, India, and the Hijaz to study with experts in the subfields of Islamic studies.

Modern Curriculum

The Sunni madrasas of Iran offer eight-, ten-, or twelve-year programs. The Hawza-yi 'ilmiyya Ahmadiyya offers a ten-year model.[123]

---

[121] Wilferd Madelung, "Taftazani," *EI*², 10:88–89; see also Thomas Würtz, *Islamische Theologie im 14. Jahrhundert* (Berlin: de Gruyter, 2016), 17–36; Khwafi, *Mujmal*, 3:124–25; Khwandamir, *Rijal*, 91–93; Khwandamir, *Habib*, 3:544–46.

[122] Qutb al-Din Muhammad Jami, *Hadiqat al-haqiqa*, ed. Hasan Nasiri Jami (Tehran: Pizhuhishgah-i 'ulum-i insani wa mutal'at-i farhangi, 1390/2011), xxiii (editor's commentary).

[123] Program communicated to me via email 1 July 2017 and 27 September 2017; discussed at interviews at Turbat-i Jam in September 2017 with officials and Husayn Jami al-Ahmadi (the son of Haji Qazi), the seminary's new principal as of 1396/2017.

TABLE 8.3 Shrine's seminary curriculum for academic year AHS 1396–97/2017–18

Level	Duration	Level	Topics	Core titles	Authors	Comments
Beginner	4 years	1	Ahmad-i Jam and Jam; Persian literature; introduction to English; introduction to computing; hygienics; al-Qur'an's sounds and tones (*savt wa lahn*) and Qur'anic studies (*'ulum-i qur'ani*)	—	—	Core curriculum Students enter with at least basic command of Arabic Not all students are from Jam; hence the study of Jam's history and culture
		2	Jurisprudence (*fiqh*)	*Mukhtasar-i Quduri*	Ahmad al-Quduri Baghdadi (d. 428/1037)	GAL I:183, bio. 12, ti. i Handbook on Hanafi *furu'* Translated texts (*tarjuma*) Pub. in Zahedan, 1362/1983f.
				Miscellaneous	—	
			Qur'an commentaries (sing. *tafsir*)	*Zad al-talibin*	Muhammad 'Ashiq Ilahi	
			Hadith	*Qisas al-nabiyin*	Abu al-Hasan 'Ali Nadwi (d. 1999)	
			History and biography (*tarikh wa sirah*)	Miscellaneous	—	
			Arabic language and literature	*Nawb-i Mir*	Ali b. Muhammad Jurjani (d. 816/1413)	Various editions in Iran
			Syntax and morphology (*nahw wa sarf*)	*Sarf-i Mir*	Ali b. Muhammad Jurjani (d. 816/1413)	Various editions in Iran
			Qur'an studies (*'ulum-i qur'ani*)	*Hila al-Qur'an*	Muhsin Musawi	Multiple levels and editions

TABLE 8.3 Continued

Level	Duration	Level	Topics	Core titles	Authors	Comments
		3	Jurisprudence	*Fiqh-i muyassar*	Abu Hanifa	Trans. Shafiq al-Rahman al-Nadwi; pub. 1393/2014f., in Turbat-i Jam
			—	—	—	Not identified
			Ethics (*akhlaq*)	*Mufid al-talibin*	Muhammad Bardak	—
			Arabic language and literature	Miscellaneous	—	—
			Morphology	*Sarf-i Baha'i*	Shaykh Baha'i	Shi'i scholar (d. *ca*. 1021/1630); pub. in Zahedan, 1380/2001f.
			—	—	—	See above
			History and biography	*Qisas al-nabiyin*	Abu al-Hasan 'Ali Nadwi	—
			Qur'an studies	Miscellaneous	—	—
			Qur'an recital (*tajwid*)	*Tartil-i Qur'an ba tajwid-i asan*	'Abd al-Majid Hanafi	Published in Jam, 1395/2016f.
		4	Jurisprudence	*Fiqh-i muyassar*	Abu Hanifa	See above
			Qur'an commentaries (*tafsir*)	Miscellaneous	—	—
			Ethics	*Ta'lim al-muta'allim*	Burhan al-Din Zarnuji (fl. 600/1203)	GAL I:606, bio. 17
			Arabic language and literature	Miscellaneous	—	—
			Morphology	*Marah al-arwah*	Ahmad b. 'Ali b. Mas'ud (d. *ca*. 613/1216)	Pub. in Qum, 1391/2012f.
			Syntax	*al-Hidaya fi al-nahw*	—	Various titles and editions
				'Awamil al-mi'a	Muhammad b. Yusuf (d. *ca*. 745/1344)	GAL I:341, bio. 5, ti. i
					'Abd al-Qahir b. Jurjani (d. *ca*. 471/1078)	See above
			History and biography	*Qisas al-nabiyin*	Abu al-Hasan 'Ali Nadwi	Pub. in Jam, 1384/2005f.
			Dialectics (*mantiq*)	*Tisir al-mantiq*	'Abdallah Ganguhi	
Intermediate	3 years	1	Jurisprudence	*Usul Shashi* [*Kitab al-usul*]	Nizam al-Din Shashi (fl. seventh/thirteenth cent.)	Cf. *GAL* I:182, bio. 8
			Qur'an commentaries (*tafsir*)			*GAL* II:250, bio. 1, ti. iii
			Hadith			—

#	Subject	Work	Author	Reference
	Rhetoric (*'ilm al-balagha*)	*Kanz al-daqa'iq fi al-furu'*	Hafiz al-Din al-Nasafi (d. 710/1310)	*GAL* I:496, bio. 30, ti. x. Pub. in Zahedan, 1385/2006f.
	Morphology	Miscellaneous	—	—
	Syntax	*Riyad al-salihin*	Abu Zakariyya Yahya al-Nawawi (d. 676/1278)	—
	Dialectics/logic (*mantiq*)	*Durus al-balagha*	Nasif Hanafi et al.	*GAL* I:367, bio. 8, ti. i
		Mubadi al-'arabiyya	Rashid Shartuni (d. 1906)	*GAL* I:608, bio. 23, ti. ii
		al-Kafiya	Ibn Hajib (d. 646/1249)	*GAL* II:278, bio. 2, ti. i
		Isaghuji	Athir al-Din al-Abhari (d. *ca.* 660–63/1263–65)	
		Tahdhib al-mantiq wa-l-kalam	Sa'd al-Din Taftazani (d. *ca.* 793/1390)	
2	Jurisprudence	*Kanz al-daqa'iq fi al-furu'*	Hafiz al-Din al-Nasafi (d. 710/1310)	See above
	Rhetoric	*Nur al-anwar*	Mullah Ahmad Jiwan (d. 1130/1717)	Commentary on *Manar al-anwar*, *GAL* II:250, bio.1, ti. i
	Syntax and morphology	—	—	Various editions in Iran
		Jawahir al-balagha	Ahmad al-Hashimi (d. 1943)	*GAL* II:266, bio. 7, ti. xi
		Sharh Jami [*al-Fawa'id al-diya'iyya*]	'Abd al-Rahman Jami (d. 898/1492)	*GAL* II:108, bio. 11, ti. ii
		Sharh Ibn 'Aqil [*Sharh alfiyyat Ibn Malik*]	'Abdallah b. 'Aqil al-Hamadani (d. 769/1367)	—
3	Jurisprudence	*al-Hidaya*	Burhan al-Din al-Marghinani (d. 593/1197)	*GAL* I:466–69, bio. 24
	Qur'an commentaries	*Nur al-anwar*		See above
	Qur'an studies	*al-Wajiz fi usul al-fiqh*		In Arabic; Farsi trans. exists

TABLE 8.3 Continued

Level	Duration	Level	Topics	Core titles	Authors	Comments
			Hadith studies	Tafsir al-Jalalayn	Mullah Ahmad Jiwan (d. 1130/1717)	GAL II:180, bio. 7., ti. vi
			Rhetoric	al-Tibyan fi 'ulum al-Qur'an	Wahbah Zuhayli (b. 1932)	Various editions worldwide
			Arabic literature	Muqaddamat min usul al-hadith		—
			Syntax and morphology	Jawahir al-balagha	Jalal al-Din Suyuti and Jalal al-Din Mahalli	GAL Supp. II: S. 215 (at p. 304)
			Dogmatics	Mukhtasar fi 'ilm al-ma'ani	Muhammad 'Ali Sabuni	Various editions in Iran
				Mukhtarat min adab al-'Arab	Najm al-Din Muhammad Darkani (n.d.)	See above
				Sharh Ibn 'Aqil	Ahmad al-Hashimi (d. 1943)	GAL I:548, bio. 2, ti. i
				al-'Aqa'id	Sa'd al-Din Taftazani (d. ca. 793/1390)	
					Abu al-Hasan 'Ali Nadwi (d. 1999)	
					'Abdallah b. 'Aqil al-Hamadani (d. 769/1367)	
					Najm al-Din al-Nasafi al-Maturidi (d. 537/1142)	
Advanced	3 years	1	Jurisprudence	al-Hidaya	Burhan al-Din al-Marghinani (d. 593/1197)	See above
			Qur'an commentaries	'Uqud rasm al-mufti		On Hanafi fiqh; fatwas
			Hadith studies	Athar al-sunan		On Hanafi fiqh; hadith

		Fara'id al-Sirajiyya	Siraj al-Din al-Sajawandi (fl. sixth/twelfth cent.)	On Hanafi *fiqh*; inheritance; GAL I:470, bio. 26, ti. i
		al-Durr al-mukhtar	Muhammad Amin b. 'Abidin Shami (d. 1836)	Commentary on Timurtashi's *Tanwir*; see GAL II:404, bio. 5
		Tafsir al-Jalalayn	Muhammad b. 'Ali al-Nimawi (d. 1904)	See above
		Taysir mustalah al-hadith	Muhammad b. 'Ali al-Haskafi (d. 1088/1677)	On hadith sciences
		—	Jalal al-Din Suyuti and Jalal al-Din Mahalli Mahmud Tahhan (n.d.)	
2	Jurisprudence	*al-Hidaya*	Burhan al-Din al-Marghinani (d. 593/1197)	See above
	History	*Tarikh al-tashri' al-islami*	Muhammad Khudari Bik (d. 1927)	History of Islamic legislation GAL I:530, bio. 25, ti. i
	Qur'an commentaries	*Tafsir al-Baydawi [Anwar al-tanzil wa asrar al-ta'wil]*	'Abdallah b. 'Umar al-Baydawi (d. *ca*. 685/1286)	— GAL I:182, bio. 7, ti. ii
	Hadith studies	*Sharh ma'ani al-athar Mishkat al-masabih*	Abu Ja'far Ahmad al-Tahawi (d. 321/933)	GAL II:249, bio. 2

TABLE 8.3 Continued

Level	Duration	Level	Topics	Core titles	Authors	Comments
					Shams al-Din M. al-Tabrizi (fl. ca. 737/1336)	
		3	Hadith	Sahih al-Bukhari	Muhammad al-Bukhari (d. 256/870)	
				Sahih Muslim	Muslim ibn al-Hajjaj (d. 261/874)	
				Jami' al-Tirmidhi	Muhammad b. 'Isa al-Tirmidhi (d. 279/892)	
				Sunan al-sughra	Ahmad al-Nasa'i (d. 303/915)	
				Sunan Ibn Majah	Muhammad b. Majah al-Qazwini (d. 273/887)	
				Sunan Abu Da'ud	Abu Da'ud Sulayman al-Sistani (d. 275/888)	

The Jami Madrasa

FIGURE 8.2 Principal, staff, and students at the Hawza-yi ʿilmiyya Ahmadiyya

Core readings have changed significantly since Yusuf-i Ahl's *ijaza* was issued. Sufism is not included in the curricula. In the medieval era, a student at a Jami madrasa obtained a solid grounding in Shafiʿi, Hanbali, and Maliki thought, but today, the emphasis is on Hanafi thought. Burhan al-Din al-Marghinani's *al-Hidaya* is the constant. Study of works by Saʿd al-Din Taftazani, Abu Zakariyya Yahya al-Nawawi (d. 676/1278), Abu Jaʿfar Ahmad al-Tahawi (d. 321/933), ʿAbdallah b. ʿUmar al-Baydawi (d. *ca*. 685/1286), and Shams al-Din Muhammad al-Tabrizi (fl. *ca*. 737/1336) reflect some degree of continuity, although different titles are occasionally referenced.[124] Abu Hamid al-Ghazali's *Ihya' 'ulum al-din* is not studied, which considering his high standing at Jam, is surprising. It should be emphasized that the titles in Table 8.3 are the "core titles" for the 1396–97/2017–18 academic year: other primary and secondary texts in Arabic or Persian will be read or referenced. There is also continuity from level to level, that is, texts from a previous year will be referenced in later years. English lessons are continued past the first year. The curriculum is subject to modifications and customizations (for individual needs) and should not be reified.

---

[124] On texts and authors in a modern madrasa, see Ebrahim Moosa, *What Is a Madrasa?* (Chapel Hill, NC: University of North Carolina Press, 2015), 108–121; and Arshad Alam, *Inside a Madrasa* (New Delhi: Routledge, 2011), 222–27.

At the end of the ten-year program, a graduate of the Ahmadiyya college becomes a qualified doctor of law (*'alim, mawlawi*), holding the rank of general practitioner (*pizishk-i 'umumi*). The program at Hibat al-Rahman college terminates after seven years. Although female students study the same topics, their program is less intensive because they cannot become ulama due to their gender. Many Jami graduates obtain teacher certifications and become public school teachers. The integration of the Jami madrasas with the educational bureaucracies of Iran facilitates the recognition of degrees conferred at Jam.

Part IV

The Sufis

9

Doctrines and Practices

Ahmad-i Jam's gnosticism, as Shafi'i Kadkani said, has a "unique flavor" (*ta'm-i wizha*). Ahmad's progeny attempted to describe his gnostic (*'irfan*) and religious concepts in their books, namely, *Hadiqat al-haqiqa* and *Khulasat al-maqamat* (both still valued at Jam). However, a Sufi methodology (*suluk* or *tariq*) attributable to Ahmad was not articulated. With novel or revived Sufi concepts wafting through Khurasan in the eighth/fourteenth and ninth/fifteenth centuries, the doctrines and practices of the Sufis of Jam shifted. The Khwajagan-Naqshbandiyya offered them fresh and exciting mystical theories and models.

Examined closely here are *dhikr* (recollection of God), *khalwat* (seclusion), *sama'* (auditory stimulation), and *rabita* (bonding one's heart with the shaykh's heart), which remain popular *'irfan* exercises. A case study of 'Aziz-Allah Jami, who was drawn to the Naqshbandiyya, demonstrates how Jamis borrowed and adapted, but remained faithful to their saint by focusing their devotion on Ahmad-i Jam. By focusing on Ahmad, sometimes through the practice of *rabita*, the fissiparous Sufi components of the cult avoided conflict over doctrines. Jami Sufis were a "broad church," bound together by love for Ahmad of Jam.

AHMAD'S GNOSTIC PATH

"The gnostic path of the shaykh of Jam is distinct from the gnostic paths of all the great masters who came before or after him" (*'irfan-i shaykh-i Jam ba 'irfan-i tamam-i buzurgan qabl az uw wa ba'd az uw mutafawit ast*).[1] Shafi'i

---

[1] Kadkani, *Darwish*, 37.

Kadkani's assessment is accurate. Ahmad-i Jam had an incisive and independent mind. It is not surprising that he would devise distinct ideas. His conceptualizations, however, had limited appeal beyond his devoted Sufi circle (*halqa*). The Chishtiyya loved Ahmad-i Jam for a couplet that pierced the core of Sufism,[2] but they did not subscribe to his concepts. Baha' al-Din Naqshband, the eponym of the Sufi order (*tariqa*), quotes one time the words of Ahmad,[3] but otherwise, Ahmad's doctrines did not penetrate Sufism's mainstream.

Ahmad-i Jam's ideas are scattered over multiple titles. There was no cohesive source for his successors, a handbook, if you will, and unfortunately, his heirs did not produce one. 'Abd al-Rahman Jami, for example, distilled the complex ideas of Ibn al-'Arabi (d. 638/1240) into a concise guide in Persian, *Lawa'ih* (*Gleams of Light*),[4] making Ibn al-'Arabi's concepts accessible to an audience of intellectuals and nonintellectuals. As Sachiko Murata wrote, "[i]n terms of attractive style and balance of poetry and prose, it is the most successful, and indeed it was the most widely read" of the works by Jami on Ibn al-'Arabi.[5] 'Abd al-Rahman distilled the eleven tenets of the Naqshbandiyya into three in *Primary Tenets of the Khwajagan Order*.[6] However, Qutb al-Din Muhammad and Shihab al-Din (Abu al-Makarim) Tirmizi Jami, authors of *Hadiqat al-haqiqa* and *Khulasat al-maqamat*, respectively, were less successful than 'Abd al-Rahman Jami in imparting knowledge in an attractive style, and in succinct and lucid prose.

AHMAD'S SUFI HEIRS

Hadiqat al-haqiqa

Qutb al-Din Muhammad Jami (d. 667/1268)[7] wrote *Hadiqat al-haqiqa*.[8] The book was finalized by Safar 643/July 1245. The intended audience for the *Hadiqat al-haqiqa* is clear from his announcement of its publication,[9] namely, ulama (= intellectuals). The book passed virtually unnoticed outside of Jam. This is still true.

---

[2] Sijzi, *Morals*, 72. Explained in Chapter 2.
[3] al-Bukhari, *Anis al-talibin*, 218–19. Noted in Chapter 2.
[4] On the importance of this work, and for a translation by William Chittick, see Sachiko Murata, *Chinese Gleams of Sufi Light* (Albany, NY: SUNY Press, 2000).
[5] Ibid., 115.
[6] 'Abd al-Rahman Jami, *Sar-rishta-i tariqa-yi Khwajagan*, ed. 'Abd al-Hayy Habibi (Kabul: Anjuman-i Jami, 1343/1964). On the eleven doctrines, see Itzchak Weismann, *The Naqshbandiyya* (New York: Routledge, 2007), 25–30.
[7] On him, see Chapters 2 and 3.   [8] Jami, *Hadiqat al-haqiqa*, xxxiii. See Appendix 3.
[9] See the announcement letter in Yusuf-i Ahl/Moayyad (ed.), *Fara'id*, 2:471–73.

The book's title translates as "the enclosed garden of the Truth," a reference to the Truth at the end of a Sufi wayfarer's Path (*tariqa*) to God. Obedience to the Shariʿa is the prerequisite for every wayfarer (*salik*): "no mystical experience can be realized if the binding injunctions of the *shariʿa* are not followed faithfully first."[10] Qutb al-Din is the landscaper of the garden: he demarcates its boundaries and footpaths, the springs from which a *salik* may quench his thirst, and he identifies the flowers and fruits that may tempt a wayfarer,[11] but which will poison him if touched or ingested.

The *Hadiqat* is not exclusively about method (*tariq, suluk*), stations (*maqamat*), and states (*ahwal*) in *ʿirfan*, although topics like repentance (*tawba*), trust (*tawakkul*), renunciation (*zuhd*), poverty (*faqr*), contentment (*riza*), audition (*samaʿ*), and ecstasy (*wajd*) are discussed.[12] The book grants the *salik* freedom to experiment with mystical exercises because he is not bound by a fixed methodology (*suluk* or *tariq*).[13] But he must adhere to God's commands irrespective of techniques. The quintessence of the *Hadiqat* is devotion to the Shariʿa and avoidance of errors. Qutb al-Din includes a list of common snares (*ghalat*); for instance, trying to traverse the mystical path without the guiding hand of a shaykh, and not working in tandem with a shaykh.

The author delivered a cumbersome book in fourteen chapters (each one called *bayan*, "clarification"), and seventy-one sections (*fasl*). According to Hasan Nasiri Jami, editor of the *Hadiqat al-haqiqa*, "important sections" of the *Hadiqat* reveal the influences of sundry *khanaqah*s of Khurasan, principally, the *khanaqah*s of Herat and Turbat-i Jam. Furthermore, he concludes that "without a doubt" Qutb al-Din's writings were based on doctrines by ʿAbdallah Ansari (d. 481/1089) of Herat. He identifies Ansari's *Sad maydan* (*The Hundred Fields*) and *Manazil al-saʾrayn* (*Stages of the Wayfarers*) as principal sources. Qutb al-Din's classification system is also based on Ansari's system.[14] The doctrines of other

---

[10] Schimmel, *Dimensions*, 98.
[11] The tempter is Satan: "the slinking whisperer / who whispers in the breasts of men" (Q114:4–5).
[12] Terms like *tariqa, maqam* (pl. *maqamat*), *hal* (pl. *ahwal*), *tawba, riza, faqr*, etc., and the Sufi Path, have been explicated in Schimmel, *Dimensions*, 98–186; Knysh, *Mysticism*, 301–25; John Renard, *Historical Dictionary of Sufism* (Oxford: Scarecrow Press, 2005); Abu al-Qasim al-Qushayri, *al-Risala al-Qushayriyya* (Cairo: Dar al-kutub al-haditha, 1966); and al-Qushayri/Knysh (trans.), *Epistle*.
[13] On Ahmad not bequeathing a mystical path, see discussion in Chapter 2.
[14] Jami, *Hadiqat*, xxxvii. One of Qutb al-Din's daughters married a descendant of Ansari. Buzjani/Moayyad (ed.), *Rawzat*, 96–97; Figure A1.2.

Sufi luminaries of Khurasan – Bistami, Kharaqani, Shibli, et al. – are manifest. It is likely that readers outside of Ahmad's devotees did not find Qutb al-Din's formulations original, which would account for the book's obscurity in Sufi literature.

Borrowing by Jami Sufis of doctrines and practices from other *khanaqah*s is a recurring issue. It is difficult to characterize their gnostic paths, especially since their views shift, even if slightly. This also makes it difficult to locate a doctrine or practice as originating with Ahmad-i Jam. Interlocutors at Jam explain that because Ahmad did not bequeath a rigid gnostic methodology (i.e., a systematic 1–2–3 method), they were free to adopt concepts and techniques that appealed to them. And borrow they did, but they were not outside the norm with this practice. Ernst and Lawrence observed that unlike Christian monastic orders with "firm lines of authority and sacrament," Sufi groups overlapped. Sufis therefore had access to an array of gnostic techniques. "[I]t is difficult to regard the constitution of Sufi orders and sainthood as a zero-sum competition . . . . It is in fact this wide collection of techniques that makes Sufism a *cumulative tradition* rather than a series of isolated and private experiences."[15]

Appropriations and doctrinal shifts were not limited to gnostic enterprises; they extended to rituals and law. Qutb al-Din's ritual practices shifted from Hanafi to Shafi'i: he performed ritual prayers according to Hanafi rites, but adopted Shafi'i rites.[16] In the *Hadiqat*'s chapter on "clarifications on the Shari'a," Hanafi and Shafi'i perspectives are incorporated.[17] In the analysis of Yusuf-i Ahl Jami's *ijaza* (Table 8.2), it was shown that Shafi'i and Hanafi titles were studied by Jamis. Although the saint cult's members today consider themselves Hanafi, I have avoided this characterization. The Jami theological-theosophical mosaic has changed its hues at numerous points over 900 years, and retains many of the disparate threads woven into it over the centuries.

Khulasat al-maqamat

Shihab al-Din (Abu al-Makarim) Tirmizi Jami (b. 796/1393f.; d. 847/1443f.),[18] authored the *Concise Spiritual Feats*.[19] It includes a section on

---

[15] Ernst and Lawrence, *Sufi Martyrs*, 28 (emphasis added). [16] Kadkani, *Darwish*, 266.
[17] Jami, *Hadiqat*, xxiii, 51–83. [18] On him, see Chapter 3.
[19] [Shihab al-Din] Abu al-Makarim ibn 'Ala' al-Mulk [Tirmizi Jami], *Khulasat al-maqamat-i hazrat-i fil subhan* (Lahore: Muhammad Jalal al-Din, 1335/1916); 'Ala' al-Mulk Jami/Jami (ed.), *Khulasat al-maqamat*; another edition of *Khulasat al-maqamat* is included in Kadkani, *Darwish*, 159–418 (see Appendix 3).

Ahmad's concepts, drawn from his writings. The topics selected by Abu al-Makarim are in twenty-four sections (*bab*), and include Ahmad's sayings (*sukhanan*) on basic tenets like God's unity (*tawhid*), obligatory prayer (*namaz*), and repentance (*tawba*); exegesis (*tafsir*) of Qur'anic verses; the Prophet's virtues (*faza'il*); and Sufi concepts like renunciation (*zuhd*), poverty (*faqr*), contentment (*riza*), and audition (*sama'*). Although Abu al-Makarim covers familiar Sufi concepts, he does not articulate a methodology (*suluk*, *tariq*) nor describe how spiritual exercises are performed. The absence of guidance on gnostic exercises is not unusual; ordinarily this information is passed directly from shaykh to darwish; for example, the inculcation of the formula for the recollection of God (*talqin al-dhikr*). Nonetheless, the book is closer to a theosophical guide than was previously available.

Abu al-Makarim excises stories by Ghaznawi (*Spiritual Feats*) about Ahmad-i Jam's miracles and inappropriate behaviors – like his pursuit of a fourteen-year-old girl when he was eighty! Indeed, one senses a degree of embarrassment on the part of the Sufis of Jam about their saint's manifestly unsaintly behaviors.[20] Moreover, stories related by Ghaznawi will have been dismissed as superstitious twaddle by sophisticated readers. This was the Timurid era, after all, where works by sophisticated thinkers like 'Ala' al-Din 'Attar, Muhammad Parsa, Najm al-Din Kubra, and others were then being studied by those interested in Sufism or actually immersed in Sufi studies.

SUFISM IN TIMURID KHURASAN

Sufi networks in Khurasan were extensive. The Timurid age ushered profound changes in Sufi doctrines and practices. Beatrice Forbes Manz wrote of the *cooperative* nature of Sufi networks in Shah-Rukh's Herat (i.e., to 850/1447);[21] whereas, Jürgen Paul wrote on the *competitive* nature of Sufi networks of Timurid Herat (ninth/fifteenth century).[22] Sufis – not all exclusively

---

[20] One interlocutor at Turbat-i Jam practically ordered me not to utilize Ghaznawi's book. Abu al-Makarim's aim was to craft a sanitized biography for his target audience: Shah-Rukh, Timurid officials, and Herat's Sufis and ulama.

[21] Manz, *Timurid Iran*, 208–44.

[22] Jürgen Paul, "The Rise of the Khwajagan-Naqshbandiyya Sufi Order in Timurid Herat," in *Afghanistan's Islam*, ed. Nile Green (Oakland, CA: University of California Press, 2017), pp. 71–86. See also Jürgen Paul, "The Khwajagan at Herat During Shahrukh's Reign," in *Horizons of the World*, ed. I. E. Binbaş and N. Kihc-Schubel (Istanbul: Ithaki Publishing, 2011), 217–50.

194   Doctrines and Practices

Sunni – offered the mystically oriented a veritable banquet of novel doctrines – and old doctrines wrapped in new packaging.

An old doctrine with renewed emphasis includes *rabita*. Silent (*khafi*) *dhikr* was advocated by the Khwajagan-Naqshbandiyya;[23] whereas the Zayniyya of Zayn al-Din Khwafi preferred the vocal (*jahri*) method.[24] Doctrine could be a source of friction; it could become a proxy for personal rivalries. There was, for instance, division among the Khwajagan of Central Asia on the most efficacious mode for *dhikr* (silent or vocal).[25] Sufi *tariqa*s had not yet crystallized by the late Timurid period, nor were Sufi doctrines immutable: experimentation was commonplace. Sufis participated in sundry currents, that is, *monogamous Sufism* – exclusive allegiance to a single *tariqa* – was not yet instituted. The Sufi subset of Ahmad's saint cult was no exception. Jami Sufis adopted a laissez-faire outlook toward gnostic choices, which persists. Jami Sufis did not publicly descend into factionalism over doctrines, although there were (and are) critical divisions in doctrines and techniques; and multiple subsets of mystics (still) flourish at Jam.

NAQSHBANDIYYA AT JAM

The Khwajagan-Naqshbandiyya were the most potent influence on Jami Sufis. Pillars of the Khwajagan, Baha' al-Din Naqshband (718–91/1318–89), Muhammad Parsa (d. 822/1419), and others, influenced Jamis, either through their writings or their intellectual discourses in Khurasan. Baha' al-Din sojourned with Zayn al-Din Taybadi at Taybad,[26] where he undoubtedly heard about Ahmad-i Jam's gnostic concepts.[27] Hasan 'Attar (d. 826/1422f.) and Yusuf 'Attar (d. *ca.* 873/1458f.), two descendants of "'Ala' al-Din 'Attar" (i.e., Muhammad b. Muhammad al-Bukhari; d. 802/1400), were active in Herat,[28] and certainly interacted with Jami Sufis. Khwaja Muhammad Parsa, "was a major influence in 'intellectualizing' the teaching of the [Khwajagan]

---

[23] Khwajagan: "[Sufi] Masters"; later known as Naqshbandiyya.
[24] On Zayn al-Din, see Manz, *Timurid Iran*, 228ff.
[25] Jürgen Paul, *Doctrine and Organization: The Khwajagan/Naqshbandiya in the First Generation after Baha'uddin* (Berlin: Das Arabische Buch, 1998), 18–21.
[26] Anon./Gusha-Gir (ed.), *Maqamat*, 57–58; Jami, *Nafahat*, 499–500.
[27] A doctrinal outlook by Ahmad-i Jam quoted by Baha' al-Din Naqshband in al-Bukhari, *Anis al-talibin*, 218–19, was probably transmitted by Zayn al-Din Taybadi.
[28] Paul, "Khwajagan at Herat."

endowing it with a philosophical-theological background it had hardly known earlier."[29]

Sa'd al-Din Kashghari (d. 858/1455) was instrumental in attracting Sufis – talent-hunting candidates – including Jamis, to the Khwajagan. Jürgen Paul observed, "[g]ifted young men did not go unnoticed in Herat ... there must have been competition over such persons among [Herat's] Sufi teachers." 'Abd al-Rahman Jami was talent hunted by Kashghari.[30] 'Aziz-Allah Jami (d. 902/1497) was another Naqshbandi Sufi trained by Kashghari. A spiritual genealogy of Kashghari's adepts includes mystics from the Jami community.[31] Kashghari's disciples, as happens, spawned collateral lineages, but which do not appear in "official" hagiologies. *Silsila*s are incomplete in most instances because only a subset of names are incorporated in official hagiologies.[32] Lineages attached to regional saint cults and collateral Sufi lines are almost invariably overlooked in the preparation of official hagiologies.[33]

BORROWING AND ADAPTING DOCTRINES

How were the doctrinal infusions received at Jam? The practices of Jami Sufis show that they were receptive to innovations and experimentations provided Ahmad-i Jam remained the focus of devotion. Flexibility in their "membership rules," and focus on Ahmad-i Jam, allowed the cult to manage the competition and preserve cohesion. Shams al-Din Muhammad Kusuyi (d. 863/1459) is an example of this principle. He is of Jami blood. Although he favored Zayniyya doctrines,[34] he remained devoted to Ahmad and honored by the cult. Kusuyi's situation is illustrative of the ephemeral character of mystical concepts of bygone epochs. It is unlikely anyone at Jam today can articulate Zayniyya doctrines, but Kusuyi's devotion to Ahmad guaranteed him a permanent place in the cult's historical memory. It was

---

[29] Paul, *Doctrine*, 74.   [30] Paul, "Khwajagan-Naqshbandiyya," 71–86, 82.
[31] See Figure A2.1.
[32] An example of an "official" hagiology is Fakhr al-Din 'Ali b. Husayn Wa'iz Kashifi, *Rashahat-i 'ayn al-hayat*, 2 vols., ed. 'Ali Asghar Mu'iniyan (Tehran: Bunyad-i nikukari-i nuriyani, 1356/1977); cf. Nur al-Din Muhammad al-Qazwini, *Silsilanama-yi Khwajagan-i Naqshband* (Paris: Bibliothèque Nationale, MS Supplément persan 1418). See Appendix 3.
[33] Spencer J. Trimingham's *The Sufi Orders in Islam* (Oxford: Oxford University Press, 1971) tends to reflect official lines. It has therefore reified for many students of Sufism the idea that (1) Sufism is comprised of orders (*tariqa*); and (2) that affiliations can be reflected in tidy organizational charts.
[34] Buzjani/Moayyad (ed.), *Rawzat*, 118–21; Jami, *Nafahat*, 496–98; Manz, *Timurid Iran*, 226–27.

Kusuyi who had read the *khutba* at Herat's Friday mosque following the investiture of Sultan-Abu Saʿid Mirza (see Chapter 3).

I trace below the contours of Jami gnostic doctrines and practices by examining critical mystical exercises: temporary seclusion (Ar. *khalwa*; Per. *khalwat*), recollection of God (Ar. *dhikr*; Per. *zikr*), auditory stimulation (*samaʿ*), and *rabita* (bonding a darwish's heart with his shaykh's heart). Interlocutors at Jam aver that temporary seclusion is practiced today by a minority. *Khalwat* as a mystical exercise withered during the Jamis' Khwajagan-Naqshbandi phase: the Khwajagan favored "solitude in society" (*khalwat dar anjuman*) over withdrawal; however, Khwajagan doctrine was not the primary reason. There was a pragmatic reason for the abandonment of *khalwat*, namely, the imperative to earn incomes. The use of Masjid-i Nur (Kuh-yi Bizd) as a *khanaqah*, and the construction of a new *khanaqah* at Kuh-yi Bizd (Figure 9.1), demonstrate that *khalwat* is still an enduring spiritual exercise for (at least) one subset of Jami gnostics.

Dhikr underwent shifts. Silent *dhikr* competed with vocal *dhikr*, with the former seen by certain Sufis as a technique superior to vocal *dhikr*. *Samaʿ* – not just in the Sufi sense of mystical music – is popular in Turbat-i Jam and its purlieus: native (*bumi*) or traditional music (*muziqi-yi sunnati*), folk dance (*raqs-i sunnati*), poetry and Qurʾan recitals are living traditions on Iran's eastern and southeastern Sunni belt. The dance and musical heritages of the region await study by ethnologists and musicologists.

GNOSTIC (*ʿIRFAN*) PRACTICES AT JAM

Khalwat

Qutb al-Din Muhammad mentions *khalwat* in passing. It was an ubiquitous and noncontroversial mystical exercise that did not warrant explanations. Shihab al-Din ʿUmar (Abu Hafs) al-Suhrawardi (d. 632/1234) had published guidance on *khalwat*.[35] His writings were studied at Jam in the Timurid era (Table 8.2), and doubtless earlier. For Jami Sufis, *khalwat* meant temporary withdrawal from society, often, the annual forty-day

---

[35] Shihab al-Din ʿUmar b. Muhammad al-Suhrawardi, *ʿAwarif al-maʿarif*, trans. Abu Mansur b. ʿAbd al-Muʾmin Isfahani, ed. Qasim Ansari (Tehran: Intisharat-i ʿilmi wa farhangi, 1386/1987), 101–6.

retreat (Ar. *arbaʿyin*; Per. *chilla*).³⁶ Seclusions took place in cells (*chillakhana*) built within the shrine's buildings and *khanaqah*s: the Kirmani Mosque's cells are extant. However, *khalwat* does not have to be conducted inside a cell. In actuality, when Sufis withdrew en masse, cells became scarce. Spiritual exercises (*riyazat*) during *khalwat* and *arbaʿyin* included Qurʾan readings and recitals, supererogatory prayers (*duʿaʾ*), *waraʿ*,³⁷ and austerities (*zuhd*). In effect, little sleep, food, and drink.³⁸ The focus is on repentance (*tawba*), prayer, and reflection on God's Message and His Grace.

The cell was the long-term home for novices in the early years of the Jami Sufi community. The cell is where the *salik* taking the first steps on his long journey learned to bring his carnal soul (*nafs*) under control, the conditio sine qua non for advancement on the Sufi Path. Repentance is the first step on the Sufi Path.³⁹ Heartfelt remorse for his trespasses, sincere apologies to God, and severing of associations with "wicked" people are expected of the novice. He must bring his *nafs* under control. If he does not succeed, he will surrender to baser desires and be unable to advance, for "the *nafs* is a persistent enjoiner of evil" (Q12:53).⁴⁰ *Riyazat* helps bring the *nafs* under control. The *nafs* is often described in lurid terms: a ravenous beast, a seductress, and so on. The novice, locked in a cell for months, possibly years, detached from family and society, eating and sleeping little, and occupying himself with worship of the Lord, learns to control his *nafs*. Some Sufis believe that mortifications – pain, suffering, and humiliation – help bring the *nafs* under control by subjugating the ego. Abu Saʿid b. Abu al-Khayr's regimen included cleaning latrines.⁴¹ Self-abasement (for some Sufis) was a pathway to God.

---

[36] *Arbaʿyin* finds support within the Qurʾan: "We appointed for Moses thirty nights, and completed (the period) with ten (more): thus was completed the term (of communion) with his Lord, forty nights" (Q7:142). The *arbaʿyin* "should not be interrupted except for the communal prayers, and it should be repeated once every year. It is conceived to be an instance of [imitating Muhammad's] custom to seclude himself in a cave on Mount Hiraʾ in anticipation of revelation." Knysh, *Mysticism*, 316–19.

[37] *Waraʿ*: prudence/abstinence. Aspects include paying scrupulous attention to feelings, to God's presence; but also strict attention to earthly matters, such as avoiding doubtful fare. I am grateful to Jürgen Paul for this clarification.

[38] "The chief means for taming and training the *nafs* [are] fasting and sleeplessness." Schimmel, *Dimensions*, 114.

[39] Jami, *Hadiqat*, 136; Nahid Angha, *Stations of the Sufi Path: The One Hundred Fields (Sad Maydan) of ʿAbdallah Ansari of Herat* (Cambridge: Archetype, 2010), 76.

[40] On *nafs* in the Qurʾan, see T. E. Homerin, "Soul," *EQ*, 5:80–84. See also Gavin Picken, *Spiritual Purification in Islam* (New York: Routledge, 2011), 123–67.

[41] Ibn Munawwar, *Asrar al-tawhid*, 1:27ff; Nicholson, *Mysticism*, 12–14.

The experiences of Qutb al-Din Muhammad Jami at the hands of his shaykh and uncle, Zahir al-Din ʿIsa b. Ahmad-i Jam, are revealing. The adept endured supervised exercises (*riyazat wa mujahadat*) and suffered abstinences and pains.[42] Qutb al-Din writes, about a year into his regimen, with his shaykh monitoring his mystical state (*hal*), he saw a frightful old woman (*ganda-piri*) enter (his cell). Her garments were tattered and bloodstained; her back was bent, her face was black and blue, with protruding yellow teeth. She had a cane in one hand and a bloody knife in the other. With one foul breath from afar, she repossessed Qutb al-Din's *nafs* (*az dam na-khwush uw az dur nafs baz girift*). Shortly thereafter, Zahir al-Din ʿIsa Jami bade his nephew farewell: "praise be to God! You have effectively severed (*qatʿ*) [your] bonds to the material world (*dunya*). After this, the world will not possess you."[43] The story has an astounding implication: Zahir al-Din's claim is that Qutb al-Din has dominion over his *nafs*. In Sufi thought, normally, the battle with the *nafs* is never over. It is akin to the taming of a wild lion. The "tame" lion is outwardly docile, but inwardly remains a dangerous creature that could turn without hesitation and maul its "master."[44]

Arbaʿyin ordinarily caters to a different level of mystics, namely, to those who have traveled farther along the Sufi Path to God. *Arbaʿyin* is still practiced by a subset of Jami gnostics who withdraw to the Masjid-i Nur in the Bizd Mountains (*Kuh-yi Bizd*) near Jam, usually in the last ten days of Shaʿban and for the month of Ramazan.[45] The forty-day retreat terminates in time for them to return home to celebrate *ʿid al-fitr* with family. Jamis believe the original Masjid-i Nur was erected by Ahmad-i Jam during his seclusion in Bizd, and that the current mosque retains wooden beams from the original. The Masjid-i Nur is cramped and has one cell. A new *khanaqah*, discreetly termed "guesthouse" (*mihman-khana*) to avoid ruffling feathers in Iranian officialdom, was erected near the Masjid-i Nur (Figure 9.1).[46] The new hospice is a labor of love for the gnostics who donate time and money for its construction and maintenance. The *khanaqah* has no cells or dormitory. Spiritual activities are communal, which fosters fellowship. Residents gather in a circle in the lodge's center and perform the *dhikr* communally.

---

[42] Buzjani/Moayyad (ed.), *Rawzat*, 86–88.   [43] Kadkani, *Darwish*, 261–62.
[44] I am indebted to Jürgen Paul for this brilliant analogy.
[45] Tradition claims the *arbaʿyin* should be performed in the thirty days of Dhu al-Qaʿda and ten from Dhu al-Hijja. See al-Suhrawardi, *ʿAwarif al-maʿarif*, 99. However, application of the tradition will impinge on the Hajj, which culminates on the tenth of Dhu al-Hijja.
[46] The structure resembles a Chishti community hall (*jamaʿat-khana*).

FIGURE 9.1 The new hospice, Khanaqah-yi Masjid-i Nur

The majority of Jami Sufis discarded *khalwat*. The virtual elimination of *khalwat* cannot be attributed directly to the influence of Naqshbandi doctrines, that is, *khalwat dar anjuman*. According to Baha' al-Din Naqshband, *khalwat dar anjuman* "is to be outwardly (*zahir*) with the people (*khalq*), and inwardly (*batin*) with God (*haqq*)."[47] Adherence to the doctrine, which emphasized companionship (*suhbat*) with the shaykh, brought Sufis out of their cells. Baha' al-Din was not innovating by promoting *khalwat dar anjuman* in lieu of *khalwat*: Sufis have long held differing opinions on the efficacy of *khalwat*.[48] Abu Nasr Sarraj is of the opinion that solitude is only for the stout, whereas most Sufis are better served by remaining in a community.[49] Hujwiri supplies the view that companionship for God's sake, in contradistinction to companionship for selfish reasons, is laudable. He warns, "solitude is fatal to the novice ... Satan is with the solitary."[50] Companionship and intellectual intercourses (*suhbat*) with one's shaykh do not preclude the conduct of *khalwat* exercises under the shaykh's supervision.

[47] al-Bukhari, *Anis al-talibin*, 120; Jami, *Nafahat*, 386; Wa'iz Kashifi, *Rashahat*, 1:42.
[48] See alternate opinions in al-Qushayri, *al-Risala*, 271–76; al-Qushayri/Knysh (trans.), *Epistle*, 122–25.
[49] Abu Nasr al-Sarraj, *Kitab al-luma' fi al-tasawwuf*, ed. R. A. Nicholson (London: Luzac, 1914), 207.
[50] al-Hujwiri, *Kashf al-mahjub*, 338.

The overriding factor, in my estimation, which relegated *khalwat* exercises to the annual forty-day retreat, is that most Jami Sufis had professions and families to feed. The Jami community were the antithesis of the romanticized Sufis who eschewed financial favors from the state and contacts with sultans. The model of the "holy man" who knows not how he will receive his daily bread, but has trust in God that He will supply it, is idealized. It is also a parasitic existence – a manifestation of which is the yogi or fakir with his outstretched bowl. A few Jamis, like the Kartid vizier's son, Shihab al-Din ʿUmar, had family wealth backstopping them, and could afford to "renounce" the material world – precisely as he did with Miranshah's lavish presents.[51] The majority of the Jamis of Timurid Iran had vocations, and contributed to the betterment of their society as litterateurs, artisans, ulama, judges, lecturers, merchants, and managers of hydrological systems and agricultural estates. For instance, in Sultan-Abu Saʿid's decree on the restoration of the Gulistan Dam,[52] Yusuf-i Ahl Jami is designated as the project's Shariʿa court lawyer.[53] In Gawhar-Shad's endowment for her eponymous mosque in Mashhad, Jamis (among others) are tasked with managing hydrological projects.[54] Some, probably most, Jami Sufis discarded *khalwat* or *arbaʿyin* for pragmatic reasons. A popular Naqshbandi precept applies to the Sufis of Jam: "the hand at work, the heart with the Friend" (*dast bih kar, dil bar yar*).

Dhikr

Recollection of God is a moral imperative and unshakeable duty. "Then do ye remember Me; I will remember you. Be grateful to Me, and reject not Faith" (Q2:152). The Qurʾan has numerous references on this imperative (Q3:41, Q5:91, Q13:28, Q24:37, Q26:227, Q29:45, Q57:16, Q58:19, and Q62:09). Al-Ghazali extols the *dhikr* in *Ihyaʾ ʿulum al-din*'s "Book of Supplications and Devotions."[55] A popular formula used in recollection is the recitation of the first part of the profession of faith (*shahada*), *la ilaha illa ʾllah* ("there is no god but God"), while its second clause, *Muhammad-*

---

[51] Buzjani/Moayyad (ed.), *Rawzat*, 111–13; Zanganah, *Sarzamin*, 149–51; Manz, *Timurid Iran*, 226. Mentioned in Chapter 3. This is a classic Sufi gesture – one that he could afford.

[52] See W. M. Clevenger, "Dams in Ḥorasan: Some Preliminary Observations," *East and West* 19/3 (1969): 387–94, 391.

[53] Nawaʾi (ed.), *Asnad*, 313; translated in Subtelny, *Timurids*, 349–50.

[54] Mahendrarajah, "Gawhar Shad Waqf."   [55] al-Ghazali, *Ihyaʾ*, 2:343ff.

un rasul-u Allah ("Muhammad is the Messenger of God") is included in different formulae.

Dhikr has two methodological wings: vocal recollection (*dhikr al-lisan*, *dhikr-i zaban*, *dhikr al-jali*, *dhikr-i jahr*, etc.) and silent recollection (*dhikr al-qalb*, *dhikr al-khafi*, etc.). Furthermore, within each *dhikr* wing are found assorted techniques. For example, the vocalized *dhikr* could be a scarcely audible murmur, or it could be quite loud, as with the "rasping" or "sawing" method (*dhikr-i arra* or *dhikr-i minshar*).

As Sufism matured in the Islamic east, and nebulous Sufi currents coalesced into identifiable *tariqa*s, sophisticated techniques on performance of *dhikr*, control of breath (*habs-i dam*), and movements of the body were propagated.[56] Training (*talqin al-dhikr*) a novice in the correct performance of *dhikr* was the duty of his directing shaykh (*shaykh al-tarbiyya*): "the teaching of the formula of recollection was one of the most important aspects of mystical initiation ... Only a *dhikr* properly inspired by the spiritual director, and constantly controlled by him, was effective."[57] An example of a *dhikr* technique may prove helpful: "one says in one breath three times *la ilaha illa 'llah*, beginning from the right side [of the breast], and brings it down to the heart, and brings forth *Muhammad-un rasul-u Allah* from the left side."[58]

Recollection with the tongue is the preferred entrée for novices at Jam. Mastery of this level helps the novice tackle harder techniques. *Dhikr* with the heart (*dhikr-i dil*) as a technique should follow *dhikr* with the tongue (*dhikr-i zaban*).[59] Al-Qushayri favors the vocal-to-silent *dhikr* sequence because "the continual remembrance of the tongue eventually brings the servant to remembrance of the heart. The true effect, however, lies in the remembrance of the heart."[60] In preferring the vocal-to-silent *dhikr* sequence, the Sufis of Jam were in the mainstream of Sufi thought.

Qutb al-Din Jami connects *dhikr* to rational contemplation (*fikr*) and reflection (*tafakkur*).[61] Vocal *dhikr* is the key that unlocks contemplation in the heart (*fikr-i dil*), and should that key slip from the *salik*'s grasp, the heart will never be unlocked.[62] *Tafakkur* is to reflect on God's creation and

---

[56] For an exposition on breathing and movement in *dhikr*, see Shahzad Bashir, *Sufi Bodies* (New York: Columbia University Press, 2011), 68–74.
[57] Schimmel, *Dimensions*, 169.
[58] Jami, *Nafahat*, 390; reproduced in Schimmel, *Dimensions*, 174.
[59] Jami, *Hadiqat*, 174–78. *Dil* is Persian for heart (*qalb*); tongue is *zaban* or *lisan*.
[60] al-Qushayri, *al-Risala*, 465; al-Qushayri/Knysh (trans.), *Epistle*, 232.
[61] Jami, *Hadiqat*, 174–78; see also Angha, *Sad Maydan*, 95–96 (*tafakkur* is the twenty-ninth station).
[62] Jami, *Hadiqat*, 175.

His bounties. 'Abdallah Ansari clarifies, "The difference between remembrance [*dhikr*] and reflection [*tafakkur*] is that reflection is seeking but remembrance is finding."[63] Qutb al-Din does not use either *muraqaba* (contemplation) or *khawatir* (thoughts) in his explications on *dhikr* and *tafakkur*;[64] but he is, nonetheless, stressing the importance of the meditations that should follow the conclusion of the *dhikr*. The Naqshbandi scholar Muhammad Parsa (writing decades after Qutb al-Din) explains: "the purpose of vocal recollection (*dhikr-i lisani*), silent recollection (*dhikr-i qalbi*), and watchfulness (*nigah dasht*) is the contemplation of thoughts (*khawatir*); [and] concentration (*yad dasht*) is the contemplation of the Divine Essence."[65] According to a subgroup of gnostics at Turbat-i Jam, performing *dhikr* after *namaz*, especially the day's first *namaz* (*salat al-fajr*), helps maintain rectitude (*sawab*) throughout the day.[66] Post-*dhikr* meditations (*khawatir*) are indispensable.

Dhikr techniques and formulae are not explicated in the *Hadiqat* or *Khulasat al-maqamat*. *Dhikr* formulae and techniques were not published in medieval Iran (to the best of my knowledge); publications of this genre began appearing in Mughal India.[67] It is evident from Qutb al-Din's explanations, and general Sufi practices, that vocal *dhikr* was a central practice at Jam, one not limited to initiations, but employed habitually by Jami mystics. Vocal *dhikr* was normally a communal activity in *khanaqah*s. Sessions were performed in a *halqa* and could last for minutes or for days depending on the target, that is, from, hypothetically, 10 to 30,000 repetitions, with intermissions for ritual prayers. The sitting concluded with a litany (*khatm*; *wird*, pl. *awrad*).

Techniques, formulae, and litanies used by the mystics of Jam remain secret, that is, they are passed from shaykh to darwish. However, a traveler recorded a *khatm/wird* by Ahmad-i Jam in use in thirteenth/nineteenth-century Jam. The litany was published by Fritz Meier under the rubric of Naqshbandi closing formulae (*khatm-i khwajagan*).[68] In interviews at

---

[63] Angha, *Sad Maydan*, 96.
[64] On *khawatir*, see Muhammad Parsa, *Tuhfat al-salikin* (Delhi: Afghani dar al-kutub, 1970), 186–87. *Khawatir* is a more complex process than "thoughts" would suggest. I am indebted to Jürgen Paul for this caveat.
[65] Muhammad Parsa, *Qudsiyya*, ed. Ahmad Tahiri 'Iraqi (Tehran: Tahuri, 1354/1975), 36.
[66] Interlocutor at Jam. Communications via Telegram in December 2017.
[67] See Buehler, *Sufi Heirs*, 234–49 (Naqshbandi literature in India); Ernst and Lawrence, *Sufi Martyrs*, 28–34 (Chishti *dhikr* methods in *Nizam al-qulub*).
[68] Fritz Meier, *Zwei Abhandlungen über die Naqsbandiyya* (Istanbul: Franz Steiner Verlag, 1994), 197–98.

Turbat-i Jam,[69] interlocutors claimed the litany originated with Ahmad-i Jam and is in use presently with (at least) one subgroup of Jami gnostics:

(1) 25 repetitions: to ask God for forgiveness;
(2) *Rabita* (bonding the heart with the shaykh);[70]
(3) 100 repetitions: Blessing upon the Prophet;
(4) 1,000 repetitions from Surat al-Raʿd (Q13:09): "He knoweth the unseen and that which is seen: He is the Great, the Most High";
(5) 100 repetitions: Blessing upon the Prophet;
(6) 10 Qurʾanic verses to be recited by a participant.

It was said of the Chishtiyya's *dhikr* sittings, which could continue for lengthy periods, "[t]he time demands of this practice also clearly prevented serious Chishtis from having regular jobs."[71] The *dhikr-i dil* was favored by Naqshbandis in part because it could be performed while the Sufi was enjoying "solitude in society," which is to be "outwardly (*zahir*) with the people, and inwardly (*batin*) with God." Just as some Jamis came to disfavor *khalwat* for impacting on their professional commitments, *dhikr-i dil* increased in popularity for reasons unconnected to the influences of the Khwajagan-Naqshbandiyya. The *dhikr* options of *dil* or *zaban* were neither binary nor binding; each method had its appropriate places and times. The silent *dhikr* could be performed when quiet moments materialized in the workplace (the shopkeeper with his prayer beads); and the vocal *dhikr* performed communally. Congregational *dhikr*, in combination with other communal gnostic activities, fostered fellowship and cohesion.

There is inferential evidence of congregational *dhikr* (*hadra, halqa, dhikr-i majlis*) practices at Turbat-i Jam in premodern times. Firstly, the above *khatm-i khwajagan* was observed at a communal *dhikr*. Secondly, ʿAli Buzjani writes, about eighty people from the vicinities of Turbat-i Jam came to his shaykh's *khanaqah* for *khalwat* in 902/1496. Their exercises were interrupted two weeks later when the shaykh, ʿAziz-Allah Jami, became ill and died (27 Rabiʿ II 902/2 January 1497).[72] Given the paucity of cells at Ahmad-i Jam's shrine and ʿAziz-Allah's *khanaqah*,[73] it is not clear how eighty Sufis observed the *khalwat*. Congregational *khalwat* is possible;[74] however, its mechanics are unclear. Congregational *dhikr*,

---

[69] Research visit in September 2017.   [70] On *rabita*, see below.
[71] Ernst and Lawrence, *Sufi Martyrs*, 31.   [72] Buzjani/Moayyad (ed.), *Rawzat*, 131–32.
[73] ʿAziz-Allah's mausoleum is where his hospice stood. It is outside the legal boundaries of Ahmad's shrine complex, in the neighborhood (*mahalla*) of Maʿd-Abad.
[74] On "communal seclusion," see Devin DeWeese, "Shamanization in Central Asia," *JESHO* 57/3 (2014): 326–63, esp. 349ff.

silent or vocal, was an activity in congregational *khalwat*. It is unlikely that eighty Sufis performed the *dhikr-i dil* inside cells. Solitary exercises were surely complemented by communal exercises; for example, a *halqa* for silent or vocal *dhikr*. The *dhikr* session will have concluded with prayers, Qur'an readings, and poetry.

Congregational *dhikr* is currently practiced at Turbat-i Jam. There are subsets of mystics at Jam; each subset has its own approaches to mysticism. One group shared its practices. They meet every morning following morning prayers (*salat al-fajr*) at one of the mosques outside the shrine: the Masjid-i Zamistan (also called Masjid-i zir-i zamin); or the *musalla* (open space) on its roof (called Masjid-i Tabistan).[75] Once the others depart, the group, which has a *dhikr* leader, forms a *halqa*. Their *general* practice follows:

(1) A member begins the *dhikr* by reading from Surat Ya-Sin (Q36:1–83);
(2) A member begins the recollection process with *la ilaha illa'llah* or *la ilaha illa'llah wa-Muhammad-un rasul-u Allah*. The *dhikr* is ostensibly the silent form (*dhikr-i khafi*), but termed colloquially as "quiet recollection" (*dhikr-i ahisti*);[76]
(3) The initiator recollects God thirty-three times; another member picks up and recollects God thirty-three times (in like manner), and so on;
(4) The sessions last from forty-five to sixty minutes. They close with a mystical *ghazal* or *bayt*, followed by closing prayers.[77]

The focus of Surat Ya-Sin is the Prophet and his conveyance of Revelation. It is said to be the "heart of the Qur'an" (*qalb al-Qur'an*) "because of its comprehensiveness, dealing with *tawhid*, prophethood, death, and the afterlife [and according to hadith] the recitation of the *Sura* at night results in the forgiveness of one's sins. It is customarily recited also at the bedside of the dying, at funerals, and when visiting graves."[78]

The number is derived from hadith on praising God thirty-three times in three ways (glory be to God, *subhan Allah*; praise be to God, *al-hamdu lillah*; and God is greatest, *Allahu akbar*), which amount to ninety-nine (33 x 3), the number of "the beautiful names of God" (*al-asma al-husna*).[79]

---

[75] Table 5.1, § X.
[76] Phonetic: *aaheste*. It means, slowly, gently, quietly. The *dhikr* is possibly not entirely silent (confined to the heart), but gently aspirated.
[77] The *dhikr* session's closing formula is not attributed to Ahmad-i Jam.
[78] Hamid Algar, email to the author, 13 December 2017.
[79] See, e.g., *Sahih Muslim*, hadith # 520a and *Sunan Abu Dawud*, hadith # 1504; cf. *Sahih al-Bukhari*, hadith # 5362 and hadith # 6318. There are thirty-three beads in prayer beads (Ar. *misbaha*, *subha*). I am very grateful to Hamid Algar for his insights.

Hamid Algar suggested that the limitation of thirty-three at a Jami *dhikr* could be connected to the Naqshbandi principle of "numerical awareness" (*wuquf-i ʿadadi*), where one must not continue endlessly with the *dhikr*, but limit the *dhikr* to a fixed number: three, five, seven, or twenty-one times.[80]

Vocalization is an element in recollection irrespective of whether the silent or the vocal technique is employed. This is manifest from the *khatm-i khwajagan*. Opening prayers and Qurʾan readings are vocalized. Some manner of vocalization is implied by the term *dhikr-i ahisti* since this mode may not be confined to the heart, but aspirated softly. It may be audible to the *halqa* members sitting nearest to him.

Hamid Algar describes the congregational *dhikr* of a Naqshbandi group in Bosnia. Aspects of this *dhikr* session, held Ramazan 1389/November–December 1969, were silent; however, the group performed the vocal *dhikr*. This is contrary to the popular belief of silent *dhikr* as universal Naqshbandi dogma. Four takeaways based on Algar's report:

Firstly, "the appeal of vocal *dhikr* is more immediate and its practice of greater facility than silent *dhikr*." This is true, especially for novices, not just for ease of practice but for the instant gratification it produces.

Secondly, the silent *dhikr* "may in a sense be regarded as suited only to an elite among the Sufis."[81] This is true with respect to the "high Sufism" espoused by a subset of Sufis of Timurid Herat. The silent *dhikr* was difficult to master, elitist, and less likely to gratify a believer's perception of spiritually connecting with God.

Thirdly, Sufi practices, observed at specific moments in time and space, diverge materially from doctrines in Sufi manuals. This parallels the earlier discussion (Chapter 2) on theoretical Islam (ortho*doxy*) versus normative Islam (ortho*praxy*).

Fourthly, the movement or the non-movement of the mystic's body was dictated by the *dhikr* technique employed. Shahzad Bashir explains: "the body was at the center of this quintessential Sufi ritual [the *dhikr*] irrespective of the production of movement or sound ... the silent [*dhikr*] version is

---

[80] See Waʿiz Kashifi, *Rashahat*, 1:47–48; cf. Ernst and Lawrence, *Sufi Martyrs*, 31 (Chishti *dhikr* and high repetition targets).
[81] Hamid Algar, "Some Notes on the Naqshbandi Tariqat in Bosnia," *Die Welt des Islams* 13/3 (1971): 168–203, 183–86, 188; and Hamid Algar, "Silent and Vocal *Dhikr* in the Naqshbandi Order," in *Akten des VII. Kongresses für Arabistik und Islamwissenschaft*, ed. Albert Dietrich (Göttingen: Vandenhoeck & Ruprecht, 1976), 39–46.

also keyed very strongly to the practitioners' consciousness of their bodies."[82]

Vocalized congregational *dhikr* facilitated the widest participation by Ahmad-i Jam's cult, and offered instant gratification: "For lovers of God, it [the *dhikr*] must be out loud!"[83] This is true for many mystics at Jam. The union of tongue and body – movement and sound – during communal *dhikr* implicates the concept of *samaʿ*.

Samaʿ

The term *samaʿ* "refers to the listening to music, singing, chanting and measured recitation designed to bring about religious emotion and ecstasy (*wajd*) ... the practice of *samaʿ* is vigorously contested among Sufi theologians, some of whom denigrate it as an illegitimate attempt by man to achieve a spiritual state granted by God."[84] *Samaʿ* is not forbidden in the Qurʾan; and hadith yield contradictory opinions.

Samaʿ receives qualified support from ulama and Sufis.[85] Al-Ghazali states that *samaʿ* should be performed at the proper time and place and with suitable companions. In *Ihyaʾ*'s "Book on Audition and Ecstasy," al-Ghazali describes *samaʿ* as a tool for the extraction of secrets (*al-saraʾir*) of the heart.[86] Secrets may lead to manifestations of the *nafs*; hence ʿAbd al-Qahir (Abu al-Najib) al-Suhrawardi's (d. 563/1168) advice: "*Samaʿ* is beneficial to him whose heart is alive and whose lower soul [*nafs*] is dead."[87] ʿAbdallah Ansari (d. 481/1089) disapproved of *samaʿ* but did not condemn it. This stems from an experience that had left him shaken: during a *samaʿ* session, Ansari "fell into a state of ecstasy .... Ansari saw this incident as a warning to himself as well as those novices who might assume that longing for God ends in a state of ecstasy, and strive for that rather than studying, practicing, and following the teachings of the Qurʾan."[88] Abu al-Najib al-Suhrawardi is dismissive of *samaʿ*: he articulates rules for comportment in *samaʿ* (Rules 135–47),[89] but remarks, "[i]t is said that only one

---

[82] Bashir, *Sufi Bodies*, 74.   [83] Ernst and Lawrence, *Sufi Martyrs*, 31 (on the Chishtiyya).
[84] Arthur Gribetz, "The *Samaʿ* Controversy: Sufi vs. Legalist," *Studia Islamica* 74 (1991): 43–62, 43.
[85] Leonard Lewisohn, "The Sacred Music of Islam: *Samaʿ* in the Persian Sufi Tradition," *British Journal of Ethnomusicology* 6 (1997): 1–33, esp. 1–15.
[86] al-Ghazali, *Ihyaʾ*, 4:410.   [87] al-Suhrawardi, *Adab*, 61.   [88] Angha, *Sad Maydan*, 38.
[89] al-Suhrawardi, *Adab*, 61–64.

whose state is weak needs the *sama'* (to arouse his spirit), but the vigorous [spirit] does not need it."[90] His rules reflect his conservatism; for example, dancing (*raqs*) is permissible only in the state (*hal*) of ecstasy (*wajd*), but the inducement of *wajd* is prohibited (Rule 139). Adolescent males are best excluded from *sama'* sessions (lest they arouse), and if present, the boys must not dance (Rule 140). Erotic descriptions and love poetry are prohibited (Rule 143).

Qutb al-Din Jami's explications on *sama'* are not novel. The novice should avoid *sama'* because he does not yet have control over his *nafs*. He lists three classes modeled on Ansari's tripartite divisions (*sama' al-'amm, sama' al-khass, sama' al-akhass*). Masters are in the highest class (*sama' al-akhass*) and permitted *sama'*; those in the lowest class (*sama' al-'amm*) include novices. The masters are "knowers of God" (*'arif*) who possess exquisite knowledge (*'ilm*) and strong faculties (*'aqil*).[91] Jami's guidance parallels Abu al-Najib al-Suhrawardi's: "[o]nly the knower (*'arif*) can properly practice *sama'* …. The *sama'* is more suitable for shaykhs than for novices."[92] Abu Hafs al-Suhrawardi says about the same as Abu al-Najib Suhrawardi.[93] In any event, *sama'* is to be appreciated spiritually (*ruhani*) and not corporeally (*jismani*).

In Abu al-Makarim Jami's *Khulasat al-maqamat*'s chapter on *sama'*, Ahmad-i Jam provides situational examples in Q&A format.[94] The topics selected by Abu al-Makarim for inclusion were based, presumably, on discussions in his *khanaqah* about permissible and impermissible *sama'*. The views do not differ materially from those discussed above. We learn from this exposition that Jami darwishes and shaykhs sat in a *halqa* for Qur'an recitals and *dhikr*. The Qur'an was read at the opening (*ibtida*) and the closing (*khatm*) of the *dhikr*. Poetry may be injected into the *dhikr*, as when someone attains a proper state (*hal-i uw rast ayad*) and (involuntarily?) utters verses (*bayt*).[95]

Poetry and Qur'an recitals are cultural imperatives at Jam as elsewhere in Iran. Mystics and non-mystics in Jam enjoy *sama'*: recitals of the Qur'an, Hafiz, Sa'adi, Rumi, 'Abd al-Rahman Jami, and Ahmad-i Jam's prose and poems. Since distant times, the cult has enjoyed listening to Ahmad's words, or words about him, with or without music. An

---

[90] Ibid., 64 (the parentheses are Milson's insertions; the square brackets are mine).
[91] Jami, *Hadiqat*, 101–9.   [92] al-Suhrawardi, *Adab*, 63.
[93] al-Suhrawardi, *'Awarif al-ma'arif*, 90–98.
[94] Kadkani, *Darwish*, 396–400. See also Ahmad-i Jam, *Uns al-ta'ibin*, 221–32.
[95] Kadkani, *Darwish*, 398–99.

anonymous poet set Ghaznawi's *Spiritual Feats* to verse;[96] Ahmad-i Jam's collections of poems (*Diwan*) remains a source of enjoyment;[97] audio of Ahmad's *Rawzat al-muznibin* at the Internet Archive demonstrates the adoption of new media for old purposes.[98]

The rhythms and cadences of Qur'an recitals (*tajwid*, *tilawat*) and Persian poetry, and choreographed movements and repetition of *la ilaha illa'llah*, can have intoxicating effects on participants and audiences as anyone who has attended an Afghan or Iranian Qur'an/poetry recital or *dhikr* session knows. The narcotic effect of *sama'* may arouse desires lurking in recesses of the heart, a reason why boys are best excluded from *sama'* sessions. *Sama'* could be employed to advance a *salik*'s quest to find God by altering his state (*hal*). The *salik*, through ecstatic behaviors (*tawajud*), may try to induce the *hal* of ecstatic rapture (*wajd*) and ecstatic finding of God (*wujud*).[99] *Sama'* opens the door to the *hal* of *wajd*. Leonard Lewisohn explains *wajd*: "the basic experience of *wajd* is that of a heightened egoless consciousness ... The subject who experiences *wajd* is temporarily absent from him or herself; it is indeed an *extasis*, an exit from self-existence and an entrance into egoless consciousness." The essence of *wajd* is "the finding (*wajada*) of an existence transcending the consciousness of the finite ego – and it is that existence which the Sufis believe is Absolute Being Itself."[100]

Mystical and non-mystical *sama'* and *raqs* in the eastern Sunni belt are pervasive. An inquiry on *sama'* and *raqs* practices at Jam belongs in a separate study.

Rabita

Rabita, bonding the darwish's heart with the shaykh's heart, was popularized by the Khwajagan-Naqshbandiyya. 'Abd al-Rahman Jami devoted a short treatise to three critical Khwajagan doctrines: *dhikr*, *rabita*, and *tawajjuh wa muraqaba* (glossed below);[101] Fritz Meier devoted a monograph to *rabita*;[102] and Arthur Buehler explicated *rabita*'s role in

---

[96] Anonymous, *Maqamat-i manzum-i Shaykh-i Jam (Zhanda-Pil)*, ed. Hasan Nasiri Jami (Tehran: Pizhuhishgah-i 'ulum-i insani wa mutala'at-i farhangi, 1391/2012).
[97] Ahmad-i Jam, *Diwan-i Shaykh Ahmad-i Jam* (Tehran: Nashriyat-i ma, 1365/1986).
[98] www.archive.org (http://tinyurl.com/rawzat) (accessed 29 May 2020).
[99] al-Qushayri, *al-Risala*, 201ff; al-Qushayri/Knysh (trans.), *Epistle*, 83–87; Schimmel, *Dimensions*, 178–79.
[100] Lewisohn, "Sacred Music," 22–23. [101] Jami, *Tariqa-yi Khwajagan*, et passim.
[102] Meier, *Zwei Abhandlungen*, Book 1: *Herzensbindung an dem Meister*.

Gnostic (*'Irfan*) Practices at Jam 209

Indian Naqshbandi Sufism.[103] The concept embodied by *rabita* was known to Sufis of Khurasan by other terms; for example, the bond of hearts between shaykh and darwish (*rabita qalbiyya*) was used by 'Abd al-Qadir Gilani;[104] Najm al-Din Kubra attributed *rabt al-qalb bi-l-shaykh* to Junayd Baghdadi (d. 298/910).[105] These concepts were surely familiar to darwishes who had studied the writings of the Sufi masters.

The quintessence of *rabita* is that the darwish bond his heart with his shaykh in order to open himself to (or make himself more receptive to) infusions of his shaykh's *fayz*. "The method used is that the adept concentrates on the outward as well as inward image of his master, whether present or absent, living or dead."[106] 'Abd al-Rahman Jami's explanations on *rabita* are thus: *suhbat* (intellectual discourses with the shaykh) is important. The darwish should regularly meet with his shaykh to obtain guidance. If a concept is unclear for any reason, then he must query his shaykh until it becomes clear to him. If his master happens to be absent, then the darwish must hold in his mind the image of his master in all aspects, internal and external, and impress it upon his heart, while banishing all distracting thoughts from his mind.[107] While it is important that the darwish love his shaykh, reciprocity by the shaykh is paramount. Jürgen Paul (quoting from *Anis al-talibin*): "To be accepted by the shaikh is a true sign of being accepted by God and His Prophet; a *murid* [darwish] who has occupied a place in the shaikh's heart has attained the privilege to be regarded by God."[108]

Shaykh-darwish bonding requires further clarification:

Bonding has distinct components: (1) *suhbat* between shaykh and darwish; (2) a darwish's love for his shaykh; and (3) the shaykh's transference of *fayz* into the darwish. As Jürgen Paul explains, *rabita* (in some way) is the "corollary to the attitude of *tawajjuh* or *tasarruf* a sheikh uses to funnel his energy into the adept."[109] The term, *rabita*, gained traction at Jam in the ninth/fifteenth century; but the concept of the shaykh transferring his spiritual energies into his darwish was known. Terms like *tawajjuh* (concentration of shaykh and darwish upon each other); *tasarruf* (power of the shaykh to shape events); and *muraqaba* (contemplation) are in Jami

---

[103] Buehler, *Sufi Heirs*, 131–46.   [104] Ibid., 132 n8; and Meier, *Zwei Abhandlungen*, 17.
[105] Michel Chodkiewicz, "Quelques aspects des techniques spirituelles dans la tariqa Naqshbandiyya," in Marc Gaborieau et al. (eds.), *Naqshbandis: Cheminements et situation actuelle d'un ordre mystique musulman* (Paris and Istanbul: ISIS, 1990), 69–82, 75; Meier, *Zwei Abhandlungen*, 18; Buehler, *Sufi Heirs*, 132 n8; Paul, *Doctrine*, 36–37 nn102, 104, 105.
[106] Paul, *Doctrine*, 36.   [107] Jami, *Khwajagan*, 15.
[108] Paul, *Doctrine*, 42 (*Anis al-talibin*, MS Tashkent IVRU 2520).   [109] Paul, *Doctrine*, 36.

literature; but without explications on the modes of transference of spiritual energies.

Tawajjuh is not a one-way process as Annemarie Schimmel noted: "The sheikh, too, would practice *tawajjuh* and thus 'enter the door of the disciple's heart' to watch him and guard him every moment."[110] To minimize confusion, only *rabita* is used with respect to Jami darwishes; and to describe *rabita*'s three distinct features: (1) *suhbat*; (2) love (*mahabb, mahabbat*); and (3) energy transference (*fayz, tawajjuh*).

RABITA AT JAM

Super Saints

'Abd al-Rahman Jami's formulations, namely, the creation of "super saints," helped Ahmad's cult attract or retain members. In the hazy past, the term *uwaysi* was applied only to mystics initiated "by the spirits of Muhammad or of pre-Islamic prophets." The *uwaysi* concept, however, was expanded by 'Abd al-Rahman to include Sufis initiated "by the spirits of great Sufi saints of earlier times."[111] By expanding the pool of eligible *uwaysi* initiators, Jami enabled the popular saints of Khurasan – Ahmad-i Jam, Abu Sa'id b. Abu al-Khayr, et al. – to enter a spiritual pantheon hitherto occupied by the likes of Abraham, Moses, and Muhammad. Ahmad-i Jam and others were ranked below the prophets (of course), but they were of superior rank to the pedestrian saints of Khurasan.[112] They were *super saints* in effect. The new super saints and *rabita* became inextricable.

Two-Shaykh Model: Living Shaykh + Deceased Shaykh

A consistent belief at Turbat-i Jam is that a wayfarer's *initiating* (i.e., teaching) shaykh (Ar. *shaykh al-ta'lim*; Per. *pir-i suhbat*) is Ahmad-i Jam; and his *directing* shaykh (Ar. *shaykh al-tarbiyya*; Per. *pir-i tarbiyyat*) is his living shaykh.[113] Ahmad's hagiologists claimed that he had received *uwaysi* initiation from Khizr (see Chapter 1); however, through recourse

---

[110] Schimmel, *Dimensions*, 237.
[111] DeWeese, "*Uvaysi*" *Sufi*, 4 and n9; and see Jami, *Nafahat*, 20–21.
[112] "Pedestrian" is not used pejoratively. Anyone who has traveled overland in Iran and Afghanistan has seen the myriads of reliquary sites peppering the landscape.
[113] The terms were described in Chapter 1.

to super saints, it was not necessary for a prophet or servant of God (like Khizr) to initiate a Sufi: A super saint – Ahmad-i Jam – could do the job.

The two-shaykh model is not unusual. The main corpus of literature on Sufism tends to focus on relationships between living shaykhs and living darwishes; moreover, later writings focused on organized (*tariqa*) Sufism (the Naqshbandiyya, Qadiriyya, etc.), not the practices of an insular regional saint cult with manifold subgroups; and where some subgroups engage in gnosticism, while other subgroups do not. A darwish could be initiated into a Sufi (gnostic) subgroup by the spirit (*ruhaniyyat*) of the cult's saint, while receiving practical training from his directing shaykh. Johan Ter Haar explains (albeit for a Naqshbandi context) that a *salik*'s bonds with his *uwaysi* initiator do not weaken his liaisons with the living shaykh. The darwish takes "his first steps on the mystical path in the physical presence of a living" director, but "owes his real initiation to a spiritual guide whom he has never met."[114]

Jami *salik*s bond their hearts with Ahmad-i Jam *and* their directing shaykh. An example of this model is Qutb al-Din Muhammad, initiated by his deceased grandfather, Ahmad-i Jam, but trained by his uncle, Zahir al-Din ʿIsa. The relationships implicated by the two-shaykh model are complementary. Ahmad-i Jam is believed to funnel his *fayz* directly into the *salik* – as when he appears in dreams – or he funnels it indirectly via the directing shaykh. The concept of Ahmad as the fount of spiritual energies is paramount because it binds the Jami saint cult: Ahmad-i Jam is the anchor.

Ahmad-i Jam's appearances in the dreams of his descendants and members of his cult pervade Jami literature.[115] Ahmad-i Jam visited Humayun (Chapter 2).[116] Shihab al-Din (Abu al-Makarim) Tirmizi Jami did not realize he was Ahmad's progeny until he dreamed about Ahmad.[117] Zayn al-Din Taybadi was initiated by Ahmad-i Jam's spirit.[118] Ahmad appeared to (putative Shiʿi) Qasim-i Anwar (d. 838/1434f.) and infused him with *fayz*.[119] Ahmad-i Jam initiated Sufis who followed other mystical paths but remained devoted to him; for example, Shams al-Din Muhammad Kusuyi

---

[114] Johan Ter Haar, "The Spiritual Guide in the Naqshbandi Order," in *The Heritage of Sufism*, ed. Leonard Lewisohn (Oxford: Oneworld, 1999), 2:311–21, 316.
[115] On the dream motif, see "Motif Index," in Moayyad and Lewis, *Colossal*, 444–49.
[116] Begam/Beveridge (trans.), *Humayun*, 145 (fol. 39b); Begim/Thackston (trans.), *Humayunnama*, 34.
[117] Buzjani/Moayyad (ed.), *Rawzat*, 110–11.   [118] Jami, *Nafahat*, 498.
[119] Samarqandi, *Tadhkirat*, 348. Noted in Chapter 2.

followed the path of Zayn al-Din Khwafi;[120] and Shihab al-Din Ahmad Birjandi (d. 856/1452f.) followed the Khwajagan-Naqshbandi path.[121] Although *ruhaniyyat* and *uwaysi* are not always expressed in the literary sources, a midnight visit from Ahmad-i Jam is laden with spiritual implications.

The literature does not make known how the two-shaykh model worked. The practices of *suhbat* and devotion comport with Jami doctrines and practices. Ahmad-i Jam warned that for a darwish to be without a shaykh and consulting him is to follow the path of *shaytan*,[122] an ominous way of emphasizing *suhbat*. Qutb al-Din Muhammad Jami warned: "the first error is in the [*salik*] not seeing his *pir* [shaykh] or serving him (*khidmat*), or conversing (*suhbat*) with him."[123] According to Abu Hafs al-Suhrawardi, master-adept relationships are characterized by the adept entrusting (*tafwiz*) himself to his shaykh's care; he learns through companionship (*suhbat*) and service (*khidmat*).[124] A shaykh has to be a pious model and show his adept the Path.[125]

To summarize: Ahmad-i Jam initiates the wayfarer's (*salik*'s) journey on the Path. The living shaykh directs the *salik*, who is in regular *suhbat* and *khidmat* with him.[126] The *salik* loves his shaykh, who must accept him into his heart (acceptance by the shaykh is critical). The *salik* practices *rabita* with both the living shaykh and the veiled shaykh. Both shaykhs funnel their spiritual energies (*fayz* or *tawajjuh*) into the *salik*.

CASE STUDY: KHWAJA 'AZIZ-ALLAH JAMI

A biography by 'Ali Buzjani of his beloved shaykh, 'Aziz-Allah Jami (d. 902/1497), a shaykh with the Naqshbandiyya,[127] offers a glimpse into material differences between textual Sufism and Sufism as practiced at Turbat-i Jam; and reveals the hybrid character of Jami gnostic doctrines and practices. It is, however, a snapshot in time:

---

[120] Buzjani/Moayyad (ed.), *Rawzat*, 118–21; Jami, *Nafahat*, 496–98; Manz, *Timurid Iran*, 226–27.
[121] Kashifi, *Rashahat*, 1:302; Manz, *Timurid Iran*, 227; see also Appendix 2.
[122] Ahmad-i Jam, *Bihar al-haqiqa*, ed. Hasan Nasiri Jami (Tehran: Pizhuhishgah-i 'ulum-i insani wa mutala'at-i farhangi, 1389/2010–11), 210. The warning is attributed to Bayazid Bistami (d. *ca.* 261/874). See al-Suhrawardi, *'Awarif al-ma'arif*, 40.
[123] Jami, *Hadiqat*, 198.   [124] al-Suhrawardi, *'Awarif al-ma'arif*, 40–46.
[125] Ibid., 33–38.
[126] *Khidmat*: loyal service to the shaykh. This is an essential component in the shaykh-darwish relationship. Service can take myriads of forms.
[127] Buzjani/Moayyad (ed.), *Rawzat*, 124–33.

Case Study: Khwaja ʿAziz-Allah Jami

(p. 124, line 10) [ʿAziz-Allah Jami] is another one of the illustrious descendants of Shaykh al-Islam Ahmad. (line 11) He is the son of Khwaja Qutb al-Din Muhammad Zahid, and he, the son of Khwaja Abu al-Maʿali. (12) [ʿAziz-Allah] was a scholar (ʿalim) trained in the exoteric and esoteric sciences (bih ʿulum-i zahiri wa batini). He was abstemious and pious; (13) he would strive to the furthest limits and powers in conforming to the Shariʿa and the path of the Prophet. His gnostic path was the tariqa-yi naqshbandiyya: (14) he was initiated into that silsila by His Excellency (hazrat) Mawlana Saʿd al-Din Kashghari, [who] (15) was one of the disciples of Khwaja ʿAla' al-Din ʿAttar, and he, one of the great disciples of Khwaja Baha' al-Din Naqshband (16) (God's blessing upon them!). [ʿAziz-Allah] came into the noble companionship of Khwaja ʿUbayd-Allah Ahrar. (17) He made the blessed pilgrimage to the two Holy Cities.

His first mystical state (hal) (18) involved austere exercises: he was continually fasting and standing all night. The veiling of the states (ahwal) (19) and concealment of [gnostic] activities is the practice of the tariqa-yi khwajagan [known as the Naqshbandiyya]; he strived diligently [in adhering to this practice]. He passed his blessed (20) days, like the darwishes, in khalwat and arbaʿyinat; and (21) [he] very quickly found himself in [the hal of] wajd. And because he had invested considerable time in spiritual training (riyazat) and striving (mujahadat), (line 22) the commands and influences of the nafs had been overpowered by the spirit (ruh) and the heart. (22–23) He would become overwhelmed by the slightest thing when in a mystical state (fi al-hal), crying out and exclaiming as the expressions of delight from the listeners (mustamiʿan) reached him.[128] (24) Sometimes, when he heard the call of the muezzin, he would shriek (p. 125, line 1) and everyone who heard this would jump out of their seats, shaken. At times, when the imam (2) read [the Qurʾan] aloud during the namaz, he would exclaim loudly, and this [expression of] pleasure would reach the assembly.

(3) One day, in the shrine of Shaykh al-Islam Ahmad (God's blessings be upon him!), a whirlwind materialized and (4) leaves from a pistachio tree fell to the ground, collected, and spun like a wheel in the middle of the portico. (5) His eyes soon shifted upon this phenomenon, and uttering a cry, he arose, and began to engage in samaʿ (bih samaʿ dar amadand).[129]

(6) One day, while [he was] sitting khalwat, a person opened the door, (7) and melancholy sounds drifted within. He exclaimed and fell into a strange hal ... [verses from the poet Saʿadi omitted]. (11) One of the servants said [of this], "one day while we were waiting for something nice to happen, suddenly the sound of the door opening reached our ears, and this peculiar state of affairs became observable" (halati ʿajib dast dad).

(12) Be it known that samaʿ is permissible (jaʾiz) for any person in the intermediate stage along the path (bih wasata-yi suluk) (13) and [in] striving and training

---

[128] Listeners or audience (sing. mustamiʿ) at samaʿ session.
[129] ʿAziz-Allah appears to have imitated the spinning of the leaves, vocally expressing his pleasure.

(*mujahadat wa riyazat*); or because "the rapture (*jadhba*) from the attraction of God [that is] equal to the two" [striving and training]; (14) and the characteristics of the carnal soul (*nafs*) having been conquered by the forces of the heart and the spirit (*ruh*); and his moral defects having been replaced by laudable [qualities]. (15) The *masha'ikh* (God's blessings upon them!) have concluded that the *sama'* is lawful (*mubah*) for such a person. However, if the *sama'* performer's (16) carnal soul should remain in command, and the qualities of the heart and spirit defeated by (17) bestial and bodily forces, when [he is] in the *hal*, the *nafs* will interrupt and spiritual pleasure (*lazzat-i ruhani*) [will] become (18) sensual and libidinous (*nafsani wa shahwani*).

The Khwajagan-Naqshbandiyya neither prescribed nor proscribed *sama'*. Baha' al-Din Naqshband personally disfavored *sama'*.[130] Irrespective of whether Khwajagan-Naqshbandi doctrines had crystallized in 'Aziz-Allah's lifetime or were still in flux, 'Aziz-Allah's biography shows that in his corner of Khurasan, shaykhs and darwishes engaged in *khalwat* and *arba'yin*; and *sama'* was permitted to those *salik*s in the intermediate stage of the Path and above.

'Aziz-Allah was an excitable person who evidently drew considerable pleasure from the sounds he encountered in daily life. The Sufi shaykhs (*masha'ikh*) who are said to have determined the lawfulness (*mubah*) of *sama'* were Khurasanian Sufi champions like Abu 'Abd al-Rahman al-Sulami (d. 412/1021).[131] 'Aziz-Allah was opposed to extreme *sama'* activities or novices engaging in *sama'*. He is thus in accord with the teachings of Khurasan's great Sufi masters and his illustrious ancestors.

On 'Aziz-Allah and *dhikr*, Buzjani writes:

(p. 126, lines 12–13) ['Aziz-Allah] performed the silent *dhikr* (*wa dhikr guftan ishan bih tariq-i khafiyya*). (13) At the devotions (*awrad*) that he hosted, readings were conducted in a low voice, but some (14) of the time, darwishes inside the mosque conducted the *awrad* [in the style] of Zayn al-Din.[132] (14–15) They sat in their devotional circle (*halqa-yi awrad*) [and] performed the vocal recollection (*dhikr-i jahr*) in concert. However, it was not known [to those outside the group] (16) if a thing was being read or listened to by them.

(17) We heard from one of our retainers that early one day in the mosque ... (18) Shams al-Din Muhammad Tabadakani[133] and some of his disciples had been reading aloud at their *awrad*. ['Aziz-Allah] (19) sat far away [from them] and occupied himself with *tawajjuh*.

---

[130] al-Bukhari, *Anis al-talibin*, 120.   [131] Buzjani/Moayyad (ed.), *Rawzat*, 126.
[132] Zayn al-Din Khwafi (d. 838/1435). On him, see Manz, *Timurid Iran*, et passim; Paul, "Khwajagan-Naqshbandiyya," 71–86, et passim.
[133] Tabadakani (d. 891/1486) was Zayn al-Din Khwafi's successor.

The snide tone reflects antipathies over doctrines: vocal *dhikr* and silent *dhikr*. Evidently, there was tension between the Zayniyya and the Jami-Naqshbandis.

CLOSING COMMENTS

In discussions on *khalwat*, *dhikr*, and *samaʿ*, I have tried to balance theory – the words of Qutb al-Din Jami, et al. – with practices. This has been a perilous navigation because *reliable* information on gnostic (mystical, Sufi) practices at Jam is scarce. Jam, like myriads of small (Sunni and Shiʿa) communities scattered across the Persian world, has unique religious and cultural traditions of great diversity. Regional traditions shift and morph over time: they become infused with fresh religious or cultural concepts, while attriting other religious or cultural concepts. The persistence of disparate Jami *dhikr* subgroups demonstrates that fissiparousness is the norm; and mystical doctrines and practices deviate from subset to subset of Jami mystics.

The diverse narratives of *fayz* infusions, *uwaysi* initiations, or visits by Ahmad's spirit (*ruh*) are revealing. Ahmad's cult did not care which path a man took as long as he venerated Ahmad-i Jam. ʿAli Buzjani's, Waʿiz Kashifi's, Dawlatshah al-Samarqandi's, and ʿAbd al-Rahman Jami's narratives of *uwaysi* initiations, or of subjects dreaming of Ahmad and receiving his *fayz*, are unlikely to have been propagated absent evidence of the subjects' genuine devotion for Ahmad-i Jam. The Sufi technique of *rabita* facilitated fidelity and devotion for Ahmad-i Jam. By not insisting on a monolithic mystical path (*monogamous Sufism*), gnostic components of Ahmad-i Jam's multifarious saint cult were able to attract members from other mystical currents. Moreover, by allowing experimentation in devotional practices, and freedom to choose one's directing shaykh (*shaykh al-tarbiyya*), while insisting only on steadfast fidelity to Ahmad-i Jam, the Jami community minimized factionalism. The Jami *Gemeinschaft* (mystics and non-mystics) is multifarious – and includes, notably, Shiʿi filaments. The Sufi components of the saint cult are fissiparous, but Sufi subgroups are not necessarily antagonistic. Ahmad-i Jam is the powerful centripetal energy that binds heterogenous Jami tendencies. Ahmad-i Jam, in various senses of the Sufi term *qutb*,[134] is the axis around which the devotional cult revolves.

---

[134] See Renard, *Historical Dictionary of Sufism*, 185 (on *qutb*: pole or axis).

Conclusion

We opened this inquiry with the questions "[w]hy has Ahmad-i Jam's shrine flourished while other Sufi shrines throughout the Islamic world have gone to ruin?"; and "[h]ow did this unapologetically Sunni community survive for 900 years, and come to thrive in the (Shiʻi) Islamic Republic of Iran?"

There are several reasons as to why the shrine has survived and thrived. Central to the shrine's longevity are Ahmad-i Jam's progeny, the product of him fathering (at least) forty-two children. His progeny number in the thousands, and still venerate his memory and protect his legacy. Progeny by themselves, however, do not account for either the shrine's or the saint cult's longevity, absent their *adaptive* strategies for (1) protecting Ahmad-i Jam's spiritual legacy and his shrine complex; and (2) interacting with Iran's rulers, from the Seljuqs to the Ayatollahs.

The Jami community's focus is singular: it is always about Ahmad-i Jam: *this, too, shall pass but Ahmad is forever*. Beatrice Forbes Manz observed that "[t]he emphasis on the founder Ahmad-i Jam ... may help to account for the family's receptiveness to a variety of teachings and its continuing adaptability to changes of political power." This book has demonstrated the accuracy of Manz's insight. Ahmad's successors protect his shrine and extract benefits from their overlords when opportunities materialize. This is evident vis-à-vis the Islamic Republic, where the Jami community has adopted a nonthreatening demeanor, which has allowed it to secure political and financial benefits.

The shrine's longevity is testament to the resilience and diplomacy of its elders, mostly males, but also females – like Hibat al-Rahman and Khandzada Fakhr al-Mulk – who managed the shrine and its endowments, and helped the Jami community navigate stormy waters. In so doing, the leadership shaped Iranian and Islamic histories. This is remarkable because the leadership, generation to generation, century to century, held the heterogenous community together and forestalled internecine strife, which often sunders families, clans, and religious communities. Although subgroups subscribed to disparate doctrines and practices they were not antagonistic. The polychromatic saint cult and its assorted Sufi subsets demonstrate that fissiparousness does not inevitably lead to factionalism. The centripetal power is Ahmad-i Jam. Visualize, if you will, the disparate mystical and non-mystical elements that constitute the saint cult as being akin to a motley collection of planetary objects revolving around the sun.

The geographical insularity of the cult (Jam's hinterland status and distance from Herat and Mashhad), and parochialism of the cult's adherents, also minimized factionalism. Scholars have queried why the Jami Sufis never spread their message through proselytism. It is likely that proselytizing activities were directed at people in the shrine's catchment area (between Nishapur and Balkh) and possibly beyond; but Jami religious propaganda appears to have principally targeted sultans, viziers, amirs, and ulama in Khurasan, Transoxiana, and India. Their targets were men and women of influence with the resources to patronize and protect the shrine.

In the centuries between the reign of Shah i'Abbas I and the founding of the Islamic Republic, the cult became politically quietist and provincial. Political-religious quiescence, insularity, and parochialism undoubtedly helped the saint cult to survive. The cult hibernated for decades, slowly awakening in the Pahlawi era, and coming to thrive under the Islamic Republic once it demonstrated it was not a threat to the Shi'i republic, and indeed, could be an asset to Tehran in bringing political quiescence to this section of Iran's Sunni borderlands. Sistan and Baluchistan province's restiveness helped it secure state funding for libraries, seminaries, archaeological preservations and such; the projects were intended to "pacify" Iranian Baluch nationalists. The districts of Jam, Khwaf, and Taybad consequently received state funding aimed at thwarting agitation by Wahhabi and CIA provocateurs operating out of Pakistan and Afghanistan.

Reflections on the foregoing discussions on saint and shrine.

The history of this Sunni institution revolves around its saint, Ahmad of Jam. As the scion of an eminent Shafi'i scholar, i'Ali of Namaq, he received a stellar education in the Islamic Sciences. Ahmad's intellectual journey is remarkable: from Shafi'i (Ash'ari?) origins to Karrami *ascetic* to Hanafi *mystic*. He settled (*ca.* 480/1087) in Mai'd-Abad village in Jam shortly after his father died, and began evangelizing (*da'wa*). Ahmad's religious activism (*tabligh*) involved badgering Muslims to repentance (*tawba*), and enforcing the quintessentially Islamic obligation to "enjoin the good and forbid the reprehensible" (*al-amr bi-l-ma'ruf wa-l-nahy i'an al-munkar*). Ahmad's hand fell hard on his Zoroastrian and Muslim neighbors, whose musical instruments and wine barrels were smashed. The epithet "Furious Elephant" (Zhanda-Pil) was conferred on Ahmad-i Jam by a wit, who mischievously played on our hero's physique and pugnacity.

Sultan Sanjar, the Seljuq ruler of Iran, became fond of Ahmad-i Jam. Sanjar's ancestors, Tughril Beg and Chaghri Beg, have a hagiological, possibly actual, connection to Abu Sa'id b. Abu al-Khayr of Mayhana, whose town had supported the Seljuqs over the Ghaznavids in their struggle for Khurasan. The outgoing rulers were patrons of the Karramiyya, who had persecuted Abu Sa'id. Ahmad hitched his spiritual wagon to Abu Sa'id and his temporal wagon to the Seljuqs. His Karrami history was whitewashed, and his spiritual connection to Abu Sa'id was embellished.

The saint cult claimed in an eighth/fourteenth-century hagiography that their saint had received a *khirqa* from the hand of Khizr, the immortal servant of God, equated in some circles with the prophet Elijah. The claim was made to burnish Ahmad-i Jam's sainthood (*walayat*) and saintdom (*wilayat*), since the Friends of God "converse with [Khizr], who wanders across the earth, on land and sea, in the plains and in the mountains, searching for someone like himself out of passionate longing for him."

As the saint cult became *silsila*-conscious in the late eighth/fourteenth and early ninth/fifteenth centuries, it manipulated Ahmad-i Jam's spiritual pedigree to interpolate the "golden chain" (*silsilat al-dhahab*), beginning with Imam Riza, the eighth Shi'i Imam and the "Sultan of Khurasan." The manipulation of *silsila*s is not by itself extraordinary as Jürgen Paul and others have demonstrated. However, it is instructive that a staunchly Sunni cult elected to insert an undeniably Shi'i pedigree as its protagonist's bridge to the Prophet. The Naqshbandiyya, which eventually morphed into a dogmatic Sunni *tariqa*, manipulated Baha' al-Din's primary link to Muhammad to be the first caliph, Abu Bakr al-Siddiq. They are the only major Sufi order to subordinate the i'Alid *silsila*.

In or around 649/1251, Ahmad-i Jam's offspring started promoting the saint as the "refuge of kings" and "protector of the realm," that is, Ahmad-i Jam, "patron saint of kings." The first king to subscribe was Shams al-Din Kart, founder of the Kartid dynasty, vassals of Iran's Mongol overlords, the

Ilkhanids. Ahmad's association with Sanjar was central to Jami propaganda. Muiʿin al-Din Jami, the Kart vizier, explained in his letter to Tamerlane that Sanjar's grandeur as king of the world and Khusraw of his age were God's favors (*niʿmah*) and blessings (*baraka*) for his fidelity to Ahmad-i Jam, a Friend of God (*wali Allah*). "When he was with the Furious Elephant, the Presence of God, Sanjar was but a slave (*ghulam*) kneading clay [for his master]." Temür was invited to drink from the same chalice as his illustrious Turkic predecessor, which he did.

Turbat-i Jam became a politically powerful and wealthy City of God under the Kartids and Ilkhanids. Ghiyath al-Din Kart was devoted to Ahmad-i Jam, and viewed his in-law, Shaykh al-Islam Shihab al-Din Ismaʿil Jami, as his preceptor and the conduit for Ahmad's *baraka* and *fayz*. The shrine, which had benefited from its first major addition in 633/1236 (*gunbad*), became a shrine complex with the addition of the "Old Mosque" (Masjid-i iʿatiq), towering *iwan*, Madrasa-i Faryumadi, Gunbad-i Safid, and Masjid-i Kirmani. The edifices were funded by Kartid, Ilkhanid, and Jami sources.

A thesis proffered here is that Ahmad-i Jam's shrine rode the crest of Ilkhanid reforms initiated by Ilkhanid sultan Ghazan Khan and vizier Rashid al-Din to increase agricultural production by restoring hydrological systems and reviving fallow lands (*ihyaʾ al-mawat*). Concomitant with Ilkhanid reforms were Kartid endeavors to restore irrigation systems serving Herat, and to improve agricultural production. By the end of the Kartid epoch, Ahmad's shrine had become the premier hydro- and agro-manager in Jam, Bakharz, and Khwaf provinces. In the Timurid period, the major shrine complexes of Khurasan – Ahmad-i Jam's (influential in the regions of Jam, Bakharz, Fushanj, Khwaf, and Kusuyi); iʿAbdallah Ansari's (Herat and its environs); Imam Riza's (Mashhad-Tus and its environs); and Imam iʿAli's (Balkh and its environs) – were utilized for this purpose. Delegation by Timurid sultans to Islamic institutions of hydro- and agro-management was rooted in Kartid and Ilkhanid practices.

The shrine's leadership jettisoned the Karts when Muʿizz al-Din Kart's son, Pir iʿAli Kart, elected to strengthen Herat's defenses and resist Temür instead of parleying for vassalage as his Twelver Shiʿa rival in Sabzavar, iʿAli Muʾayyad, was to do. The Jamis were joined by a subset of the upper echelon of Khurasanian notables, who were fearful of a redux of 619/1222, when Chingiz Khan desolated Herat. Betrayal by the Jamis of their kinsmen was not without risks: traitors are rarely respected or trusted. However, Temür, a superstitious man who collected *baraka* hither and tither, and was astute and pragmatic as to secure temporal support from influential religious families of Transoxiana and Iran, accepted their offer, because "assistance in the world of spirits (*i'alam-i arwah*) is superior to all the armies, treasures, and defenses."

The shrine's association with Timurid royals and high officials lasted 125 years and brought architectural, financial, and political bounties to the shrine and its Sufis. In addition to fiscal and legal protections by the Timurid court and officials, the Madrasa-i Firuzshah, Gunbad-i Firuzshah, and Masjid-i jami'-i naw were sponsored by Amir Jalal al-Din Firuzshah, who served as a military commander for Temür and Shah-Rukh. Ghiyath al-Din Amir Shah-Malik, the governor of Khwarzam and *atabeg* to Ulugh Beg b. Shah-Rukh, sponsored the Madrasa-i Amir Shah Malik. The shrine complex's architectural contours were frozen in place with Shah-Rukh's death (850/1447). Although Sultan-Abu Sa'id and Sultan-Husayn Bayqara continued patronage and protection (*i'inayat wa himayat*) for the shrine and its leadership, there is no evidence of devotion to Ahmad by either Timurid sultan. Neither the sultans nor their officials sponsored any building activity.

Shaykh al-Islam Shihab al-Din Isma'il Jami (d. *ca.* 738/1338) negotiated with the Mongols when Herat was besieged. The administrator of the shrine's *khanaqah*s, Ziya al-Din Yusuf Jami (d. 797/1394), hosted Temür at Turbat-i Jam in Dhu al-Hijja 782/February–March 1381 when he came to venerate Ahmad-i Jam. Yusuf, and his cousin, Shihab al-Din Isma'il (d. 809/1407), accompanied Temür on campaign as spiritual advisors. Shihab al-Din Isma'il (Abu al-Makarim) Tirmizi Jami (d. 847/1443f.) was Shah-Rukh b. Temür's preceptor and envoy to Bengal. The above accounts reflect the different ways in which Jami shaykhs al-Islam served their community by serving their sultans. The Kartids, Ilkhanids, and Timurids rewarded Ahmad-i Jam's shrine and Jami shaykhs. Shah-Rukh and Gawhar-Shad included benefits for the Jami shrine in their waqf for the Gawhar-Shad Mosque. Economic surpluses, namely, agricultural wealth, were utilized to "feed the people" (*takafful-i umur*), an Indo-Persian cultural tenet that obliges the affluent to offer "social services" to the indigent and infirm; and to literally feed the people during hard times: when pestilences or epidemics (*waba'* or *ta'un*) afflict livestock and peoples, or famine (*qaht*) strikes in the wake of war, pestilence, or drought.

The triumph of Shah Isma'il I, Safavi, over the Aq-Quyunlu heralded the beginning of the end of Sunni political hegemony in Iran. The Safavid-Uzbek wars brought intense sectarian violence to Khurasan. Jamis fled to India and were welcomed by Humayun, his wife, Hamida Banu Bigum, and later, their son, Akbar the Great. Shi'i policies toward the shrine were flexible under the Safavids. Shah Ismai'il I renewed fiscal immunities for a shrine custodian, who had kissed the floor and showed faith in the exalted family of the Imamate. Shah i'Abbas I sponsored restorative work on the *iwan*. Nonetheless, the shrine declined as conversion to Shi'ism in Khurasan inexorably advanced. The saint cult lost its Indian foothold when Mughal emperor Akbar the Great turned to the Chishtiyya.

The outlook for Turbat-i Jam's Sunnis is not unlike in the past. They do not see their situation as ideal, but appreciate that Iran will always be a Twelver Shi'a land, an Islamic Republic, and that Sunnis will be a permanent minority. They neither foresee nor seek restoration of the monarchy. Interlocutors are not anti-Shi'a, although many are amused by the excessive expressions of devotion by the Shi'a to *ahl al-bayt*, weeping for the Immaculate Imams; and chest-beating i'Ashura commemorations accompanied by passion plays (*ta'ziya*); but annoyed by the proscriptions on sundry social activities in Muharram and Safar that adversely impact on social and economic activities in Jam; for instance, the ban on weddings in Muharram and Safar.[1] The complaints of Sunnis echo the complaints of Iranians from other confessions: the abysmal state of Iran's economy and foreign interference in Iranian affairs; the nonstop violence in Afghanistan, Iraq, Syria, and Libya; the long history of Russian, Soviet, American, and British interference in Iran – coups, occupation, famine, and epidemic; and the failed promises of the JCPOA (the P5+1 agreement) – bond pragmatic Sunnis to the Islamic Republic.

It behooves the Shi'i Islamic Republic of Iran to support Ahmad-i Jam's shrine in tangible and intangible ways. The shrine is part of Iran's rich cultural heritages and the center of Friday prayers for Turbat-i Jam's Sunnis. Favorable socioeconomic policies toward the region's Sunnis is astute security policy. Funding for Sunni seminaries is not solely to advance Islamic studies, but serves to channel Sunnis into Iranian seminaries supervised by state officials. This reduces the likelihood that they will travel overseas to secure an education in the Islamic Sciences, where they will be at risk of indoctrination by Wahhabis. Iranian Sunnis have noted with satisfaction that Sunni militancy in Iran is negligible (mostly confined to Baluch militants); and that Wahhabi terrorists in Syria and Iraq do not include Iranians.[2] The shrine's seminaries have profited from official

---

[1] One year when I was sojourning in Jam, I was astounded by the number of weddings being held in the neighboring wedding hall. A friend explained the rush to wed before the end of the Hijri year.

[2] A study of Sunni militants suggests this may be correct. E. Pokalova, *Returning Islamist Foreign Fighters* (Cham, Switzerland: Palgrave, 2020), esp. 29–58 (Iraq: 2003–11; Syria: 2011–20).

policies; hence the swelling of library collections and student enrollments at Hawza-yi i'ilmiyya Ahmadiyya and Hawza-yi i'ilmiyya Hibat al-Rahman.

Ayatollah Khomeini inclined to *i'irfan*, including the mystical philosophy of Ibn al-i'Arabi (d. 638/1240).[3] Thus, while *sufi* today has dark connotations to certain Iranian officials, *i'irfan* does not. The gnostics of Jam practice select aspects of *i'irfan*, principally, *dhikr*, *sama'*, and *rabita*. Gnostic enterprises at Jam are diverse, and probably have been diverse since Ahmad-i Jam's death. *Khanaqah*s are not illegal, but since Safavid times, they have been viewed with suspicion. Jami mystics have mostly discarded *khalwat* and *arba'yin*, but one subgroup withdraws to Kuh-yi Bizd. They erected a hospice near the Masjid-i Nur, which is their center for *dhikr* and *arba'yin*. Silent *dhikr* is practiced by (at least) one subgroup; whereas (at least) one subgroup prefers the vocal *dhikr*: for these lovers of God, the *dhikr* must be performed communally and vocally.

I have tried here to present the story of an Islamic institution in a niche within Islam's expanses that thrives nearly 900 years after its emergence. That this adamantly Sunni institution prospers in the Shi'i Islamic Republic of Iran is particularly remarkable considering the destruction in Afghanistan, Pakistan, Iraq, and Syria of Sufi shrines; the Taliban's destruction of cultural heritages; and the destruction of mausolea and cupolas by the Saudi-Wahhabi armies when they captured Karbala and the Hijaz, including the desecration of the sanctified graves of *ahl al-bayt* and the Prophet of Islam.

The history of the shrine is also a history of its catchment area, an ethnically, linguistically, and culturally variegated corner of Khurasan. The polychromatic cult reflects the catchment area because it has welcomed any male or female, Sunni or Shi'a, Turk, Turco-Mongol, Tajik, or Hazara, mystic or non-mystic, offering all-comers the unifying image of Ahmad-i Jam to impress on their heart. The message is simple: Love Ahmad-i Jam. He is your conduit to God. By focusing on Ahmad as the wellspring for God's favors (*ni'mah*) and blessings (*baraka*); and by employing gnostic techniques like *tawajjuh* and *rabita* to bond hearts with Ahmad and receive his *fayz*, Ahmad's shrine and saint cult survive hard times and thrive in good times. While political conditions today are not ideal, and economic conditions are not good, the indubitably Sunni saint cult is enjoying a renaissance under the Shi'i Islamic Republic of Iran.

---

[3] See Alexander Knysh, "*Irfan* Revisited: Khomeini and the Legacy of Islamic Mystical Philosophy," *Middle East Journal* 46/4 (1992): 631–53; A. A. Seyed-Gohrab, "Khomeini the Poet Mystic," *Die Welt des Islams* 51/3 (2011): 438–58.

Appendix 1 Jami Genealogies

Ahmad-i Jam fathered thirty-nine sons and three daughters, but only a few names are found in literary sources. Latifa is the only daughter identified. She was exceptionally devout, a mystic, and an ascetic. She married the judge (*qadi*) of Bizd (in Jam province). They had one son, Kamal al-Din, who died in childhood.[1]

The fourteen sons are not discussed by ʿAli Buzjani or Ibrahim Zanganah by their order of birth. They have been listed below in birth order as stipulated by Shihab al-Din (Abu al-Makarim) Tirmizi Jami in his *Khulasat al-maqamat*.[2]

(1) Rashid al-Din (ʿAbd al-Rashid), like his brothers, bears the title *shaykh al-Islam*. He was a scholar and mystic based in Turshiz province; he had two sons, neither of whom produced any offspring. ʿAbd al-Rashid was a member of a *jawanmard* (akin *futuwwa*) and died fighting Ismaʿilis (Sevener Shiʿa).[3]

(2) Jamal al-Din (Abu al-Fath). He lived in the Maghrib. His two sons developed a sizeable clan in the Maghrib about which nothing is known.[4]

(3) Safi al-Din Mahmud. He lived in Anatolia and had three sons,[5] perhaps four.[6] A significant Jami clan is said to have flourished in Anatolia.

(4) Qutb al-Din Muhammad. He lived in *b-r-s* in the environs of Nishapur. He fathered a son, Razi al-Din Ahmad (d. *ca.* 650/1252f.), who had fourteen children,[7] but none of them can be connected to activities in medieval Khurasan.

---

[1] Buzjani/Moayyad (ed.), *Rawzat*, 52; Zanganah, *Sarzamin*, 95.
[2] Kadkani, *Darwish*, 179–83; ʿAlaʾ al-Mulk Jami/Jami (ed.), *Khulasat al-maqamat*, 23–26.
[3] Buzjani/Moayyad (ed.), *Rawzat*, 61–62; Zanganah, *Sarzamin*, 86–87.
[4] Buzjani/Moayyad (ed.), *Rawzat*, 61–62; Zanganah, *Sarzamin*, 88.
[5] Kadkani, *Darwish*, 180.
[6] Buzjani/Moayyad (ed.), *Rawzat*, 63–64; Zanganah, *Sarzamin*, 88–89.
[7] Buzjani/Moayyad (ed.), *Rawzat*, 64–65; Zanganah, *Sarzamin*, 89–90.

(5) Fakhr al-Din (Abu al-Hasan). He is buried in a dependency of Jam. He had one son, Shaykh ʿAmu. We know nothing about father or son.[8]

(6) Najm al-Din (Abu Bakr). He died in Kirman. His son, Ibrahim, had no offspring.[9]

(7) Burhan al-Din Nasr. He was Ahmad-i Jam's locum tenens as the custodian. He studied in Shirwan and Sarakhs before settling in Kariz-i Saʿad in the Zir-i Pul ("below the bridge") region (south of Malan Bridge, Herat). His only child, Hibat al-Rahman, married Siraj al-Din Ahmad, the only child of his brother, Ziya al-Din Yusuf.[10] Two grandsons from this union originated two lineages known by the *nisba* of "Karizi" and "Kusuyi."

(8) Ziya al-Din Yusuf. He inherited his father's Sufi mantle (the *khirqa* supposedly given to Ahmad-i Jam by Abu Saʿid b. Abu al-Khayr) that is said to have stayed with Ziya al-Din's descendants in Kusuyi. He was an active Sufi with many darwishes; he was *khalifa* (shaykh) for all villages of Jam province; and is buried beside Ahmad.[11] It would appear that Ziya al-Din was Ahmad-i Jam's locum tenens with respect to the *khanaqah*, which makes sense since Burhan al-Din Nasr, the designated locum tenens, lived near Herat.

(9) ʿImad al-Din (ʿAbd al-Rahim). He had a son, Sharaf al-Din (ʿAbd al-Karim), who died in 617–18/1221 during the Mongol irruptions. His line expired with him.[12]

(10) Shams al-Din Mutahhar (Abu al-Maʿali). He studied the religious sciences in Herat and resided in Qatmiran, near Herat. He had five children, but only one child, Qutb al-Din Muhammad (577–667/1181–1268), is named. The others were probably females. Qutb al-Din Muhammad became the patriarch of his generation and accumulated wealth for the shrine. The most important lineages descend from Shams al-Din, with hundreds of descendants in Jam, Bakharz, Khwaf, Nishapur, and Samarqand. In fact, most of Ahmad-i Jam's progeny in the region are descended from Shams al-Din Mutahhar.[13]

(11) Badr al-Din Saʿad (d. 566/1170f.). He is buried near the Masjid-i Nur in Kuh-yi Bizd, where Ahmad is said to have passed his seclusionary years.[14] He had no children.[15]

(12) Hamid-al-Din ʿAbdallah. No children.[16]

---

[8] Buzjani/Moayyad (ed.), *Rawzat*, 65–66.   [9] Ibid., 66; Zanganah, *Sarzamin*, 93.
[10] Buzjani/Moayyad (ed.), *Rawzat*, 52–60; Zanganah, *Sarzamin*, 85–86.
[11] Buzjani/Moayyad (ed.), *Rawzat*, 66–69; Kadkani, *Darwish*, 180.
[12] Buzjani/Moayyad (ed.), *Rawzat*, 69–72.   [13] Ibid., 72–73; Kadkani, *Darwish*, 181.
[14] The grave is extant (visited 9 September 2017). The new hospice is located here.
[15] Buzjani/Moayyad (ed.), *Rawzat*, 73–74.   [16] Ibid., 74–75.

Appendix 1

(13) Zahir al-Din ʿIsa (Abu al-Mufakhar). He was the intellectual force of his generation. He studied in Syria and the Hijaz, and returned to Herat to be near Shams al-Din Mutahhar. He founded a *khanaqah* and trained many darwishes. He was shaykh to his nephew, Qutb al-Din Muhammad b. Shams al-Din Mutahhar. Zahir al-Din was a prolific writer, but his books have not survived. One title was dedicated to Khwarazm-Shah, ʿAlaʾ al-Din Takish (r. 567–96/1172–1200). Zahir al-Din was a confidant of Fakhr al-Din Razi (d. 606/1209);[17] and the Ghurid sultan, Ghiyath al-Din Muhammad (r. 558–99/1163–1203). Zahir al-Din ʿIsa was a bachelor. He is buried in the Herat region.

(14) Shihab al-Din Ismaʿil. He was born late in Ahmad's life. Shihab al-Din Ismaʿil Jami became ill fleeing the Mongol vanguards and died in 617/1220. His remains were returned to Jam and buried in a passageway in the shrine. He was a bachelor.[18]

---

[17] Ibid., 75–78; Zanganah, *Sarzamin*, 103–5.
[18] Buzjani/Moayyad (ed.), *Rawzat*, 78–79; Kadkani, *Darwish*, 182.

226 Appendix 1

Ahmad-i Jam

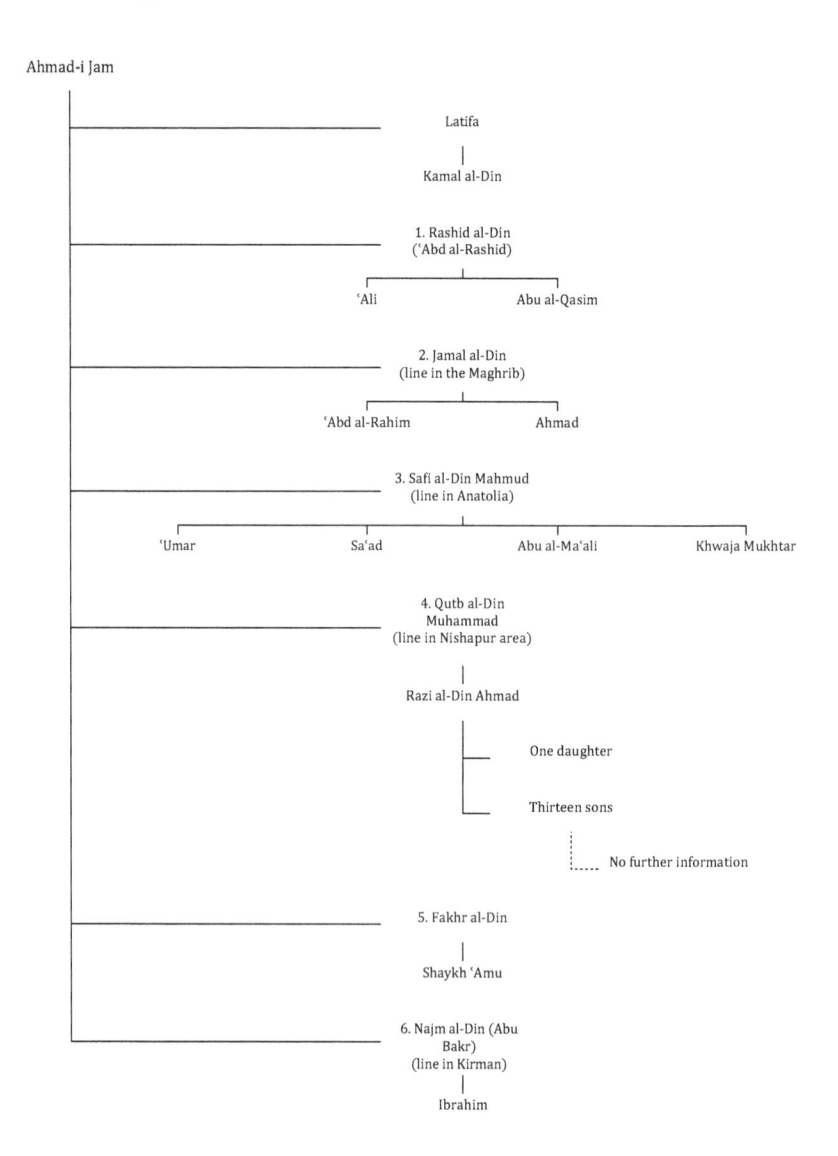

- Latifa
  - Kamal al-Din
- 1. Rashid al-Din ('Abd al-Rashid)
  - 'Ali
  - Abu al-Qasim
- 2. Jamal al-Din (line in the Maghrib)
  - 'Abd al-Rahim
  - Ahmad
- 3. Safi al-Din Mahmud (line in Anatolia)
  - 'Umar
  - Sa'ad
  - Abu al-Ma'ali
  - Khwaja Mukhtar
- 4. Qutb al-Din Muhammad (line in Nishapur area)
  - Razi al-Din Ahmad
    - One daughter
    - Thirteen sons
      - No further information
- 5. Fakhr al-Din
  - Shaykh 'Amu
- 6. Najm al-Din (Abu Bakr) (line in Kirman)
  - Ibrahim

FIGURE A1.1A Ahmad-i Jam's immediate descendants (part 1 of 2)

Appendix 1

Ahmad-i Jam

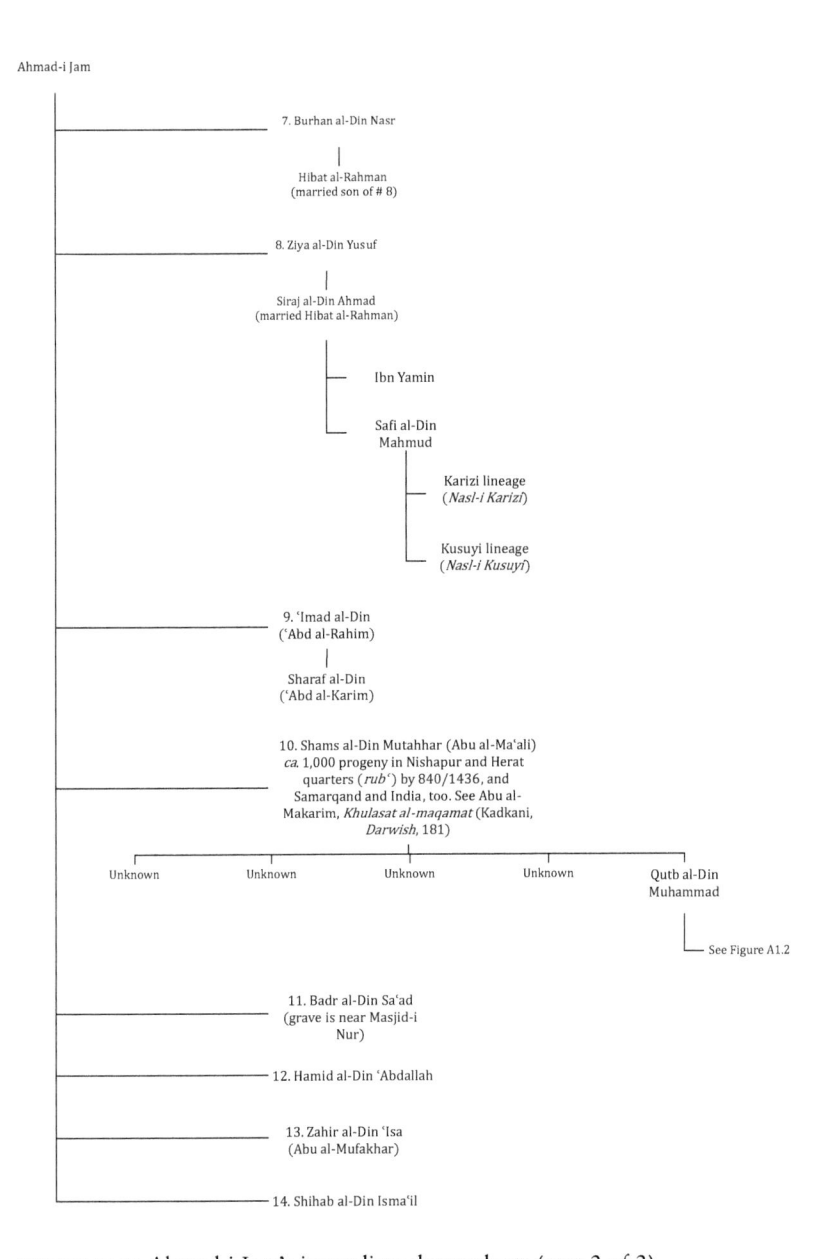

- 7. Burhan al-Din Nasr
  - Hibat al-Rahman (married son of # 8)
- 8. Ziya al-Din Yusuf
  - Siraj al-Din Ahmad (married Hibat al-Rahman)
    - Ibn Yamin
    - Safi al-Din Mahmud
      - Karizi lineage (*Nasl-i Karizi*)
      - Kusuyi lineage (*Nasl-i Kusuyi*)
- 9. 'Imad al-Din ('Abd al-Rahim)
  - Sharaf al-Din ('Abd al-Karim)
- 10. Shams al-Din Mutahhar (Abu al-Ma'ali) ca. 1,000 progeny in Nishapur and Herat quarters (*rub'*) by 840/1436, and Samarqand and India, too. See Abu al-Makarim, *Khulasat al-maqamat* (Kadkani, *Darwish*, 181)
  - Unknown
  - Unknown
  - Unknown
  - Unknown
  - Qutb al-Din Muhammad
    - See Figure A1.2
- 11. Badr al-Din Sa'ad (grave is near Masjid-i Nur)
- 12. Hamid al-Din 'Abdallah
- 13. Zahir al-Din 'Isa (Abu al-Mufakhar)
- 14. Shihab al-Din Isma'il

FIGURE A1.1B Ahmad-i Jam's immediate descendants (part 2 of 2)

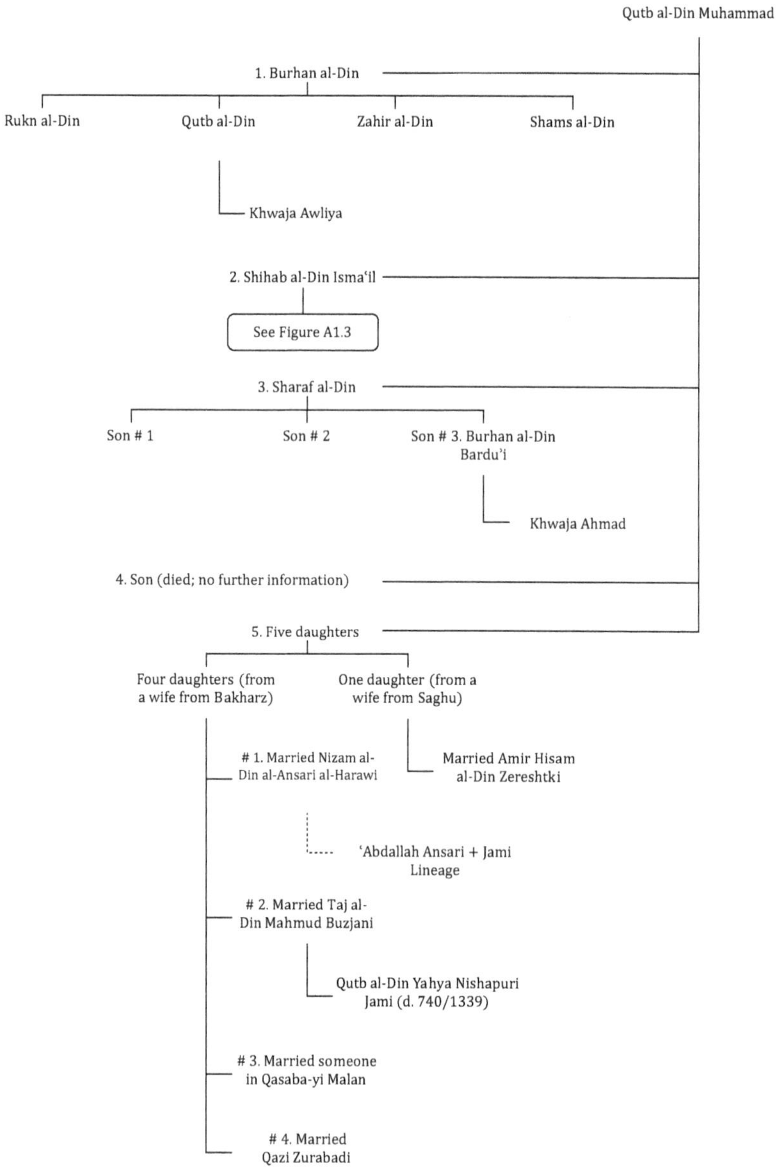

228   Appendix 1

```
                                                               Qutb al-Din Muhammad
                         1. Burhan al-Din ─────────────────────────────┤
      ┌──────────┬──────────────┬──────────────┐                       │
  Rukn al-Din   Qutb al-Din   Zahir al-Din   Shams al-Din              │
                    │                                                  │
                Khwaja Awliya                                          │
                                                                       │
                     2. Shihab al-Din Isma'il ────────────────────────┤
                         ┌──────────────────┐                          │
                         │ See Figure A1.3  │                          │
                         └──────────────────┘                          │
                     3. Sharaf al-Din ────────────────────────────────┤
      ┌──────────┬──────────────┬──────────────┐                       │
   Son # 1      Son # 2      Son # 3. Burhan al-Din                    │
                                  Bardu'i                              │
                                    │                                  │
                                Khwaja Ahmad                           │
                                                                       │
         4. Son (died; no further information) ───────────────────────┤
                                                                       │
                     5. Five daughters ───────────────────────────────┘
      ┌────────────────────────┬──────────────────────┐
  Four daughters (from    One daughter (from a
  a wife from Bakharz)    wife from Saghu)
         │                        │
      # 1. Married Nizam al-    Married Amir Hisam
      Din al-Ansari al-Harawi   al-Din Zereshtki
              ┆
              ┆    'Abdallah Ansari + Jami
              ┆         Lineage
         │
      # 2. Married Taj al-
      Din Mahmud Buzjani
              │
           Qutb al-Din Yahya Nishapuri
           Jami (d. 740/1339)
         │
      # 3. Married someone
      in Qasaba-yi Malan
         │
      # 4. Married
      Qazi Zurabadi
```

FIGURE A1.2 Qutb al-Din Muhammad Jami's descendants

Appendix 1

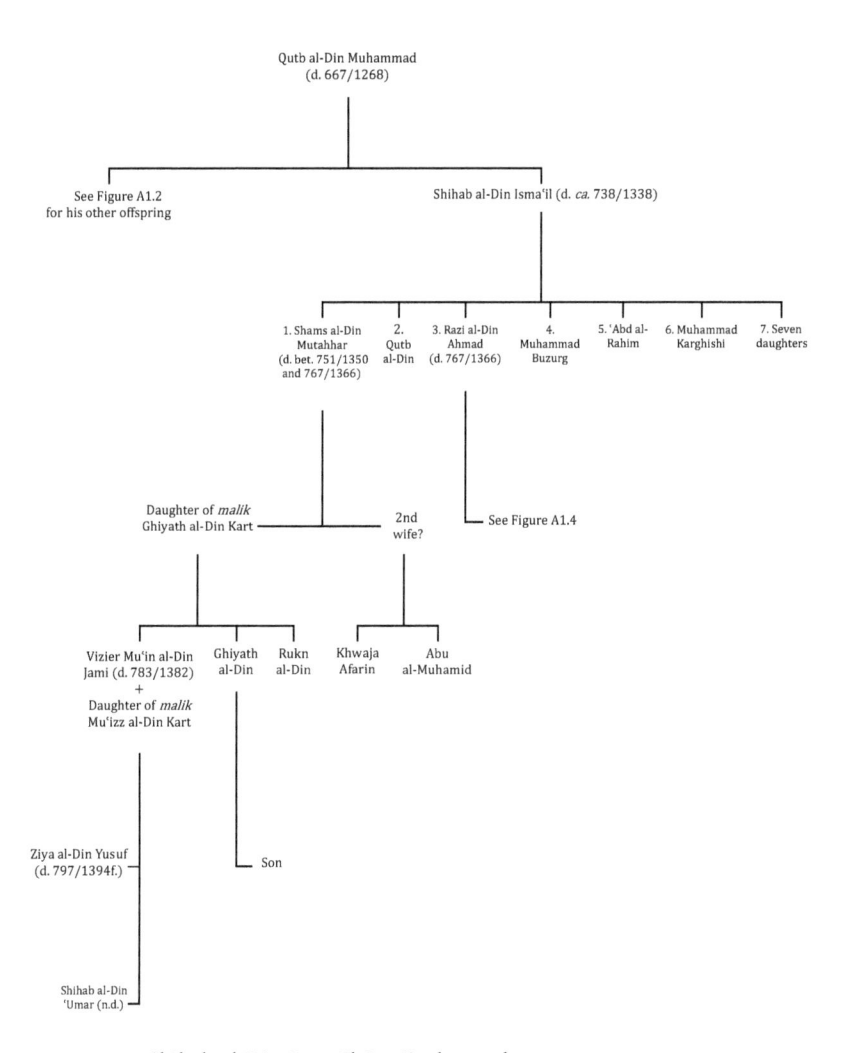

FIGURE A1.3 Shihab al-Din Isma'il Jami's descendants

230 Appendix 1

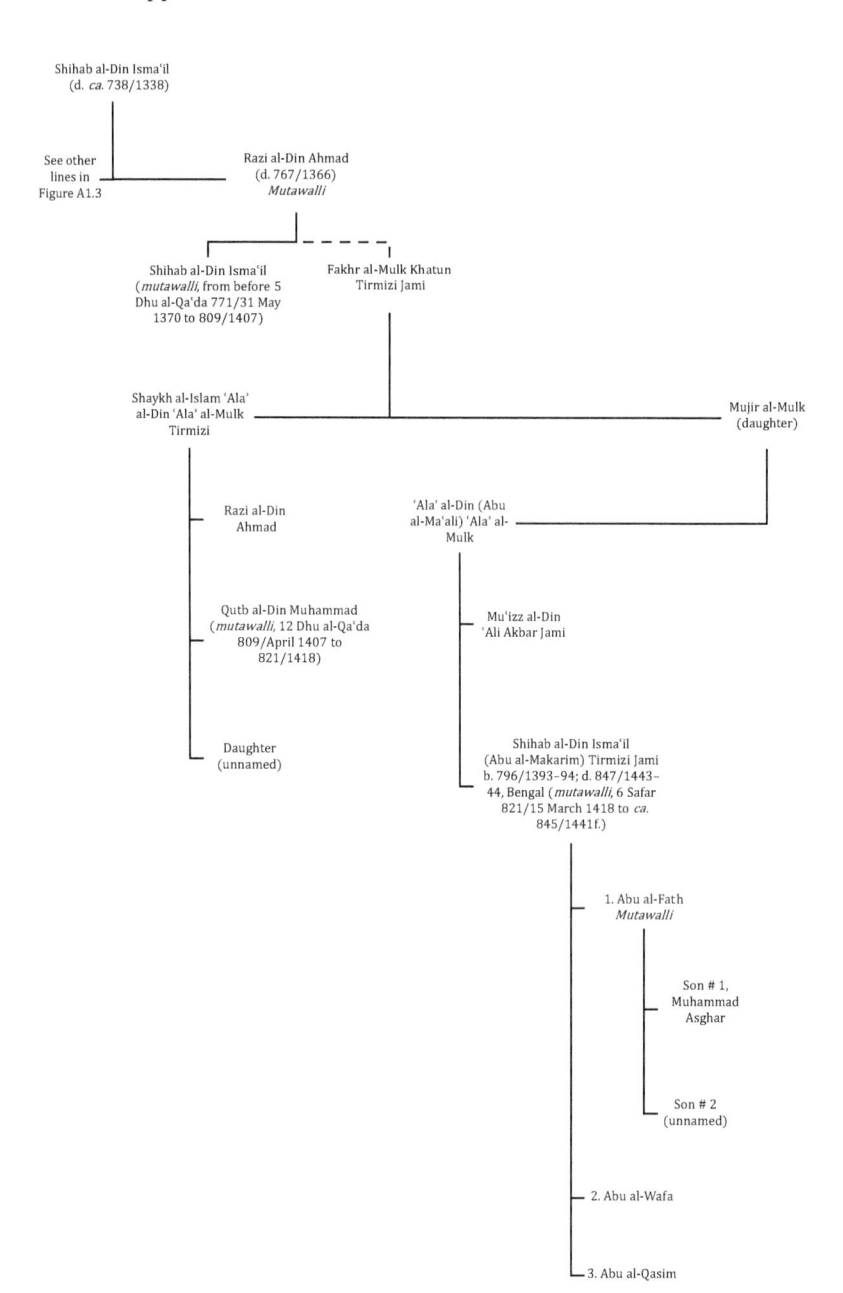

```
Shihab al-Din Isma'il
(d. ca. 738/1338)
│
├── See other lines in Figure A1.3
│
└── Razi al-Din Ahmad
    (d. 767/1366)
    Mutawalli
    │
    ├── Shihab al-Din Isma'il
    │   (mutawalli, from before 5
    │   Dhu al-Qa'da 771/31 May
    │   1370 to 809/1407)
    │
    └──── Fakhr al-Mulk Khatun
          Tirmizi Jami
          │
          ├── Shaykh al-Islam 'Ala' al-Din 'Ala' al-Mulk Tirmizi
          │   │
          │   ├── Razi al-Din Ahmad
          │   │
          │   ├── Qutb al-Din Muhammad
          │   │   (mutawalli, 12 Dhu al-Qa'da
          │   │   809/April 1407 to 821/1418)
          │   │
          │   └── Daughter (unnamed)
          │
          └── Mujir al-Mulk (daughter)
              │
              └── 'Ala' al-Din (Abu al-Ma'ali) 'Ala' al-Mulk
                  │
                  ├── Mu'izz al-Din 'Ali Akbar Jami
                  │
                  └── Shihab al-Din Isma'il
                      (Abu al-Makarim) Tirmizi Jami
                      b. 796/1393-94; d. 847/1443-44,
                      Bengal (mutawalli, 6 Safar
                      821/15 March 1418 to ca.
                      845/1441f.)
                      │
                      ├── 1. Abu al-Fath Mutawalli
                      │   │
                      │   ├── Son # 1, Muhammad Asghar
                      │   │
                      │   └── Son # 2 (unnamed)
                      │
                      ├── 2. Abu al-Wafa
                      │
                      └── 3. Abu al-Qasim
```

FIGURE A1.4 Tentative reconstruction of Transoxiana branch of Jami family

Appendix 1

```
                    ┌─────────────────────────────┴──────────────────────────────┐
         Malik Ghiyath al-Din                                        Jami (d. ca. 738/1338)
            Muhammad Kart                                               Shaykh al-Islam
              (d. 729/1329)                                          Shihab al-Din Isma'il
    ┌──────────────┬──────────────┬──────────────┐            ┌──────────────┬──────────────┐
 Sons: Shams al-Din   Son: Mu'izz al-Din   Daughter ◄┄┄   Shams al-Din         Other
 Muhammad (d. ca. 730/1330)  Muhammad Kart                    Mutahhar          children
 Hafiz (d. ca. 732/1332)    (d. 771/1370)              (d. bet. 751/1350    (see Figure A1.3)
 Muhammad Baqir                                        and 767/1366)
 (fl. 753/1353)
```

Sons: Shams al-Din Muhammad (d. ca. 730/1330) Hafiz (d. ca. 732/1332) Muhammad Baqir (fl. 753/1353)

Son: Mu'izz al-Din Muhammad Kart (d. 771/1370)

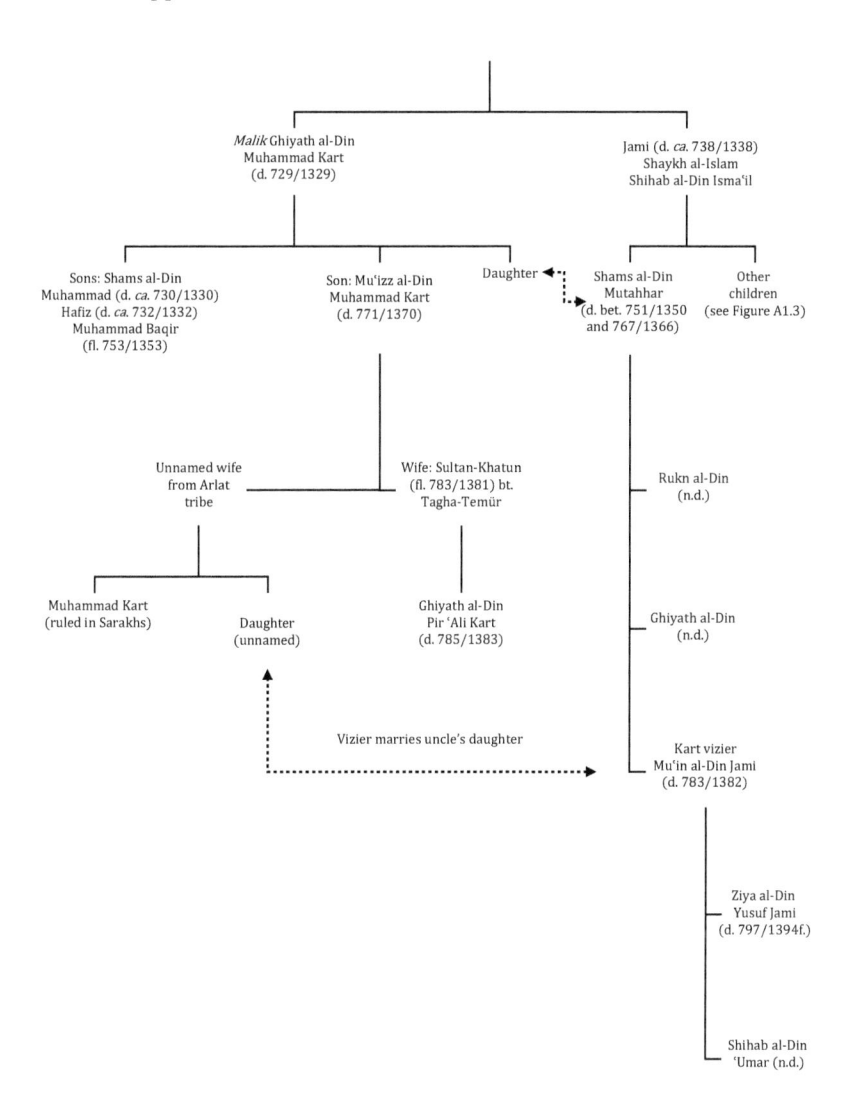

- Unnamed wife from Arlat tribe
- Wife: Sultan-Khatun (fl. 783/1381) bt. Tagha-Temür

Children:
- Muhammad Kart (ruled in Sarakhs)
- Daughter (unnamed)
- Ghiyath al-Din Pir 'Ali Kart (d. 785/1383)

Shams al-Din Mutahhar line:
- Rukn al-Din (n.d.)
- Ghiyath al-Din (n.d.)
- Kart vizier Mu'in al-Din Jami (d. 783/1382)
  - Ziya al-Din Yusuf Jami (d. 797/1394f.)
  - Shihab al-Din 'Umar (n.d.)

Vizier marries uncle's daughter

FIGURE A1.5 Jami family marriage ties to the Kart dynasty of Herat

Appendix 2 Khwajagan-Naqshbandi *Silsila* and Jami Sufis

Sa'd al-Din Kashghari (d. 858/1455) was an active recruiter for the Khwajagan in Herat.[1] His Khwajagan precedessors, namely, the progeny of 'Ala' al-Din Attar (d. 802/1400), had prepared the ground in Herat.[2] Jami Sufis first came into contact with the Khwajagan when one of Ahmad's most notable devotees, Zayn al-Din Taybadi (d. 791/1389), hosted Baha' al-Din Naqshband (d. 791/1389) as he passed through Khurasan on his way to Mecca.[3]

Figure A2.1 is a reconstruction of Kashghari's initiatic lines based on multiple sources.[4] Jami oral history avers that many Jamis were attracted to the Khwajagan path; however, the literary sources offer few links that corroborate this claim. 'Aziz-Allah Jami is the only firm connection to Ahmad-i Jam's bloodlines. Pir 'Ali Jami's pedigree is unclear. Shihab al-Din Ahmad Birjandi is a putative connection because the story surrounding his birth reflects a familiar Jami topos: Birjandi's father dreamed of Ahmad-i Jam, who bade him: "you must name [the baby] after us because he is one of us."[5] A later parallel topos is Ahmad-i Jam's night appearance to Humayun announcing the conception of the Mughal emperor Akbar the Great.

Kashghari's role in shaping Khwajagan-Naqshbandi history is considerable. 'Abd al-Rahman Jami is Kashghari's most famous adept. Jami accepted only a few adepts, and helped popularize the Khawajagan, in part through his *Nafahat al-uns*; in part through a guide, *The Primary Tenets of the Khwajagan Order*,[6] which

---

[1] Paul, "Khwajagan-Naqshbandiyya," 71–86.   [2] Paul, "Khwajagan at Herat," 217–50.
[3] Anon./Gusha-Gir (ed.), *Maqamat-i Taybadi*, 57–58; Jami, *Nafahat*, 499–500.
[4] Kashifi, *Rashahat*, et passim; al-Qazwini, *Silsilanama*, fol. 14b–19b; Buzjani/Moayyad (ed.), *Rawzat*, 124–33; 'Ali Akbar Husayni Ardistani, *Majma' al-awliya'* (London: British Library, Ethé 645), fol. 398b–415b; Muhammad Baqir, *Tarikh-i ghariba* (London: British Library, Ethé 636), fol. 3a–8b. See Appendix 3 regarding the manuscripts.
[5] Wa'iz Kashifi, *Rashahat*, 1:302; see also Manz, *Timurid Iran*, 227.
[6] Jami, *Tariqa-yi Khwajagan*.

Appendix 2

```
Sa'd al-Din Kashghari
    │
    ├──────────────────────── Jami lines
    │       ┌────────────────────┬───────────────────┐
    │   Shihab al-Din         Pir 'Ali Jami      'Aziz-Allah Jami
    │   Ahmad Birjandi
    │   (putative Jami)
    │
    ├──────────────────────── 'Abd al-Rahman Jami
    │       ┌────────────────────┬───────────────────┐
    │   Shahidi Qummi      Ziya al-Din Yusuf Jami   'Abd al-Ghafur Lari
    │                      ('Abd al-Rahman's son)
    │
    ├──────────────────────── Other disciples
    │                       ├── Muhammad Jami
    │                       │   ('Abd al-Rahman's brother)
    │                       │
    │                       ├── Shams al-Din Muhammad Ruji
    │                       │   (has spiritual lines in
    │                       │   Herat, Marw, and Fars)
    │                       │
    │                       ├── 'Ala' al-Din Abizi Quhistani
    │                       │   (his adept wrote
    │                       │   Rawzat al-salikin)
    │                       │
    │                       ├── Hafiz Isma'il Ruji
    │                       │
    │                       ├── Ahmad Karizi
    │                       │
    │                       ├── 'Ala' al-Din Kirmani
    │                       │
    │                       ├── 'Ala' al-Din Maktub
    │                       │   (has spiritual lines)
    │                       │
    │                       └── Has spiritual lines in
    │                           Kashan and Qazvin
    │
    └──────────────────────── Kashghari's sons
            ┌────────────────────┬────────────────────┐
        Muhammad Akbar                        Muhammad Asghar
        (Khwaja Kullan)                       (Khwaja Khurd)
```

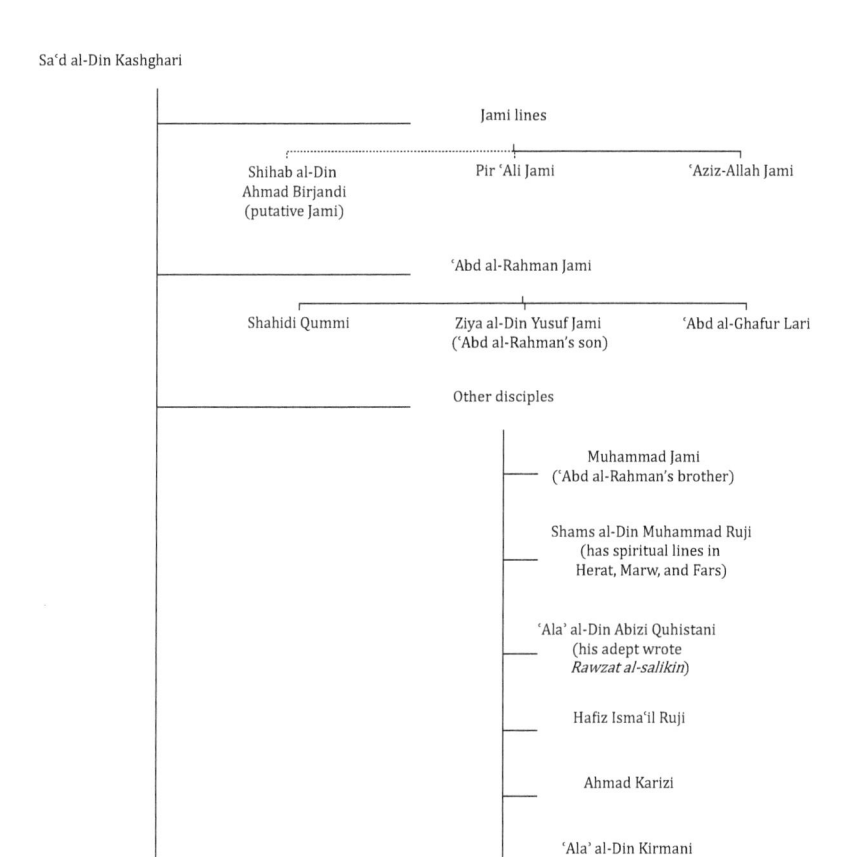

FIGURE A2.1 Kashghari's novitiates

simplified concepts, helping novices to focus on three of the eleven Khwajagan-Naqshbandiyya doctrines.[7]

---

[7] On the eleven doctrines, see Weismann, *Naqshbandiyya*, 25–30.

'Abd al-Ghafur Lari wrote the *Takmila*, "completion" of the *Nafahat al-uns*.[8] Shams al-Din Muhammad Ruji's adept, Fakhr al-Din 'Ali, wrote the *Rashahat-i 'ayn al-hayat*. In addition to spiritual lines in Iran, Kashghari had lines in Central Asia.

---

[8] Razi al-Din 'Abd al-Ghafur Lari, *Takmila-yi hawashi-i nafahat al-uns*, ed. 'Ali Asghar Bashir Harawi (Kabul: Anjuman-i Jami, 1343/1964).

Appendix 3 Bibliographical Survey

AHMAD-I JAM'S WRITINGS

A discussion by Heshmat Moayyad and Franklin Lewis about Ahmad-i Jam's writings is in *The Colossal Elephant and His Spiritual Feats*.[1] A discussion on the sources relating to Ahmad-i Jam and his heirs is in John Dechant's dissertation.[2]

Ahmad-i Jam authored fourteen books according to the author of the *Khulāṣat al-Maqāmāt* (see below), who provides the year of composition and details for each title.[3] A volume of poetry, *Dīwān-i Shaykh Aḥmad-i Jām*, has survived,[4] but doubts persist as to the authorship of select poems. Only seven of Ahmad's prose works have survived: *Miftāḥ al-najāt*,[5] *Uns al-tā'ibīn*,[6] *Rawżat al-muznibīn*,[7] *Kunūz al-ḥikmah*,[8] *Biḥār al-ḥaqīqah*,[9] *Sirāj al-sā'irīn*,[10] and *Risāla al-*

---

[1] Moayyad and Lewis, *Colossal Elephant*, 28–40.
[2] John Dechant, "The 'Colossal Elephant' Shaykh Ahmad-i Jam: Legacy and Hagiography in Islam" (unpublished PhD diss., Indiana University, 2015), 17–27.
[3] Muḥammad Riżā Shafī'ī Kadkanī, *Darwīsh-i sitīhandah: az mīrās-i 'irfānī-i Shaykh-i Jām* (Tehran: Intishārāt-i sukhan, 1393/2014), 184–88; Shihāb al-Dīn b. 'Alā' al-Mulk [Tirmizi] Jami, *Khulāṣat al-maqāmāt-i ḥażrat-i fīl subḥān*, ed. Ḥasan Naṣīrī Jāmī (Tehran: Pizhūhishgāh-i 'ulūm-i insānī wa muṭāla'āt-i farhangī, 1397/2018), 27–31.
[4] Aḥmad-i Jām, *Dīwān-i Shaykh Aḥmad-i Jām* (Tehran: Nashriyāt-i mā, 1365/1986).
[5] Aḥmad-i Jām, *Miftāḥ al-najāt*, ed. 'Alī Fāżil (Tehran: Pizhūhishgāh-i 'ulūm-i insānī wa muṭāla'āt-i farhangī, 1373/1994).
[6] Aḥmad-i Jām, *Uns al-tā'ibīn*, ed. 'Alī Fāżil (Tehran: Intishārāt-i Ṭūs, 1368/1989).
[7] Aḥmad-i Jām, *Rawżat al-muznibīn wa jannat al-mushtāqīn*, ed. 'Alī Fāżil (Tehran: Pizhūhishgāh-i 'ulūm-i insānī wa muṭāla'āt-i farhangī, 1372/1993).
[8] Aḥmad-i Jām, *Kunūz al-ḥikmah*, ed. 'Alī Fāżil (Tehran: Pizhūhishgāh-i 'ulūm-i insānī wa muṭāla'āt-i farhangī, 1387/2008).
[9] Aḥmad-i Jām, *Biḥār al-ḥaqīqah*, ed. Ḥasan Naṣīrī Jāmī (Tehran: Pizhūhishgāh-i 'ulūm-i insānī wa muṭāla'āt-i farhangī, 1389/2010).
[10] Aḥmad-i Jām, *Sirāj al-sā'irīn*, ed. Ḥasan Naṣīrī Jāmī (Tehran: Pizhūhishgāh-i 'ulūm-i insānī wa muṭāla'āt-i farhangī, 1389/2010).

Samarqandiyya.[11] A translation of the last title, *Epistle to the Samarqandians*, is in Heshmat Moayyad and Franklin Lewis, *The Colossal Elephant*.[12]

WORKS BY AHMAD-I JAM'S DESCENDANTS

Early descendants of Ahmad contributed their views on his legacy and Sufi path.

(1) *Risāla dar isbāt-i buzūrgī-yi Shaykh-i Jām* (*Treatise to Prove the Greatness of the Shaykh of Jām*),[13] by Aḥmad's youngest son, Shihāb al-Dīn Ismaʿil (d.*ca.* 617/1220).

(2) *Ḥadīqat al-ḥaqīqah* (*Enclosed Garden of Truth*) by Aḥmad-i Jam's grandson, Quṭb al-Dīn Muḥammad (d. 667/1268). An edition based on one manuscript was published in 1964.[14] Dr. Ḥasan Naṣīrī Jāmī accessed several manuscripts for his 2011 edition.[15]

(3) The *Khulāṣat al-Maqāmāt*,[16] by Shihāb al-Dīn (Abū al-Makārim) b. ʿAlāʾ al-Mulk Tirmizī Jāmī. Hitherto, a lithograph of *Khulāṣat al-Maqāmāt* from Lahore was the principal source; however, when Professor Shafīʿī Kadkanī published his exposition on Aḥmad-i Jam, *Darwīsh-i sitīhandah* (*The Bellicose Mystic*),[17] he included a superb critical edition of *Khulāṣat al-Maqāmāt* based on eight recensions,[18] including the Lahore text.[19] An edition of *Khulāṣat al-Maqāmāt* by Ḥasan Naṣīrī Jāmī, long delayed, appeared in 1397/2018.[20]

The *Khulāṣat al-Maqāmāt* draws on a "lost" *maqāmāt* about Aḥmad-i Jām by Aḥmad Turkhastānī. The *Khulāṣat* references works by Tāj al-Dīn Maḥmūd Būzjānī, and Zayn al-Dīn (Abū Bakr) Taybādī (d. 791/1389).[21] Zayn al-Dīn Taybādī was associated with the Kartid-era Jamis. Shafīʿī Kadkanī doubts that Turkhastānī even existed.[22] He also postulates that the author of the *Maqāmāt-i*

---

[11] Aḥmad-i Jām, *Risāla al-Samarqandiyya*, ed. Ḥasan Naṣīrī Jāmī (Tehran: Pizhūhishgāh-i ʿulūm-i insānī wa muṭālaʿāt-i farhangī, 1396/2017). Recension included in Ghaznawī, *Maqāmāt-i Zhanda-Pīl*, 329–47.

[12] Moayyad and Lewis, *Colossal Elephant*, 423–41 (translation of the *Epistle*).

[13] Shihāb al-Dīn Ismāʿīl b. Aḥmad Jāmī, *Risāla dar isbāt-i buzurgī-yi Shaykh-i Jām*, ed. Ḥasan Naṣīrī Jāmī (Tehran: Pizhūhishgāh-i ʿulūm-i insānī wa muṭālaʿāt-i farhangī, 1391/2012).

[14] Quṭb al-Dīn Muḥammad b. Shams al-Dīn Muṭahhar b. Aḥmad-i Jām, *Ḥadīqat al-ḥaqīqah*, ed. Muḥammad ʿAlī Muwaḥḥid (Tehran: Bungāh-i tarjuma wa nashr-i kitāb, 1343/1964).

[15] Quṭb al-Dīn Muḥammad b. Shams al-Dīn Muṭahhar b. Aḥmad-i Jām, *Ḥadīqat al-ḥaqīqah*, ed. Ḥasan Naṣīrī Jāmī (Tehran: Pizhūhishgāh-i ʿulūm-i insānī wa muṭālaʿāt-i farhangī, 1390/2011).

[16] Shihāb al-Dīn (Abū al-Makārim) b. ʿAlāʾ al-Mulk [Tirmizī] Jāmī, *Khulāṣat al-maqāmāt-i ḥażrat-i fīl subḥān* (Lahore: Muḥammad Jalāl al-Dīn, 1335/1916–17).

[17] Shafīʿī Kadkanī, *Darwīsh*.

[18] Ibid., 159–418 (annotated text of the *Khulāṣat al-maqāmāt*).

[19] Shafīʿī Kadkanī, *Darwīsh*, 151–57 (discussion on the sources).

[20] Jāmī/Jāmī (ed.), *Khulāṣat*.   [21] Shafīʿī Kadkanī, *Darwīsh*, 176.   [22] Ibid., 73–75.

Appendix 3

Taybādī (*The Spiritual Feats of [Zayn al-Dīn] Taybādī*), a Timurid-era hagiography, was Būzjānī.[23]

HAGIOGRAPHIES

The best-known hagiology of Ahmad-i Jam is *Maqāmāt-i Zhanda-Pīl* (*The Spiritual Feats of the Furious Elephant*),[24] and translated by Heshmat Moayyad and Franklin Lewis. *Maqāmāt-i Taybādī* includes information on the Jami shaykhs.[25] The *Nafaḥāt al-uns* (*Breaths of Intimacy*) of ʿAbd al-Raḥman Jāmī has multiple notices for Jāmī shaykhs.[26]

EPISTOLARY COLLECTIONS (*INSHĀʾ*)

Inshāʾ are chancery documents and correspondence. The *Farāʾid-i Ghīyāṣī* by Jalāl al-Dīn Yūsuf-i Ahl Jāmī is an important source on Jami history. He compiled letters by or to his illustrious ancestors; for example, letters to Seljuq sultan Sanjar, Tamerlane, and the Delhi Sultans. It is a collection of 654 (possibly more) unique documents. Two volumes, totalling 318 letters, were published in 1977 and 1979 by Professor Heshmat Moayyad.[27] The remainder, 336 (or more) documents, remain in manuscript. There were six known manuscripts when Moayyad prepared his index.[28]

The *Farāʾid-i Ghīyāṣī* has ten chapters (*bāb*), each of which is a class of document;[29] for example, letters to sultans; chapters on letters to judges (sing. *qāḍī*), notables (*nuqabaʾ*); dispatch of congratulations and condolences. Most of the letters are composed in ornate styles, with rhymed prose (*sajʿ*) and poetry,

---

[23] Ibid., 75–78.
[24] Sadīd al-Dīn Ghaznawī, *Maqāmāt-i Zhanda-Pīl*, ed. H. Moayyad (Tehran: Intishārāt-i ʿilmī wa farhangī [Bungāh-i tarjuma wa nashr-i kitāb], 1388/2009 [reprint of 1340/1961 ed.]).
[25] Anonymous [Tāj al-Dīn Maḥmūd Būzjānī?], *Maqāmāt-i Taybādī*, ed. Sayyid ʿAlāʾ al-Dīn Gūsha-Gīr (Dizfūl [Khūzistān]: Intishārāt-i afhām, 1382/2003); Anonymous [Tāj al-Dīn Maḥmūd Būzjānī?], *Malfūẓ-i Ḥażrat Shaykh Zayn al-Dīn Taybādī* (Oxford: Bodleian Ms. Ind. Inst. Pers. 46).
[26] ʿAbd al-Raḥmān Jāmī, *Nafaḥāt al-uns min ḥażarāt al-quds*, ed. Mehdī Tawḥīdī-Pūr (Tehran: Kitāb-furūshī-yi Maḥmūdī, 1336/1957); ʿAbd al-Raḥmān Jāmī, *Nafaḥāt al-uns min ḥażarāt al-quds*, ed. Mahmud ʿĀbadī (Tehran: Intishārāt-i iṭṭalāʿāt, 1382/2003).
[27] Yūsuf-i Ahl [Jāmī], *Farāʾid-i Ghīyāṣī*, ed. Heshmat Moayyad (Tehran: Intishārāt-i bunyād-i farhang-i Īrān, vol. I, 1356/1977; vol. II, 1358/1979). Moayyad prepared a four-volume set of the 654 documents for Asatir Publications (*Intishārāt-i Asāṭīr*), Tehran, ca. 2004; however, the publisher has yet to honor the agreement. My last query to Asatir's management on the status of the MS elicited a response on 10 June 2020 that there are no immediate plans to publish it. The Jami community is seeking to purchase the MS from Asatir.
[28] See Yūsuf-i Ahl/Moayyad (ed.), *Farāʾid-i Ghīyāṣī*, 1:xxxix–lxi.
[29] See discussion in Gottfried Herrmann, "Zur Institulatio timuridischer Urkunden," *ZDMG*, Supp. II, XVIII (1972): 498–521.

interspersed with hadith and Qur'an fragments. They delight scholars of Persian literature, but dismay historians who must wade through muck in search of gems. The most important material (for historians) is in *Bāb* 7: Decrees. Included are edicts by Öljeitü, Kart *malik*s, Temür, Shāh Rukh, and others relating to immunities, grants, and confirmations for shrine *mutawallī*s. Not every manuscript is complete. Tehran 4756,[30] and Fatih 4012,[31] are near to complete. Berlin Ms. Orient. Fol. 110[32] is ostensibly complete (it appears to be the author's personal copy). However, since the Berlin MS is written in an atrocious "experimental *nasta'līq*" script (according to Dr. Saqib Baburi of the British Library), it is difficult to decipher.

Recueil de documents diplomatiques, de lettres et de pièces littéraires is an eclectic corpus of correspondence, *farmān*s, and *soyūrghāl*s in manuscript. It includes documents relating to the Jami Sufis.[33] The corpus was described in vapid terms by Edgar Blochet;[34] however, it is a goldmine for historians. The manuscript was composed in the sixteenth century (or latest, seventeenth century), in western Iran. Includes documents from the Mongols to Safavids, and regional Iranian dynasties. Select letters and decrees were published by Dr. 'Abd al-Ḥusayn Nawā'ī.[35] Two compendia of *inshā'* with Jami material are *Manshā' al-inshā'* (edited by Dr. Humāyūn-Farrukh),[36] and *Asnād wa nāmah-hā-yi tārīkhī* (edited by Dr. S̱ābitī).[37]

PROSOPOGRAPHIES AND MISCELLANEOUS SOURCES

Rawżat al-Riyāḥīn (*Garden of Sweet Herbs*), a prosopography and hagiology, was completed by 929/1523, which is when the author, 'Alī Būzjānī, expired.[38] Būzjānī was a devotee of Ahmad-i Jam and disciple of the Jami-Naqshbandi Sufi 'Azīz-Allāh Jāmī (d. 902/1497), who was initiated by Sa'd al-Dīn Kāshgharī (d. 858/1455), who also initiated 'Abd al-Raḥman Jāmī. A new edition of *Rawżat al-Riyāḥīn* appeared in 2018.[39]

---

[30] Tehran 4756 (Tehran: Central Library of the University of Tehran).
[31] Fatih 4012 (Istanbul: Süleymaniye Kütüphanesi).
[32] Berlin: Staatsbibliothek zu Berlin. W. Pertsch, *Verzeichniss der Persischen Handschriften der Königlichen Bibliothek zu Berlin* (Berlin: A. Asher & Co., 1888), 1010–11, Cat. No. 1060.
[33] Anonymous, *Recueil de documents diplomatiques, de lettres et de pièces littéraires* (Paris: Bibliothèque nationale de France, MS Supplément persan 1815).
[34] Edgar Blochet, *Catalogue des manuscrits persans de la Bibliothèque Nationale*, 4 vols. (Paris: Bibliothèque Nationale, 1905–34), 4:277–79; Catalogue No. 2336.
[35] 'Abd al-Ḥusayn Nawā'ī (ed.), *Asnād wa mukātibāt-i tārīkh-i Īrān: az Tīmūr tā Shāh Ismā'īl* (Tehran: Bungāh-i tarjuma wa nashr-i kitāb, 1341/1963).
[36] Niżām al-Dīn 'Abd al-Wāsi' Niżāmī [Niżāmī Bakhārzī], *Manshā' al-inshā'*, ed. Rukn al-Dīn Humāyūn-Farrukh (Tehran: Dānishgāh-i millī-yi Īrān, 1357/1978f.).
[37] 'Alī Mu'ayyid S̱ābitī (ed.), *Asnād wa nāmah-hā-yi tārīkhī* (Tehran: Ṭahūrī, 1346/1967).
[38] Darwīsh 'Alī Būzjānī, *Rawżat al-Riyāḥīn*, ed. Heshmat Moayyad (Tehran: Bungāh-i tarjuma wa nashr-i kitāb, 1345/1966).
[39] Darwīsh 'Alī Būzjānī, *Rawżat al-Riyāḥīn*, ed. Ḥasan Naṣīrī Jāmī (Tehran: Pizhūhishgāh-i 'ulūm-i insānī wa muṭāla'āt-i farhangī, 1396/2017).

Numerous studies on Ahmad have appeared in recent decades, particularly by Dr. ʿAlī Fāżil (d. 1382/2004).[40] Fāżil, like Heshmat Moayyad (d. 2018), became fascinated with Ahmad-i Jam and his oeuvre. Both did much to bring Ahmad's writings to light.

An invaluable resource is the prosopography by Ibrāhīm Zanganah, *Sarzamīn-i Jām wa rijāl ān (Jām Region and Its Eminent Peoples)*.[41] It is a quasi-primary source: his bibliography lists eighty-nine different sources, including the *Maqāmāt-i Awlād-i Shaykh-i Jām (The Spiritual Feats of the Progeny of the Shaykh of Jām)*, but for which Zanganah failed to provide a citation. ʿAlī Būzjānī relied on a volume with this title for *Rawżat al-Riyāḥīn*. Mr. Nasir al-Din Qiwam Ahmadi, director of the shrine's library, was unable to locate this title.

Jami devotees published their own interpretations of Ahmad-i Jam's legacy. Many works are deemed lost, although periodically one will surface, like the anonymous versified *Maqāmāt-i Zhanda-Pīl*.[42] In recent years, publications by devotees of Ahmad-i Jam, on topics from ʿirfān, tafsīr, fiqh, al-Qurʾān, and ḥadīth, have proliferated.[43] Noteworthy books include two by Yaʿqūb Nidāʾī.[44] Dr. Ḥasan Jāmī has picked up Fāżil's baton and continues the labors of editing manuscripts. He has also published on the music of Jām.[45]

NAQSHBANDI-JAMI LITERATURE

An illustrated spiritual genealogy by Nūr al-Dīn al-Qazwīnī reveals links between Jamis and the Khwājagān-Naqshbandī through Saʿd al-Dīn Kāshgharī.[46] Kāshifī's *Rashaḥāt-i ʿayn al-ḥayāt* is a resource,[47] although its foci are the *ṭarīqa*'s luminar-

---

[40] ʿAlī Fāżil, *Kār-nāma-yi Aḥmad-i Jām* (Tehran: Intishārāt-i Ṭūs, 1383/2004); ʿAlī Fāżil, *Sharḥ-i aḥwāl wa naqd wa taḥlīl-i āsār-i Aḥmad Jām* (Tehran: Intishārāt-i Tūs, 1373/1994); ʿAlī Fāżil, *Az jām-i Shaykh-i Jām: guzīdah-i āsār-i Shaykh-i Jām* (Tehran: Intishārāt-i sukhan, 1376/1997).

[41] Ibrāhīm Zanganah, *Sarzamīn-i Jām wa rijāl ān* (Turbat-i Jām: Intishārāt-i Shaykh al-Islām Aḥmad-i Jām, 1384/2006).

[42] Anonymous, *Maqāmāt-i manẓūm-i Shaykh-i Jām (Zhanda-Pīl)*, ed. Ḥasan Naṣīrī Jāmī (Tehran: Pizhūhishgāh-i ʿulūm-i insānī wa muṭālaʿāt-i farhangī, 1391/2012).

[43] These items are best located in the catalogue for the National Library and Archives of the I. R. of Iran (www.nlai.ir/). They do not always appear in WorldCat.

[44] Yaʿqūb Nidāʾī Aḥmadī, *Dīdgāh-hā-yi ʿirfānī-yi Shaykh-i Jām* (Mashhad: Dastūr, 1391/2011); Yaʿqūb Nidāʾī Aḥmadī, *Manāzil wa maqāmāt* (Mashhad: Dastūr, 1393/2014). He recently published *Jughrāfiyā-yi tārīkhī-yi Jām* (Mashhad: Dastūr, 1398/2019).

[45] Ḥasan Naṣīrī Jāmī, *Taḥlīl-i sakhtār wa darūnamāyah-i tarānah-hā-yi kuhan-i sharqī: bar asās-i tarānah-hā-yi Jām* (Mashhad: Intishārāt-i muḥaqqiq, 1380/2002).

[46] Nūr al-Dīn Muḥammad al-Qazwīnī, *Silsila-nāma-yi Khwājagān-i Naqshband* (Paris: Bibliothèque Nationale de France, Supplément persan 1418). There are multiple recensions at the Süleymaniye Kütüphanesi in Istanbul; for example, Esad Efendi 1487, Lala Ismail 155, Laleli 1381, and Sehid Ali Pasa 2893.

[47] Fakhr al-Dīn ʿAlī b. Ḥusayn Wāʿiẓ-i Kāshifī, *Rashaḥāt-i ʿayn al-ḥayāt*, 2 vols., ed. ʿAlī Aṣghar Muʿīniyān (Tehran: Bunyād-i nīkūkārī-i nūriyānī, 1356/1977).

ies. Propospographies in manuscript (see Hermann Ethé)[48] with potential include al-Kūrānī's, *Rawżat al-sālikīn*;[49] Bāqir's, *Tārīkh-i gharība*;[50] and Ardistānī's, *Majmaʿ al-awliyāʾ*.[51]

The contributions of ʿAbd al-Raḥman Jāmī and disciple Rażī al-Dīn (ʿAbd al-Ghafūr) Lārī in influencing Jami Sufis is open to further investigation.[52] Jāmī, *The Primary Tenets of the Khwajagan Order*,[53] is discussed in Chapter 9.

SOURCES ON IRANIAN HISTORY

The historical sources are listed in the bibliography. References to Jami shaykhs or Ahmad-i Jam's shrine are scattered in miscellaneous histories and chronicles.

[48] Hermann Ethé, *Catalogue of Persian Manuscripts in the Library of the India Office*, 2 vols. (Oxford: vol. I, India Office, 1903; vol. II, Clarendon Press, 1937).
[49] Ibid., 1:260–61; Catalogue No. Ethé 632 (access as I.O. Islamic 698).
[50] Ibid., 262–63; Catalogue No. Ethé 636 (access as I.O. Islamic 1426).
[51] Ibid., 270–74; Catalogue No. Ethé 645 (access as I.O. Islamic 1647).
[52] Rażī al-Dīn ʿAbd al-Ghafūr Lārī, *Takmila-yi ḥawāshī-i nafaḥāt al-uns*, ed. ʿAlī Aṣghar Bashīr Harawī (Kabul: Intishārāt-i anjuman-i Jāmī, 1343/1964).
[53] ʿAbd al-Raḥman Jāmī, *Sar-rishta-i ṭarīqa-yi Khwājagān*, ed. ʿAbd al-Ḥayy Ḥabībī (Kabul: Intishārāt-i anjuman-i Jāmī, 1343/1964).

Bibliography

PRIMARY SOURCES (INCLUDES TRANSLATIONS, COMPILATIONS, AND TRAVELOGUES)

Abu al-Fazl. *The History of Akbar.* 3 vols. Ed. and trans. Wheeler Thackston. Cambridge, MA: Harvard University Press, 2015. (Persian and English texts.)
Abu Ruh Lutfallah b. Abi Saʿid. *Halat wa sukhanan-i Abu Saʿid-i Abu al-Khayr.* Ed. Muhammad Riza Shafiʿi Kadkani. Tehran: Intisharat-i sukhan, 1384/2005.
Ahmad-i Jam. *Bihar al-haqiqah.* Ed. Hasan Nasiri Jami. Tehran: Pizhuhishgah-i ʿulum-i insani wa mutalaʿat-i farhangi, 1389/2010–11.
Ahmad-i Jam. *Diwan-i Shaykh Ahmad-i Jam.* Tehran: Nashriyat-i ma, 1365/1986.
Ahmad-i Jam. *Kunuz al-hikmah.* Ed. ʿAli Fazil. Tehran: Pizhuhishgah-i ʿulum-i insani wa mutalaʿat-i farhangi, 1387/2008.
Ahmad-i Jam. *Miftah al-najat.* Ed. ʿAli Fazil. Tehran: Pizhuhishgah-i ʿulum-i insani wa mutalaʿat-i farhangi, 1373/1994.
Ahmad-i Jam. *Rawzat al-muznibin wa jannat al-mushtaqin.* Ed. ʿAli Fazil. Tehran: Pizhuhishgah-i ʿulum-i insani wa mutalaʿat-i farhangi, 1372/1993.
Ahmad-i Jam. *Siraj al-saʾirin.* Ed. Hasan Nasiri Jami. Tehran: Pizhuhishgah-i ʿulum-i insani wa mutalaʿat-i farhangi, 1389/2010.
Ahmad-i Jam. *Uns al-taʾibin.* Ed. ʿAli Fazil. Tehran: Intisharat-i Tus, 1368/1989.
ʿAli, ʿAbdullah Yusuf. *The Meaning of the Holy Qurʾan.* 11th ed. Beltsville, MD: Amana, 2004.
Amin, Munshi Muhammad Kazim b. Muhammad. *ʿAlamgir Nama.* Ed. Khadim Husayn and ʿAbd al-Hayy. Calcutta: Royal Asiatic Society, 1868.
Angha, Nahid. *Stations of the Sufi Path: The One Hundred Fields (Sad Maydan) of ʿAbdallah Ansari of Herat.* Cambridge: Archetype, 2010.
Anonymous. *Hudud al-ʿalam.* 2nd ed. Trans. Vladimir Minorsky. Cambridge: E. J. W. Gibb Memorial Trust, 1982.
Anonymous. *Iran Statistical Yearbook.* Tehran: Statistical Center of Iran, 1392/2014.

Bibliography

Anonymous. *Malfuz-i Hazrat Shaykh Zayn al-Din Taybadi*. Oxford: Bodleian Ms. Ind. Inst. Pers. 46.
Anonymous. *Maqamat-i manzum-i Shaykh-i Jam (Zhanda-Pil)*. Ed. Hasan Nasiri Jami. Tehran: Pizhuhishgah-i 'ulum-i insani wa mutala'at-i farhangi, 1391/2012.
Anonymous. *Maqamat-i Taybadi*. Ed. Sayyid 'Ala' al-Din Gusha-Gir. Dizful [Khuzistan]: Intisharat-i afham, 1382/2003.
Anonymous. *Recueil de documents diplomatiques*. Paris: Bibliothèque nationale de France, Supplément persan 1815.
Anonymous. *Tadhkirat al-Muluk: A Manual of Safavid Administration*. Trans. Vladimir Minorsky. Cambridge: E. J. W. Gibb Memorial Trust, 1980.
Ansari, Rafi'a Jabiri. *Mirza Rafi'a's Dastur al-Muluk: A Manual of Later Safavid Administration*. Trans. M. I. Marcinkowski. Kuala Lampur: International Institute of Islamic Thought and Civilization, 2002.
Ansari, Rafi'a Jabiri. *The Dastur al-Moluk: A Safavid State Manual*. Trans. Willem Floor and M. H. Faghfoory. Costa Mesa, CA: Mazda Publishers, 2006.
Ardistani, 'Ali Akbar Husayni. *Majma' al-awliya'*. London: British Library, Ethé 645.
'Attar, Farid al-Din. *Tadhkirat al-awliya'*. Ed. R. A. Nicholson. Tehran: Intisharat-i asatir, 1379/2000.
Babur, Zahir al-Din. *Babur-nama in English*. 2 vols. Trans. Annette S. Beveridge. London: Luzac, 1922.
Babur, Zahir al-Din. *The Baburnama*. Trans. Wheeler Thackston. New York: Modern Library, 2002.
al-Baghdadi, 'Abd al-Qahir. *al-Farq bayn al-firaq*. Ed. Muhammad 'Uthman Khisht. Cairo: Maktabat Ibn Sina, n.d. [1988].
al-Baghdadi, 'Abd al-Qahir. *Moslem Schisms and Sects [al-Farq bayn al-firaq]*. Trans. A. S. Halkin. Philadelphia, PA: Porcupine Press, 1978.
Bakri, Sayyid Muhammad Ma'sum. *Tarikh-i Sind*. Ed. 'Umar b. Muhammad Da'udputah. Tehran: Intisharat-i asatir, 1382/2003.
Baqir, Muhammad. *Tarikh-i ghariba*. London: British Library, Ethé 636.
Baqli, Ruzbihan. *Kashf al-asrar wa mukashafat al-anwar*. Ed. Maryam Husayni. Tehran: Intisharat-i sukhan, 1393/2014.
Baqli, Ruzbihan. *The Unveiling of Secrets*. Trans. Carl Ernst. Chapel Hill, NC: Parvardigar Press, 1997.
Bayazid Bayat. *Tarikh-i Humayun*. In *Three Memoirs of Homayun*. Trans. Wheeler Thackston. Costa Mesa, CA: Mazda Publishers, 2009.
Bayhaqi, Abu al-Fazl Muhammad b. Husayn. *The History of Beyhaqi [Tarikh-i Mas'udi]*. 3 vols. Trans. C. E. Bosworth. Rev. Mohsen Ashtiany. Boston, MA, and London: Ilex, 2011.
al-Bukhari, Salah b. Mubarak. *Anis al-talibin wa 'uddat al-salikin*. Ed. Khalil Ibrahim Sari-Ughli. Tehran: Sazman-i intisharat-i kayhan, 1371/1993.
Buzjani, 'Ali. *Rawzat al-riyahin*. Ed. Heshmat Moayyad. Tehran: Bungah-i tarjuma wa nashr-i kitab, 1345/1966.
Buzjani, 'Ali. *Rawzat al-riyahin*. Ed. Hasan Nasiri Jami. Tehran: Pizhuhishgah-i 'ulum-i insani wa mutala'at-i farhangi, 1396/2017f.
Byron, Robert. *The Road to Oxiana*. London: Pimlico, 2004.

Bibliography

de Khanikoff, Nicholas. *Mémoire sur la partie méridionale de l'Asie centrale*. Paris: Imprimerie de L. Martinet, 1861.

al-Dhahabi, Muhammad b. Ahmad. *al-'Ibar fi khabar man ghabar*. 4 vols. Ed. Abu Hajar Muhammad al-Saʿid b. Basyuni Zaghlul. Beirut: Dar al-kutub al-ʿilmiyya, 1985.

al-Dhahabi, Muhammad b. Ahmad. *Tarikh al-Islam*. 53 vols. Ed. ʿUmar Tadmuri. Beirut: Dar al-kitab al-ʿArabi, 1992–2000.

Dughlat, Mirza Haydar. *Tarikh-i-Rashidi: A History of the Khans of Moghulistan*. In *Classical Writings of the Medieval Islamic World: Persian Histories of the Mongol Dynasties*. 3 vols. Trans. Wheeler Thackston. London: I.B. Tauris, 2012.

Dughlat, Muhammad Haidar. *Tarikh-i Rashidi*. Ed. N. Elias. Trans. E. D. Ross. London: Sampson Low, 1895.

Elgood, Cyril. *A Medical History of Persia and the Eastern Caliphate*. Cambridge: Cambridge University Press, 1951.

al-Farisi, Abu al-Hasan. *al-Mukhtasar min kitab al-siyaq li-tarikh Naysabur*. Ed. Muhammad Kazim al-Mahmudi. Tehran: Miras-i maktub, 1384/2005.

al-Farisi, Abu al-Hasan. *al-Muntakhab min al-siyaq li-tarikh Naysabur*. Ed. Muhammad Ahmad ʿAbd al-ʿAziz. Beirut: Dar al-kutub al-ʿilmiyya, 1989.

Ferrier, J. P. *Caravan Journeys and Wanderings in Persia, Afghanistan, Turkistan and Beloochistan*. Trans. W. Jesse. London: John Murray, 1856.

Fraser, J. B. *Narrative of a Journey into Khorasan*. New Delhi: Oxford University Press, 1984.

al-Ghazali, Abu Hamid. *Ihyaʾ ʿulum al-din*. 10 vols. Jeddah: Dar al-minhaj, 2011.

al-Ghazali, Abu Hamid. *The Remembrance of Death and the Afterlife*. Trans. T. J. Winter. Cambridge: The Islamic Texts Society, 1989.

Ghaznawi, Sadid al-Din. *Maqamat-i Zhanda-Pil*. Ed. Heshmat Moayyad. Tehran: Intisharat-i ʿilmi wa farhangi, 1388/2009.

Gul-Badan Begam. *The History of Humayun*. Trans. Annette S. Beveridge. London: Royal Asiatic Society, 1902.

Gulbadan Begim. *Humayunnama*. In *Three Memoirs of Homayun*. Trans. Wheeler Thackston. Costa Mesa, CA: Mazda Publishers, 2009.

Hafiz-i Abru. *Tarikh-i salatin-i Kart* [*The History of the Kart Kings*]. Ed. Mir-Hashim Muhaddis. Tehran: Markaz-i pizhuhishi-i miras-i maktub, 1389/2010.

Hafiz-i Abru. *Zayl-i jamiʿ al-tawarikh-i Rashidi*. Ed. Khanbaba Bayani. Tehran: Intisharat-i anjuman-i asar-i milli, 1350/1971.

Hafiz-i Abru. *Zubdat al-tawarikh*. 2 vols. Ed. Kamal Hajj Sayyid Jawadi. Tehran: Nashr-i nay, 1372/1993.

al-Harawi, Qasim b. Yusuf Abu Nasr. *Irshad al-ziraʿa* [*Guidance on Agriculture*]. Ed. Muhammad Mushiri. Tehran: Danishgah-yi Tehran, 1346/1968.

al-Harawi, Qasim b. Yusuf Abu Nasr. *Risala-yi tariq-i qismat-i ab-i qulb* [*Treatise on Apportioning Waters through Sluice-gates*]. Ed. Mayil Harawi. Tehran: Intisharat-i bunyad-i farhang-i Iran, 1347/1969.

al-Harawi, Sayf. *Tarikhnamah-yi Harat*. Ed. Ghulam-Riza Tabatabaʾi-Majd. Tehran: Intisharat-i asatir, 1383/2004.

al-Hujwiri, ʿAli. *Kashf al-mahjub*. Trans. R. A. Nicholson. London: Luzac, 1911.

Ibn Athir, *al-Kamil fi al-tarikh*. 10 vols. Ed. Abu al-Fidaʾ ʿAbdallah Qadi. Beirut: Dar al-kutub al-ʿilmiyya, 1987.

Ibn Battuta. *The Travels of Ibn Battuta*. Vol. 3. Trans. H. A. R. Gibb. Cambridge: Cambridge University Press, 1971.
Ibn Munawwar, Muhammad. *Asrar al-tawhid fi maqamat-i Shaykh Abi Sa'id*. 2 vols. Ed. Muhammad Riza Shafi'i Kadkani. Tehran: Agah, 1366–67/1987–88.
al-'Imad, 'Abd al-Hayy b. Ahmad b. *Shadharat al-dhahab fi akhbar man dhahab*. Ed. 'Abd al-Qadir al-Arna'ut and Mahmud al-Arna'ut. Beirut: Dar Ibn Kathir, 1986.
Isfizari, Zamchi. *Rawzat al-jannat fi awsaf-i madinat-i Harat*. 2 vols. Ed. Muhammad Kazim Imam. Tehran: Danishgah-i Tehran, 1338/1959.
Jahangir, Nur al-Din Muhammad. *Jahangir Nama*. Ed. Muhammad Hashim. Tehran: Intisharat-i bunyad-i farhang-i Iran, 1359/1980.
Jami, 'Abd al-Rahman. *Munsha'at-i Jami*. Ed. 'Abd al-'Ali Nur Ahrari. Turbat-i Jam: Intisharat-i Shaykh al-Islam Ahmad-i Jam, 1383/2004.
Jami, 'Abd al-Rahman. *Nafahat al-uns min hazarat al-quds*. Ed. Mehdi Tawhidi-Pur. Tehran: Intisharat-i kitabfurushi-i Mahmudi, 1336/1957.
Jami, 'Abd al-Rahman. *Namaha-yi dastniwis-i Jami*. Ed. 'Asam al-Din Urunbayif and Mayil Harawi. Kabul: Matba'ah-i dawlati, 1364/1985.
Jami, 'Abd al-Rahman. *Sar-rishta-i tariqa-yi Khwajagan*. Ed. 'Abd al-Hayy Habibi. Kabul: Anjuman-i Jami, 1343/1964.
Jami, Hasan Nasiri. *Maktab-i Harat wa shi'r-i Farsi*. Tehran: Intisharat-i mawla, 1393/2014f.
[Jami], Jalal al-Din Yusuf-i Ahl. *Fara'id-i Ghiyasi*. Berlin: Staatsbibliothek zu Berlin, Ms. Orient. Fol. 110.
[Jami], Jalal al-Din Yusuf-i Ahl. *Fara'id-i Ghiyasi*. Ed. Heshmat Moayyad. Tehran: Intisharat-i bunyad-i farhang-i Iran, vol. I, 1356/1977; vol. II, 1358/1979.
[Jami], Jalal al-Din Yusuf-i Ahl. *Fara'id-i Ghiyasi*. Istanbul: Süleymaniye Kütüphanesi, Fatih 4012.
[Jami], Jalal al-Din Yusuf-i Ahl. *Fara'id-i Ghiyasi*. Istanbul: Süleymaniye Kütüphanesi, Aya Sofya 4155.
[Jami], Jalal al-Din Yusuf-i Ahl. *Fara'id-i Ghiyasi*. Tehran: University of Tehran, 4756.
Jami, Qutb al-Din Muhammad. *Hadiqat al-haqiqa*. Ed. Hasan Nasiri Jami. Tehran: Pizhuhishgah-i 'ulum-i insani wa mutal'at-i farhangi, 1390/2011.
[Jami], [Shihab al-Din] Abu al-Makarim b. 'Ala' al-Mulk. *Khulasat al-maqamat-i hazrat-i fil subhan*. Lahore: Muhammad Jalal al-Din, 1335/1916.
[Jami], [Shihab al-Din] Abu al-Makarim b. 'Ala' al-Mulk. *Khulasat al-maqamat-i hazrat-i fil subhan*. In *Darwish-i sitihandah: az miras-i 'irfani-yi Shaykh-i Jam*. Ed. Muhammad Riza Shafi'i Kadkani. Tehran: Intisharat-i sukhan, 1393/2014.
[Jami], [Shihab al-Din] Abu al-Makarim b. 'Ala' al-Mulk. *Khulasat al-maqamat-i hazrat-i fil subhan*. Ed. Hasan Nasiri Jami. Tehran: Pizhuhishgah-i 'ulum-i insani wa mutala'at-i farhangi, 1396/2018.
Jami, Shihab al-Din Isma'il b. Ahmad-i Jam Namaqi. *Risala dar isbat-i buzurgi-yi Shaykh-i Jam*. Ed. Hasan Nasiri Jami. Tehran: Pizhuhishgah-i 'ulum-i insani wa mutala'at-i farhangi, 1391/2012.
Jawhar Aftabachi. *Tazkirat al-waqi'at*. In *Three Memoirs of Homayun*. Trans. Wheeler Thackston. Costa Mesa, CA: Mazda Publishers, 2009.

al-Jawzi, Abu al-Faraj ʿAbd al-Rahman b. ʿAli b. *al-Muntazam fi tarikh al-mulukwa-l-umam*. 19 vols. (incl. index). Ed. Muhammad ʿAbd al-Qadir ʿAta' and Mustafa ʿAbd al-Qadir ʿAta'. Beirut: Dar al-kutub al-ʿilmiyya, 1992.
Juvaini, ʿAla' al-Din ʿAta'-Malik. *The History of the World-Conqueror*. 2 vols. Trans. John Andrew Boyle. Manchester: Manchester University Press, 1958.
al-Kalabadhi, Abu Bakr Muhammad b. Ishaq. *The Doctrine of the Sufis [Kitab al-taʿarruf li-madhhab ahl al-tasawwuf]*. Trans. A. J. Arberry. Cambridge: Cambridge University Press, 1935.
al-Kalabadhi, Abu Bakr Muhammad b. Ishaq. *Kitab al-taʿarruf li-madhhab ahl al-tasawwuf*. Ed. Ahmad Shams al-Din. Beirut: Dar al-kutub al-ʿilmiyya, 1993.
Khan, Shah Nawaz. *Maʾathir al-umara'*. 4 vols. Ed. ʿAbd al-Rahim and Ashraf ʿAli. Calcutta: Royal Asiatic Society, 1888–95.
Khan, Shah Nawaz. *Maʾathir al-umara'*. 3 vols. Trans. Henry Beveridge and B. Prashad. Calcutta: Royal Asiatic Society, 1941–64.
Khwafi, Ahmad Fasih. *Mujmal-i Fasihi*. 3 vols. Ed. Muhammad Farrukh. Mashhad: Intisharat-i bastan, 1339/1960.
Khwafi, Ahmad Fasih. *Mujmal-i Fasihi*. 3 vols. Ed. Muhsin Naji Nasrabadi. Tehran: Intisharat-i asatir, 1386/2007f.
Khwandamir, Ghiyath al-Din. *Habib al-siyar*. 4 vols. Ed. Muhammad Dabir Siyaqi. Tehran: Intisharat-i markazi khayyam piruz, 1333/1954.
Khwandamir, Ghiyath al-Din. *Habib al-siyar*. 2 vols. Trans. Wheeler Thackston. Cambridge, MA: Sources of Oriental Languages and Literatures, 1994.
Khwandamir, Ghiyath al-Din. *Rijal-i kitab-i habib al-siyar*. Ed. ʿAbd al-Husayn Nawa'i. Tehran: Anjuman-i athar wa mafakhir-i farhang, 1379/2000.
Lari, Razi al-Din ʿAbd al-Ghafur. *Takmila-yi hawashi-i nafahat al-uns*. Ed. ʿAli Asghar Bashir Harawi. Kabul: Anjuman-i Jami, 1343/1964.
Matthiesen, Toby. *The Other Saudis: Shiism, Dissent and Sectarianism*. Cambridge: Cambridge University Press, 2015.
Meri, Josef (trans.). *A Lonely Wayfarer's Guide to Pilgrimage: ʿAli ibn Abi Bakr al-Harawi's Kitab al-isharat ila maʿrifat al-ziyarat*. Princeton, NJ: Darwin, 2004.
Mirkhwand, Muhammad. *Rawzat al-safa*. 10 vols. Tehran: Intisharat-i markazi khayyam piruz, 1339/1960.
Mirkhwand, Muhammad. *Tarikh-i rawzat al-safa i sirat al-anbiya' wa al-muluk wa al-khulafa'*. 15 vols. Ed. Jamshid Kiyanfar. Tehran: Intisharat-i asatir, 1380/2001.
Moayyad, Heshmat and F. Lewis (trans.). *The Colossal Elephant and His Spiritual Feats: Shaykh Ahmad-e Jam. The Life and Legend of a Popular Sufi Saint of 12th Century Iran*. Costa Mesa, CA: Mazda Publications, 2004.
Monshi, Eskander Beg. *History of Shah ʿAbbas the Great [Tarikh-i ʿAlamara-yi ʿAbbasi]*. 2 vols. Trans. Roger Savory. Boulder, CO: Westview, 1978.
Munshi, Muhammad ʿAli. *Safarnamah-yi Rukn al-Dawla*. Ed. Muhammad Gulban. Tehran: Intisharat-i sahr, 2536/1977.
al-Muqaddasi, Muhammad b. Ahmad. *Ahsan al-taqasim fi maʿrifa al-aqalim*. Ed. M. J. de Goeje. Leiden: Brill, 1906.
Mustawfi, Hamd-Allah. *Nuzhat al-Qulub*. London: Brill, 1915.
Mustawfi, Hamd-Allah. *The Geographical Part of the Nuzhat al-Qulub*. Trans. Guy Le Strange. Leiden: Brill, 1919.

Nawa'i, 'Abd al-Husayn (ed.). *Asnad wa mukatibat-i tarikh-i Iran: az Timur ta Shah Isma'il*. Tehran: Bungah-i tarjuma wa nashr-i kitab, 1341/1963.

Nishaburi, Hakim. *Tarikh-i Nishabur*. Ed. Muhammad Riza Shafi'i Kadkani. Tehran: Agah, 1375/1996.

[Nizami Bakharzi], Nizam al-Din 'Abd al-Wasi' Nizami. *Mansha' al-insha'*. Ed. Rukn al-Din Humayun Farrukh. Tehran: Danishgah-i milli-i Iran, 1357/1978–79.

Nizam al-Mulk. *The Book of Government or Rules for Kings*. Trans. Hubert Darke. London: Routledge & Kegan Paul, 1960.

Parsa, Muhammad. *Qudsiyya*. Ed. Ahmad Tahiri 'Iraqi. Tehran: Tahuri, 1354/1975.

Parsa, Muhammad. *Tuhfat al-salikin*. Delhi: Afghani dar al-kutub, 1970.

Qawlawaya, Ja'far b. Muhammad b. *Kamil al-ziyarat*. Qum: Nashr al-faqahat, 1429/2009.

al-Qayini, Jalal al-Din. *Nasa'ih-i Shah-Rukhi*. Vienna: Nationalbibliothek, Cod. A. F. 112.

al-Qazwini, Nur al-Din Muhammad. *Silsilanama-yi Khwajagan-i Naqshband*. Paris: Bibliothèque Nationale, MS Supplément persan 1418.

al-Qazwini, Nur al-Din Muhammad. *Silsilanama-yi Khwajagan-i Naqshband*. Istanbul: Süleymaniye Kütüphanesi, MSS Esad Efendi 1487, Lala Ismail 155, Laleli 1381, and Sehid Ali Pasa 2893.

al-Qushayri, Abu al-Qasim. *Al-Qushayri's Epistle on Sufism*. Trans. Alexander Knysh. Reading: Garnet, 2007.

al-Qushayri, Abu al-Qasim. *al-Risala al-Qushayriyya*. Cairo: Dar al-kutub al-haditha, 1966.

Rashid al-Din. *Athar wa ahya'*. Ed. Manuchihr Sutudah and Iraj Afshar. Tehran: McGill University and Tehran University, 1368/1989.

Rashid al-Din. Jami' al-tawarikh. In *Classical Writings of the Medieval Islamic World: Persian Histories of the Mongol Dynasties*. 3 vols. Trans. Wheeler Thackston. London: I.B. Tauris, 2012.

Rumlu, Hasan. *Ahsan al-tawarikh*. 3 vols. Ed. 'Abd al-Husayn Nawa'i. Tehran: Intisharat-i asatir, 1384/2005.

Ruzbihan Khunji, Fazl-Allah b. *Mihmannamah-yi Bukhara*. Ed. Manuchihr Sutudah. Tehran: Bungah-i tarjumah wa nashr-i kitab, 1341/1962.

Saljuqi, Fikri. *Risalah-i mazarat-i Harat: shamil-i sih hisah*. Afghanistan: Markaz-i nashrati Faruqi, 1379/2001.

al-Salmani, Taj. *Tarikhnamah: Shams al-husn*. Ed. Akbar Saburi. Tehran: Intisharat-i Duktur Mahmud Afshar, 1393/2014–15.

al-Sam'ani, 'Abd al-Karim. *Kitab al-ansab*. 13 vols. Ed. 'Abd al-Rahman al-Yamani et al. Hyderabad: Osmania Oriental Publications Bureau, 1962–82.

al-Samarqandi, 'Abd al-Razzaq. *Matla'-i sa'dayn wa majma'-i bahrayn*. 4 vols. Ed. 'Abd al-Husayn Nawa'i. Tehran: Pizhuhishgah-i 'ulum-i insani wa mutala'at-i farhangi, vol. I, part 1, 1372/1993; vol. 1, pt. 2, and vol. 2, pts. 1 and 2, 1383/2004–5.

al-Samarqandi, Dawlatshah. *Tadhkirat al-shu'ara'*. Ed. E. G. Browne. Leiden: Brill, 1900.

al-Sarraj, Abu Nasr. *Kitab al-luma' fi al-tasawwuf*. Ed. R. A. Nicholson. London: Luzac, 1914.
Sayyidi, Mehdi (ed.). *Masjid wa mawqufat-i Gawhar Shad*. Tehran: Bunyad-i pizhuhish wa tawsi'a-yi farhang-i waqf, 1386/2007.
Shabankara'i, Muhammad b. 'Ali b. Muhammad. *Majma' al-ansab*. Ed. Mir-Hashim Muhaddis. Tehran: Amir Kabir, 1363/1984.
al-Shahrastani, Muhammad. *al-Milal wa-l-nihal*. 2 vols. Ed. Amir 'Ali Muhanna and 'Ali Hasan Fa'ur. Beirut: Dar al-ma'rifa, 1993.
Sijzi, Amir Hasan. *Nizam ad-Din Awliya: Morals for the Heart [Fawa'id al-fu'ad]*. Trans. Bruce Lawrence. New York: Paulist Press, 1992.
Subki, Taj al-Din 'Abd al-Wahhab b. 'Ali. *Tabaqat al-Shafi'iyya al-kubra*. Ed. Mahmud Muhammad Tanahi and 'Abd al-Fattah Muhammad Hulw. Cairo: 'Isa al-Babi al-Halabi, 1964.
al-Suhrawardi, ['Abd al-Qahir b. 'Abdallah] Abu Najib. *Kitab adab al-muridin*. Trans. M. Milson. Cambridge, MA: Harvard University Press, 1975.
al-Suhrawardi, Shihab al-Din 'Umar b. Muhammad. *'Awarif al-ma'arif*. Trans. Abu Mansur b. 'Abd al-Mu'min Isfahani. Ed. Qasim Ansari. Tehran: Intisharat-i 'ilmi wa farhangi, 1386/1987.
al-Sulami, Abu 'Abd al-Rahman Muhammad b. al-Husayn. *Tabaqat al-Sufiyya*. Ed. Mustafa 'Abd al-Qadir 'Ata'. Beirut: Dar al-kutub al-'ilmiyya, 2010.
Talaee, Zahra and Ilahi Mahbub Farimani. *Guzida-yi asnad-i masjid-i Gawhar Shad az Safaviyya ta Qajariyya*. Mashhad: Sazman-i kitabkhana-ha, muzi-ha, wa markaz-i asnad-i Astan-i Quds-i Rizawi, 1396/2017.
al-Tirmidhi, al-Hakim. *The Concept of Sainthood in Early Islamic Mysticism: Two Works by al-Hakim al-Tirmidhi*. Trans. Bernd Radtke and John O'Kane. Richmond: Curzon Press, 1996.
Wa'iz, Asil al-Din 'Abdallah. *Maqsad al-iqbal al-sultaniyya*. Ed. Mayil Harawi. Tehran: Pizhuhishgah-i 'ulum-i insani wa mutala'at-i farhangi, 1386/2007.
Wa'iz Kashifi, Fakhr al-Din 'Ali b. Husayn. *Rashahat-i 'ayn al-hayat*. 2 vols. Ed. 'Ali Asghar Mu'iniyan. Tehran: Bunyad-i nikukari-i nuriyani, 1356/1977.
Yate, C. E. *Khurasan and Sistan*. Edinburgh: William Blackwood, 1900.
Yazdi, Sharaf al-Din 'Ali. *Zafarnama*. 2 vols. Ed. Muhammad 'Abbasi. Tehran: Amir Kabir, 1336/1957.
Zanganah, Ibrahim. *Sarzamin-i Jam wa rijalan*. Turbat-i Jam: Intisharat-i Shaykh al-Islam Ahmad-i Jam, 1384/2006.

SECONDARY SOURCES

Abrahamian, Ervand. *A History of Modern Iran*. Cambridge: Cambridge University Press, 2008.
Abrahamian, Ervand. *Iran between Two Revolutions*. Princeton, NJ: Princeton University Press, 1982.
Aigle, Denise. "Among Saints and Poets: The Spiritual Topography of Shiraz." In *Cities of Medieval Iran*. Ed. David Durand-Guédy et al., *Eurasian Studies* 16/1–2 (2018): 142–76.

Aka, Ismail. "The Agricultural and Commercial Activities of the Timurids in the First Half of the 15th Century." *Oriente Moderno* 15/2 (1996): 9–21.
Alam, Arshad. *Inside a Madrasa*. New Delhi: Routledge, 2011.
Albera, Dionigi and M. Couroucli (eds.). *Sharing Sacred Spaces in the Mediterranean: Christians, Muslims and Jews at Shrines and Sanctuaries*. Bloomington, IN: Indiana University Press, 2012.
Algar, Hamid. "A Brief History of the Naqshbandi Order." In *Naqshbandis: Cheminements et situation actuelle d'un ordre mystique musulman*. Ed. Marc Gaborieau et al. Paris: ISIS, 1990, pp. 3–44.
Algar, Hamid. "Silent and Vocal *Dhikr* in the Naqshbandi Order." In *Akten des VII. Kongresses für Arabistik und Islamwissenschaft*. Ed. Albert Dietrich. Göttingen: Vandenhoeck & Ruprecht, 1976, pp. 39–46.
Algar, Hamid. "Some Notes on the Naqshbandi Tariqat in Bosnia." *Die Welt des Islams* 13/3 (1971):168–203.
Algar, Hamid. *Religion and State in Iran, 1785–1906*. Berkeley, CA: University of California Press, 1969.
Algar, Hamid. *Wahhabism*. Oneonta, NY: Islamic Publications, 2002.
Allen, Terry. *A Catalogue of the Toponyms and Monuments of Timurid Herat*. Cambridge: Aga Khan Program for Islamic Architecture, 1981.
Allen, Terry. *Timurid Herat*. Wiesbaden: Reichert, 1983.
Allsen, Thomas. *Culture and Conquest in Mongol Eurasia*. Cambridge: Cambridge University Press, 2001.
Allsen, Thomas. *Mongol Imperialism: The Policies of the Grand Qan Möngke in China, Russia, and the Islamic Lands, 1251–1259*. Berkeley, CA: University of California Press, 1987.
Amanat, Abbas. *Apocalyptic Islam and Iranian Shi'ism*. London: I.B. Tauris, 2009.
Amanat, Abbas. *Iran: A Modern History*. New Haven, CT: Yale University Press, 2017.
Anderson, Jon. "There Are No Khans Anymore: Economic Development and Social Change in Tribal Afghanistan." *Middle East Journal* 32/2 (1978): 167–83.
Ando, Shiro. "The Shaykh al-Islam as a Timurid Office: A Preliminary Study." *Islamic Studies* 33/2 (1994): 253–80.
Ando, Shiro. *Timuridische Emire nach dem Muʿizz al-ansab*. Berlin: Klaus Schwarz, 1992.
Anonymous. "*Musahaba ba* (Interview with) Mawlana Sharaf al-Din Jami al-Ahmadi." *Faslnamah-yi Habl al-matin* 4 (Winter 1394/2015–16): 8–16.
Ansari, Ali M. *Modern Iran since 1921*. Edinburgh: Pearson, 2003.
Ansari, Ali M. *The Politics of Nationalism in Modern Iran*. Cambridge: Cambridge University Press, 2012.
ʿArab-Timuri, ʿAbd al-Latif. "Hawza-yi ʿilmiyya Ahmadiyya." *Faslnamah-yi Habl al-matin* 4 (Autumn 1394/2015): 172–81.
Arjomand, Said Amir. "Religious Extremism (*Ghuluww*), Sufism and Sunnism in Safavid Iran: 1501–1722." *JAH* 15/1 (1981): 1–35.
Arjomand, Said Amir. "The Law, Agency, and Policy in Medieval Islamic Society: Development of the Institutions of Learning from the Tenth to the Fifteenth Century." *Comparative Studies in Society and History* 41/2 (1999): 263–93.

Bibliography

Arjomand, Said Amir. *The Shadow of God and the Hidden Imam*. Chicago, IL: University of Chicago Press, 1984.

Arjomand, Said Amir. *The Turban for the Crown*. New York: Oxford University Press, 1988.

Aubin, Jean. "Comment Tamerlan prenait les villes." *Studia Islamica* 19 (1963): 83–122.

Aubin, Jean. "La fin de l'État Sarbadar du Khorassan." *Journal Asiatique* 262 (1974): 95–118.

Aubin, Jean. "Le Khanat de Čaġatai et le Khorassan (1334–1380)." *Turcica* 8/2 (1970): 16–60.

Aubin, Jean. "Le Quriltai de Sultan-Maydan (1336)." *Journal Asiatique* 279 (1991): 175–97.

Azad, Arezou. *Sacred Landscape in Medieval Afghanistan: Revisiting the Fada'il-i Balkh*. Oxford: Oxford University Press, 2013.

Baldick, Julian. *Imaginary Muslims: The Uwaysi Sufis of Central Asia*. London: I.B. Tauris, 1993.

Ball, Warwick. *The Monuments of Afghanistan*. London: I.B. Tauris, 2008.

Barfield, Thomas. *Afghanistan: A Cultural and Political History*. Princeton, NJ: Princeton University Press, 2010.

Barthold, V. V. *Four Studies on the History of Central Asia: Ulugh Beg*. Trans. Vladimir and T. Minorsky. Brill: Leiden, 1958.

Barthold, V. V. *Turkestan Down to the Mongol Invasion*. 4th ed. Cambridge: E. J. W. Gibb Memorial Trust, 1977.

Barzegar, Karim. "The Nuqtavi Movement and the Question of Its Exodus during the Safavid Period (Sixteenth Century AD): A Historical Survey." *Indian Historical Review* 40/1 (2013): 41–66.

Bashir, Shahzad. "Between Mysticism and Messianism: The Life and Thoughts of Muhammad Nurbaks (d. 1464)." Unpublished PhD diss., Yale University, 1997.

Bashir, Shahzad. "Naqshband's Lives: Sufi Hagiography between Manuscripts and Genre." In *Sufism in Central Asia*. Ed. Devin DeWeese and Jo-Ann Gross. Leiden: Brill, 2018, pp. 75–97.

Bashir, Shahzad. *Sufi Bodies*. New York: Columbia University Press, 2011.

Bellew, Henry Walter. *The Indus to the Tigris*. London: Trubner & Co., 1874.

Betteridge, Anne H. "*Ziarat*: Pilgrimage to the Shrines of Shiraz." Unpublished PhD diss., University of Chicago, 1985.

Blow, David. *Shah Abbas*. London: I.B. Tauris, 2009.

Bonner, Michael. "The *Kitab al-kasb* Attributed to al-Shaybani: Poverty, Surplus, and the Circulation of Wealth." *JAOS* 121/3 (2001): 410–27.

Bosworth, C. E. *The Ghaznavids*. Edinburgh: Edinburgh University Press, 1963.

Bosworth, C. E. "The Rise of the Karamiyyah in Khurasan." *Muslim World* 50/1 (1960): 5–14.

Brockelmann, Carl. *Geschichte der arabischen Litteratur*. Leiden: Brill, 1937–42.

Brockelmann, Carl. *History of the Arabic Written Tradition*. 2 vols. and 3 supp. vols. Trans. Joep Lameer. Leiden: Brill, 2017–19.

Brown, Peter. *Augustine of Hippo: A Biography*. Berkeley, CA: University of California Press, 2000.

Brown, Peter. *The Cult of the Saints*. Chicago, IL: University of Chicago Press, 1981.
Browne, E. G. *The Persian Revolution of 1905–1909*. Cambridge: Cambridge University Press, 1910.
Buehler, Arthur. *Sufi Heirs of the Prophet*. Columbia, SC: University of South Carolina Press, 1998.
Bulliet, R. W. *Islam: The View from the Edge*. New York: Columbia University Press, 1994.
Bulliet, R. W. *The Patricians of Nishapur*. Cambridge, MA: Harvard University Press, 1972.
Burton, Audrey. "The Fall of Herat to the Uzbegs in 1588." *Iran* 26 (1988): 119–23.
Chabbi, Jacqueline. "Remarques sur le développement historique des mouvements ascétiques et mystiques au Khurasan: IIIe/IXe siècle–IVe/Xe siècle." *Studia Islamica* 46 (1977): 5–72.
Chodkiewicz, Michel. "Quelques aspects des techniques spirituelles dans la tariqa Naqshbandiyya." In *Naqshbandis: Cheminements et situation actuelle d'un ordre mystique musulman*. Ed. Marc Gaborieau et al. Paris and Istanbul: ISIS, 1990, pp. 69–82.
Clevenger, W. M. "Dams in Ḫorasan: Some Preliminary Observations." *East and West* 19/3 (1969): 387–94.
Cook, Michael. *Commanding Right and Forbidding Wrong in Islamic Thought*. Cambridge: Cambridge University Press, 2000.
Cook, Michael. *Forbidding Wrong in Islam*. Cambridge: Cambridge University Press, 2003.
Crone, Patricia. *Slaves on Horses*. Cambridge: Cambridge University Press, 1980.
Cronin, Stephanie. *Tribal Politics in Iran: Rural Conflict and the New State, 1921–1941*. London: Routledge, 2007.
Curzon, George. *Persia and the Persian Question*. 2 vols. London: Longmans, 1892.
Dabashi, Hamid. *Authority in Islam*. New Brunswick, NJ: Transaction Publishers, 1989.
Daftary, Farhad. *A History of Shi'i Islam*. London: I.B. Tauris, 2013.
Daftary, Farhad. *Ismailis in Medieval Muslim Societies*. London: I.B. Tauris, 2005.
Daniel, Elton. *The Political and Social History of Khurasan under Abbasid Rule, 747–820*. Minneapolis, MN, and Chicago, IL: Bibliotheca Islamica, 1979.
Dechant, John. "The 'Colossal Elephant' Shaykh Ahmad-i Jam: Legacy and hagiography in Islam." Unpublished PhD diss., Indiana University, 2015.
DeWeese, Devin. *An "Uvaysi" Sufi in Timurid Mawarannahr*. Bloomington, IN: Research Institute for Inner Asian Studies, 1993.
DeWeese, Devin. "Shamanization in Central Asia." *JESHO* 57/3 (2014): 326–63.
DeWeese, Devin. "'Stuck in the Throat of Chingiz Khan.'" In *History and Historiography of Post-Mongol Central Asia and the Middle East*. Ed. J. Pfeiffer and S. Quinn. Wiesbaden: Harrassowitz, 2006, pp. 23–60.
Dudoignon, Stéphane. *The Baluch, Sunnism and the State in Iran: From Tribal to Global*. Oxford: Oxford University Press, 2017.
Dupree, Louis. *Afghanistan*. Princeton: Princeton University Press, 1980.

Bibliography

Dupree, Louis. "Saint Cults in Afghanistan." *South Asia Series* 20/1 (Hanover: American Universities Field Staff Reports, 1976): 1–21.
Ebrahimnejad, Hormoz. *Medicine, Public Health and the Qajar State*. Leiden: Brill, 2004.
Elias, Jamal J. "The Sufi Lords of Bahrabad: Saʿd al-Din and Sadr al-Din Hamuwayi." *Iranian Studies* 27/1 (1994): 53–75.
Elias, Jamal J. "The Sufi Robe (*Khirqa*) as a Vehicle of Spiritual Authority." In *Robes and Honor: The Medieval World of Investiture*. Ed. Stewart Gordon. New York: Palgrave, 2001, pp. 275–89.
Elias, Ney. "Notice of an Inscription at Turbat-i-Jam, in Khorasan, about Half-way between Meshed and Herat." *JRAS* (1897): 47–48.
Elling, R. C. *Minorities in Iran*. New York: Palgrave, 2013.
Eraly, Abraham. *Emperors of the Peacock Throne*. New Delhi: Penguin, 1997.
Ernst, Carl W. *Ruzbihan Baqli*. Richmond: Curzon Press, 1996.
Ernst, Carl W. *The Shambhala Guide to Sufism*. Boston, MA: Shambhala, 1997.
Ernst, Carl W. and Bruce B. Lawrence. *Sufi Martyrs of Love: Chishti Sufism in South Asia and Beyond*. New York: Palgrave, 2002.
Faruqui, Munis D. *The Princes of the Mughal Empire, 1504–1719*. Cambridge: Cambridge University Press, 2012.
Fazl, ʿAli. *Az jam-i Shaykh-i Jam: guzidah-i asar-i Shaykh-i Jam*. Tehran: Intisharat-i sukhan, 1376/1997.
Fazl, ʿAli. *Karnama-yi Ahmad-i Jam*. Tehran: Intisharat-i Tus, 1382/2003.
Fazl, ʿAli. *Sharh-i ahwal wa naqd wa tahlil-i asar-i Ahmad Jam*. Tehran: Intisharat-i Tus, 1373/1994.
Fernandes, Leonor. *The Evolution of a Sufi Institution in Mamluk Egypt: The Khanqah*. Berlin: Klaus Schwarz, 1988.
Foltz, Richard. "Central Asians in the Administration of Mughal India." *JAH* 31/2 (1997): 139–54.
Garcia-Arenal, Mercedes. *Messianism and Puritanical Reform*. Leiden: Brill, 2006.
Gascoigne, Bamber. *The Great Moghuls*. London: Robinson, 1971.
Geertz, Clifford. *Islam Observed*. Chicago, IL: University of Chicago Press, 1968.
Gellner, Ernest. *Muslim Society*. Cambridge: Cambridge University Press, 1981.
Ghereghlou, Kioumars. "On the Margins of Minority Life: Zoroastrians and the State in Safavid Iran," *BSOAS* 80/1 (2017): 45–71.
Godard, André. *The Art of Iran*. New York: Praeger, 1965.
Goldsmid, F. J. (ed.). *Journeys of the Persian Boundary Commission*. 2 vols. London: Macmillan, 1876.
Golombek, Lisa. "A Thirteenth Century Funerary Mosque at Turbat-i Shaykh Jam." *Bulletin of the Asia Institute* 1 (Shiraz, 1969): 13–26.
Golombek, Lisa. "The Chronology of Turbat-i Shaykh Jam." *Iran* 9 (1971): 27–44.
Golombek, Lisa and Donald Wilber. *The Timurid Architecture of Iran and Turan*. 2 vols. Princeton, NJ: Princeton University Press, 1988.
Grabar, Oleg. "The Earliest Islamic Commemorative Structures, Notes and Documents." *Ars Orientalis* 6 (1966): 7–46.
Gramlich, Richard. *Die Wunder der Freunde Gottes*. Stuttgart: Steiner, 1987.
Green, Nile. "The Religious and Cultural Roles of Dreams and Visions in Islam." *JRAS* 13/3 (2003): 287–313.

Gribetz, Arthur. "The *Sama'* Controversy: Sufi vs. Legalist." *Studia Islamica* 74 (1991): 43–62.
Halm, Heinz. "Der Wesir al-Kunduri und die *Fitna* von Nishapur." *Die Welt des Orients* 6/2 (1971): 205–33.
Hanaoka, Mimi. *Authority and Identity in Medieval Islamic Historiography.* Cambridge: Cambridge University Press, 2016.
Harrow, Leonard. "The Tomb Complex of Abu Sa'id Fadl Allah b. Abi'l-Khair at Mihna." *Iran* 43 (2005): 197–215.
Hasluck, F. W. *Christianity and Islam under the Sultans.* Oxford: Clarendon, 1929.
Hawting, G. R. "The Disappearance and Rediscovery of Zamzam and the 'Well of the Ka'ba.'" *BSOAS* 43/1 (1980): 44–54.
Hiro, Dilip. *Cold War in the Islamic World: Saudi Arabia, Iran, and the Struggle for Supremacy.* Oxford: Oxford University Press, 2018.
Hope, Michael. *Power, Politics, and Tradition in the Mongol Empire and the Ilkhanate of Iran.* Oxford: Oxford University Press, 2016.
Hopkins, B. D. *The Making of Modern Afghanistan.* New York: Palgrave, 2008.
Hopkirk, Peter. *The Great Game.* New York: Kodansha, 1994.
al-Houdalieh, S. H. "Visitation and Making Vows at the Shrine of Shaykh Shihab al-Din." *Journal of Islamic Studies* 21/3 (2010): 377–90.
Hunter, Shireen. *Iran's Foreign Policy in the Post-Soviet Era.* Santa Barbara, CA: Praeger, 2010.
Husain, Afzal. "Growth of Irani Element in Akbar's Nobility." *PIHC* 36 (1975): 166–79.
Husain, Afzal. "Provincial Governors under Akbar (1580–1605)." *PIHC* 32 (1970): 269–77.
Hussaini, A. S. "Uways al-Qarani and the Uwaysi Sufis." *Muslim World* 57/2 (1967): 103–13.
ul-Huda, Qamar. "The Light beyond the Shore in the Theology of Proper Sufi Moral Conduct (*Adab*)." *Journal of the American Academy of Religion* 72/2 (2004): 461–84.
Issawi, Charles (ed.). *The Economic History of Iran, 1800–1914.* Chicago, IL: University of Chicago Press, 1971.
Ivanow, Vladimir. "A Biography of Shaykh Ahmad-i-Jam." *JRAS* (1917): 291–365.
Jackson, Peter. *The Mongols and the Islamic World.* London and New Haven, CT: Yale University Press, 2017.
Johansen, Baber. *The Islamic Law on Land Tax and Rent.* London: Croom Helm, 1988.
Jones, Norman. *Governing by Virtue.* Oxford: Oxford University Press, 2015.
Kamali, Mohammad Hashim. *Principles of Islamic Jurisprudence.* Cambridge: The Islamic Texts Society, 2003.
Kamiar, Mohammad. "The Qanat System in Iran." *Ekistics* 50/303 (1983): 467–72.
Karamustafa, Ahmet T. *God's Unruly Friends.* Oxford: Oneworld, 2006.
Karamustafa, Ahmet T. "Reading Medieval Persian Hagiography through the Prism of *Adab*: The Case of *Asrar al-tawhid*." In *Ethics and Spirituality in Islam: Sufi Adab.* Ed. F. Chiabotti et al. Leiden: Brill, 2017, pp. 131–41.

Bibliography

Karamustafa, Ahmet T. *Sufism: The Formative Period*. Edinburgh: Edinburgh University Press, 2007.

Khan, Afzal. "Iranis in the Mughal Nobility: A Case Study of the Khawafis." *PIHC* 41 (1980): 248–64.

Khan, Iqtidar. "The Nobility under Akbar and the Development of His Religious Policy, 1560–80." *JRAS* 1/2 (1968): 29–36.

Khanbaghi, Aptin. *The Fire, the Star and the Cross: Minority Religions in Medieval and Early Modern Iran*. London: I.B. Tauris, 2006.

Kissling, Hans J. "Die Wunder der Derwische." *ZDMG* 107 (1957): 348–61.

Kiyani, Muhsin. *Tarikh-i khanaqah dar Iran*. Tehran: Intisharat-i Tahuri, 1369/1990.

Knysh, Alexander. "*Irfan* Revisited: Khomeini and the Legacy of Islamic Mystical Philosophy." *Middle East Journal* 46/4 (1992): 631–53.

Knysh, Alexander. *Islamic Mysticism*. Leiden: Brill, 2000.

Krawulsky, Dorothea. *Ḫorasan zur Timuridenzeit*. 2 vols. Wiesbaden: Ludwig Reichert, 1982–84.

Lambton, A. K. S. *Continuity and Change in Medieval Persia*. London: I.B. Tauris, 1988.

Lambton, A. K. S. *Landlord and Peasant in Persia: A Study of Land Tenure and Revenue Administration*. London: I.B. Tauris, 1991.

Lambton, A. K. S. "The Evolution of the *Iqta'* in Medieval Iran." *Iran* 5 (1967): 41–50.

Lane, George. *Early Mongol Rule in Thirteenth-Century Iran*. London: RoutledgeCurzon, 2003.

Lassner, Jacob. *Medieval Jerusalem*. Ann Arbor, MI: University of Michigan Press, 2017.

Lawrence, C. H. *Medieval Monasticism*. London: Longman, 1984.

Lewis, Bernard. *The Assassins*. New York: Basic Books, 2003.

Lewisohn, Leonard. "Sufism in Late Mongol and Early Timurid Persia, from 'Ala' al-Dawla Simnani (d. 736/1326) to Shah Qasim Anvar (d. 837/1434)." In *Iran after the Mongols*. Ed. Sussan Babaie. London: I.B. Tauris, 2019, pp. 177–209.

Lewisohn, Leonard. "The Sacred Music of Islam: *Sama'* in the Persian Sufi Tradition." *British Journal of Ethnomusicology* 6 (1997): 1–33.

Lifchez, R. *The Dervish Lodge*. Berkeley, CA: University of California Press, 1992.

Lowther, William and Colin Freeman. "US Funds Terror Groups to Sow Chaos in Iran." *Daily Telegraph*, 25 February 2007.

MacGregor, C. M. *Narrative of a Journey through the Province of Khorassan*. 2 vols. London: W. H. Allen, 1879.

Madelung, Wilferd. *Religious Trends in Early Islamic Iran*. Albany, NY: Persica, 1988.

Mahendrarajah, Shivan. "A Revised History of Mongol, Kart, and Timurid Patronage of the Shrine of Shaykh al-Islam Ahmad-I Jam." *Iran* 54/2 (2016): 107–28.

Mahendrarajah, Shivan. "Tamerlane's Conquest of Herat and the 'Politics of Notables.'" *Studia Iranica* 46/1 (2017): 49–76.

Mahendrarajah, Shivan. "The Gawhar Shad Waqf: Public Works and the Commonweal." *JAOS* 137/4 (2018): 821–57.

Mahendrarajah, Shivan. "The Sarbadars of Sabzavar: Re-examining Their 'Shiʿa' Roots and Alleged Goal to 'Destroy Khurasanian Sunnism.'" *Journal of Shiʿa Islamic Studies* 5/4 (2012): 379–402.

Mahendrarajah, Shivan. "The Shaykh al-Islam in Medieval Khurasan." *Afghanistan* 1/2 (2018): 257–81.

Mahendrarajah, Shivan. "The Shrine of Shaykh Ahmad-i Jam: Notes on a Revised Chronology and a *Waqifiyya*." *Iran* 50 (2012): 145–48.

Mahendrarajah, Shivan. "The Sufi Shaykhs of Jam: A History, from the Il-Khans to the Timurids." Unpublished PhD diss., University of Cambridge, 2014.

Majd, Mohammad Gholi. *A Victorian Holocaust: Iran in the Great Famine of 1869–1873*. London: Hamilton, 2018.

Majd, Mohammad Gholi. *Iran under Allied Occupation in World War II*. Lanham, MD: University Press of America, 2016.

Malamud, Margaret. "Sufi Organizations and Structures of Authority in Medieval Nishapur." *IJMES* 26/3 (1994): 427–42.

Malamud, Margaret. "The Politics of Heresy in Medieval Khurasan: The Karramiyya in Nishapur." *Iranian Studies* 27/1 (1994): 37–51.

Manz, Beatrice Forbes. *Power, Politics and Religion in Timurid Iran*. Cambridge: Cambridge University Press, 2007.

Manz, Beatrice Forbes. *The Rise and Rule of Tamerlane*. Cambridge: Cambridge University Press, 1989.

Marsham, Andrew. *Rituals of Islamic Monarchy*. Edinburgh: Edinburgh University Press, 2009.

Massignon, Louis. *Essay on the Origins of the Technical Language of Islamic Mysticism*. Trans. B. Clark. Notre Dame: University of Notre Dame Press, 2003.

McChesney, R. D. "Economic and Social Aspects of the Public Architecture of Bukhara in the 1560's and 1570's." *Islamic Art* 2 (1987): 217–37.

McChesney, R. D. "Reliquary Sufism: Sacred Fiber in Afghanistan." In *Sufism in Central Asia*. Ed. Devin DeWeese and Jo-Ann Gross. Leiden: Brill, 2018, pp. 192–237.

McChesney, R. D. "The Conquest of Herat 995–6/1587–8." In *Etudes safavides*. Ed. J. Calmard. Paris: Institut français de recherche en Iran, 1993, pp. 69–107.

McChesney, R. D. "Waqf and Public Policy: The Waqfs of Shah ʿAbbas, 1011–1023/1602–1614." *Asian and African Studies* 15 (1981): 165–90.

McChesney, R. D. *Waqf in Central Asia*. Princeton, NJ: Princeton University Press, 1991.

McChesney, R. D. and M. M. Khorrami (trans.). *The History of Afghanistan: Fayz Muhammad Katib Hazarah's Siraj al-tawarikh*. 6 vols. Leiden: Brill, 2013–16.

Meier, Fritz. *Abu Saʿid-i Abu l'Ḥayr (357–440/1049): Wirklichkeit und Legende*. Leiden: Brill, 1976.

Meier, Fritz. "Ḫurasan und das Ende der klassichen Sufik." In *Bausteine I*. Ed. Erika Glassen and Gudrun Schubert. Istanbul: Franz Steiner, 1992, pp. 131–56.

Meier, Fritz. "Zur Biographie Ahmad-i Gam's und zur Quellenkunde von Gami's Nafahatʾl-uns." *ZDMG* 97 (1943): 47–67.

Meier, Fritz. *Zwei Abhandlungen über die Naqsbandiyya*. Istanbul: Franz Steiner, 1994.

Melchert, Christopher. *The Formation of the Sunni Schools of Law, 9th–10th Centuries C.E.* Leiden: Brill, 1997.
Melville, C. P. "*Padishah-i Islam*: The Conversion of Sultan Mahmud Ghazan Khan." *Pembroke Papers* 1 (1990): 159–77.
Melville, C. P. "Persian Famine of 1870–1872: Prices and Politics." *Disasters* 12/4 (1988): 309–25.
Melville, C. P. "The Chinese-Uighur Animal Calendar in Persian Historiography of the Mongol Period." *Iran* 32 (1994): 83–98.
Melville, C. P. *The Fall of Amir Chupan and the Decline of the Ilkhanate, 1327–37: A Decade of Discord in Mongol Iran*. Bloomington, IN: Research Institute for Inner Asian Studies, 1999.
Melville, C. P. "The Itineraries of Shahrukh b. Timur (1405–47)." In *Turko-Mongol Rulers, Cities and City Life*. Ed. David Durand-Guédy. Leiden: Brill, 2013, pp. 285–315.
Meri, Josef. "Aspects of *Baraka* (Blessing) and Ritual Devotion among Medieval Muslims and Jews." *Medieval Encounters* 5/1 (1999): 46–69.
Meri, Josef. *The Cult of Saints among Muslims and Jews in Medieval Syria*. Oxford: Oxford University Press, 2002.
Meri, Josef. "The Etiquette of Devotion in the Islamic Cult of Saints." In *The Cult of Saints in Late Antiquity and the Middle Ages: Essays on the Contribution of Peter Brown*. Ed. J. Howard-Johnston and P.A. Hayward. Oxford: Oxford University Press, 1999, pp. 263–86.
Minorsky, Vladimir. "A 'Soyurghal' of Qasim b. Jahangir Aq-qoyunlu (903/1498.)" *BSOAS* 9/4 (1939): 927–60.
Mir-Kasimov, Orkhan. *Words of Power: Hurufi Teachings between Shi'ism and Sufism in Medieval Islam*. London: I.B. Tauris, 2015.
Mojaddedi, Jawid. *Beyond Dogma*. Oxford: Oxford University Press, 2012.
Momen, Moojan. *An Introduction to Shi'i Islam*. London: Yale University Press, 1985.
Moosa, Ebrahim. *What Is a Madrasa?* Chapel Hill, NC: University of North Carolina Press, 2015.
Mortel, Robert T. "Madrasas in Mecca during the Medieval Period: A Descriptive Study Based on Literary Sources." *BSOAS* 60/2 (1997): 236–52.
Mortel, Robert T. "'Ribats' in Mecca during the Medieval Period: A Descriptive Study Based on Literary Sources." *BSOAS* 61/1 (1998): 29–50.
Mottahedeh, Roy. *Loyalty and Leadership in an Early Islamic Society*. 2nd ed. London and New York: I.B. Tauris, 2001.
Mühlbacher, Engelbert (ed.). *Die Urkunden der Karolinger*. Hanover: Hahnsche Buchhandlung, 1906.
Munt, Harry. *The Holy City of Medina: Sacred Space in Early Islamic Arabia*. Cambridge: Cambridge University Press, 2014.
Muqaddam, Faramarz Sabr. *Mazar-i Shaykh Ahmad-i Jam*. Turbat-i Jam: Nashr-i sunbalah 1383/2004.
Murata, Sachiko. *Chinese Gleams of Sufi Light*. Albany, NY: SUNY Press, 2000.
Nasr, Vali. "The Rise of Sunni Militancy in Pakistan: The Changing Role of Islamism and the Ulama in Society and Politics." *Modern Asian Studies* 34/1 (2000): 139–80.

Nattaj, V. H. and Z. Sanaati. "Recognition of the Persian Garden Plan in Sheikh Ahmad-e Jam Complex." *Manzar* 11/46 (Spring 2019): 6–13.
Newman, Andrew. *Safavid Iran*. London: I.B. Tauris, 2006.
Nicholson, R. A. *Studies in Islamic Mysticism*. Cambridge: Cambridge University Press, 1921.
Noelle-Karimi, Christine. *The Pearl in Its Midst: Herat and the Mapping of Khurasan (15th–19th Centuries)*. Vienna: Österreichischen Akademie der Wissenschaften, 2014.
Nurbakhsh, Javad. *In the Tavern of Ruin*. New York: Khaniqahi Nimatullahi, 1978.
O'Kane, Bernard. "Natanz and Turbat-I Jam: New Light on Fourteenth Century Iranian Stucco." *Studia Iranica* 21 (1992): 85–92.
O'Kane, Bernard. "Taybad, Turbat-i Jam and Timurid Vaulting." *Iran* 17 (1979): 87–104.
O'Kane, Bernard. "The Madrasa al-Ghiyasiyya at Khargird." *Iran* 14 (1976): 79–92.
O'Kane, Bernard. "Timurid Architecture in Khurasan." Unpublished PhD diss., University of Edinburgh, 1982.
O'Kane, Bernard. *Timurid Architecture in Khurasan*. Costa Mesa, CA: Mazda Publishers, 1987.
Otto, Rudolf. *The Idea of the Holy*. 2nd ed. Trans. J. W. Harvey. London: Oxford University Press, 1950.
Palmer, Aiyub. *Sainthood and Authority in Early Islam: al-Hakim al-Tirmidhi's Theory of Wilaya and the Reenvisioning of the Sunni Caliphate*. Leiden: Brill, 2020.
Parodi, Laura. "Of Shaykhs, Bibis and Begims: Sources on Early Mughal Marriage Connections and the Patronage of Babur's Tomb." In *Mediaeval and Modern Iranian Studies: Proceedings of the 6th European Conference of Iranian Studies (Vienna, 2007)*. Ed. M Szuppe et al., *Cahiers de Studia Iranica* 45 (2011): 121–38.
Parodi, Laura and B. Wannell, "The Earliest Datable Mughal Painting." *Asianart* (18 November 2011). www.asianart.com/articles/parodi/ (accessed 13 June 2020).
Paul, Jürgen. "Archival practices in the Muslim world prior to 1500." In *Manuscripts and Archives: Comparative Views on Record-Keeping*. Ed. Alessandro Bausi et al. Berlin: de Gruyter, 2018, pp. 339–60.
Paul, Jürgen. "Balkh, from the Seljuqs to the Mongol Invasion." In *Cities in Medieval Iran*. Ed. David Durand-Guédy et al., *Eurasian Studies* 16/1–2 (2018): 313–51.
Paul, Jürgen. "Constructing the Friends of God: Sadid al-Din Ghaznavi's *Maqamat-i Zinda-Pil* (with Some Remarks on Ibn Munawwar's *Asrar al-tawhid*)." In *Narrative Pattern and Genre in Hagiographic Life Writing*. Ed. Stephan Conermann. Berlin: E.B.-Verlag, 2014, pp. 205–26.
Paul, Jürgen. *Doctrine and Organization: The Khwajagan/Naqshbandiya in the First Generation after Baha'uddin*. Berlin: Das Arabische Buch, 1998.
Paul, Jürgen. "Forming a Faction: The *Himayat* System of Khwaja Ahrar." *IJMES* 23 (1991): 533–48.

Paul, Jürgen. "Local Lords or Rural Notables: Some Remarks on the *Ra'is* in Twelfth Century Eastern Iran." In *Medieval Central Asia and the Persianate World*. Ed. A. C. S. Peacock and D. G. Tor. London: I.B. Tauris, 2015, pp. 174–209.

Paul, Jürgen. "Scheiche und Herrscher im Khanat Čaġatay." *Der Islam* 67/2 (1990): 278–321.

Paul, Jürgen. "The Khwajagan at Herat during Shahrukh's Reign." In *Horizons of the World*. Ed. I. E. Binbaş and N. Kihc-Schubel. Istanbul: Ithaki Publishing, 2011, pp. 217–50.

Paul, Jürgen. "The Rise of the Khwajagan-Naqshbandiyya Sufi Order in Timurid Herat." In *Afghanistan's Islam*. Ed. Nile Green. Oakland, CA: University of California Press, 2017, pp. 71–86.

Paul, Jürgen. "Where Did the Dihqāns Go?" *Eurasian Studies* XI (2013): 1–34.

Paul, Jürgen. "Zerfall und Bestehen: Die Ǧaun-i qurban im 14. Jahrhundert." *Asiatische Studien/Études Asiatiques* 65/3 (2011): 695–733.

Peacock, A. C. S. *Early Seljuq History*. New York: Routledge, 2010.

Peacock, A. C. S. *The Great Seljuq Empire*. Edinburgh: Edinburgh University Press, 2015.

Peters, F. E. *The Hajj*. Princeton, NJ: Princeton University Press, 1994.

Petrushevsky [Petrushevskiĭ], I. P. *Kishawarzi wa munasabat-i arzi dar Iran-i 'ahd-i Mughul*. 2 vols. Trans. Karim Kishawarz. Tehran: Intisharat-i nil, 1347/1968.

Petrushevsky [Petrushevskiĭ], I. P. "The Socio-economic Conditions of Iran under the Il-Khans." In *Cambridge History of Iran*. Vol. 5. Ed. J. A. Boyle. Cambridge: Cambridge University Press, 1968, pp. 483–537.

Picken, Gavin. *Spiritual Purification in Islam*. New York: Routledge, 2011.

Pokalova, E. *Returning Islamist Foreign Fighters*. Cham, Switzerland: Palgrave, 2020.

Pope, Arthur Upham (ed.). *A Survey of Persian Art*. 6 vols. Oxford: Oxford University Press, 1938–58.

Potter, Lawrence G. "The Kart Dynasty of Herat: Religion and Politics in Medieval Iran." Unpublished PhD diss., Columbia University, 1992.

Radtke, Bernd. "The Concept of *Wilaya* in Early Sufism." In *The Heritage of Sufism*. Vol. 1. Ed. Leonard Lewisohn. Oxford: Oneworld, 1999, pp. 483–96.

Renard, John. *Friends of God*. Berkeley, CA: University of California Press, 2008.

Renard, John. *Historical Dictionary of Sufism*. Oxford: Scarecrow Press, 2005.

Rudolph, Ulrich. *Al-Maturidi and the Development of Sunni Theology in Samarqand*. Trans. Rodrigo Adem. Leiden: Brill, 2015.

Safi, Omid. "Bargaining with *Baraka*: Persian Sufism, 'Mysticism,' and Pre-modern Politics." *Muslim World* 90 (2000): 259–87.

Safi, Omid. *The Politics of Knowledge in Premodern Islam*. Chapel Hill, NC: University of North Carolina Press, 2006.

Sanasarian, Eliz. *Religious Minorities in Iran*. Cambridge: Cambridge University Press, 2004.

Savory, Roger. *Iran under the Safavids*. Cambridge: Cambridge University Press, 1980.

Schimmel, Annemarie. *Islamic Names*. Edinburgh: Edinburgh University Press, 1989.

Schimmel, Annemarie. *Mystical Dimensions of Islam*. Chapel Hill, NC: University of North Carolina Press, 1975.
Schimmel, Annemarie. *The Empire of the Great Mughals*. London: Reaktion Books, 2004.
Schurmann, Franz. "Mongolian Tributary Practices of the Thirteenth Century." *Harvard Journal of Asiatic Studies* 19/3 (1956): 304–89.
Seyed-Gohrab, A. A. "Khomeini the Poet Mystic." *Die Welt des Islams* 51/3 (2011): 438–58.
Shafi'i Kadkani, Muhammad Riza. *Chashidan-i ta'm-i waqt: az miras-i 'irfani-yi Abu Sa'id Abu al-Khayr*. Tehran: Intisharat-i sukhan, 1385/2006.
Shafi'i Kadkani, Muhammad Riza. *Darwish-i sitihandah: az miras-i 'irfani-yi Shaykh-i Jam*. Tehran: Intisharat-i sukhan, 1393/2014.
Shafi'i Kadkani, Muhammad Riza. *Janib-i 'irfani-yi madhhab-i Karramiyya*. Unpublished.
Shafi'i Kadkani, Muhammad Riza. *Qalandariyya dar tarikh*. Tehran: Intisharat-i sukhan, 1386/2007.
Shafi'i Kadkani, Muhammad Riza. "Rawabit-i Shaykh-i Jam ba Karramiyan-i 'asr-i khwish." *Majalla-i danishkada-i adabiyyat wa 'ulum-i insani* 2/6–8 (1374/1995): 29–50.
Shakeb, M. Z. A. *A Descriptive Catalogue of Miscellaneous Persian Mughal Documents from Akbar to Bahadur Shah II*. London: India Office Library and Records, 1982.
Shuster, W. Morgan. *The Strangling of Persia*. New York: Century, 1912.
Silvers, Laury. "The Teaching Relationship in Early Sufism: A Reassessment of Fritz Meier's Definition of the *Shaykh al-Tarbiya* and the *Shaykh al-Ta'lim*." *Muslim World* 97 (2003): 69–97.
Smith, Adam. *An Inquiry into the Nature and Causes of the Wealth of Nations*. Ed. Edwin Cannan. Chicago, IL: University of Chicago Press, 1976 [2012 reprint].
Smith, Anthony. *Blind White Fish in Persia*. New York: E. P. Dutton, 1953.
Smith, John Masson, Jr. "Mongol and Nomadic Taxation." *Harvard Journal of Asiatic Studies* 30 (1970): 46–89.
Smith, John Masson, Jr. *The History of the Sarbadar Dynasty 1336–1381 A.D. and Its Sources*. The Hague: Mouton, 1970.
Soudavar, Abolala. "Between the Safavids and the Mughals: Art and Artists in Transition." *Iran* 37 (1999): 49–66.
Standish, J. F. "The Persian War of 1856–1857." *Middle East Studies* 3/1 (1966): 18–45.
Steingass, Francis J. *The Student's Arabic–English Dictionary*. London: Crosby Lockwood & Son, 1884.
Subtelny, Maria Eva. "A Persian Agricultural Manual in Context: The *Irshad al-zira'a* in Late Timurid and Early Safavid Khorasan." *Studia Iranica* 22 (1993): 167–217.
Subtelny, Maria Eva. "A Timurid Educational and Charitable Foundation: The Ikhlasiyya Complex of 'Ali Shir Nava'i in 15th-Century Herat and Its Endowment." *JAOS* 111/1 (1991): 38–61.
Subtelny, Maria Eva. "Centralizing Reform and Its Opponents in the Late Timurid Period." *Iranian Studies* 21/1 (1988): 123–51.

Subtelny, Maria Eva. "Scenes from the Literary Life of Timurid Herat." In *Logos Islamikos*. Ed. Roger Savory and D. A. Agius. Toronto: Pontifical Institute of Mediaeval Studies, 1984, pp. 137–55.
Subtelny, Maria Eva. "Socioeconomic Bases of Cultural Patronage under the Later Timurids." *IJMES* 20/4 (1988): 479–505.
Subtelny, Maria Eva. *Timurids in Transition*. Leiden: Brill, 2007.
Subtelny, Maria Eva and Anas Khalidov. "The Curriculum of Islamic Higher Learning in Timurid Iran in the Light of the Sunni Revival under Shah-Rukh." *JAOS* 115 (1995): 210–36.
Szuppe, Maria. *Entre Timourides, Uzbeks et Safavides*. Paris: Association pour l'Avancement des Études Iraniennes, 1992.
Taylor, Christopher S. *In the Vicinity of the Righteous: Ziyara and the Veneration of Muslim Saints in Late Medieval Egypt*. Leiden: Brill, 1999.
Taylor, Christopher S. "Reevaluating the Shi'i Role in the Development of Monumental Islamic Funerary." *Muqarnas* 9 (1992): 1–10.
Ter Haar, Johan. "The Spiritual Guide in the Naqshbandi Order." In *The Heritage of Sufism*. Vol. 2. Ed. Leonard Lewisohn. Oxford: Oneworld, 1999, pp. 311–21.
Tor, D. G. "'Sovereign and Pious': The Religious Life of the Great Seljuq Sultans." In *The Seljuqs: Politics, Society, and Culture*. Ed. Christian Lange and Songül Mecit. Edinburgh: Edinburgh University Press, 2011, pp. 39–62.
Trimingham, J. Spencer. *The Sufi Orders in Islam*. Oxford: Oxford University Press, 1971.
Tsadik, Daniel. "Identity among the Jews of Iran." In *Iran Facing Others*. Ed. Abbas Amanat and Farzin Vejdani. New York: Palgrave, 2012, pp. 221–44.
U.S. State Department. *Country Reports on Terrorism 2011*. Washington, DC, July 2012.
van Ess, Josef. *Ungenutzte Texte zur Karramiya*. Heidelberg: Sitzungsberichte der Heidelberger Akademie der Wissenschaften, 1980.
Vikør, Knut S. *Between God and the Sultan: A History of Islamic Law*. New York: Oxford University Press, 2005.
Watabe, Ryoko. "Census-taking and the *Qubchur* Taxation System in Ilkhanid Iran." *Memoirs of the Toyo Bunko* 73 (2015): 27–63.
Weismann, Itzchak. *The Naqshbandiyya*. New York: Routledge, 2007.
Werbner, Pnina. "*Langar*: Pilgrimage, Sacred Exchange, and Perpetual Sacrifice in a Sufi Saint's Lodge." In *Embodying Charisma*. Ed. Pnina Werbner and Helene Basu. London: Routledge, 1998, pp. 95–116.
Werner, Christoph. "Soziale Aspekte von Stiftungen zugunsten des Schreins von Imam Riza in Mashhad, 1527–1897." In *Islamische Stiftungen zwischen juristischer Norm und sozialer Praxis*. Ed. A. Meier et al. Berlin: Akademie Verlag, 2009, pp. 167–89.
Wheatley, Paul. *The Places Where Men Pray Together*. Chicago, IL: University of Chicago Press, 2001.
Wilber, Donald. "Qavam al-Din ibn Zayn al-Din Shirazi: A Fifteenth-Century Timurid Architect." *Architectural History* 30 (1987): 31–44.
Wilber, Donald. *The Architecture of Islamic Iran: The Il Khanid Period*. Princeton, NJ: Princeton University Press, 1955.
Wink, Andre. *Akbar*. Oxford: Oneworld, 2009.

Woods, J. E. "Turco-Iranica II: Notes on a Timurid Decree of 1396/798." *JNES* 43/4 (1984): 331–37.

Wulff, H. E. "The Qanats of Iran." *Scientific American* 218/4 (1968): 94–105.

Würtz, Thomas. *Islamische Theologie im 14. Jahrhundert*. Berlin: de Gruyter, 2016.

Zakaria, K. "Uways al-Qarani: Visages d'une Légende." *Arabica* 46 (1999): 230–58.

Zysow, Aron. "Two Unrecognized Karrami Texts." *JAOS* 108/4 (1988): 577–87.

Index

Abu ʿAbdallah. *See* Ibn Karram
Abu al-ʿAbbas Ahmad b. Muhammad Qassab, 14
Abu Bakr Shibli, 15
Abu al-Fazl Hasan Sarakhsi, 11
Abu Nasr Sarraj, 11, 199
Abu al-Qasim Babur b. Baysunghur, 69
Abu al-Qasim Nasrabadi, 15
Abu Saʿid b. Abu al-Khayr, 11, 13, 15, 26, 29, 46, 197, 218
  and Seljuqs, 21
  his *khanaqah*, 30, 164
  his *khirqa*, 12, 13, 14
  his shrine, 47, 68, 142
  his *silsila*, 11, 12
  his *walayat*, 36
  in Nishapur, 19, 20
Abu Saʿid Bahadur Khan, 62, 109, 112, 124, 135
Abu Tahir-i Saʿid, 14, 15, 16
Abu Tahir Kurd, 11, 14
Afsharids, 3, 82
agriculture, 69, 76, 132, 133, 136
  fallow lands, 128
  rationalization of, 136
ahl al-bayt, 75, 221
ahl-i sunnat, 97
Ahmad Sirhindi, 14
Ahmad-i Jam
  and divine appointment, 45
  and Sanjar, 17, 21, 44, 45, 46
  as *shaykh al-taʿlim*, 31

  biography, 3, 4, 6, 9, 16, 21, 24, 25, 27, 28
  guardian of kings, 44, 45, 46, 51, 150, 218
  hagiography, 12, 13, 14, 24
  his *baraka*, 62, 219, 222
  his *fayz*, 40, 62, 152, 211, 215, 219
  his Karrami leanings, 25, 26
  his *khanaqah*, 9, 31, 57, 58
  his *khirqa*, 12, 13, 14, 16, 37, 218
  his progeny, 55, 56, 79, 195, 213, 216
  his *silsila*, 9, 11, 14, 15, 30
  his spirit (*ruh*), 211. *See also ruhaniyyat*
  his view of Ibn Karram, 27
  his writings, 16, 28, 35, 41
  in Bizd, 14, 198
  in Buzjan, 24, 146
  in Maʿd-Abad, 25
  in Nishapur, 26
  intellectual journey, 28, 29, 31
karamat, 9
khatm by, 203
lineage, 23. *See also* al-Namaqi, ʿAli
marketing of, 4, 45, 46, 47, 81, 218
miracles, 26, 27, 36, 37, 40, 41, 78, 150
personality, 13, 55, 193
pilgrims to his tomb, 42, 43, 46, 47, 49, 62, 66, 68, 102, 152
sainthood, 32, 37, 219
super saint, 211
the Furious Elephant, 31, 40, 46, 51, 218, 219
ummi, 16, 24
uwaysi, 37, 210

Index

Ahmad-i Jam shrine
  agro-manager, 125, 130, 219
  catchment area, 82, 84
  gunbad, 58, 65, 103, 106, 108
  Gunbad-i Firuzshah, 2, 109
  Gunbad-i Safid, 108
  iwan, 78, 109
  khanaqah, 5, 102, 164, 165, 167, 168
  khanaqah-i saracha, 108
  Kirmani Mosque, 108, 197
  Madrasa-i Amir Shah-Malik, 110, 167
  Madrasa-i Faryumadi, 108, 167
  Madrasa-i Firuzshah, 109
  Masjid-i 'atiq, 2, 107
  Masjid-i jami'-i naw, 110
  necrology, 43, 102, 162
  renaissance, 88
  Safavid cistern, 78, 111
  sanctified space, 150
  source of *baraka*, 152
  Summer Mosque, 111
  typology of pilgrims, 159
  wealth, 124, 125, 141
  Winter Mosque, 111
al-Ahmadi Jami, Haji Qazi Sharaf al-Din, 86, 89, 111, 122, 141
Ahrar, 'Ubayd-Allah, 213
Akbar, Jalal al-Din Muhammad, 5, 48, 77, 81, 82
  birth of sons, 81
  his birth predicted, 48
  his birth realized, 48
  his saintly pedigree, 51
  kidnapped, 49
  patrimony secured, 51
  protected by Ahmad-i Jam, 51
  remarks by Beveridge, 81
'Ala' al-Dawla b. Baysunghur, 69, 114
'alam-i arwah (spirit world), 158, 220. *See also* pilgrimages
Algar, Hamid, 15, 205
Amir Shah-Malik, Ghiyath al-Din, 110, 113, 220
al-amr bi-l-ma'ruf wa-l-nahy 'an al-munkar, 9, 20, 218
animal calendar, 75, 139, 140
Aq-Quyunlu, 71, 73
asceticism. *See* Sufi terms
Ash'ari, 19, 28
  in Nishapur, 20
'Attar, 'Ala' al-Din, 194, 213

'Attar, Hasan, 194
'Attar, Yusuf, 194

Babur, Zahir al-Din, 48, 71, 74
al-Baghdadi, 'Abd al-Qahir (Abu Mansur) b. Tahir, 22, 23
al-Bajistani, Ahmad b. Ibrahim, 27
Baluch, 2, 89, 98
baraka, 5, 43, 62, 68, 150, 152, 163, 219
  and COVID-19, 151
  and light, 26
  at Jam, 160, 162
  holy water, 151
  quest for, 151
Barfield, Thomas, 64
bast (asylum), 161
bay'a (oath), 161
Birjandi, Shihab al-Din Ahmad, 212

Chaghatai, 63
  Arlat, 63, 64
Chingiz Khan, 57, 63, 74, 219
Chishtiyya, 51
  and Ahmad-i Jam, 190
  couplet by Ahmad-i Jam, 41
  dhikr practices, 203
  Mu'in al-Din Chishti, 81
  Nizam al-Din Awliya, 36
  Salim Chishti, 81
Christians, 3, 73, 85, 86, 88
Chupan Suldus, 61, 62, 109, 112, 135, 162

da'wa (proselytizing), 31, 218
Dawud Ta'i, 11
directing shaykh. *See* Sufi terms

Faryumadi, 'Ala' al-Din Muhammad, 61, 108, 112, 131
fayz, 5, 209, 210, 212
feed the people. *See takafful-i umur*
Firuz-Jang b. Husayn, 78
Firuzshah, Jalal al-Din, 110, 113, 114, 220
futuwwa, 27, 28, 165, 223

Gawhar Shad, 4, 16, 113, 114
  benefaction to, 68
  execution of, 71
Ghazan Khan, 59, 60, 127, 161, 219
  reforms. *See* Rashid al-Din (Ilkhanid vizier)

Index

al-Ghazali, Abu Hamid, 30, 154, 185, 200, 206
Ghaznavids, 17, 18, 20, 21, 28, 218
  and Karramiyya, 19, 20
  Dandanqan, 17, 20
  Mahmud b. Sebüktigin, 20
  Mayhana, 21
Ghiyath al-Din Muhammad b. Rashid al-Din, 112
Ghurids (Shansabani dynasty), 43
Golden Chain. *See silsilat al-dhahab*
Golombek, Lisa, 98
granary (*anbar-i ghalla*), 134

Habib 'Ajami, 11
hagiologist
  'Abd al-Rahman Jami, 11, 24
  'Ali Buzjani, 59, 134, 146, 161, 165, 167, 212, 214
  Muhammad Ibn Munawwar, 11, 13
  Sadid al-Din Ghaznawi, 12, 26, 35, 44, 193
al-Hakim al-Tirmidhi, 4, 33
  eight proofs, 34, 36
  firasa or *firasat*, 34
  ilham, 34
  karama or *karamat*, 34
  on Khizr, 34
Hamida Banu Bigum, 48, 80, 81
  at Jam, 49, 80
  in Iran, 48
  mother to Akbar, 48
  panegyrics for, 51
al-Hammuya, Sadr al-Din Ibrahim, 60
Hanafi, 9, 28
  in Nishapur, 19, 20
haram. *See* sacred spaces
Hasan Basri, 11, 15
Hawza-yi 'ilmiyya Ahmadiyya, 103, 111, 165, 178, 222
Hawza-yi 'ilmiyya Hibat al-Rahman, 112, 186, 222
Haydar Dughlat, 74
al-Haysam, 'Ali, 25, 26
al-Haysam, Muhammad b., 25
Hazaras, 2, 98, 160
hima. *See* sacred spaces
himayat, 139, 140
Hindu, 'Ala' al-Din, 61, 112, 130
al-Hiri, Ahmad (Abu Bakr) b. al-Hasan al-Harashi, 22, 23

al-Hujwiri, 'Ali, 29, 34, 199
Hülegü, 44, 127
Humayun, 5, 47, 48, 80
  at Jam, 49, 80
  death of, 51
  faith in Ahmad, 49
  in Iran, 48
  reversal of fortune, 49
  vision of Ahmad, 48, 211
hydrological systems, 5, 76, 124, 125, 126, 128, 129, 219
  and Jamis, 168, 200
  band, 94, 133
  hawz, 133
  juy-bar, 94, 131
  juy-i tahuna, 133
  mirab, *mard-i juy*, 133
  nataruh, 94, 133
  qulb, 94, 133

Ibn al-'Arabi, 190, 222
Ibn Battuta, 1, 61, 95, 124
Ibn Karram, 17, 25, 26, 27
  birthplace, Sistan, 26
  source of *baraka*, 27
Ibrahim-Sultan b. Amir Shah-Malik, 113
ihtiyat. *See taqiyya*
ihya' al-mawat, 127, 219
Ilkhanids, 4, 60, 127, 219
Imam 'Ali, 11, 14, 15, 79
  his charisma, 15
  in *silsila*, 15
imam-jum'a, 2, 86, 155, 160
Imam Riza, 9, 15
  in *silsila*. *See silsilat al-dhahab*
  Sultan of Khurasan, 15, 162, 218
'inayat wa himayat, 32, 46, 47, 144, 220
iqta', 130
'irfan. *See* Sufi terms
Islamic Republic of Iran, 1, 2, 3, 85, 217, 222
  destabilization of, 85, 86, 87
  loyalties to, 86, 87
  nationalism in, 86, 88
  sacrifices by Sunnis, 86
Isma'ilis, 19, 20, 27, 28. *See* motifs
  and Ahmad-i Jam, 28, 44
  fidayin, 28
  in Nishapur, 19

Index

Jahangir b. Akbar the Great, 81
Jami
  as *takhallus*, 79, 80
Jami, ʿAbd al-Rahman (d. 898/1492), 6, 11, 72, 195, 232
  desecration of grave, 76
  devotion to Ahmad, 72
  *khatm al-shuʿara*ʾ, 6, 72
  Sufi writings, 190, 208, 209, 210
Jami, ʿAli Akbar (n.d.), 48
Jami, ʿAziz-Allah (d. 902/1497), 6, 195, 203, 212, 213, 214
Jami, Ghiyath al-Din (master weaver), 79
Jami, Ghiyath al-Din b. Shams al-Din Mutahhar b. Shihab al-Din Ismaʿil (d. *ca.* 738/1338), 109
Jami, Hibat al-Rahman bt. Burhan al-Din Nasr, 57, 58, 102, 156, 216
  buried beside Ahmad, 162
Jami, Ibn Yamin, 58
Jami, ʿImad al-Din (ʿAbd al-Rahim) b. Ahmad-i Jam, 161
Jami, Jalal al-Din (Abu al-Qasim) (d. 920/1514f.), 72, 74, 75, 172
  at court of Shah Ismaʿil, 75
Jami, Jalal al-Din (n.d.), 70
Jami, Jalal al-Din Yusuf-i Ahl, 59, 173, 200
  his *ijaza*, 173, 192
Jami, Muʿin al-Din, 62, 63, 158, 178, 219
  Arlat wife, 63
  in jail, 65
  letter to Temür, 45, 66
Jami, Qutb al-Din Ahmad (n.d.), 70, 140
Jami, Qutb al-Din Muhammad (d. 667/1268), 43, 56, 58, 102, 117, 134, 178, 198, 211, 212
  and India, 58, 59
  his *Hadiqat*, 190, 191, 196
  his Sufi training, 198
Jami, Qutb al-Din Muhammad (d. 821/1418), 67, 139, 168
Jami, Qutb al-Din Muhammad Zahid, 213
Jami, Qutb al-Din Yahya Nishapuri, 112
Jami, Rashid al-Din (ʿAbd al-Rashid) b. Ahmad-i Jam, 27, 165
Jami, Razi al-Din Ahmad (d. 767/1366), 64, 65, 66, 109, 117
  lineage in Transoxiana, 67
Jami, Razi al-Din Ahmad (d. 908/1502f.), 70
Jami, Razi al-Din Ahmad b. Jalal al-Din Jami (d. *ca.* 884/1479), 172

Jami, Safi al-Din Mahmud, 58
Jami, Shams al-Din Mutahhar (Abu al-Maʿali) b. Ahmad-i Jam (n.d.), 56, 102
Jami, Shams al-Din Mutahhar b. Shihab al-Din Ismaʿil (d.*ca.* 738/1338), 62, 66, 109
Jami, Sharaf al-Din (ʿAbd al-Karim) b. ʿImad al-Din, 57
Jami, Shihab al-Din (Abu al-Makarim) al-Mulk (d. 847/1443f.), 68, 142, 145, 172
  as *mutawalli*, 68
  his *Khulasat*, 190, 192
  preceptor to, 68, 69
Jami, Shihab al-Din Ismaʿil (d. *ca.* 738/1338), 58, 59, 62, 63, 109, 112, 117, 130, 131, 134, 135, 138, 144, 146, 148, 161, 219, 220
  and Nawruz, 59, 60
  and Öljeitü, 60, 61
  his magnanimity, 61
  his social network, 60
  preceptor to, 62
Jami, Shihab al-Din Ismaʿil (d. 809/1407), 66, 67, 117, 145, 148, 220
Jami, Shihab al-Din Ismaʿil b. Ahmad-i Jam, 11, 15, 56, 57, 163
Jami, Shihab al-Din ʿUmar b. Muʿin al-Din, 67, 200
Jami, Zahir al-Din ʿIsa b. Ahmad-i Jam, 43, 56, 58, 198, 211
Jami, Ziya al-Din Yusuf (d. 797/1394f.), 66, 145, 178, 220
Jami, Ziya al-Din Yusuf b. Ahmad-i Jam, 56
jawanmard. See *futuwwa*
Jebe, 57
Jews, 73, 85, 86
Judaism, 3, 88
Junayd Baghdadi, 11, 15, 209

Kadkani, Shafiʿi, 16, 22, 24, 25, 27
  on Ahmad-i Jam, 30, 40, 190
Kamran Mirza, 48, 49
Karramiyya, 4, 9, 16, 18, 28, 29, 37, 218
  activism, 18, 19, 20, 22, 24
  and Ahmad-i Jam, 21
  in Nishapur, 29
  in retreat, 20, 21
  subsects, 26
Kart, Fakhr al-Din, 60, 61, 131, 133, 161
Kart, Ghiyath al-Din (Pir ʿAli), 63, 64, 65, 219

Index

Kart, Ghiyath al-Din Muhammad, 4, 45, 61, 64, 106, 108, 109, 112, 132, 133, 134, 135, 160, 219
  and Öljeitü, 61
  devotee of Ahmad-i Jam, 62
  inscription at Jam, 107
Kart, Muhammad b. Muʿizz al-Din, 63, 64
  at Sarakhs, 65
Kart, Muhammad Baqir, 64, 65
  farman by, 135
Kart, Muʿizz al-Din Muhammad, 63, 106, 132, 133, 135, 219
  death of, 65
  deposition of, 64, 65
  inscription at Jam, 106
  manshur by, 147
  parley at Jam, 162
  patronage at Herat, 64
  patronage at Jam, 65
Kart, Shams al-Din Muhammad, 4, 43, 61, 160, 218
  burial at Jam, 162
  murder of, 51
  pilgrimage to Jam, 42, 152
Kartid, 42, 62, 64, 125, 145, 219
Kashghari, Saʿd al-Din, 6, 195, 213, 232
Khalifa Mir Yahya, 163
khanaqah, 163, 166, 173, 222
  Karrami, 9, 19, 21, 164
kharaj, 126
al-Kharaqani, ʿAli b. Ahmad, 14
khirqa, 12, 13, 58
Khizr, 13, 14, 34, 37, 210, 218. See also *uwaysi*
Khomeini, Ayatollah Rohullah, 85, 222
Khwafi, Ghiyath al-Din Pir Ahmad, 112
Khwafi, Majd al-Din Muhammad, 113
Khwafi, Zayn al-Din, 212, 214. See also Zayniyya
Khwajagan. See Naqshbandiyya
Körgüz, 59
al-Kunduri, ʿAmid al-Mulk, 20
Kusuyi, Shams al-Din Muhammad (d. 863/1459), 71, 195, 211

Lewisohn, Leonard, 208
locus sanctus. See sacred spaces

madhhab
  Hanafi, 18
  Karrami, 4, 18, 27, 29

Shafiʿi, 18, 24
Maham Bigum, 48, 80
Mahmashadh, Ishaq (Abu Yaʿqub) b., 25, 26
Mahmashadh, Muhammad (Abu Bakr) b. Ishaq b., 25
Malamatiyya, 28
malik-panah, 44
Manicheans, 163
manshur, 67, 70, 168, 172
Manz, Beatrice, 3, 193, 216
Maʿruf Karkhi, 11, 15
Maryam-Makani. See Hamida Banu Bigum
Maʿsud Kirmani (architect), 163
al-Maydani, Ahmad b. Ibrahim al-Bajistani, 26
mihna, 20, 28
miracles
  istidraj, 35
  karamat, 35
  makhraqa, 35
  maʿsum v. *mahfuz*, 36
  muʿjizat v. *karamat*, 35
  views of Ahmad-i Jam, 35
  views of Ruzbihan Baqli, 35
Miranshah b. Temür
  governor of Khurasan, 67
  pilgrimage to Jam, 67, 200
Miras-i Farhangi, 5, 85, 103
Mirza Sultan-Sanjar, 69
Moayyad, Heshmat, 41
  on Ahmad-i Jam, 30
Möngke, 42, 44, 61, 127
  yarligh by, 42
motifs
  anti-Ismaʿili, 44
  anti-Shiʿa, 28
  divine guardian, 45
  Jami propaganda, 44, 51
  light, 26
  poison and kings, 45
  spiritual guide, 45
  transubstantiation, 36
  vision or dream of Ahmad, 48
muʿafi, 124, 137, 138, 139, 140, 141
Muhammad (Prophet), 11, 14, 15
  his charisma, 15
  in *silsila*, 15. See also *silsilat al-dhahab*
Muhammad Bik Jawni-Qurban, 162
Muhammad Juki, 114
Muhammad Shaybani Khan, 73
Muhammad al-Sulami, 15

Muhammad Taraghay (Ulugh Beg), 113
al-Mulk, 'Ala' al-Din 'Ala' al-Mulk, 139
al-Mulk, 'Ali Asghar, 140
al-Mulk, Khandzada Fakhr al-Mulk Khatun, 67, 139, 140, 216
al-Mulk, Razi al-Din Ahmad [Jami] (n.d.), 139
mulk-panah, 32, 44, 45, 160
Murta'ish Baghdadi, 11
musa'ada, 126
mutakaffil-i umur. *See* takafful-i umur
Mutasim Agha Jan (Taliban minister), 87
mutawalli, 66, 122, 125, 168
Mu'tazila, 19, 28
  in Nishapur, 20
muzara'a, 126
mystic. *See* Sufi terms
mysticism. *See* Sufi terms

al-Namaqi, 'Ali, 21, 22, 23, 24, 217
Naqshband, Baha' al-Din, 11, 14, 41, 190, 194, 213, 232
  on *khalwat dar anjuman*, 199
Naqshbandiyya, 6, 194, 208, 214, 215, 218
  and *wuquf-i 'adadi*, 205
  eleven principles, 190
  khalwat dar anjuman, 199
  Shi'i persecutions of, 76
  silent *dhikr*, 203
Nawa'i, 'Ali Shir, 72
Nawruz b. Arghun Aga, 59, 60, 161
nazr (vow), 161
ni'mah, 62, 150, 151, 152, 222
al-Nishapuri, al-Husayn (Abu 'Ali) b. 'Ali b. al-Husayn, 23
al-Nishapuri, Zahir (Abu al-Qasim) b. Tahir al-Shahhami, 22, 24
Nizam al-Mulk, 21, 28
Nuqtawiyya, 77, 78

Ögödei, 132
Öljeitü, 60, 62, 112, 130, 160
  and *altun tamgha*, 131
  yarligh by, 61, 62, 130, 138
Ottomans, 64, 74

Pahlawis, 2, 97
  Muhammad Riza Shah, 85
  nationalism, 86
  Riza Shah, 85
Parsa, Muhammad, 194, 202

Paul, Jürgen, 146, 193, 198, 202, 209
pietism or pietist. *See* Sufi terms
pilgrimages, 152
  and *du'a*, 153
  and *fayz*, 152
  and *'ibada*, 153
  and intimate friend, 154
  and invisible companion, 154
  and sacred exchange, 157
  and Timurids, 158
  and women, 156
  legality of, 153, 154
  protocols (*adab*), 152, 155
  reprehensible actions, 155
  spirit world, 157, 158
  spiritual journey, 157
  views of Abu Hamid al-Ghazali, 154
  views of Asil al-Din Wa'iz, 155, 156
  views of Ibn Taymiyya, 153, 154
  views of Ruzbihan Khunji, 154, 156
  views of Taqi al-Din Subki, 154

Qajars, 2, 82, 96
  Lord Curzon on, 83
  ruin of Iran, 82, 83, 84
  Treaty of Paris, 83
Qalandariyya, 28
qanat or *kariz*. *See* hydrological systems
Qasim-i Anwar, 40, 152, 211
al-Qayini, Jalal al-Din, 173, 177
Qizilbash, 74, 76
Qubilai Khan, 127
al-Qushayri, Abu al-Qasim, 29
Qutlugh-Shah, 60

ra'is, 24, 125, 146
Rashid al-Din (Ilkhanid vizier), 112, 137, 219
  reforms, 127, 128, 129, 130, 132
rijal al-ghayb, 14
ruhaniyyat, 14, 40, 152, 211, 212

sacred spaces
  and light, 26
  haram, 149
  hima, 149
  sanctification of, 150
  shared by Christians and Muslims, 158
  spiritual powers, 149
Safavids, 3, 5, 51, 78, 82, 116

Index

saint cults
  and *ikhtilaf*, 39
  devotion, 37
  orthodoxy v. orthopraxy, 39
  popular v. orthodox, 38, 39
  views of Augustine of Hippo, 38
  views of Carl Ernst, 37
  views of Ernest Gellner, 39
  views of Louis Dupree, 38
  views of Orientalists, 37
  views of Peter Brown, 38
saintdom. *See wilayat*
sainthood. *See walayat*
salatin-panah. See mulk-panah
Sanjar, Ahmad, 10, 17, 21, 218
  demise of, 51
  faith in Ahmad-i Jam, 46
  ghulam of Ahmad-i Jam, 46
  idealized king, 45
  Isma'ili *fidayin*, 28, 44
  Qarajih al-Saqi, 45
Sari Saqati, 11, 15
Saudi Arabia, 3, 154
  funding for extremists, 87
Sayyids of Tirmiz. *See specific individuals under* al-Mulk
Sazman-i Hifazat, 85
Sazman-i Miras-i Farhangi. See Miras-i Farhangi
Seljuqs, 3, 17, 18, 20, 21, 28, 218. *See also mihna*
  Ahmad Sanjar (r. 511–52/1118–57). *See* Sanjar, Ahmad
  Alp Arslan (d. 465/1072), 10
  and Abu Sa'id b. Abu al-Khayr, 21
  and Ahmad-i Jam, 44
  Chaghri Beg (d. *ca.* 452/1060), 21
  in Mayhana, 21
  Malikshah (d. 485/1092), 10
  Tughril Beg (d. 455/1063), 21
service and fidelity. *See* Shaykh al-Islam
Shafi'i, 9, 28
  in Nishapur, 19, 20
Shah 'Abbas I, 5, 77, 217
  massacre at Khwaf, 78
  patronage at Jam, 78, 109
Shah Isma'il I, Safavi, 5, 73, 74
  in Khurasan, 74
  soyurghal by, 74
Shah Isma'il II, Safavi, 77

Shah-Rukh, 4, 14, 70, 111, 113, 114, 136, 140, 142, 220
  at Jam, 46, 161
  death of, 69
  devotee of Ahmad-i Jam, 68
  governor of Khurasan, 67
  his pilgrimages, 16
  manshur by, 67, 68, 168, 172
  on agriculture, 136
  supporters at Jam, 67
Shah Tahmasp, 49, 77
Shaykh al-Islam
  as arbitrator, 60, 146, 220
  khidma and *wafa'*, 144, 145
  nasab and *hasab*, 147
  obligations, 125
  of Herat, 74, 177
  of Jam, 61, 66, 70, 74, 147
  political actions, 63, 64, 66
  public service, 146, 147
Shirazi, Haji Zayn b. Mahmud, 114
Shirazi, Qiwam al-Din, 114
silsila
  collateral lineages, 195
  later emphasis on, 11, 218
  official lineages, 195
silsilat al-dhahab, 15, 218
Simnani, Rukn al-Din 'Ala' al-Dawla, 60
soyurghal, 70, 72, 124, 130, 137, 138, 139, 140, 141
  loss of, 69
  return of, 70
soyurghamishi, 137, 142
Sübedei, 57
Sufi Path, 197
  tariq or *suluk*, 16
Sufi terms
  'abid, 29
  ahwal, 16, 26, 29, 191, 213
  arba'yin, 197, 198, 200, 214
  baqa', 42
  baqa' wa-fana', 42
  batin, 13, 16, 165
  chilla. See arba'yin
  chilla-khana (cells), 197
  dhikr, 6, 201
  dhikr, and Surat al-Ra'd, 203
  dhikr, and Surat Ya-Sin, 204
  dhikr, at Jam, 202, 204, 205, 207, 214, 222
  dhikr, changes, 196

Index

Sufi terms (cont.)
  dhikr, communal, 203, 205, 206
  dhikr, silent v. vocal, 203, 205
  dhikr, views of ʿAbdallah Ansari, 202
  dhikr, views of Muhammad Parsa, 202
  dhikr, views of Qutb al-Din Jami, 201
  dhikr-i ahisti, 205
  dhikr-i jahri, 6, 194, 201, 214
  dhikr-i khafi, 6, 194, 201
  dhikr-i majlis (communal *dhikr*), 203
  duʿaʾ, in Sufi context, 197
  fanaʾ, 42
  faqr, 191
  fikr, 201
  fikr-i dil, 201
  ghalat, 191
  habs-i dam, 201
  hadra, 203
  hal, 198, 213
  halqa, 203, 214
  ʿibada, 18
  ʿirfan, 29, 58, 222
  jadhba, 214
  khalwa or *khalwat*, 6
  khalwat, 196, 200, 203, 213, 214
  khalwat, communal, 203
  khalwat dar anjuman, 196
  khatm. See *wird*
  khatm, at Jam, 202, 207
  khatm-i khwajagan, 202, 203, 205
  khawatir, 202
  khidmat, 212
  maqamat, 16, 29, 191
  mujahadat, 198, 213
  muraqaba, 202, 209
  nafs, 42, 197, 198, 213, 214
  pir-i suhbat, 14, 210
  pir-i tarbiyyat, 210
  rabita, 6, 194, 208, 210, 212, 222
  rabita and *fayz*, 209
  rabita and *suhbat*, 209
  rabita in *khatm*, 203
  rabita qalbiyya, 209
  rabita, works by ʿAbd al-Rahman Jami, 208
  rabita, works by Arthur Buehler, 208
  rabita, works by Fritz Meier, 208
  rabt al-qalb, 209
  raqs, 19, 208
  riyazat, 165, 197, 198, 213
  riza, 191
  salik, 191, 197
  samaʿ, 6, 19, 191, 206, 208, 213, 214
  samaʿ, narcotic effect, 208
  samaʿ, views of ʿAbdallah Ansari, 206
  samaʿ, views of Abu Hamid al-Ghazali, 206
  samaʿ, views of Ahmad-i Jam, 207
  samaʿ, views of ʿAziz-Allah Jami, 214
  samaʿ, views of Bahaʾ al-Din Naqshband, 214
  samaʿ, views of Qutb al-Din Jami, 207
  samaʿ, views of al-Suhrawardi, Abu Hafs, 207
  samaʿ, views of al-Suhrawardi, Abu al-Najib, 206, 207
  samaʿ, views of al-Sulami, 214
  shaykh al-taʿlim, 30, 210
  shaykh al-tarbiyya, 30, 201, 210, 215
  sufi, a mystic, 28
  suhbat, 199, 209, 210, 212
  suluk, 16, 191
  tafakkur, 201
  talqin al-dhikr, 201
  tariq, 16, 191
  tasarruf, 209
  tasawwuf, 29
  tawajjuh, 152, 209, 210, 212, 214, 222
  tawakkul, 57, 191
  tawba, 9, 191, 197
  two-shaykh model, 211, 212
  wajd, 191, 208
  waraʿ, 197
  wird (pl. *awrad*), 202, 214
  zahid, 27
  zahir, 13, 16, 165
  zuhd, 18, 191, 197
al-Suhrawardi, ʿAbd al-Qahir (Abu al-Najib), 30, 164, 206, 207
al-Suhrawardi, Shihab al-Din ʿUmar (Abu Hafs), 196, 207, 212
al-Sulami, ʿAbd al-Rahman, 29, 214
Sultan-Abu Saʿid Mirza, 47, 69, 70, 220
  and Asil al-Din Waʿiz, 156
  coronation of, 71
  manshur by, 70, 141, 172
  soyurghal by, 70, 72, 140
Sultan-Husayn Bayqara, 47, 71, 72, 79, 136, 141, 220
  manshur by, 72, 172
Sultan-Khatun bt. Tagha-Temür, 63, 133
  patronage at Herat, 64

Index

Sultan-Muhammad b. Baysunghur, 69
suluk (Sufi Path), 5

Tabadakani, Shams al-Din Muhammad. *See* Zayniyya
tabligh (religious activism), 31
Taftazani, Saʿd al-Din Masʿud, 177, 185
Taftazani, Sayf al-Din Ahmad, 74
Tagha-Temür, 63
Tahirids, 17
Taj al-Din ʿAli Shah, 112
Tajiks, 1, 2, 97, 136, 160
takafful-i umur, 5, 148, 220
Tamerlane or Temür, 4, 65, 113, 172, 219
   Amir-i Buzurg?, 168
   and Ahmad-i Jam, 45, 46
   at Jam, 46, 66, 109, 145, 161, 220
   his *khanaqah*s, 46, 109
   letters from Jam, 66
   on agriculture, 135
   superstitions, 47, 158, 219
   yarligh by, 67, 139
taqawi, 126, 129
taqiyya (dissimulation), 79
tariq or *tariqa* (Sufi Path), 5
tariqa-yi khwajagan. *See* Naqshbandiyya
Taybadi, Zayn al-Din (Abu Bakr), 3, 46, 114, 135, 158, 194, 211
   letter to Temür, 46
teaching shaykh. *See* Sufi terms
Timurids, 3, 47, 116, 220
tiyul, 130
Tolui, 57, 136, 219
toponyms
   Agra to Ajmer, walk by Akbar, 82
   Balkh, Abu Nasr Parsa Shrine, 2
   Balkh, Imam ʿAli shrine, 2
   Binalud Mountains, 57
   Bizd, *khanaqah* at, 173
   Bizd, Masjid-i Nur, 173, 196, 198, 222
   Buzjan, 24
   Damascus, Ibn al-ʿArabi shrine, 2
   Ghur, Chishtiyya in, 43
   Hamadan, Esther and Mordecai tomb, 3
   Hasan-Abad, *khanaqah* at, 172
   Herat, ʿAbdallah Ansari shrine, 2, 115
   Herat, *buluk-i Injil*, 132
   Herat, Gawhar-Shad complex, 114
   Herat, Shah-Rukh's buildings, 115
   Herat, Sufi networks in, 193
   Jam, battle at, 75
   Jam, capture or pillage of, 76
   Jam, description of, 95, 97
   Jam, drought, 95
   Jam, in Gujarat, 81
   Jam, Mongols in, 57
   Jam, Sunni seminaries at, 89
   Juy-yi Baghand, 131
   Kadkan, 16, 21
   Khargird, tomb of Qasim-i Anwar, 40
   Khurasan, famine in, 76
   Khurasan, Sufi networks in, 193
   Khwaf, Sunni seminaries at, 89
   Kusuyi, 13
   Lahore, Humayun at, 48
   Maʿd-Abad, 9, 10, 25, 57
   Marw, 17, 136
   Mashhad, Gawhar-Shad Mosque, 4, 16, 114, 117
   Mashhad, Imam Riza shrine, 16, 114
   Mayhana, 13, 21
   Nama, 21
   Namaq, 9, 21, 25
   Nishapur, 16
   Pasargadae, 3
   Persepolis, 3
   Ribat-i Pay, Fushanj, 43
   Sikri, Mughal capital, 82
   Sistan and Baluchistan, 87
   Sultan-Maydan, *quriltai* at, 63
   Taybad, Sunni seminaries at, 89
   Tirmiz, sayyids of, 68
   Turbat-i Haydariyya, 16
   Turshiz, 27
   Yazd, fire temple, 3
   Zahedan, Sunni seminaries at, 89
   Zaranj, Ibn Karram birthplace, 17
   Zir-i Pul, 131
Turk, 2
Twelver Shiʿism
   official confession, 73

ʿUmar Shaykh b. Temür, 71
United States, 85, 87
ʿushr, 126
uwaysi, 13, 14, 16, 210, 211, 212, 215. *See also rijal al-ghayb*
Uzbeks, 73, 74, 75, 76

Wahhabi, 3, 39, 87, 88, 151, 154, 217, 222
walayat, 33, 35, 37, 218
wali Allah, 33, 40, 219

waqf
  by Gawhar-Shad, 68
  by Khadijah Khatun, 165
  in general, 96, 115, 116, 129
  Jami shrine, 117, 122, 123, 141
  Maria Subtelny on, 115
  Robert McChesney on, 116
wilayat, 33, 37, 218

Yadgar Muhammad, 71
yarligh, 43, 62
Yasa'ur, 134

Zamzam well, 151
Zand, 82
zandaqa (heresy), 20
Zayniyya, 194, 195, 215
Zhanda-Pil (the Furious Elephant), 31, 40, 48, 218
al-Ziyadi, Muhammad (Abu Tahir) b. Muhammad b. Muhammadish, 22, 23
Zoroastrian, 3, 10, 23, 40, 73, 85, 86, 88
Zysow, Aron, 25, 29

Other Titles in the Series

Agricultural Innovation in the Early Islamic World: The Diffusion of Crops and Farming Techniques, 700–1100, Andrew M. Watson
Muslim Tradition: Studies in Chronology, Provenance and Authorship of Early Ḥadīth, G. H. A. Juynboll
Social History of Timbuktu: The Role of Muslim Scholars and Notables 1400–1900, Elias N. Saad
Sex and Society in Islam: Birth Control before the Nineteenth Century, B. F. Musallam
Towns and Townsmen of Ottoman Anatolia: Trade, Crafts and Food Production in an Urban Setting 1520–1650, Suraiya Faroqhi
Unlawful Gain and Legitimate Profit in Islamic Law: Riba, Gharar and Islamic Banking, Nabil A. Saleh
Men of Modest Substance: House Owners and House Property in Seventeenth-Century Ankara and Kayseri, Suraiya Faroqhi
Roman, Provincial and Islamic Law: The Origins of the Islamic Patronate, Patricia Crone
Economic Life in Ottoman Jerusalem, Amnon Cohen
Mannerism in Arabic Poetry: A Structural Analysis of Selected Texts (3rd Century AH/9th Century AD–5th Century AH/11th Century AD), Stefan Sperl
The Rise and Rule of Tamerlane, Beatrice Forbes Manz
Popular Culture in Medieval Cairo, Boaz Shoshan
Early Philosophical Shiism: The Ismaili Neoplatonism of Abū Yaʻqūb al-Sijistānī, Paul E. Walker
Indian Merchants and Eurasian Trade, 1600–1750, Stephen Frederic Dale
Palestinian Peasants and Ottoman Officials: Rural Administration around Sixteenth-Century Jerusalem, Amy Singer
Arabic Historical Thought in the Classical Period, Tarif Khalidi
Mongols and Mamluks: The Mamluk–Īlkhānid War, 1260–1281, Reuven Amitai-Preiss
Knowledge and Social Practice in Medieval Damascus, 1190–1350, Michael Chamberlain
The Politics of Households in Ottoman Egypt: The Rise of the Qazdağlıs, Jane Hathaway
Hierarchy and Egalitarianism in Islamic Thought, Louise Marlow
Commodity and Exchange in the Mongol Empire: A Cultural History of Islamic Textiles, Thomas T. Allsen
State and Provincial Society in the Ottoman Empire: Mosul, 1540–1834, Dina Rizk Khoury
The Mamluks in Egyptian Politics and Society, Thomas Philipp and Ulrich Haarmann (eds.)
The Delhi Sultanate: A Political and Military History, Peter Jackson
European and Islamic Trade in the Early Ottoman State: The Merchants of Genoa and Turkey, Kate Fleet

The Ottoman City between East and West: Aleppo, Izmir, and Istanbul, Edhem Eldem, Daniel Goffman, and Bruce Masters
The Politics of Trade in Safavid Iran: Silk for Silver, 1600–1730, Rudolph P. Matthee
The Idea of Idolatry and the Emergence of Islam: From Polemic to History, G. R. Hawting
A Monetary History of the Ottoman Empire, Şevket Pamuk
Classical Arabic Biography: The Heirs of the Prophets in the Age of al-Ma'mūn, Michael Cooperson
Empire and Elites after the Muslim Conquest: The Transformation of Northern Mesopotamia, Chase F. Robinson
Poverty and Charity in Medieval Islam: Mamluk Egypt, 1250–1517, Adam Sabra
Culture and Conquest in Mongol Eurasia, Thomas T. Allsen
Christians and Jews in the Ottoman Arab World: The Roots of Sectarianism, Bruce Masters
Arabic Administration in Norman Sicily: The Royal Diwan, Jeremy Johns
Law, Society and Culture in the Maghrib, 1300–1500, David S. Powers
Revival and Reform in Islam: The Legacy of Muhammad al-Shawkānī, Bernard Haykel
Tolerance and Coercion in Islam: Interfaith Relations in the Muslim Tradition, Yohanan Friedmann
Guns for the Sultan: Military Power and the Weapons Industry in the Ottoman Empire, Gábor Ágoston
Marriage, Money and Divorce in Medieval Islamic Society, Yossef Rapoport
The Empire of the Qara Khitai in Eurasian History: Between China and the Islamic World, Michal Biran
Domesticity and Power in the Early Mughal World, Ruby Lal
Power, Politics and Religion in Timurid Iran, Beatrice Forbes Manz
Postal Systems in the Pre-modern Islamic World, Adam J. Silverstein
Kingship and Ideology in the Islamic and Mongol Worlds, Anne F. Broadbridge
Justice, Punishment and the Medieval Muslim Imagination, Christian Lange
The Shiites of Lebanon under Ottoman Rule, 1516–1788, Stefan Winter
Women and Slavery in the Late Ottoman Empire, Madeline Zilfi
The Second Ottoman Empire: Political and Social Transformation in the Early Modern World, Baki Tezcan
The Legendary Biographies of Tamerlane: Islam and Heroic Apocrypha in Central Asia, Ron Sela
Non-Muslims in the Early Islamic Empire: From Surrender to Coexistence, Milka Levy-Rubin
The Origins of the Shi'a: Identity, Ritual, and Sacred Space in Eighth-Century Kufa, Najam Haider
Politics, Law, and Community in Islamic Thought: The Taymiyyan Moment, Ovamir Anjum
The Power of Oratory in the Medieval Muslim World, Linda G. Jones
Animals in the Qur'an, Sarra Tlili
The Logic of Law Making in Islam: Women and Prayer in the Legal Tradition, Behnam Sadeghi

Empire and Power in the Reign of Süleyman: Narrating the Sixteenth-Century Ottoman World, Kaya Şahin
Law and Piety in Medieval Islam, Megan H. Reid
Women and the Transmission of Religious Knowledge in Islam, Asma Sayeed
The New Muslims of Post-conquest Iran: Tradition, Memory, and Conversion, Sarah Bowen Savant
The Mamluk City in the Middle East: History, Culture, and the Urban Landscape, Nimrod Luz
Disability in the Ottoman Arab World, 1500–1800, Sara Scalenghe
The Holy City of Medina: Sacred Space in Early Islamic Arabia, Harry Munt
Muslim Midwives: The Craft of Birthing in the Premodern Middle East, Avner Giladi
Doubt in Islamic Law: A History of Legal Maxims, Interpretation, and Islamic Criminal Law, Intisar A. Rabb
The Second Formation of Islamic Law: The Ḥanafī School in the Early Modern Ottoman Empire, Guy Burak
Sexual Violation in Islamic Law: Substance, Evidence, and Procedure, Hina Azam
Gender Hierarchy in the Qurʾān: Medieval Interpretations, Modern Responses, Karen Bauer
Intellectual Networks in Timurid Iran: Sharaf al-Dīn ʿAlī Yazdī and the Islamicate Republic of Letters, Ilker Evrim Binbaş
Authority and Identity in Medieval Islamic Historiography: Persian Histories from the Peripheries, Mimi Hanaoka
The Economics of Ottoman Justice: Settlement and Trial in the Sharia Courts, Metin Coşgel and Boğaç Ergene
The Mystics of al-Andalus: Ibn Barrajān and Islamic Thought in the Twelfth Century, Yousef Casewit
Muhammad's Heirs: The Rise of Muslim Scholarly Communities, 622–950, Jonathan E. Brockopp
The First of the Modern Ottomans: The Intellectual History of Ahmed Vasif, Ethan Menchinger
Non-Muslim Provinces under Early Islam: Islamic Rule and Iranian Legitimacy in Armenia and Caucasian Albania, Alison Vacca
Women and the Making of the Mongol Empire, Anne F. Broadbridge
Slavery and Empire in Central Asia, Jeff Eden
Christianity in Fifteenth-Century Iraq, Thomas A. Carlson
Child Custody in Islamic Law: Theory and Practice in Egypt since the Sixteenth Century, Ahmed Fekry Ibrahim
Ibadi Muslims of North Africa: Manuscripts, Mobilization and the Making of a Written Tradition, Paul M. Love Jr.
Islamic Law of the Sea: Freedom of Navigation and Passage Rights in Islamic Thought, Hassan S. Khalilieh
Law and Politics under the Abassids: An Intellectual Portrait of al-Juwayni, Sohaira Z. M. Siddiqui
Friends of the Emir: Non-Muslim State Officials in Premodern Islamic Thought, Luke B. Yarbrough

The Crisis of Kingship in Late Medieval Islam: Persian Emigres and the Making of Ottoman Sovereignty, Christopher Markiewicz
Collective Liability in Islam: The ʿĀqila and Blood Money Payments, Nurit Tsafrir
Arabic Poetics: Aesthetic Experience in Classical Arabic Literature, Lara Harb

Lightning Source UK Ltd.
Milton Keynes UK
UKHW020958111122
411963UK00011B/47